MEDIEVAL ARMENIAN CULTURE

University of Pennsylvania
Armenian Texts and Studies

Supported by the Sarkes Tarzian Fund

SERIES EDITOR
Michael E. Stone

MEDIEVAL ARMENIAN CULTURE

edited by
Thomas J. Samuelian
and
Michael E. Stone

Scholars Press
Chico, California

MEDIEVAL ARMENIAN CULTURE

Proceedings of the Third Dr. H. Markarian Conference
on Armenian Culture

edited by
Thomas J. Samuelian
and
Michael E. Stone

© 1984
University of Pennsylvania
Armenian Texts and Studies

Library of Congress Cataloging in Publication Data

Dr. H. Markarian Conference on Armenian Culture (3rd :
  1982 : University of Pennsylvania)
  Medieval Armenian culture.

  (University of Pennsylvania Armenian texts and
studies ; no. 6)
  "Proceedings of the Third Dr. H. Markarian
Conference on Armenian Culture"—T.p. verso.
  1. Armenia—Civilization—Congresses. I. Samuelian,
Thomas J. II. Stone, Michael E., 1938– .
III. Title. IV. Series.
DS171.D7 1982   956.6'201   83-14298
ISBN 0–89130–642–0

Printed in the United States of America

CONTENTS

Editors' Preface

The Third Dr. H. Markarian Conference on Armenian Culture was held November 7-10, 1982 at the University of Pennsylvania under the auspices of the Tarzian Chair in Armenian History and Culture. The conference, which dealt with Armenian culture from the seventh to fourteenth centuries, was the sequel to the Conference on Classical Armenian Culture held in November 1979. Just as many of the papers presented at the first conference were collected and published as Classical Armenian Culture, so nearly all the participants in the Conference on Medieval Armenian Culture are represented in the present volume.[*]

To make the book easier to read and use, notes and names have been standardized as far as possible, and an index of proper names has been compiled. Since a comprehensive bibliography was not economical for a book of such diverse contents, the names of authors cited, either in the text or in the notes, have been listed in the index as well. Throughout the book, Armenian forms of proper and place names have been preferred and have been transliterated according to the practice of the Revue des Etudes Arméniennes, with the exception of ç , which for typographic reasons had to be transliterated ĕ instead of ә , and o , which has been transliterated o. A transliteration chart has been provided below for the reader's convenience.

Many thanks are due Kirk Typing Service, Prof. R. Kraft and the Computer Project in the Department of Religious Studies, and Prof. Vartan Gregorian, who saw to making the conference and proceedings possible.

The editors and convenors wish to express their special thanks to the participants in the conference for their efforts in understanding Armenian culture and for their cooperation in both the conference and the subsequent preparation for publication.

TJS
MES

---

[*]The only papers read at the conference which are not published in this volume are N. Garsoian, "The City in Medieval Armenian—An Alien Element?" and E. Isaac, "The Use of Ethiopian Parchment in the Binding of Certain Armenian Manuscripts."

LIST OF MAPS

LIST OF ILLUSTRATIONS

Armenian Transliteration Key

Ս	Բ	Գ	Դ	Ե	Զ	Է	Ը	Թ	Ժ
ա	բ	գ	դ	ե	զ	է	ը	թ	ժ
a	b	g	d	e	z	ē	ĕ	t'	ž

Ի	Լ	Խ	Ծ	Կ	Հ	Ձ	Ղ	Ճ	Մ
ի	լ	խ	ծ	կ	հ	ձ	ղ	ճ	մ
i	l	x	c	k	h	j	ł	č	m

Յ	Ն	Շ	Ո	Չ	Պ	Ջ	Ռ	Ս	Վ
յ	ն	շ	ո	չ	պ	ջ	ռ	ս	վ
y	n	š	o	č'	p	ǰ	ṙ	s	v

Տ	Ր	Ց	Ի	Փ	Ք	Օ	Ֆ	Ու
տ	ր	ց	ւ	փ	ք	օ	ֆ	ու
t	r	c'	w	p'	k'	ō	f	u

MEDIEVAL ARMENIAN CULTURE

A SECTION FROM THE GREEK-ARMENIAN LEXICON
TO GALEN

John A. C. Greppin

Cleveland State University

Though never edited and printed in modern times, the Galen Lexicon is a fairly well known text,[1] cited with some frequency in lexicographic and linguistic works.[2] It is a source of uncommon and rather technical Armenian vocabulary, being composed primarily of names of plants used in pharmaceutical preparations, names of the parts of the body, and stray natural science terms. If we can trust our texts, there even appears to be evidence for Armenian words that are hitherto unrecorded.

The greatest lexicographic value of the dictionary is that it gives us precise Greek-Armenian glosses, and thus provides evidence for the meanings of some Armenian words that are otherwise poorly understood. The dictionary is also of special interest since it is most likely among the very oldest of the lexicons ever prepared in the Armenian language. This claim can be made on the basis that it certainly precedes the Middle Armenian period, a point that is confirmed in the method of transliteration used. In this lexicon Gk. φ and χ are transliterated as Arm. p' and k', rather than f and x, which allows us to date the original version sometime earlier than the twelfth century. Further, there is evidence for the use of vocabulary that was largely restricted to the Gold and Silver Age, and which was most uncommonly used in the Middle Armenian period. Arm. xord is an early word that was replaced in Middle Armenian times by krunk. The existence of xord in the Galen Lexicon, glossing Gk. γέρανος 'crane,' is thus an indication of the early date of the composition of this lexicon.

From the existing manuscripts it is clear that the lexicon existed in

T. Samuelian & M. Stone, eds. Medieval Armenian Culture. (University of Pennsylvania Armenian Texts and Studies 6). Chico, CA: Scholars Press, 1983. pp. 3 to 12.

at least two separate recensions. The earlier edition arranged the Greek lexical entries alphabetically by the first letter only. Thus all entries with initial a- were grouped together with no further regard for alphabetical order. The same was true for b- and g-, and so forth. The second recension shows certain improvements in the efficiency of the text, for certain copies prepared in the eighteenth century show alphabetization by first two letters. Thus ab-, ag-, ad-, etc.

There seems to be evidence for a still earlier stage, and this is based on irregularities in alphabetical order that appear when one attempts to normalize the text.[3] Frequently when the Greek entries are reconstructed it becomes clear that the Greek word does not begin with a letter appropriate to that section of the dictionary. In the section for the letter g- we find the entry gemos—biž. Yet Arm. biž 'rheum in the eye' cannot be the equivalent of any Greek word approximated as gemos; rather Arm. biž can only be the equivalent of Gk. λήμη 'rheum in the eye and nose,' and it would have been written, in Armenian letters, as łeme, with Arm. ł eventually being miscopied as g, and the final -e erroneously turned into the common -os.[4] As one will note when looking at the entries for g-, which follow, the spelling errors made by the copyist can be bizarre.

There are other instances of irregularities which confirm that there were later additions to the text. Arabic words can be noted,[5] and there are clear indications that Greek words are entered with Western Armenian transliteration. Arm. xruk 'mercuric sulfide, HgS' is given as a gloss for a Greek word most commonly written in the manuscripts as gunaprē. The correct spelling of the Greek word, according to the eastern transliteration, used elsewhere, would be kinabari = Gk. κιννάβαρι 'mercuric sulfide, HgS.' This clear use of a Middle Armenian transliteration system provides satisfactory evidence that there were later additions to the lexicon.[6]

The exact use of the text is not yet clear. Because manuscripts of the lexicon seem to be rather common and because the lexicon itself went through two revisions following its original compilation, there is every reason to believe that it was in considerable demand. It would not have been sufficient in size to use for translating whole Greek Galenic manuscripts. Rather it was probably used as an ancillary to Armenian medical texts whose original was attributed to Galen. In Armenian medical texts, as shown above in our discussion of the Arabic vocabulary in Mxit'ar Herac'i, technical vocabulary was frequently kept in the language of the original. It would seem that the Galen lexicon was used to provide glosses of Greek words that were left untranslated in Armenian versions of the Greek medical writers.

That the dictionary was initially composed to serve Galen alone is unclear since we cannot establish clearly the original content of the lexicon. However, in the following text I have noted when the word in question appears in Galen, and in Dioscorides as well.[7]

The following is an edited text for the entries with an initial g-. They are based on readings from about forty manuscripts held in the Yerevan Matenadaran and of two texts held in the Vienna collection.[8]

[gazgazuk]		ew abata pᶜauł '?'	
զազգազուկ	8x	եւ աբատա փառւն	5x
զադգադուկ	1x	եւ աբայտա փայուն	3x
զազմազուկ	1x	սամնորււ տարփան	1x
		եւ աբատ ապայուր	1x

γαλέη 'weasel'		akᶜis 'weasel'	
զաղիա	4x	աքիս	9x
զաղեա	4x	աքի	4x
զաղա	1x		
զաղղեա	3x		
զաւղեա	1x		

Dioscorides II.25, Galen XII.321

γαργαρεών 'uvula'		sosord 'throat'[9]	
զարզարեոն	4x	սոր	2x
զարզարեւոն	1x	սոսոր	1x
զարդարէոն	1x	սառորդ	7xᵉ
զարզարեոն	4x	սոր	1x
զարզարէոն	1x	սրսոր	3x
		սաւսիր	1x
Galen XIX.368		սոսորր	1x

γεντιανή 'gentian'[10]		bogoy armat 'gentian root'		
զենդիանէ	11x	բոբոյ	8x	արմատ
զերդիանէ	3x	բոխոյ	3x	արմատն
զինդաանէ	1x	բոքլոյ	1x	
		բոզայ	1x	
		բոզբո	1x	
		բոբոյ	1x	

Dioscorides III.3, Galen XIII.822

γεράνιον 'geranium'		igrika '?'	
զերիանու	7x	իզրիկա	4x
		իզիրկա	1x
		իւզրիւզա	2x
Dioscorides III.116			

γέρανος 'crane'		xord 'crane'	
զերանու	13x	խորդ	8x
		խորթ	5x
Galen III.535			

γλαύξ 'wartcress'		bu 'owl'[11]	
զղուկաս	4x	բու	10x
զղիւկայ	4x	բուրդ 'wool'	1x
զղուկա	5x	բու իփայ սնկո	2x
Dioscorides IV.138, Galen II.857			

γλαφυρία 'brightness'		pᶜayl-oł/-umn/-akn 'id'[12]	
զաղափիւրայ	5x	փայլող 'shine'	3x
զղափուրա(յ)	8x	փայլումն 'brilliance'	8x
զզափուրա	1x	փայլակն 'lightning'	2x
դափուրա	1x	զայլող	2x

γλεῦκος 'new wine'		kᶜałcᶜu 'new wine'	
զղղուկու	11x	քաղցու	14x
զղղակու	4x	քաղցոյ	3x
ողղկու	2x		
Dioscorides V.6, Galen VI.575			

γλοιός	'glutinous substance'		orpēs pᶜrpᶜur aler kᶜamuac 'like flour-froth extracted from grain'	
գլիւոյ	9x		որպէս փրփուր ալեւր քամաց gորենոյ	8x
գիւոյ	1x			
գրիւոյ	1x		որպէս փրփուր ալեր քամաց gորեսա	2x
			որպէս փրկուր ալիւր քամաց gորենոյ	1x

Dioscorides I.30 (γλοιός), Galen XIX.91 (γλοιώδης)

γλυκύρριζα 'licorice root'		matutaki armat 'id'	
գդիկերեդին	2x	մատուտակի արմատ	14x
qqիկիգրելին	2x	մատուտակն	5x
գդիկուրեդին	1x	մատիտակ	5x
գդիծո(յ)	4x	մատուտակի տոմար	1x
գդղիծու	1x	մատուտակ տակ	3x
գդիկոյ	5x		
գդիկուղդդին	1x		
գդիկիւրէնի	4x		
գդիկիւրելի(ն)	6x		
գդիկիկիւրեդին	1x		
գդիկոտեդին	1x		

Dioscorides V.63 (γλυκύρριζα)
Galen XI.858 (γλυκυρρίζη)

γλυκύς 'sweet'		corenoy ōšarak 'syrup of bayberry'	
գղ-կին	2x	ծորենոյ շարաq	6x
գղակին	7x	ծարենոյ շարաq	3x
գղակին	2x	ծարենոյ օշարակ	4x
գղղկին	3x	ծթորենոյ օշարակ	1x

Dioscorides III.24,   Galen XVIII.B.611

γογγυλίς 'turnip'		šaɫgam 'turnip'	
գանդի	7x	*շաղգամ*	14x
գանդ	8x	*շաՖգամ*	2x
գանդիա	2x	*շաշգամ*	1x

Dioscorides II.110, Galen XI.861

γῦρις 'finely ground meal'		p°oši ĵaɫac°ac° 'mill dust'	
գորիս	4x	*գու-իշի Ֆրաղաց*	1x
գիւրիս	6x	*փշիՖաղագաց*	1x
գւրիս	1x	*փոշիՖաղագաց*	5x
գարեն	1x	*փոշիՖաղացի*	1x
գարգարեն	2x	*փողի Ֆաղոցի*	1x
		փոշի Ֆաղաց ներքի բերդին 1x	
		Ֆրաղացի	1x
		փոշիՖրաղացաց	1x
		սագուրի փոշիՖաղացաց 2x	

Dioscorides II.85

γύφος 'chalk'		buɫ 'lime, plaster'	
գիփոս	4x	*բուղ*	9x
գիրոս	7x	*բուր կ կիր*	4x
գիփոսոն	2x		

Dioscorides V.116, Galen XIV.142

γύψ 'vulture'		angɫ 'vulture'	
գիփա	3x	*անգղ*	6x
գիփայ	8x	*անղղ*	3x
		անկղ	2x

Galen XIX.730

καστόριον 'testicles of the beaver'		kɫbu ju 'egg (testicle) of the beaver'	
զուդի	5x	կղրու ծու	5x
զուդ	3x	կղբի ձծու	1x
զունդի	3x	խիլ կ կղբի ծու[13]	4x
		զղբի ծու	1x
		խիլ բաբաւի ծու[14]	1x

Dioscorides II.24,   Galen XII.337

κιννάβαρι 'mercuric sulfide'		xruk 'mercuric sulfide'	
զունապրէ	14x	խրուկ	6x
զունապէ	2x	կրուկ	2x
		կրունկ	1x
		խիրուկ	3x
		խրուկ	4x

Dioscorides V.94,   Galen XII.221

λήμη 'rheum of eye or nose'		biž 'rheum of the eye'	
զբմնու[15]	2x	բիժ	2x

Galen XVIII.A.579

NOTES

[1]This dictionary is elsewhere described in my article in "Preliminary Comments on the Greek-Armenia Lexicon to Galen," REArm 16 (1982) 69-80. Other material, and further bibliography on the Armenian versions of Galen can be found in Greppin, "Preliminaries to the Galenic Corpus in Classical Armenian," Newsletter of the Society of Ancient Medicine, April 1982, 11-13.

[2]The Galen lexicon is cited in both the Nor Baŕgirk' and Ačaŕyan's Hayeren armatakan baŕaran under the heading Gal, an abbreviation for Galianos, a common medieval Greek representation of Galen's name.

[3]The earliest dictionaries of Indo-European and Semitic languages were not always alphabetic. More frequently they listed words in homogeneous groups. Thus a dictionary of animal names would have groupings under, say, domestic animals, flesh eating animals, snakes, birds, etc. Arrangement within these headings was haphazard.

[4]Another clear example of words appearing out of alphabetical order once the text has been edited would be the entry alrasan, which appears under a-, and is glossed as Arm. k'uŕat' 'leek.' Yet the Greek word for leek is πράσον and the initial Armenian p was misread as al-, as could logically happen, considering the shape of the Armenian letters involved.

[5]We find an entry for akrkarhay = Arm. boɫoy tak ('the root of the pellitory'). Yet akrkarhay can only be Arabic āqirqarḫā 'pellitory,' a term that is used in the text of Mkhitar Heratsi (Venice 1832-83), well known for its Arabic content, and in a text of Amirdovlat, recorded in the Haybusak (p. 365).

[6]Note also gud(i) and gundi which somehow are glossed as kɫbi ju 'the testicle (egg) of the beaver' and thus must be Gk. καστόριον 'id,' a very specialized term. The testicles of the beaver were specially noted by the ancients since beaver testicles do not drop at puberty, but remain within the belly. This is a common feature of many aquatic animals.

[7]Galen (129-199 A.D.) was probably the greatest of the ancient physicians and certainly the most prolofic. His anatomical works were valuable up until the nineteenth century. Dioscorides (first century AD) is best known for his Materia medica, a systematic compilation of drugs.

[8]My special thanks go to Dr. Babken Chukaszian of the Matenadaran and to Onik Yeganian, whose knowledge of the manuscripts in that huge collection is phenomenal. Thanks also must go to Dr. Julian Plante, director of the Hill Monastic Manuscript Library where the whole Vienna Armenian collection is held in microfilm. The numbers of the Yerevan texts are given in REArm 16 (1982) 71.2. The Viennese manuscript numbers are 6 and 916.

[9]Arm. kokord is the more common word in the earliest texts though sosord does seem to be witnessed as well in fifth century texts.

[10]The word for gentian appears elsewhere in the lexicon, being entered as ĵndian, where it is glossed as ernĵnaki takn 'root of the gentian.' The lead entry, ĵndian, is obviously from the Arabic ĵinṯīānā 'gentian' rather than Gk. γεντιανή.

[11]Clearly the compiler of the lexicon was unaware that Gk. γλαύξ stood for more than just 'owl.'

[12]The exact significance of this word in a medical text remains obscure; Gk. γλαφυρός can also mean 'hairless, bald,' but this cannot be the meaning of the stem p'ayl-. In all likelihood Arm. p'ayl- is an incorrect translation of γλαφυρός which should have been rendered in a specialized sense as Arm. kntak 'bald.'

[13]The word xil, elsewhere understood only as 'search, inquiry,' is uniquely used here with the value of kłbi ju and thus constitutes a new word if the textual tradition can be relied on.

[14]Arm. ju 'egg' is the standard slang term in Modern Armenian for 'testicle'; however the writing of k'ak'awi ju (a misspelling for kak'awi ju) 'partridge egg' implies that at least one copyist was unfamiliar with the slang term, and 'improved' the text with k'ak'awi ju.

[15]Manuscript tradition varies here. One tradition lists the word under gemos, another more appropriately lists biž with łemos.

ARMENIAN DIALECTS AND THE LATIN-ARMENIAN
GLOSSARY OF AUTUN

J. J. S. Weitenberg

University of Leiden (Netherlands)

In 1882 the French scholar H. Omont published a short Latin-Armenian glossary containing 90 entries he found on the last two pages of a manuscript in the library of Autun, France.[1]   The remainder of the manuscript contains the text of the Letters of St. Jerome.   Six years later, A. Carrière republished this text, identified the Armenian words of the glossary and added valuable comments.[2]

In this paper we will consider the value of this document for study in the continuity of the development of the Armenian language.   I shall not go into the question of the purpose of this 'manuel de conversation' (Omont) or 'glossaire' (Carrière) or into the historical implications of the document.[3]   By kind permission of M. J. Perrat, Conservateur de la Bibliothèque Municipale of Autun, I am able to present a photograph of the glossary.[4]   A comparison of the photograph with Omont's and Carrière's editions shows that some improvements, mainly of a technical nature, are necessary, but on the whole they turn out to be adequate.[5]

The following facts are important in connection with this document:
1)   The Armenian text is written in Latin characters.   The manuscript was dated by Omont to the end of the ninth or beginning of the tenth century on paleographic grounds.   Inspection of the photograph confirms this, although the later date seems more probable.[6]
2)   Apart from inscriptions, the glossary thus constitutes one of the oldest documents in the Armenian language: the oldest manuscript, Matenadaran 6200 (887 AD).   In fact, the text of the glossary might even be older:

T. Samuelian & M. Stone, eds.   Medieval Armenian Culture.   (University of Pennsylvania Armenian Texts and Studies 6).   Chico, CA: Scholars Press, 1983.   pp. 13 to 28.

Carrière adduces arguments for the fact that it was recopied. A study of the photograph offers some confirmation of Carrière's view. Entries (68)-(73) run as follows: (68) scirt, (69) handam, (70) gernac, (71) andam, (72) scunch, (73) uluec. On the photograph there are traces of an additional entry after (69) that possibly reads (69a) genu: scunch, identical to (72). We might suppose that the copist mistakenly wrote (69a) after (69) handam, misreading it for (71) andam, then noticed his mistake and erased it. In addition, the confusion of paleographically similar t and c; e.g. (11) khuert [cl. Arm., č'ork'] as opposed to (4) Khurec xapte [Cl. Arm. č'orek' šabt'i], is explicable only if the text had been recopied.[7]

3)   The person who wrote down the first version of the glossary did not know Armenian. From some Latin translations of the entries it is clear that he pointed to objects and wrote down the word as he heard it. This accounts for some incorrect Latin meanings being assigned to the Armenian words (as (58) pectus 'breast' scirt 'heart').

In all, we have 90 words, most of them belonging to the basic vocabulary of language, written down by someone who was not influenced by the immense weight of orthographic conventions of Classical Armenian. These words date from a period in which reliable information on the spoken language is largely lacking and can only be traced by incidental mistakes in inscriptions and manuscripts. The value of this glossary is yet greater when we realize that it shows many deviations from classical usage in its lexicon and phonetics.

In his edition, Carrière expressed the hope that the text would soon be analyzed from a linguistic point of view. Indeed, Meillet and to a lesser extent Karst and Feydit used the glossary in their publications. The state of Armenian dialectology at the turn of the century did not permit the incorporation of the material of the glossary into a coherent picture. Since then, as far as I know, the glossary has not been drawn upon in twentieth century publications on Middle or Modern Armenian dialectology. This is surprising in view of the fact that the Modern Armenian dialects took shape in the seventh to eleventh centuries, for which this glossary is the oldest, and most extensive source available.[8]

We know nothing about the background of the Armenian who served as the linguistic informant for the glossary, except that he was in Europe at the beginning of the tenth century, or earlier, nor do we know what his business was. Nevertheless we can try to trace his language back to its native sources. In other words, we can try to connect the language of the glossary to a specific dialect-area of Armenia, taking into account the thousand-year gap between the glossary and the attestation of modern Armenian dialects.

A complete analysis of the glossary is outside the scope of this paper. Instead I will concentrate on distinctive phonetic features. Whether the orthography of the glossary is reliable for a linguistic enquiry can be answered positively; the glossary is remarkably consistent in its orthography and, of course, follows the orthographic conventions of the Romance European area of the time. Even the Armenian affricates are rendered in Latin script in such a way that we can draw conclusions about them.

First I will give an example of how the glossary fits into the known facts. The loss of final postvocalic -y in polysyllables is attested in (38) luna: lucenga: Cl. Arm. lusnkay. This loss is common to all modern dialects and is in fact attested as early as the beginning of the seventh century. Judging from an inscription on 887, we can date complete loss of final -y in polysyllables in the ninth century.[9]   The glossary offers no unexpected development in this respect.

Certain phonetic features make it possible to give a negative characterization of the dialect represented in the glossary. For example, entry (19) XXX: Erchun [Cl. Arm. eresun] exhibits the elision of unstressed, medial -e-. The glossary shows that the syncopation of unstressed -e- began a century earlier than previously thought.[10] The syncopated form is attested in nearly all, except the easternmost dialects (Erevan, Agulis, Nor Ĵuła, Łarabał, Goris and Šamaxi) of Modern Armenian. In Tiflis the disyllabic yarsun coexists with the trisyllabic yarasun. By comparison with the distribution of dialect forms, it is clear that the glossary does not represent one of these eastern dialects. Further corroboration can be found by a comparison of the dialectical forms of eresun with those of k'aṙasun. It turns out that all dialects that lost medial -e- in eresun also lose interior unstressed -a- in k'aṙasun; those dialects that preserve interior -e- in eresun likewise preserve the medial -a- in k'arasun.[11] This is no coincidence. The explanation lies in the fact that precisely those dialects that preserve the trisyllabic forms eresun and k'arasun retracted the classical accent from the last to the penultimate syllable.[12]

In more general terms, it seems probable that loss of medial unstressed -e- and -a- originated at the same time. The glossary attests to loss of -e- in erchun and loss of -a- in (49) dens : atmunc : [Cl. Arm.

atamunk'].[13]   Here again the glossary gives the earliest attestation by almost a century of the syncopation of unstressed -a-.[14]   However, the glossary unexpectedly preserves -a- in (20) XXXX: karraschun [Cl. Arm. k'arasun]. How do we account for this?   The possibility that loss of -e- was earlier than loss of -a- seems excluded by the form atmunc in the glossary and by coextensive distribution of disyllabic [syncopated] forms in the modern dialects.   I think that karraschun may have preserved its -a- under the influence of the literary language.   This same explanation is possible for literary Cilician Armenian that shows eresun [with medial e intact], although syncopation of unstressed interior -e- is attested in this dialect as well.[15]

In sum, the glossary here shows an innovation that did not take place in the Agulis-Łarabał-Erevan area.   This is a first negative indication on the dialect-area of the glossary.

Another clue to the dialect-area of the glossary is found in the treatment of Classical Armenian o and e.   The facts were clearly stated by Meillet some years ago: in unstressed position Classical Armenian e and o are not diphthongized; in that position o is written in the glossary with u, which shows that Classical Armenian o tended to become more closed.[16] Examples: (9) II: ergout [Cl. Arm. erku]; (37) sol: arechac [Cl. Arm. aregakn]; (4) feria IIII: Khurec xapte [Cl. Arm. č'orek'šabt'i]; (73) crus: uluec [Cl. Arm. olok'/g].   In stressed position Classical Armenian e and o are diphthongized as in (10) III: eriec [Cl. Arm. erek']; (53) facies: eriesc [Cl. Arm. eresk']; (11) IIII: khuert [Cl. Arm. č'ork']; (67) dorsum: cuelc [Cl. Arm. kołk'].   Whereas classical stressed o in interior position always appears as - ue-, the glossary writes (h)ua- in initial stressed position: (66) spina: hualn [Cl. Arm. ołn]; (74) pes: uaden [Cl. Arm. otn].[17]   Classical e is never diphthongized e.g. (80) deus: ter [Cl. Arm. tēr]; (88) presbiter: eresc [Cl. Arm. erēc'].   As far as I know, the earliest attestations of diphthongization of classical e in stressed position are found in Greek transcriptions of Armenian toponyms in the work of Constantine Porphyrogenetes (who died in 959).[18]   The glossary provides slightly older and more extensive material witnesses to this development.   Indeed, Ĵahukyan goes as far as to date the diphthongization of stressed o and e to classical or even pre-classical times.[19]

The situation sketched here is found in literary Cilician Armenian.[20] This does not mean, however, that the dialect of the glossary is a direct ancestor of literary Cilician Armenian: the distribution of the diphthongization in modern Armenian dialects must be taken into account before we can make reliable statements on this isogloss.

The geographical distribution of diphthongized stressed e̲ and o̲ in the modern dialects can be traced easily through J̌ahukyan's work.[21] Diphthongization of stressed e̲ occurs in 28% of the dialects, of o̲ in 31%. Since diphthongization of o̲ and e̲ occur together in the glossary, I refrain from giving those instances where diphthongization of only one of these two vowels occurs.

Diphthongization of stressed e̲ and o̲ is found in one contiguous area and in some isolated regions. The contiguous area is centered in the region west of lake Urmia and around Lake Van. It includes the southern part of the Xoy-Urmia dialect (Garibjari̇̀s group 7); all the terrritory of the Van-dialect (group 7); the southern part of the Muš-dialect (group 2), i.e. the cities north of Lake Van and Muš itself; and the central part of the Sassun-dialect (group 4).[22] The scattered areas together form a semi-circle around the Sivas and Karin-Erevan area (groups 1 and 2) but are very isolated. They include: The Zeytun-area (group 4); the area round Sivas (group 1); Xotorǰur (east of Trabzon; group 2); a line Leninakan-Lor̄i (group 2).[23]

This isogloss tells us that diphthongization originated from the center of this region, spread over a vast area and was subsequently neutralized, at least in part, by the spread of some other dialect that did not diphthongize. We have no direct evidence as to the origin of this spread, although the Urmia-Van-Muš area is a likely candidate. In particular, since the Erevan-Karin dialect does not diphthongize it is not probable that the glossary belongs to this group. But before the dialect of the glossary can be conclusively identified, evidence on the consonantism of the glossary must be examined.

The Classical Armenian occlusives [b, d, g, j, ǰ; p, t, k, c, č; p', t', k', c', č'] are represented the following way in the glossary:

Classical voiced stops[24] are unchanged in medial position after nasal: (69) renes: handam; (71) coxa: andam, [Cl. Arm. andam]. This is a general feature of all dialects and therefore a very early development that can not provide decisive evidence for the question at hand.[25]

Classical voiced stops in all other positions appear as voiceless stops in the glossary.[26] In initial position: E.g. (30) vinum: chini [Cl. Arm. gini]; (47) os: peran [Cl. Arm. beran]; in medial intervocalic position (7) feria VII: sabpat [Cl. Arm. šabat']; (39) sol: arechac [Cl. Arm. aregakn]; in other medial positions: (2 etc.) xapte [Cl. Arm. -šabt'i]; (6) feria VI: urpat [Cl. Arm. urbat']; in final position: (12) V: hinc [Cl. Arm. hing]; (84) sanctus: supr (showing metathesis?) [Cl. Arm. surb].[27]

Classical voiceless stops have a twofold representation in the glossary: voiced and voiceless. As a rule, the glossary has voiced stops for a Classical voiceless stops in the environment of n, between vowels and after r; i.e., in voiced environments. Here are some examples:

Classical voiceless stops are retained in initial position: ((17) X: taz [Cl. Arm. tasn]; (31) caseus: paner [Cl. Arm. panir];[28] in final position: (57) guttur: kcerchac [Cl. Arm. xřč'ak]; (78) mulier: kenic [Cl. Arm. knik]; after s: (39) stellae: astil [Cl. Arm. astł].

Classical voiceless stops appear as voiced stops in the glossary: near n: (38) luna: lucenga [Cl. Arm. lusnkay] (in the position before -n the phonetic realisation was -Cěn; the glossary always writes ě [schwa] as a vowel; here too, Classical voiceless stop is voiced in the glossary: (33) piscis: chugen [Cl. Arm. jukn]; (74) pes: uaden [Cl. Arm. otn]; voicing in voiced surroundings occurs in: the group r+ consonant + vowel: (9) II: ergout [Cl. Arm. erku]; (36) celum: erginc [Cl. Arm. erkink']; (45) cilium: ardevanunc [Cl. Arm. artewanunk']; the group VCV: (40) terra: kcedinc [Cl. Arm. getink']; (54) auris: aganch [Cl. Arm. akanǰ(k')]; (61) humerus: tigunc: [Cl. Arm. t'ikunk'].[29]

As for the classical voiced and voiceless affricates the notation of the glossary is such that it cannot give independent evidence on their development. But there are some indications that the development of the affricates followed the pattern of the stops. Just as Classical voiced stops are preserved after nasals (as in (h)andam) we may suppose the same for voiced affricates. The z in (41) homo: anzen [Cl. Arm. anjn] thus indicates a voiced sound, (Classical Armenian j (dz)). By contrast, ch or sc in the glossary indicates a voiceless affricate: (33) piscis: chugen [Cl. Arm. jukn]; (32) ovum: chu [Cl. Arm. ju]; (77) testiculi: scuc [Cl. Arm. ju-k']; (35) aqua: chure [Cl. Arm. ǰur]; (54) auris: aganch [Cl. Arm. akanǰ(k')]. So we may suppose that Classical voiced affricates (j and ǰ) are devoiced in the glossary.[30]

Classical voiceless č remains voiceless in final position: (75) cabilia: cuech [Cl. Arm. koč]. As for classical voiceless c, it remains voiceless in initial position but becomes voiced between vowels: (59) mamilla: cize [Cl. Arm. cic] with unexplained final -e.[31]

As for Classical voiceless aspirated stops, they are hardly noted as such in the glossary. Classical t' is always written t; Classical k' is written c (ch before i as in (46) nasus: chit [Cl. Arm. k'it'] or k (in (20) XXXX: karraschun [Cl. Arm. k'aṫasun]). Only in the case of (65) pugnus: prunhc [Cl. Arm. bṙunk'] we may assume that aspiration is notated by writing h before the stop. Classical p' is written p initially ((56) gula: puelc [Cl. Arm. p'oɫk']) but b in final position (only (63) manus: hab [Cl. Arm. ap']).[32] I assume that the dialect of the glossary nevertheless possessed aspirated voiceless consonants on account of the spelling of the aspirated affricates and in view of the fact that all the modern dialects retain Classical p', t', k' as voiceless aspirated stops.[33]

If we compare the consonantism of the glossary as established above with the consonantism of the modern dialects we get the following picture:

	Cl. Arm.	Initial Position			Intervocalic		
		t	d	t'	t	d	t'
group 1	Sivas	d	d'	t'	d	d'	t'
2	Erevan	t	d'	t'	d	t'	t'
3	Trabzon	d	d	t'	d	t'	t'
4	Sasun	d	t	t'	d	t	t'
5	Malatya	d	t'	t'	d	t'	t'
6	Agulis	t	d	t'	t	d	t'
7	Van	t	t	t'	t	t	t'
8	(Ɫarabaɫ - Loṙi)				t	t'	t'
Autun		t	t	t'	d	t	t'

We immediately see that the consonantism of the glossary does not correspond exactly to any of the dialects: in initial position the consonantism of the glossary is identical with the situation in Van, in intervocal position with that of Sassun, but there is no single Modern dialect which matches both positions. This is not surprising inasmuch as there is a 1000 year gap between the glossary and the modern dialects. Before proceeding further, information on the earlier development of the modern dialects is necessary. Such information is provided by Kortlandt's study on the relative chronology of the development of consonantism in the Armenian dialects.[34] I shall try to fit the situation of the glossary into the stages of development established in Kortlandt's relative chronology.

The starting-point for the development of the modern dialects is found in the central dialect of Agulis where the consonantism is unchanged from the Classical language. The glossary cannot belong to this dialect (group 6) as it developed classical voiced stop into a voiceless stop. This is in accordance with two facts already established: that neither syncopation (Autun erechun vs. Cl. Arm. eresun) nor diphthongization of o and e are attested in Agulis dialect.

In broad terms, the other dialects orginated from the central area by two consecutive waves of phonetic change: the first one characterized by the aspiration in voiced consonants (Cl. Arm. d dialectical d'), comprising the dialects of Erevan-Karin-Mus (group 2) and the second one characterized by devoicing of unaspirated voiced consonants (Cl. Arm. d dialectical t), comprising the dialects of Łarabał-Xoy-Urmia-Van (group 7). The other dialects originated from these two groups in later stages.

It is apparent immediately that the glossary does not belong to the dialect-group that originated in the first wave (Erevan-Karin-Muš), as it does not aspirate but devoices the Classical voiced consonants. This also is in accordance with the facts already established: the syncopation of -e- did not reach the Erevan-dialect and the diphthongization of e and o does not affect the Erevan-Karin area, but only the southern part of the Muš-dialect.

So the dialect of the glossary belongs to the group that originated in the second wave. This is in accordance with the devoicing of classical b, d, g (> p, t, k) in the glossary. We can restrict the area a little bit further. The glossary does not belong to the Łarabał-area as both the syncopation of -e- and the diphthongization of e and o did not reach that area. That leaves the Xoy-Urmia-Van area.

But the dialect is not identical with the western dialects of group 7 as it shows voicing of classical t (> d) in voiced surroundings. It must have developed one step further.

According to Kortlandt's relative chronology, the third development involved the voicing of voiceless (glottalized) stops (Cl. Arm. t etc.> d etc.). In absolute sense, loanwords enable us to date this development to the 7th-10th centuries. As far as the Xoy-Urmia-Van area is concerned this third development resulted in the origin of dialect-group 4 (the Sasun-Zeytun-Syria or Cilician area with some scattered areas elsewhere, especially the western or Janik area of the Hamšen dialect at the border of the Black Sea).

Looking now at the glossary we see that classical voiceless stops are only partly voiced, in voiced surroundings only. This leads to the conclusion that the dialect of the glossary represents an intermediate stage between stage 2 (Cl. Arm. t̲ etc. is still voiceless) and stage 3 (Cl. Arm. t̲ etc. is voiced d̲ etc.). This fits in with the absolute chronology mentioned above. The origin of this dialect must be sought somewhere south or west of lake Van.

With these indications of the type and origin of the dialect represented by the glossary, is it possible to indicate its geographical position in the tenth century more precisely? When we look for a place that belongs to dialect-group 4 and also shows diphthongization of e̲ and o̲ we find either the Zeytun or the Sasun area. This means that the dialect of the glossary does not belong to the most southern, Syrian part of dialect-group 4 as the diphthongization did not reach this far-off area. But it does not mean that the Armenian who dictated the glossary to some monk in Western Europe originated either from Sasun or Zeytun. The geographical relation of the scattered southern groups of the dialect-group 4 (Sasun-Zeytun-Syria) is such that it suggests an earlier contiguous area that now is split up by intrusion of the later formed dialect-group 5 (Malatya-Tigranakert-Urfa) that shows no diphthongization. So the Armenian informant could have come from anywhere near the line Zeytun-Malatya-Sasun-Lake Van.

This preliminary conclusion on the type and place of origin of the dialect that is represented in the Autun glossary is a first approximation made on the basis of only a few features of this interesting document. A more detailed study will certainly be worth the reward.

NOTES

*I am indebted to Prof. F. Kortlandt for valuable comments on the subject-matter of this paper.

[1]H. Omont, "Manuel de conversation arménien-latin du Xe siecle," Bibliothèque de l'école des chartes 43 (1882) 563-564. The manuscript is kept in the Bibliothèque Muncipale of Autun (France) bearing the number 17 A (S 17). The glossary is found on Fol. 156 and 156 Vo. A short description of the manuscript was published in the Catalogue général des manuscrits des bibliothèques publiques des départements (Paris, 1849) 1, 13.

[2]A Carrière, Un ancien glossaire latin (Paris: Imprimerie Nationale,

1886). In the following I cite the entries by the number assigned to them by Carrière.

[3]The historical value of this document is briefly discussed in K. Kostaneanc', Hayagitut'iwn arewmtean Ewropayum (Tiflis: 1910) XZ. The fact that the Autun glossary is the earliest extant Armenian work of its kind is stressed by G. K. Gasparyan, Hay Bařaranagrut'yan Patmut'yun (Erevan: AN ArmSSR, 1968) 46-47.

[4]I thank Mr. Perrat for his kindness in putting the photograph at my disposal and permitting its publication. I did not see the manuscript itself.

[5]I am indebted to Prof. Dr. J. P. Gumbert, head of the department of western paleography at the Leiden University, for advising me on paleographic matters. One of the main corrections to Carrière's edition is entry (62) brachium: struch, where Prof. Gumbert rather reads stuuh.

[6]Prof. Gumbert prefers the later date on account of the form of internal -s- in entries like (20), (22), (23). There is external evidence to the dating: a note in manuscript Autun 22 mentions that manuscript 17 A belonged to those works that were given to the library of Autun by Walterius, who was an abbott of the Autun monastery in the tenth century (Catalogue général, 16-17).

[7]Recopying also accounts for some corrupted forms: (87) monachus: apiigahalts; (89) levita: aottroets (Carrière, Glossaire, 17 notes 2.3). See also n. 17 below.

[8]Carrière's publication was reviewed in Paul de Lagarde, Göttingische gelehrte Anzeigen 8 (1887) 292-294, who added some comment on consonantism and vocalism of the glossary. A short appraisal in general terms of Carrière's edition was given by A. Meillet, "Auguste Carrière," Annuaire de l'Ecole pratique des hautes Etudes. Section des Sciences historiques et philologiques 1903 (Paris 1902) 26-27.

[9]See the material presented by A. A. Abrahamyan, "Past'er hayereni patmakan hnč'yunap'oxut'yan mi k'ani erevuyt'neri žamanakašrĵani veraberyal," HSSH GA Tełekagir (1957) 4: 78-82.

[10]The earliest inscriptional evidence for loss of unstressed medial -e- dates from the eleventh century. See the discussion in A. A. Avagyan, Vimakan Arjanagrut'yunneri Hnč'yunabanut'yun (Erevan: HSSH GA, 1973)

104-107.   H. G. Muradyan, "Hnč'yunabanut'yun," 9-165 in <u>Aknarkner mijin</u> <u>grakan hayereni patmut'yan</u> (Erevan: HSSH GA, 1972) 1. 82 cites only relatively late examples.

[11]Data on the dialectical forms are taken from H. Ačaṙyan, <u>Hayeren</u> <u>Armatakan Baṙaran</u> (Repr. Erevan: HSSH GA, 1971-1979) s.vv. <u>eresun</u>, <u>k'aṙasun</u>. I have no material for '40' in the dialects of Ozmi, Hawarik and Akn, all of which show loss of -e- in <u>eresun</u>.

[12]On this retraction of the accent see H. Ačaṙyan, <u>Hayoc' Lezvi</u> <u>Patmut'yun</u> (Erevan: Haypethrat, 1951) 2. 372 and (for the Larabal-dialects) K. A. Davt'yan, <u>Leṙnayin Ḷarabaḷi barbaṙayin k'artezě</u> (Erevan: HSSH GA, 1966) 84-85.   This fact is important for relative chronology.

[13]It is interesting to note that the glossary preserves the classical word <u>atamn</u> 'tooth' whereas most modern dialects replaced it by <u>akṙay</u> (except the dialects of Erevan, Moks, Maraḷa, Salmast/P'ayajuk, Van, Ozmi and Muš): see Ačaṙyan, <u>Armatakan Baṙaran</u> s.v. <u>atamn</u>; M. H. Muradyan, "Baṙagitut'yun," 167-296 in <u>Aknarkner mijin grakan hayereni patmut'yan</u> 1. 192.

[14]The earliest inscriptional evidence for loss of unstressed medial -a- dates from 1036 (Tekor): see Avagyan, <u>Vimakan arjanagrut'yunneri hnč'-</u> <u>yunabanut'yun</u>, 381; Muradyan, "Hnč'yunabanut'yun," 74-76.

[15]See J. Karst, <u>Historische Grammatik des Kiliksch-Armenischen</u> (Strassburg: Trübner, 1901) 41-44 (loss of -a-); 51-52 (loss of -e-); 216-217 (numerals).   There seems to be no attestation of '40' in literary Cilician Armenian; Karst assumes *k'aṙsun. The accentual conditions under which unstressed -a- (and probably also -e-) were lost are explained by Meillet, <u>Esquisse d'une Grammaire comparée de l'Arménien classique</u> (and. ed.; Vienne: Imprimerie des PP. Mékhitaristes, 1936) 20.

[16]A. Meillet, "Remarques sur la Grammaire historique de l'Arménien de Cilicie de M. J. Karst," <u>Zeitschrift für armenische Philologie</u> 2 (1904) 25 [reprinted in <u>Etudes de Linguistique et de Philologie arméniennes</u> (Louvain: Imprimerie Orientaliste, 1977) 2. 121].

[17]This difference in diphthongization of classical <u>o</u> in medial and initial position is found to be preserved in the Polish Armenian dialect; Meillet, "Remarques," 25. F. Feydit, <u>Considérations de l'Alphabet de Saint</u>

Mesrob (Wien: Mechitaristen-Buchruckerei, 1964) 122-124 points to the development in the dialect of J̌uła. The discrepancy of (3) eriec xapte [Cl. Arm. erek'šabt'i] against (4) khurec xapte [Cl. Arm. č'orek'šabt'i might be explained by the nature of the vowel in the preceding syllable. In (83) tevavoet [probably Cl. Arm. t'ewawor] stressed -o- is diphthongized as expected, but written oe. For (51) lingua: lizu: class. lezu see Meillet, "Remarques," 25; Esquisse, 11. For (62) brachium: striuch [Cl. Arm. jeřk'] see n. 5 above. The word may be corrupted.

[18]Feydit, Considérations, 103-104.

[19]G. B. J̌ahukyan, Hay barbaŕagitut'yan neracut'yun (Erevan: HSSH GA, 1972) 268-269.

[20]Karst, Grammatik 18-21 (where he is unsure about o > uo). Muradyan, "Hnč'yunabanut'yun," 63-67 (on e > ye); 67-72 (on o). Literary Cilician Armenian is further developed in that initial unstressed Cl. Arm. e before liquids appears as i; Autun eriec vs. Cilician irek' ([iryek']) [Cl. Arm. erek'] (Karst, Grammatik 49-50).

[21]J̌ahukyan, Hay barbaŕagitut'yan neracut'yun, 63: isogloss No. 30 (e > ye) and No. 31 (o > uo) with table 3.

[22]The dialects are numbered in groups according to A. S. Garibjan's classification (based on consonantism) in "Ob armjanskom konsonantizme," Voprosy Jazykoznanija (1959) 5: 81-90 (reprinted in Armjanskij Konsonantizm v ocenke meždunarodnoj lingvistiki (Erevan: AN ArmSSR, Sektor naučnoj informacii po obščestvennym naukam, 1975) 1-10. For details see A. Pisowicz, "Materiaux pour servir à la recherche du consonantisme arménien," Folia Orientalia 17 (1976) 197-216. The places where e and o are diphthongized are (with the numbers assigned to them by J̌ahukyan, Hay barbaŕagitut'yan neracut'yun, 33-36): Xoy-dialect: P'ayaǰuk/Salmast (118), Urmia (119); Van-dialect: Bast (67), Van (68), Šatax (69), Moks (70), Ozm (71), Vardenis (east of lake Sevan) (72); Muš-dialect: Muš (55), Manazkert (59), Arčeš (65), Arcke (66) (but not Bitlis (63) and Xlat' (64)); Sasun-dialect: Aygetun (60), Nič' (61).

[23]More exact: the line T'omarza (27; belonging to the Arab-kir-dialect, group 3)—Haǰen (32)—Zeytun (33); the places Sivas (22) and Brgnik (23); Xotorǰur (44); the line Leninakan (42)—Gyařgyař (83)—Łalač'a (82); Kamo (near lake Sevan; 85).

[24]The Glossary writes /d̲/ with the sign d̲, /g̲/ with the sign g̲. There are no examples for /b̲/.

[25]See A. Pisowicz, Le Développement du Consonantisme arménien (Polske Akademia Nauk. Oddział w Krakowie. Prace Komisji jezykonawstwa. 43; Wrocław-Warszawa-Kraków-Gdánsk: Ossolineum, 1976) 60-62.

[26]The glossary shows the following notations for voiceless stops: /t̲/ written t̲; /p̲/ written p̲ or bp̲ (sabpat); as for /k̲/, we find representations in accordance with the spelling habits of the Romance European area: [ke] written che ((1) kyrache) or ke ((78) kenic, but also unexpectedly kce ((40) kcedinc), whereas ce denotes a fricative in (38) lucenga [Cl. Arm. lusnkay; [ki] written ky ((1) kyrache) or chi ((30) chini), whereas ci denotes a fricative ((59) cize [Cl. Arm. cic]); for [ka] we only find cha in (38) arechac; in other positions /k̲/ is written c̲: cu in (67) cuelc; nc in (12) hinc; cl in (76) cliu. It is noteworthy that the 'aberrant' writings bp (/p̲/) cha and kce (/k̲/) only occur in cases where the voiceless stop represents a Classical voiced stop; therefore, they may express some additional feature. A fricative is notated by kce and cha in (57) guttur: kcerchac [Cl. Arm. xr̄č'ak].

[27]The form (12) hinc [Cl. Arm. hing] is surprising in that we would expect a voiced stop here, as the preservation of the voiced feature after nasal (as in (h)andam) applies to word-final position too. In (5) hync xapte [Cl. Arm. hingšabt'i] the original voiced -g may be assimilated to the following voiceless š̲. Entry (72) genu: scunch may denote the plural form cung-k' rather than the modern singular cung.

[28]The only exception is (70) renes: gernac [Cl. Arm. kr̄nak].

[29]Some Classical voiceless stops, however, do not become voiced between vowels. The two cases (1) dies dominica: kyrache [Cl. Arm. kiwrake]; (81) altare: patarac [Cl. Arm. patarag] retained their Classical form on account of religious connotation (other instances of this influence in dialects gives Pisowicz, Développement, 61). I have no explanation for (64) digitus: matun [Cl. Arm. matun(k')] (plural of matn). In the case of (8) I: meche: mēk the -e is problematical in that none of the modern dialects has a form *meke or *mekḛ. This unexpected -e occurs quite often in the glossary ((35) chure [Cl. Arm. ǰur]; (55) vise [Cl. Arm. viz]; (59) cize [Cl. Arm. cic]; (60) puerhe [Cl. Arm. p'or]). I hesitate to interpret this -e as the definite article -ḛ (as Carriere does), for that seems to have arisen much

later.

[30]The devoicing of final ǰ after nasal in aganch [Cl. Arm. akanǰ(k')] is to be compared with hinc [Cl. Arm. hing]; see n. 27 above.

[31]The evidence of (8) meche [Cl. Arm. mēk] and (59) cize [Cl. Arm. cic] is contradictory, however; see n. 29 above. As for the sign z, it denotes a voiced sound between vowels (as in (27) hazar [Cl. Arm. hazar]; (42) mazen [Cl. Arm. maz(n)]; (59) cize [Cl. Arm. cic]) and after nasals ((41) anzen), but a voiceless sound in final position ((17) taz [Cl. Arm. tas(n)]; (28) panis: haz [Cl. Arm. hac']).

[32]This is the only occurrence of single b in the glossary the group -bp- ((7) sabpat [Cl. Arm. šabat'] denotes /p/.

[33]As there is for the most part no difference in the writing of voiceless and aspirated stops in the glossary, one could assume that voiceless and aspirated stops fell together in an aspirated stop. This possibility is excluded, however, by the writing of the affricates that in some cases seem to distinguish between voiceless and aspirate. Thus, class. č is written ch (75) whereas Cl. Arm. č' appears as kh ((11) IIII: khuert [Cl. Arm. č'ork'] or hc ((43) oculus: hahc: class. ač'(k'); (82) crux: chahc [Cl. Arm. xač'] where pre-posed h might note the aspiration. Both combinations reflect exclusively classical č'. In (57) guttur: kcerchac [Cl. Arm. xrč'ak] the pattern is disturbed, however. Classical c appears as c or sc (and -z- in (59) cize [Cl. Arm. cic]) whereas Classical c' is written -t ((13) VI: viit [Cl. Arm. vec']) -z ((28) panis: haz [Cl. Arm. hac']) and also -sc ((88) presbiter: eresc [Cl. Arm. erēc']).

[34]Frederik Kortlandt, "Notes on Armenian historical phonology II (the second consonant shift)," Studia Caucasica 4 (1978) 9-16.

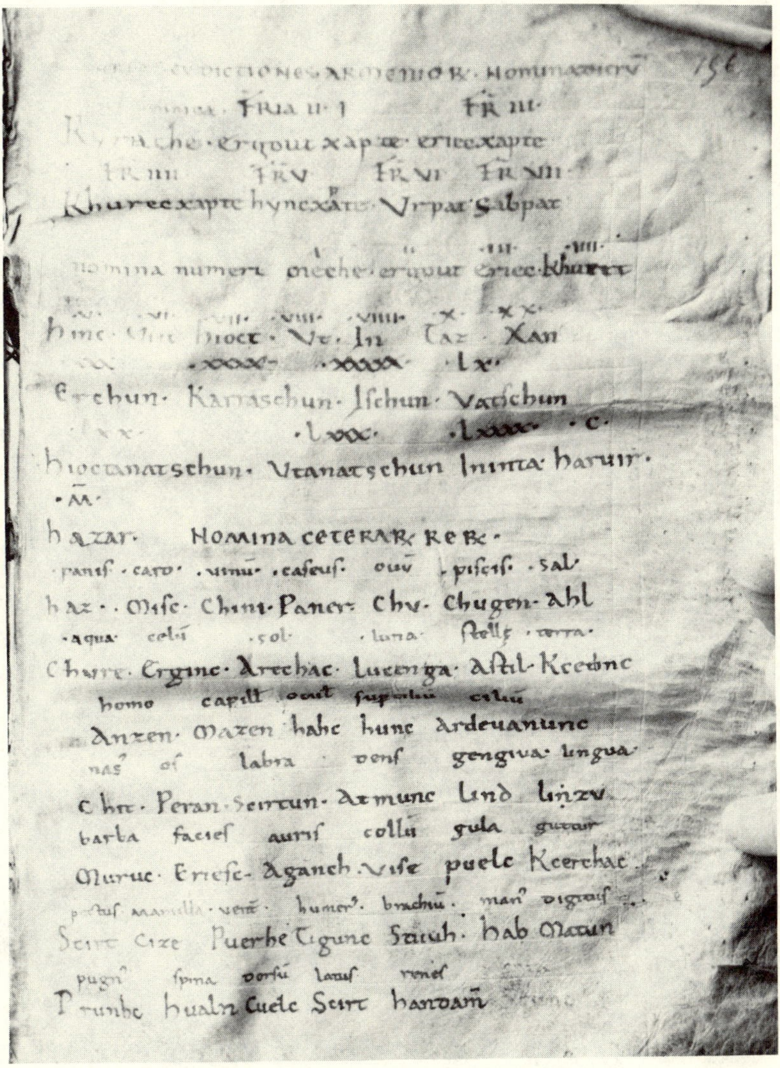

Figure 1. The Latin-Armenian Glossary of Autun

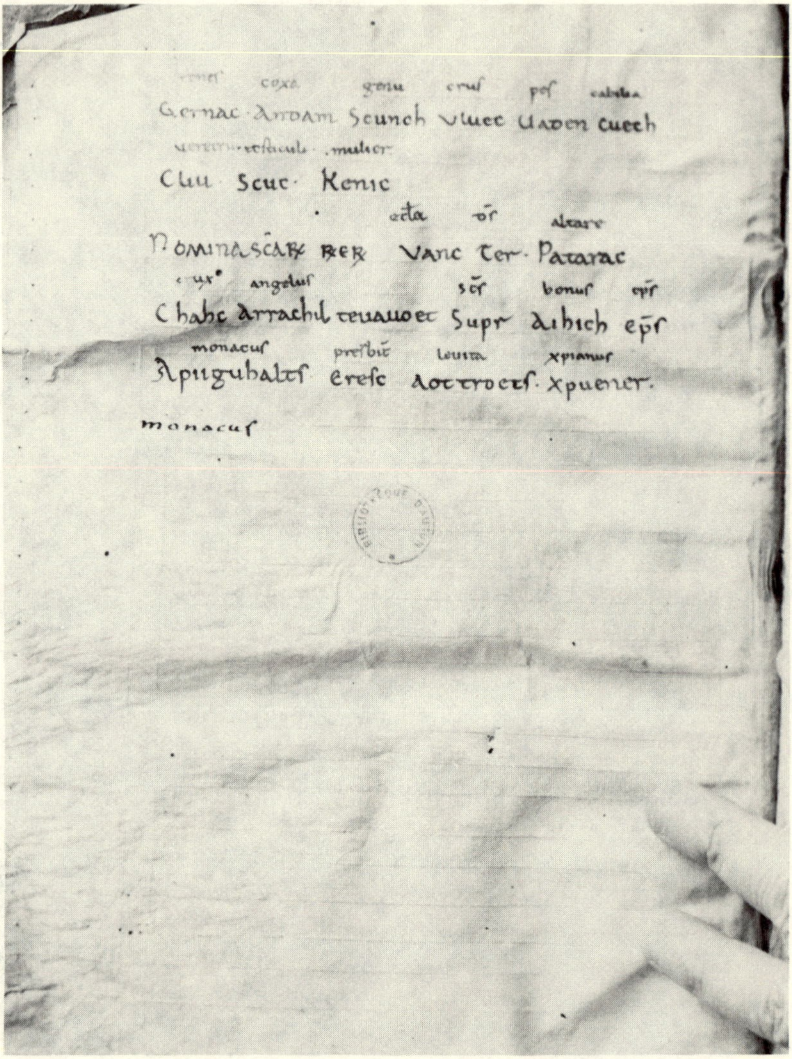

Figure 2. The Latin-Armenian Glossary of Autun

A PIONEER OF ARMENIAN ETYMOLOGY

Giancarlo Bolognesi

Università Cattolica del Sacro Cuore (Milan)

The earliest pioneers of lexicography and etymology, especially in the non-European languages, have long been neglected. We are prone to forget that although the comparative study of these languages was put on a scientific footing only recently, the ground was broken long ago.

One of these pioneers was the German orientalist Heinrich Julius Klaproth (Berlin II October 1783—Paris 28 August 1835). At the beginning of the last century, he gathered a lot of lexical material about the most disparate Asiatic languages. He gathered material not only from existing written and literary sources, but especially from people's own lips by means of interviews in the field.

His father was Martin Heinrich, the great chemist who discovered uranium and zirconium. When he was fourteen, Heinrich Julius Klaproth began to study Chinese by himself. Then he attended the Halle University and in 1804 went to St. Petersburg as "Adjunkt bei der Akademie der Wissenschaften." In 1805 he took part in a diplomatic mission to China and while travelling he learned new Asiatic languages and wrote ethnographic notes and collected books and rare texts. When he came back home in 1807, he was appointed member of the Academy of Sciences of St. Petersburg. In the same year he led a scientific expedition for geographical, ethnographical, political researches in Caucasus and Georgia, where he lived until 1809. During these two journeys he could gather a rich corpus of interesting and original material on which he based his following works.

We can agree with the judgement that "Seine beiden Expeditionen stellen ihn unter die bedeutendsten Forschungsreisenden seiner Zeit."[1]

T. Samuelian & M. Stone, eds. Medieval Armenian Culture. (University of Pennsylvania Armenian Texts and Studies 6). Chico, CA: Scholars Press, 1983. pp. 29 to 41.

From 1811 to 1814 he went to Berlin in order to elaborate all the material found during his travel and to prepare the publication. After that he did not leave Paris, except for a visit to Berlin shortly before his death (1835).

Through the good offices of W. von Humboldt, he was named to the chair of Oriental Languages at the Berlin University in acknowledgement of his scientific activity. At the same time he was exempted from his academic duties so as to be able to stay in Paris where he set to work on the Asiatic languages. He was also given 80,000 francs for their publication. This large sum of money led the French to suspect that he was a spy for the Prussians.

His difficult moods and impossible disposition, the harshness of his reviews and the liveliness of his polemics did not make him popular; nevertheless on the second centenary of his birth this Orientalist deserves to be commemorated. The breadth of his knowledge let him range nearly the whole Asiatic continent from Caucasus to Siberia, Mongolia, China and even Japan; the variety of his scientific interests led him to study linguistic, philological, historical and geographical problems of Asia.

He was one of the founders of the Société Asiatique of Paris and the important journal Journal Asiatique (Paris 1822) that is still published. He was among the founders, publishers and collaborators of other scientific journals such as Asiatisches Magazin, Annales des voyages, de la géographie et de l'histoire (Paris 1807) renamed Nouvelles annales des voyages in 1819 and other publications. His main works are: Reise in den Kaukasus und nach Georgien unternommen in dem Jahre 1807 und 1808, mit Anhang Kaukasische Sprachen, 2(3) vols. 1812-14; Asia polyglotta, with a Sprachatlas (Paris 1923; II ed. 1831), Mémoires relatifs à l'Asie, contenant des recherches historiques, géographiques et philologiques sur les peuples de l'Orient, 3 vols. 1824-28. He did not succeed in finishing a critical edition of 'Il Milione' by Marco Polo, which he worked on all his life long.

It is interesting and useful to study H. J. Klaproth's manifold activity, in particular, what he has to say about the Armenian language in his most important work Asia polyglotta. This work yet more interesting because it was published so early in the development of comparative linguistics (1823).

In order to understand the importance of H. J. Klaproth's work in this field, one must pay attention to his starting point, consisting of the works of comparative lexicography from the end of the eighteenth century. Among these Klaproth draws heavily upon lexical material collected from two hundred languages which was commissioned by Catherine II and carried out by the German P. S. Pallas, with the following title: Linguarum totius orbis vocabularia comparativa: Augustissimae cura collecta (St. Petersburg 1786-89). In it, Armenian is placed among the Turkish dialects and the Caucasian languages. It is most interesting to notice that, according to Klaproth, the misclassification of Armenian, is attributable to Pallas's inability to distinguish Classical Armenian from Modern Armenian "das eine Menge Turkischer und fremder Wörter enthält."[2]

Among the earlier works Klaproth also cites one by Johann Christoph Adelung, dedicated to the polyglot king of ancient Pontus. Adelung places Armenian among the Semitic and Caucasian languages, but he points out that it does not have any relationship with any other known language: "Die (scil. Arm.) Sprache ist eine eigene, mit keiner der bekannten verwandte Sprache, wie schon aus den Wörtern der ersten Bedurfnisses erhellt."

After examining twenty Armenian words (about relationship, the parts of the human body, some basic things) he concludes that: "Selbst die Zahlwörter, welche sich doch in so vielen sonst ganz verschiedenen Sprachen ähnlich sind, sind hier eigen."[3] Klaproth also mentions Fr. Adelung, Johann Cristoph's nephew, who "in seiner kindischen Leporelloliste von 3064 vorgeglichen Sprach- und Dialektnamen (St. Petersburg 1820, S.29), das Armenische, den Semitischen Sprachen folgen, und dem Georgischen und den Kaukasischen Sprachen vorangehen lässt."[4]

Klaproth criticizes the earlier theories about the Armenian language, and points out that: "Obgleich fur dieselbe (scil. Arm.Sprache) hinlangliche Hilfsmittel vorhanden waren, so haben dennoch die Sprachforscher bisher nicht recht gewusst mit ihr fertig zu werden." He is quite sure that Armenian is an Indo-European language and the Armenians "sind der sechste und letrte Zweig des Indo-Germanischen Stammes in Asien." The other Asiatic Indo-European languages are Sanskrit, Afghan, Persian, Kurdish and Ossetic. As Afghan, Persian, Kurdish and Ossetic are not considered to belong to the same Iranian group, but Asiatic "Zweige" of Indo-European, we cannot surely infer that Klaproth regards Armenian as a branch independent of Iranian. That would really have been ahead of its time.

Klaproth thinks that these Asiatic languages are linked together with other European languages (such as Latin, Greek, Germanic and Slavic) as part of the same Indo-European linguistic family. This fact is a clear sign that the German orientalist knew the contributions of several scholars who recognized this linguistic family around the beginning of the nineteenth century.   Among these scholars Klaproth ignores, or anyway does not mention, Friederich Schlegel who, perhaps better than anyone else, had clearly pointed out that Armenian belongs to the Indo-European family, even if the relations of Armenian with Sanskrit seem to be less obvious than those between Sanskrit and Greek, Latin, Persian and the Germanic languages. On the first page, too, of his well-known work Ueber die Sprache und Weisheit der Indier Fr. Schlegel had written: "Mit der armenischen, den slavischen Sprachen und naechstdem mit der celtischen, ist die Verwandtschaft des Indischen entweder gering, oder steht doch in gar keinem Verhaeltniss zu der grossen Uebereinstimmung mit jenen zuvor genannten Sprache (scil. mit der roemischen und grieschischen so wie mit der germanischen und persischen Sprache), die wir aus ihr ableiten." Fr. Schlegel continued: "Ganz zu uebersehen ist diese obwohl geringe Verwandtschaft aber dennoch nicht, da sie in der Ordnung, wie diese Sprachen genannt worden sind, sich selbst noch wenigstens in einigen grammatischen Formen kund giebt, in solchen Bestand-theilen die nicht unter die Zufaelligkeiten der Sprachen gerechnet werden koennen, sondern zur innern Structur derselben gehoeren."

And later on Fr. Schlegel gives a short but meaningful list of lexical and morphological connections between Armenian and other Indo-European languages, which comes to the following conclusion: "Gewiss ist das Armenische ein merkwuerdiges Mittelglied, und kann ueber die Entstehung und Geschichte der asiatischen und europaeischen Sprachen manchen Auf-schluss geben."[5]

It is most interesting to compare the lexical Armenian cognates given by Schlegel and those by Klaproth. First of all it is striking that the list of the cognates given by Klaproth is much broader than the one by Schlegel. A good place to start is with an examination of the cognates, still valid today, which are given by Klaproth, but absent from Schlegel's earlier work.

It should be noted that the Armenian words recorded by Klaproth "nach der Aussprache der Armenier von Konstantinopel" are quoted here in classical Armenian, and in the transliteration which is currently in use. Similarly words from other languages have here been "normalized" according to current systems of transliteration. Whenever an Armenian word is compared with words from several languages, only those whose comparison is correct will be noted.

	Klaproth	Schlegel
Arm. gišer	O.Sl. věčerŭ	vacat
Arm. cer	Pers. zar, Av. zaurva-, Oss. zarond	vacat
Arm. akn, pl. ač'k'	O.Sl. oko, du. oči, Russ. očki,	
	Germ. Auge, Lett. acs, Skr. akşi,	vacat
Arm. arĵ	Oss. ars, Kurd. hirč, Pers. zirs,	
	Lat. ursus	vacat
Arm. du	Ganz Indo-Germ.	vacat
Arm. ankiwn	Lat. angulus	vacat
Arm. armukn	Germ. Arm	vacat
Arm. jukn	Kriwo Liw. zuve	
	(cf. Lith. žuvìs, Lett. zuvs, zivs)	vacat
Arm. mis	O.Sl. męso	vacat
Arm. ber-k'	Pers. bar	vacat
Arm. otn	Ganz Germanisch. Angelsächsisch	
	und Schwedisch fot, etc.	vacat
Arm. mec	Gr. mega	vacat
Arm. karkut	O.Sl. gradŭ, Lat. grando[6]	vacat
Arm. jeřn	Gr. khéir	vacat
Arm. tun	Lat. domus, O.Sl. domŭ	vacat
Arm. sirt	Russ. serdce, Lith. širdìs, Lett. siřds	vacat
Arm. lsem	Russ. slušu, slušat', Engl. listen,	
	Germ. lausche	vacat
Arm. šun	Skr. śuni-, Lith. šuñs, Lett. suns,	
Arm. es	O.Sl. azŭ, Oss. äz, Kurd. az, Av. azəm,	
	Lith. aš (old eš), Lett. es	vacat
Arm. cunr, pl. cungk'	Afg. zangŭn	vacat
Arm. oskr	Lat. os, Bret. askourn, Welsh asgwrn,	
	Corn. ascorn	vacat
Arm. glux	Russ. golová	vacat
Arm. kov	Ganz Indo-Germanisch	vacat
Arm. mard	Av. mərəta-, Pahl. mart, Pers. mard,	
	Kurd. mir	vacat
Arm. mēǰ	Germ. Mitte, etc.	vacat
Arm. amis	O.Sl. měseci, Russ. mesjac	vacat
Arm. mayr	Ganz Germanisch	vacat
Arm. ełungn	Lat. unguis, ungula, Irish ionga	vacat

Arm. anun	Pers. nām, Germ. Name, Oss. nom,	
	etc., Irish anim, Gr. ónoma	vacat
Arm. mēg[7]	Pers. mēγ	vacat
Arm. arawr	Lat. arare, aratrum	vacat
Arm. awaz	Gr. ammos[8]	vacat
Arm. naw[9]	Skr. nauḫ, Pers. nāv, Lat. navis, etc.	vacat
Arm. awj[10]	Pers. až-dar, až-dahā	vacat
Arm. kul	Pers. gulū (galū), Beng. galā,	
	Lat. gula, Germ. Kehle, etc.	vacat
Arm. jiwn	Gr. khion	vacat
Arm. k'oyr	Pers. xvahar, Kurd. xōh (or xōr),	
	Afgh. xor, Bret. c'hoar	vacat
Arm. arcat'	Lat. argentum	vacat
Arm. astł	Gr. astēr	vacat
Arm. tiw	Lat. dies	vacat
Arm. durn	Germ. Thür, Thor, etc.	vacat
Arm. dustr	Germ. Tochter, Pers. duxtar	vacat
Arm. meṙeal[11]	Lat. mors, etc.	vacat
Arm. i veroy	Germ. über	vacat
Arm. hayr	Irish athir	vacat
Arm. ǰerm	Pers. garm, Germ. warm, Gr. therme	vacat
Arm. kin	Gr. gunḗ, Goth. qino, etc.	vacat
Arm. mek'	O.Sl. my[12]	vacat
Arm. atamn	Gr. ódoús, ódóntos	vacat
Arm. ost	Germ. Ast	vacat
Arm. č'ork'	Pers. čahār, čār, Beng. čār, O.Sl. četyre	vacat
Arm. vec'	Bret. c'houec'h, Welsh chwech	vacat
Arm. ewt'n	Gr. épta, Pers. haft	vacat
Arm. ut'	Lat. octo, Ital. otto	vacat
Arm. inn	Germ. neun, Gr. ennéa	vacat
Arm. tasn	O.Sl. desętĭ, Russ. desjat', Skr. daśa,	
	Oss. dās	vacat

Also the comparison of Arm. gini 'wine' with Georg. γvino, Bret. Welsh gwin, Germ. Wein, etc. can be accepted, with the obvious remark that this is not an original Indo-European word, but a word from the Mediterranean substratum, which Celtic and Germanic languages have borrowed from the Latin vinum.

The relationship between Arm. ēš 'ass', Lat. asinus, Engl. ass, Turk. ešek is as well acceptable if we remember that this word has been incorporated in different forms in the Indo-European languages from the Sumerian ansu or from an old Anatolian Mediterranean substratum, and that the Latin word arrived in the English via the Celtic.

J. Klaproth rightly remarks that Arm. katu 'cat' corresponds to Germ. Kater and to Lat. cattus, even though, for phonetic, historical and cultural reasons, the word was borrowed into Armenian from another language.[13]

Without discussing their validity, it should however be noted that other comparisons which have been afterwards suggested, had already been recognized much earlier by J. Klaproth. For example, V. Pisani considered the possibility of comparing the Armenian word karč 'short' with Germ. kurz,[14] and J. Klaproth had already established a comparison between the same Armenian word and the same German word.

Klaproth found an exact parallel with other Indo-European languages for more than fifty Armenian words. These words are not present in the previous list by Schlegel and, as far as I know, for the most part had never been comparatively explained by other scholars.

Klaproth also puts forth some cognates of other Armenian words of which Schlegel had already noted, and some relations with other Indo--European languages. It is most interesting to notice that at times the comparison made by Schlegel is incorrect, while Klaproth introduces a new element which is still valid today. For example, Schlegel related the Armenian word amenayn with Lat. omnis, and Klaproth with Lat. omnis and Pers. hama 'all.' While the reference to Lat. omnis cannot be accepted, the one to Pers. hama is most valid still today.

Sometimes the cognates given by Schlegel are exactly like those by Klaproth, who compares, however, the Armenian word with a larger number of languages. The results are clear from the following list:

	Schlegel	Klaproth
Arm. hing	Lat. quinque	Lat. quinque, Ital. cinque, French cinq
Arm. utem	Lat. edo	Lat. edere, Plattdeutsch eten
Arm. tam	Lat. do	Lat. dare, Pers. dādan

In Schlegel's and Klaproth's analysis we can point out different forms among the Armenian words and among the terms of those languages on which the comparison is based:

	Schlegel		Klaproth
Arm. lusaworim	Lat. luceo		Arm. loys, Lat. lux, Dan. lius
Arm. atim	Lat. odium		Arm. atem, Lat. odio

Schlegel gives a few exact cognates of Armenian words which Klaproth did not note:

	Schlegel	Klaproth
Arm. k'an	Lat. quan	vacat
Arm. mi 'one'	Gr. mía	vacat
Arm. mi 'prohibitive negative'	Gr. mḗ	vacat
Arm. lucanem	Gr. lúō	vacat
Arm. arnum	Gr. ắrnymai	vacat
Arm. dnem	Gr. theĩnai	vacat
Arm. lnum	Lat. plenus	vacat
Arm. em	Engl. I am	vacat
Arm. berem	Lat. fero, Pers. burdan	vacat

Of the morphological coincidences, pointed out by Schlegel between Armenian and Latin, the verbal inflections are most important:

Arm. luanam	Lat. lavo
Arm. luanas	Lat. lavas
Arm. luanay	Lat. lavat
Arm. luanan	Lat. lavant

Also the comparison of Armenian participles in -eal with the corresponding Slavic ones in -lŭ is quite right.

In Klaproth's favor there is the recognition that Armenian has in common with other languages (mainly the Iranian ones) many other words which, are not to be considered as coming from the common source but are rather as lexical loans:

	Klaproth		Schlegel
Arm. kapik	Pers. kabī		vacat
Arm. bazuk	Pers. bāzū, Kurd. bāsk, bāzk		vacat
Arm. tapar	Pers. tabar, tawar, Kurd. tefer, tewir, Russ. topor		vacat
Arm. terew	Syr. ṭəref		vacat
Arm. kapoyt	Pers. kabūd(ī)		vacat
Arm. kapar	Arab. and Pers. kabar[15]		vacat
Arm. dašt	Pers. dašt		vacat
Arm. p'ił	Pers. pīl		vacat

Arm. bad or bat	Arab. baṭṭ[16]	vacat
Arm. bazē	Pers. bāz	vacat
Arm. čarp	Pers. čarb	vacat
Arm. dat	Pers. dād	vacat
Arm. laxt	Pers. laxt	vacat
Arm. t'agawor	Pers. tāǰ	vacat
Arm. ark'ay	Gr. árkhōn[17]	vacat
Arm. płinj	Pers. birinǰ; in ganz Westasien verbreitet	vacat
Arm. margarit	Gr. margarítēs	vacat
Arm. k'ahanay	Arab. kāhin[18]	vacat
Arm. seaw	Pers. siyāh	vacat
Arm. čakat	Pers. čakād	vacat
Arm. k'ałak'	Georg. k'alak'i[19]	vacat
Arm. dew	Pers. dēv	vacat
Arm. zēn	Pers. zēn	vacat
Arm. kařk'	Germ. Karre[20]	vacat
Arm. spitak	Kurd. sipī, Afgh. spīn, Pers. sipēd	vacat
Arm. žamanak	Arab. zamān[21]	vacat
Arm. połovat	Pers. pōlād.	vacat

We must recognize that Klaproth was among the first scholars (more than anyone else) to point out a great number of lexical connections between Armenian and other languages which still hold today. He was working without scientific method and, therefore, without regard for correct phonetic correspondences, so at times he wrongly posited cognates. Nevertheless, starting from Adelung's statement that Armenian did not have any relationship with any other known language, Klaproth succeeded in showing a lot of Armenian connections with other languages of the Indo-European linguistic family. He deserved, therefore, to be at least mentioned by Joseph Karst in his history of Armenian philology.[22]

Klaproth did not succeed in distinguishing the inherited core of Indo-European origin from the later acquisitions through pre-historical and historical contacts with other linguistic traditions. On this subject it is interesting to point out that the distinction in the Armenian vocabulary between the original lexical items and those borrowed from another source had already been noted by a previous researcher, unknown to Klaproth and little known or unknown to later researchers in the field. As we shall see in greater depth in another study, from the beginning of the eighteenth century Johannes Joachim Schroder had realized that loan-words from Parthian, Greek, Syriac and Arabic had been added to the original lexical core of Armenian through successive historical contacts with other cultural traditions.   For example, Arm. dašt 'plain, field' had already been clearly recognized as borrowed from the Parthian; Arm. k'ahanay 'sacerdos' as borrowed from the Syriac, and Arm. ark'ay from the Greek.[23]

Even without the necessary distinction between original lexical elements and loans, the main lexical elements that have enriched the primary Indo-European vocabulary of Armenian, are noted in Klaproth's comparisons. The most important source was Iranian and, to a lesser extent, Greek and Syriac.   In this regard the connection between Arm. terew and Syr. təref is most interesting.

From Klaproth's comparisons it appears that he draws more on the modern than the ancient languages: more than to Old Iranian he refers to modern Persian, Kurdish, Ossetic and Afghan; more than Gothic he refers to German, Danish, Swedish and Plattdeutsch, more than old Celtic languages he refers to Breton and Welsh. He often mentions Russian beside Old Slavic, the Romance languages beside Latin. Thus, we can understand that Klaproth drew the material for his comparisons on the huge knowledge he had of spoken languages more than on dictionaries and grammars. He is very proud, indeed, of this: "Eine grosse Sammlung von Wörterbuchern und Grammatiken und ruhmredige Zeitungsartikel, machen niemanden zum Sprachforscher; man muss Sprachen gelernt haben, um über sie zu urtheilen, sonst schreibt man unnütze Bucher und macht sich lächerlich."[24]

That is a rule we think always topical and well-grounded above all in our times, when "oft schreibt man unnütze Bucher und macht sich lächerlich" because the authors of many books about linguistic theory forget that "man muss Sprachen gelernt haben, um über sie zu urtheilen." Both in his positive and negative aspects Klaproth's work must be regarded as the work by an ingenious "Bahnbrecher' of the Armenian and Oriental studies during an age full of spurs and rich in scientific discoveries like the one which immediately follows the first innovating works by Bopp, Rask, J. Grimm and came before the period when the new linguistic science found a more consistent and lasting framework.

In conclusion we can agree to what the great linguist Hans George Conon von der Gabelentz wrote about J. Klaproth: "Die Jugendgeschichte der modernen, ganz Asien umfassenden Orientalistik ist an seinen Namen geknupft wie an keinen zweiten."[25]

NOTES

[1]G. Naundorf, "Heinrich Julius Klaproth," 11 (1977) 706-707 in Historische Kommission bei der bayerischen Akademie der Wissenschaften (ed.), Neue deutsche Biographie (Berlin: Dunker & Humblot, 1977) 707.

[2]J. Klaproth, Asia polyglotta (Paris: A. Schubart, 1823) 97.

[3]J. C. Adelung, Mithridates, oder allgemeine Sprachenkunde mit dem Vater Unser als Sprachprobe in bey nahe funfhundert Sprachen und Mundarten (Berlin: Vossische Buchhandlung, 1806-1817) 1,421.

[4]J. Klaproth, Asia polyglotta, 98.   F. Adelung's Leporelloliste was translated into Italian by F. Cherubini under the title Prospetto nominativo di tutte le lingue note e dei loro dialetti (Milano: G. B. Bianchi e C. 1824) 30-31.

[5]F. Schlegel, Ueber die Sprache und Weisheit der Indier. Ein Beitrag zur Begruendung der Alterthumskunde (Heidelberg: Mohr und Zimmer, 1808) 3-4; 77-79.

[6]The etymology is as suggested by A. Meillet, and accepted by R. Solta, neither of whom had noticed that it had already been suggested much earlier by J. Klaproth: A. Meillet, "Etymologies arméniennes," MSL 10 (1898) 280; A. Ernout & A. Meillet, Dictionnaire etymologique de la langue latine (Paris: C. Klincksieck, 1959) 281; R. Solta, Die Stellung des Armenischen im Kreise der indogermanischen Sprachen.   Eine Untersuchung der indogermanischen Bestandteile des armenischen Wortschatzes (Studien zur armenischen Geschichte, 9; Wien: Mechitharisten-Buchdruckerei, 1960) 311.

[7]According to E. Benveniste this Armenian word could have been borrowed from Iranian: E. Benveniste, "Mots d'emprunt iraniens en arménien," BSL 53 (1957-58) 60.

[8]With reference to Latin sabulum, A. Meillet wrote: "Il y a un rapport avec d'autres noms du 'sable,' gr. psámmos, ammos, psamathos, et ámathos . . ., avec v. isl. sandr et v.h.a. sampt, et meme avec arm. awaz" (A. Ernout & A. Meillet, Dictionnaire etymologique de la langue latine, 585.

[9]This Armenian word could also be borrowed from Iranian: cf. G. Bolognesi, "Contributo allo studio della piu antica terminologia marinaresca armena e dei suoi rapporti con quella delle altre lingue indeuropee," Bollettino dell'Atlante linguistico Mediterraneo 18-19 (1976-77) 195-197.

[10]Cf. G. Bolognesi, "Tradition and Innovation in the Armenian," 125-141 in T. J. Samuelian (ed.), Classical Armenian Culture: Influences and Creativity (Proceedings of the First Dr. H. Markarian Conference on Armenian Culture. Philadelphia: University of Pennsylvania, 1982) 130-131.

[11]Arm. mah "death" is however borrowed from the Parthian.

[12]Cf. A. Meillet, Le slave commun (2nd ed., Paris: H. Champion, 1934) 454.

[13]H. Hubschmann, Armenische Grammatik. Erster Teil: Armenische Etymologie (Lepizig: Breitkopf & Hartel; 1897) 307.

[14]V. Pisani, "Armenische Miszelle," Die Sprache 12 (1966) 231-232 [reprinted in V. Pisani, Mantissa (Brescia: Paideia, 1978) 341-342.]

[15]H. Hubschmann also puts Arm. kapar among the "Persische Worter," comparing it not only with the Pers. kabar, but also with the Greek kápparis, and concludes: "Wohl direct aus dem Griech. entlehnt" (Armenische Grammatik, 165). In fact, Arm. kapar can be found in an Old Testament context, where it is used to translate Greek kápparis.

[16]The same word can also be found however in Iranian (cf. Pers. bat) from which the Armenian is directly derived.

[17]"On écarte malaisément l'idée que le mot arkhay 'chef' proviendrait de arkhōn; seul, un intermediaire araméen—par voie parthe—expliquerait à la rigueur le passage"; A. Meillet, "De l'influence parthe sur la langue arménienne," REA 1 (1920) 11-12.

[18]To be more precise, the Armenian word is borrowed from Syriac kàhnā which corresponds to kāhin in Arabic.

[19]The Georgian word is however to be considered as borrowed from the Armenian.

[20]The Armenian word is considered a loan from Lat. carrus which in turn is derived from Gallie carros, cf. A. Meillet, Esquisse d'une grammaire comparée de l'arménien classique (2nd ed.; Vienne: Imprimerie des PP.

Mékhitharistes, 1936) 144; and similarly: "Zu Beginn unsrer Zeitrechnung haben Germanen an ihrer Westgrenze lat. carrus 'Wagen' entlehnt, das aus gall. carros (*krsos) stammt":   F. Kluge & W. Mitzka, Etymologisches Worterbuch der deutschen Sprache (Berlin-New York: W. De Gruyter, 1975) 354.

[21]These Armenian and Arab words are borrowed from Iranian, and the first is derived from Parthian jm'n, the second from Pers. zamān; cf. G. Bolognesi, Le fonti dialettali degli imprestiti iranici in armeno (Milano: Vita e Pensiero, 1960) 44-45.

[22]J. Karst, Armeno-Pelasgica. Geschichte der armenischen Philologie in kritischer Beleuchtung nach ihren ethnologischen Zusammenhänge dargestellt, mit Beilagen und Exkursen über die asianisch-mediterraneische Vorgeschichte (Heidelberg: C. Winter, 1930).   Klaproth is also ignored by Placido Sukias Somal, who deals with "Degli Europei coltivatori dell'armena lingua" as an appendix to his Quadro della storia letteraria di Armenia (Venezia: Tipografia armena di S. Lazzaro, 1829) 201-208.

[23]J. J. Schröder, Thesaurus Linguae Armenicae, antiquae et hodiernae (Amstelodami: 1711) 43-47.

[24]J. Klaproth, Asia polyglotta, 98.

[25]H. G. Conon von der Gabelentz, "Heinrich Julius Klaproth," in J. S. Ersch & J. G. Gruber (ed.), Allgemeine Encyclopädie der Wissenschaften und Künste (Leipzig: 1818-89) II 36.359.

THE KINGDOM OF ARC'AX[*]

Robert H. Hewsen

Glassboro State College

One of the peculiarities of Armenian historiography in the West has been a neglect of the history of the Armenian Plateau in the period between the Battle of Manzikert of 1071 and the rise of the early Armenian liberation movement in the late seventeenth century. Captivated by the emergence of the remarkable state of Armeno-Cilicia, Western historians have tended to lose interest in events taking place in Armenia proper once it was overrun by the Turks, passing over with a few broad strokes the invasions, campaigns, wars and conquests which they examine in minute detail when discussing the Urartian, Roman, Byzantine, Arab, or Bagratid periods.[1] Not until the recent appearance of Histoire des Arméniens (under collective authorships, editor G. Dédéyan), which devoted slightly more than two of its sixteen chapters to this period, was any serious attempt made in the West to come to grips with the detailed history of these admittedly confusing and obscure centuries.[2]

The reason for the neglect of such a lengthy and relatively recent period in Armenian history is not a dearth of sources, for these are ample—at least for the first half of the period. Nor is it due to the lack of a history worth relating, for much of great importance was taking place in Armenia at this time. The reason, I believe, for slighting these six centuries is the lack of enthusiasm on the part of many historians for a period of Armenian history which they perceive to be primarily the history of alien peoples ruling over an Armenian population no longer master in its own homeland. The alarums and excursions of Cilician history are much more arresting for those interested in the Armenian odyssey, and the story of the later Armenian political, cultural and ecclesiastical revival is perhaps thought to be more

---

T. Samuelian & M. Stone, eds. Medieval Armenian Culture. (University of Pennsylvania Armenian Texts and Studies 6). Chico, CA: Scholars Press, 1983. pp. 42 to 68.

edifying, and more relevant for others less interested in the earlier periods. Yet, even if the history of Armenia is considered to be more the history of the Armenian people themselves than that of the Armenian plateau and of the comings and goings of the foreign powers which have dominated it, we should still be aware that in this period there are numerous examples of national endeavor on the part of the Armenians of the homeland proper, and that there was not a moment during these long centuries when all of the Armenian people lost their independence or control over the destiny of at least a part of their native land.

Space does not permit a thorough examination of the various centers of Armenian independence which survived after the Turkish deluge had broken over the high plateau. Therefore, I shall confine myself to the circumstances which surrounded and made possible the survival of autonomous enclaves in Eastern Armenia; that is, in Siwnik' and Karabagh (Łarabał), and in particular to what I shall call the "Kingdom of Arc'ax," which flourished, however feebly or fitfully, from the eleventh through thirteenth centuries. I shall not elaborate upon the history of the Armenian meliks, who appear at a later date and with whom I have dealt elsewhere.[3]   Rather I shall concentrate on their predecessors, those dynasts who bridge the period between the fall of the principality of Albania in the early ninth century and the emergence of the melik houses in the fifteenth. A brief examination of the history of this part of Armenia in this period will, I think, demonstrate the significance and excitement of the events which took place here in the Armenian "dark ages," many of which events still await their historian.

I

As the Caliphate weakened in the ninth and tenth centuries, a number of independent states emerged from among the various Armenian principalities which had survived in Armenia during the period of the Arab domination, their rulers one by one achieving recognition of royal status from both the Caliphate and the Byzantine Empire. The largest of these states, eventually centered at Ani, in Širak, appeared under the Bagratuni dynasty in 885.[4]   This was followed by Vaspurakan (under the Arcrunids) in 908;[5] by Dizak or K't'iš in southern Arc'ax (under the Aṙanšahikids), calling itself the "Kingdom of Albania" in c. 922;[6] and by Siwnik' (under its native dynasty) in c. 961.[7]   Thereafter, there emerged, as offshoots of the Kingdom of Ani, two more independent Bagratid Kingdoms, one centered at Kars, in the earlier principality of Vanand, in 962,[8] and the other at Loři, in Tašir, in 982, also calling itself the "kingdom of Albania."[9]

Finally, from c. 1000 to 1266, the Princes of Xačʻēn, the earlier land of Arcʻax, today known as Karabagh (Łarabał), also assumed the royal title, forming yet a third "Kingdom of Albania" or, alternatively, "Kingdom of Arcʻax,"[10] and obviously laying claim to the same Albanian inheritance as the Bagratid Kings at Loři and the Ařanšahikids of Dizak. To distinguish these Kings of Albania in Arcʻax-Xačʻēn from the other claimants to the same dignity, I shall refer to them as the "Kings of Arcʻax," a unique and more accurate title, which on occasion they themselves used. Thus, by the end of the first millenium A.D., no less than seven Armenian kingdoms were functioning upon the Armenian Plateau.

Few of these political formations were fated to last for long. Spearheads of the Seljuk Turkish invasion forced the King of Vaspurakan to cede his state to the Byzantines as early as 1021, while Ani passed under Byzantine rule in 1045. Then, under the leadership of Alp Arslan, a full-scale Turkish invasion of Armenia was launched. Ani was taken in 1064, and after the Battle of Manzikert in 1071, the Byzantines were cleared from the plateau forever, and the Turks were left virtual masters of Anatolia. Kars had fallen to them by 1065, while Manzikert had given them Vaspurakan. Of the seven Armenian kingdoms only four remained: Loři-Albania, whose king, Gurgen (1046-1081), saved his state only be accepting Turkish sovereignty and giving his daughter to Alp Arslan; southern Siwnikʻ (Siwnikʻ-Bałkʻ), Dizak-Kʻtʻiš, and Xačʻēn, all of which had accepted Turkish overlordship as well.[11]

The Seljuk domination of Armenia coincided with the rise of the Georgian state, which had united into a single kingdom in 1008, and which, after the coming of the Mongols in the thirteenth century, created a pan-Caucasian state of formidable proportions. As the Turks and their various Muslim vassals began to falter in the twelfth century, Georgia expanded into northern and eastern Armenia, capturing Ani, Dvin and Kars, and all of Siwnikʻ, wisely placing these regions under Armenian vassal princes, and reducing to the same vassalage the rulers of Dizak and Xačʻēn.[12] We shall not concern ourselves here with the Bagratid Kings of Loři, who lingered on until the late thirteenth century, or with such Armenian vassals of the Georgian kings as the Xałbakids of Vayocʻ Jor, the Orbelids of Siwnikʻ, or the Mxargrjelids, Gagelids and Mankaberdelids to the east of Lake Sevan, all of whom profited from the Georgian domination of Armenia. Rather we shall focus upon the various branches of the Siwnid house ruling in the regions to the south and southeast of the lake. Let us examine briefly the history of this dynasty so as to understand how the Kingdom of Arc'ax emerged under its aegis.

II

The Princes Siwni, a family which may have been of Scythian origin, were the immemorial dynasts of the land of Siwnik', the largest principality of ancient Armenia (Map I), but are known only since the conversion of Armenia to Christianity,[13] in the early fourth century, at which time Antovk (Antiochus) Siwni was head of the house.   Antiochus' granddaughter, P'aranjem, was the consort of King Aršak II of Armenia,[14] and her nephew, the arch-traitor Prince Vasak of Siwnik', was the Persian viceroy of Armenia at the time of the Vardananc' war almost a century after.[15] Still later, in the seventh century, Gregory II Novirak, Prince of Siwnik', who had married the daughter of Xosrov II, Shah of Iran, died fighting for the Persians against the Arabs at the Battle of Qadisiya.[16] Thereafter, the family may be traced with only a few breaks and uncertain filiations until the time of Vasak III (d. 821), when our sources became abundant, and when we find for the first time, to our knowledge, the territory of Siwnik' being divided among different branches of the family (Map II).[17]

Now, from earlier times, Armenia had been composed of a number of autonomous states each ruled by a sovereign prince (išxan). The lands of the prince were family domains, indivisible, and passed from father to son, or, lacking a son, to the Prince's oldest brother. This system began to break down in the Arab period (c. 650-c. 960), when the other male members of the house (sepuh-s), began to seek autonomy over specific lands held by them within the family domain.[18]

This process must have begun by the end of the eighth century for at the beginning of the ninth we find the principality of Siwnik' being divided and redivided among the various scions of the house.[19] The senior line, which we may call the branch of West Siwnik', always held the bulk of the family domains, and, when the principality achieved international recognition as a kingdom in c. 961, it was the prince of West Siwnik' alone who possessed the royal title, being recognized within the family as "Great Geniarch" (mec nahapet) over the other branches of the house. This senior line became extinct, however, in c. 1019, when King Vasak VI died leaving a single daughter Kotramide (Catherine), who had been married to King Gagik I, Bagratid ruler of Armenia at Ani, and now, apparently having inherited the bulk of her father's domains, would have had to bring them into the hands of her husband.[21]

The second branch of the Siwnid family, the line of North Siwnik' or Gełark'unik' had already disappeared in c. 912. Its lands, lying in the basin of Lake Sevan, may have been annexed by the Bagratids, who were expanding easternward under Ašot II at just about this time (922) making themselves masters of Utik' and of the other lands lying between Lake Sevan and the River Kur[22] (Map III).

The third branch of the Siwnid House, the line of South Siwnik' or Kovsakan-Bałk' is the only one in Siwnik' which survived both the Bagratid annexations and the Turkish conquest. Having inherited the royal title after the death of Vasak VI, it continued the kingdom of Siwnik' (in Bałk') as late as 1071.[23] In that year, however, King Gregory III, who married Šahanduxt, sister of King Sennacherib of Dizak and had no children of his own, left Bałk' and its throne to his brother-in-law, whose territory—Dizak—would have thereby doubled in size. This Sennacherib, son of Dakin-Sevada, was of the House of Aṙanšahik, which until the first century A.D. had ruled Albania, and which had apparently survived all these centuries here in Arc'ax. This principality, known both as Dizak or as K't'iš after its center, lay in what was later southern Karabagh, and adjoined that of Bałk' on the east. Sennacherib had saved his principality at the time of the Seljuk invasion by accepting the overlordship of Alp Arslan's son, Sultan Malik Shah, who, occupied elsewhere, had adopted a policy of maintaining local Christian rulers in Caucasia in return for submission and payment of taxes.[24] King George II of Georgia (1072-1089) had gone in person to make his obeisance to the Sultan at Ispahan, and Sennacherib, now King of Dizak and Bałk', did the same.[25]

After the death of Malik Shah in 1093, the order which he had established began to break down. In 1097, the Crusaders arrived in Syria. Meanwhile various Seljuk chieftains and rebellious lieutenants had begun struggling for possession of the newly conquered Turkish lands. The resulting turmoil soon spread to Armenia. According to Stephen Orbelean, King Sennacherib, while at Ispahan, had thoughtlessly promised the hand of his daughter to Č'ort'man, Sultan Malik Shah's favorite slave. Once freed and raised to high rank, Č'ort'man expected to receive his bride. The king, however, now apparently back in Dizak-Bałk', refused to render his daughter, and in 1103 Č'ort'man began launching attacks on his territory. Leading a force of Kurdish infantry, he surrounded Łap'an in Bałk', and though its citadel held, the town itself was taken and its population massacred.[26] Sennacherib, taken by treachery, was slain.

Over the next sixty years, the Turks continuously raided Bałk' gradually seizing one portion of it after another until in 1166 its political center, the fortress of Bałaberd, was captured.[27] We do not know if these Turkish raids extended as far as Dizak, the eastern half of the kingdom. In any case, we continue to hear of a "King of Bałk'" for another ninety-five years following the fall of Bałaberd, although—and this is something not always appreciated—by this title we must understand "King of Dizak" and only titular King of Bałk'; that is, King of the eastern half of the kingdom ruled by Sennacherib prior to c. 1072, which had originally belonged to Aṙanšahikids before they inherited Bałk', and where they continued to rule under the title "King of Bałk'" taken when Sennacherib had acquired Bałk' from his wife's brother, King Gregory III (Map IV).[28]

Now, directly to the north of Dizak lay the lands of the fourth line of the Siwnid House which we may call the eastern branch, the line of Xač'ēn, whose background we shall examine presently. Close ties bound the two states of Dizak and Xač'ēn. King Gregory IV of Dizak married his daughter Kata (Catherine) to Hasan the Great, Prince of Xač'ēn,[29] and, when Hasan's grandson, Hasan II, known as Hasan-Jalal-Dōla (c. 1214-1266) married the daughter of the last king of Dizak-Bałk', the two states were merged, Hasan-Jalal-Dōla taking the title "King of Arc'ax and of Bałk'," and subsuming into this title all of the earlier Siwnid, Aṙanšahikid and Mihranid claims.[30] Let us now examine this fourth or eastern branch of the House of Siwnik'. Its origin is interesting and it is the Siwnid line which founded the Kingdom of Arc'ax and from which most of the melik houses of Eastern Armenia originated. This branch alone survived the medieval period, and individual families descended from it survive today—from Karabagh to Moscow, and around the globe to Rome, Paris, New York, Washington, San Francisco and Hollywood.[31]

III

As far as we can tell, the land of Arc'ax originally had no princes off its own. Who owned it or how it was governed when it was passed to Albania in 387 are unknown to us.[32] All we can be sure of is that when the Principality of Albania collapsed in the ninth century, Arc'ax was in the hands of the Aŕanšahikid dynasty, which was descended from the earliest royal family of Albania.[33] In 822, when the last Presiding Prince of Albania was murdered by a close relative of the Siwnid House, his widow took her only surviving child, a daughter, Spŕam, to the castle of Xač'ēn deep in the mountains near the frontier between the Siwnid and Albanian lands. Shortly thereafter she married her daughter to Atrnerseh, a Siwnid prince, whose father, Sahl, son of Smbat, had forcibly seized Gełark'unik' from the Siwnid family domains.[34] Having married the heiress of the last Prince of Gardman and last ruler of Albania, Atrnerseh (821-853) took the title "Prince of Gardman and Albania" and lost no time moving into Arc'ax (apparently seizing the northern part of it—Vaykunik'—from the Aŕanšahikids). There he built the fortress of Handaberd and erected a palace at Vaykunik', a hot spring which had been the site of the royal baths of the old Albanian rulers.[35] Since we know that Atrnerseh already owned the district of Sōdk' (the eastern half of Gełark'unik'),[36] we must assume that Sōdk' was his share of his father's ill-gotten gains, for as we have seen, the Siwnid line of Gełark'unik' disappears in c. 912; Atrnerseh's descendants, on the other hand, continued to hold Sōdk' until the eighteenth century.[37]

Atrnerseh's son, Gregory, extended the holdings of his line in Arc'ax, and his son, Isaac-Sewada, subjected the district of Gardman or Parisos and other lands to the north[38] which, of course, were his by right of inheritance through his grandmother, Princess Spŕam. The expansionism of Atrnerseh and his descendants makes it clear that we are witnessing a conscious attempt on the part of his house to reconquer step by step the old Albanian lands inherited, at least in theory, through Atrnerseh's marriage to Princess Spŕam. It was in this way that the East Siwnid state of Xač'ēn or northern Arc'ax, ruled by this fourth Siwnid line, rose to prominence during the ninth and tenth centuries, and it is not surprising to find John-Sennacherib II, a sixth generation descendant of Atrnerseh and Spram, styling himself "King of Albania" as late as 1000,[39] or of his seventh generation descendant, Hasan I, using the title "Prince of Xač'ēn and King of Siwnik'," as late as 1142.[40]

It is this state, founded by the fourth line of the House of Siwnik' in 821, which became a kingdom by the year 1000.[41]   Ulubabyan calls it the principality of Xač'ēn.   I prefer to call it, at least for the period when its rulers possessed the royal title, the "Kingdom of Arc'ax."

Now Hasan I, called "The Great," was an important prince ruling over all of the northern half of Arc'ax[42] but, after abdicating to enter a monastery in 1182, he apparently divided his kingdom between two of his sons: the elder, Vaxt'ank II, called Tonk'ik (p. 1201-p. 1214), received the southern half of the realm, namely Xač'ēn, and a younger son, Gregory surnamed "The Black," was given the northern half, i.e. the lands adjoining the southeast corner of Lake Sevan (Sōdk' and Vaykunik' or Car, Map V).[43] From Vaxt'ank-Tonk'ik was descended the Siwnid line of the Vaxt'ankeank' Princes of Xač'ēn, from whom issued the House of Hasan-Jalalean, Meliks of Xač'ēn, the senior line among the later melik houses of Eastern Armenia.[44] From Gregory the Black was descended the younger Siwnid line of the Dop'eank' so-called from Gregory's wife Susan-Dop', daughter of Sargis II, prince Mxargrjeli.[45]   From these Dop'eank' there were issued several other of the other melik houses (Šahnazarean, Beglarean, etc.).[46]

But although the Kingdom of Arc'ax was thus divided, it did not cease to expand.   Having married the daughter of the last Aŕanšahikid King of Balk', who reigned in Dizak to the south, the son of Vaxt'ank, Hasan Jalal-Dōla (p. 1214-1266), inherited his father-in-law's domains and took the title "King of Arc'ax and Bałk'" (Map VI).[47]

Several aspects of Hasan Jalal's geneaology come into play here. First, Hasan-Jalal's wife was the last surviving member of the ancient House of Aŕanšahik, the Princes of Dizak and Bałk', who had ruled as the Kings of Albania a millenium before. Second, it was through absorption into this house that the first and third branches of the house of Siwnik' had become extinct. Finally, Hasan-Jalal was descended in the female line from the Mihranid Princes of Gardman, who had been the Presiding Princes of Albania under the Arabs, and he, himself, represented the senior male member of the last surviving branch of the House of Siwnik'. Thus there devolved upon this one prince all of the earlier titles and claims possessed both by his ancestors and by those of his wife, and through them, all of the major inheritances of the various dynasties of Albania and Eastern Armenia. At one and the same time, then, Hasan Jalal Dōla could legitimately style himself King of Siwnik', King of Bałk', King of Arc'ax, and King of Albania, not to mention Prince of Gardman, Dizak and Xač'ēn—as well as Presiding Prince of Albania—as he chose. He selected, as we have seen, the title "King of Arc'ax and Bałk'." And this was 200 years after the fall of Ani. So much for the tenacity of the rulers of Arc'ax.

IV

Geographically, the Kingdom of Arc'ax included all of the earlier land of Arc'ax, the adjoining principality of Gardman-Pařisos to the north, and the northwest Siwnian lands of Gełark'unik' and Sōdk'. It thus comprised almost 10,000 sq. km. and was a more than double the size of present-day Highland Karabagh (4388 sq. km. Map IV). The kingdom had no permanent capital, no cities and, except for Pařisos, no towns, both Ganǰa and Šamxor lying outside of its limits. The castle of Xoxanaberd[48] or Xač'ēn was its first center but Hasan the Great preferred to live at the large village of Car[49] with its hot springs, and Hasan-J̌alal's preferred residence was the castle of Akana.[50] Eventually the family settled at the fortress of Hat'erk' on the Terter River.[51] There were about fifteen forts, fortresses and castles in the kingdom. Besides those already mentioned, we may cite Berdkunk', Berdakur, Getabaks, Gardman, K't'iš and Tři, Hakarakaberd, Handaberd, Xavkaxałac' and Sōdk'.[52]

Politically Arc'ax was a unified state for over three and one half centuries until Hasan the Great partitioned it between two of his sons in 1182. Shortly thereafter, however, the acquisition of Dizak by Hasan J̌alal-Dōla gave the kingdom a third section. Each third was then ruled by a different line of the same Fourth Siwnid branch, the senior line, the Vaxt'ankeank' reigning in the central land of Xač'ēn in the Terter Valley; then the Dop'eank' to the north and northwest in Gełark'unik', Gardman, Sōdk' and Car; and finally, what I choose to call the "Avaneank'" holding Dizak to the south (Map VII).[53]

The kingdom of Arc'ax elaborated its foreign policy—its own local Weltpolitik. It accepted the suzerainty of Georgia during its ascendancy under Queen T'amar the Great (1187-1213), and quickly accepted Mongol domination when forced to do so in the mid-thirteenth century.[54] Its rulers intermarried regularly with neighboring Gagelids, Mxargrjelids, Mankaberdelids, Orbelids of Siwnik', the Bagratids of Lori and Kars, and even with their Mongol overlords.[55] The survival of the state and the preservation of its autonomy were, of course, its foremost concerns.

As far as military power was concerned Arc'ax, of course, was a feeble state, feudal in nature, and its rulers relied upon an unprofessional army composed of warrior peasants who, led by local magnates and village headmen, rallied to the banner of their lord upon his call. Always defensive, these forces are not reported to have been launched upon a campaign beyond th frontiers of the realm unless, as in the case of Hasan-Jalal, their lord himself was required to attend his suzerain with a more or less repectable force of men-at-arms.[56]

Needless to say, the Kingdom of Arc'ax attracted its share of Muslim predators eager to despoil its rulers of their modest means. In the Albanian Chronicle of Mxit'ar Goš, for example, we learn that in the year 1144/5 the Turkish emir, "Djōli, growing arrogant, turned against the region of Xač'ēn, captured all its fortresses, demolished the churches, and burned down the monasteries."[57]

In 1145/6 Djōli was back a second time:

> "For the fortresses he took on the first occasion did not remain in his hands . . . for some of the nobles who had been hiding in forest caves retook them and rebelled . . . Angered by this, Djōli marched against them seeking revenge. He was not able to capture the fortresses, but he completely laid waste the entire land. He also burned down the holy monastery of Dadivank'."[58]

Similarly, in a colophon of an Armenian manuscript dated 1417 we read that:

> In our land of Xač'ēn, there was a pious prince named Zaz who departed this life . . . and the survivors of his family . . . are all subjects of the lawless ones, and thus, the authority in our Haykazean land was diminished.[59]

In a moment we shall be reading a colophon from yet another manuscript where we will hear about another despoilation of the region by the Muslims and about how the Dop'eank' Princes of the Siwnid house responded to this in a vigorous and effective way.

For its basic needs, the kingdom relied upon its rich crops, its flocks and herds, its dense forests, its mines of copper and gold, and its skilled craftsmen. A few luxuries such as silk and salt were brought in from outside via the old trade route of the Arab period, which connected the city of Ganja with both central Armenia and Naxičevan and which followed the Terter

Valley directly past the castle of Hat'erk'.[60]

Ecclesiastically, the Kingdom of Arc'ax lay within the jurisdiction of the Catholicossate of Albania, a subdivision the administrative structure of the Armenian Church, and roughly speaking, the kingdom was coterminous with this jurisdiction.[61]   The Hasan-Jalaleans early got control of this catholicossate whose primate by the fifteenth century was always a member of the family.   The title "Catholicos of Albania" passed from uncle to nephew, and his ecclesiastical lands, finances and influence was thus always available to the house.[62] Located at the Monastery of Amaras in Dizak after the destruction of Partav,[63] the Catholicossate was transferred to the large and handsome monastery of St. John the Baptist at Gandjasar founded by Hasan-Jalal-Dōla and completed in 1238, and there it remained until the office was suppressed by the Russians in 1828.[64]   There were more than a dozen monasteries in the kingdom.   In addition to the two just mentioned, we may cite Dadivank'.[65]   Vanakan, Mak'enoc', Xot'avank', Xat'ravank', Cicernakavank' and Xoranašat.   Moreover, the ruling house supplied abbots and bishops to other monasteries and sees as far afield as Hałbat and Sanahin.[66]

As in Ani, Kars, Vaspurakan and elsewhere, where the Armenian monarchies had been restored, a certain cultural renaissance took place in Arc'ax and its vicinity in the tenth to thirteenth centuries.   It is within the context of this renaissance that we must place the eastern Armenian literary activity, which has been called the "Albanian School" of Armenian literature, and which produced, among others, such writers as the historian of Albania, Movsēs Dasxurenac'i (tenth century);[67] the philosopher and scientist, Yovhannēs Sarkawag (d. 1129);[68] the first Armenian jurist, Davit', son of Alavik (d. 1140);[69] the codifier of Armenian law, Mxit'ar Goš (d. 1213), who founded the monastery and cultural center of Nor Getik;[70] his pupil Vanakan, vartabed (d.c. 1250), who founded the monastery of Xoranašat,[71] and his pupil, Malak'ia the Monk 1272.[72]   Finally, we must not omit the three great historians of the thirteenth century, Vardan of the East (Arevelc'i),[73] called "The Great," who was also known as a geographer and writer of fables (d.c. 1270);[74] and Step'anos Ōrbelean, historian of the House of Siwnik' (d. 1305).[75]

Finally, a few words must be said about the ethos or Weltanschauung of this obscure and tiny state.   There is no question whatsoever that the Kings of Arc'ax and their successors, the princes and Meliks of Xač'ēn, were conscious of their role as one of the last centers of Armenian independence in the increasingly deepening ocean of Islam which was engulfing southeast Caucasia.[76]   In inscriptions,[77] colophons[78] and other documents,[79] they often refer to themselves as being of the House of Albania or the House of Armenia, and, when their melik descendants addressed letters to the Pope or to Peter the Great, they did not shrink from speaking on behalf of the entire Armenian people, recognizing in themselves the last remnant of the Armenian nobility of old, the traditional leaders and spokesmen of the nation as a whole.[80]   In the values and way of life of these meliks, we detect clear echoes, however feeble, decadent or impoverished, of the ethos of the great naxarar houses of ancient and medieval Armenian as described by Ełišē, Movsēs Xorenac'i and others a millenium or more before.

V

In the time of Hasan-J̌alal-Dōla, the Mongols reached Armenia. He submitted to them and led his troops in their army. Unfortunately, he fell afoul of the Emir Arghoun and was decapitated at Qazvin in 1266.[81] Thereafter, although his descendants continued to rule in Arc'ax, they no longer, to our knowledge, possessed the royal title, being content to style themselves by the earlier title "Princes of Xač'ēn."[82]   Meanwhile, Dizak, acquired by Hasan-J̌alal-Dōla, had, after his execution, passed to his cousin Vaxt'ank, ancestor of the later Meliks-Avanean of Dizak.[83] Hatir Melik, a seventh-generation descendant of Hasan-J̌alal-Dōla, became the first Melik of Xač'ēn in the time of the Black Sheep Turkoman Lord of Armenia, Jehan Shah, about 1457.[84]   His descendant, Allahverdi II, who died in 1813, was ruling Xač'ēn when the Russians came to Karabagh in 1805, and was the last Melik of his house.[85] The Hasan-J̌alalids played a major role in the early Armenian independence movement, and in 1786 the Albanian Catholicos, Yovhannēs XII, Hasan-J̌alalean was executed by the Persians for his traffic with the agents of Catherine the Great.[86]

As for the younger lines of the Siwnid House of Arc'ax, they too had their distinction. Among the Dop'eank', for example, we hear of Prince Šahinšah the Great, who fell on the field of honor together with several of his sons, defending his people against the invasion of Timur (c. 1390).[87]   In a colophon of a fifteenth-century manuscript, we read of this Sahinsah,

> in whose time the Muslims became powerful and the house of
> Armenia was overthrown, and all our princes having been

dispersed, foreign invaders confiscated the domains of the great
Prince Hasan. The great Prince Aytin, having gone to their
court, succeeded after three years of effort and much expense,
in freeing the monasteries and villages from the hands of the
infidels. May the God of the Universe grant him the rewards
for his labors. [88]

The colophonist neglects to mention the more earthly award received by
Aytin, for it was he who engineered the restoration of the Siwnid princes in
their ancestral lands in Arc'ax-Karabagh, and the recognition of their status
with the conferral upon them of the title "melik" (Map VII).[89]   As another
later example, among the Meliks of Dizak, we find Melik Avan II, a close
friend of the last Safavid Shah.[90] After the fall of the Safavids, Avan served
under Peter the Great, was recognized by the Tsar as an Armenian prince,
and was one of the first of the long line of Armenians to serve as an officer
in the Russian army.[91]   Finally, Israel Ori, founder of the Armenian
liberation movement in the seventeenth century;[92] the famed Russian-
Armenian General Prince Valerian Madatov;[93] as well as Xač'atur Abovian,
the first Armenian novelist and founder of the modern Eastern Armenian
literary language,[94] were all three of royal Siwnid origin, descendants of the
Kings of Arc'ax.

The Kingdom of Arc'ax, under one name or another, lasted from about
1000 A.D. to 1266—a period of over 250 years. I have traced its background
and origins, and have followed its echoes down to the nineteenth century. I
have also briefly sketched its political and dynastic history, but I have only
begun to penetrate the subject. The kingdom also has its social history, as
well as its ecclesiastical and cultural development, all of which need further
investigation. What I have attempted to do here, following the guidelines of
this conference, has been to demonstrate how the apparently insignificant
dynasts and petty states of post-Bagratid Armenian served as a source of
continuity between the period of the reassertation of Armenian independence
in the ninth to eleventh centuries, and the rise of a new Armenian
independence movement in the late-seventeenth century. This continuity
between medieval and modern Armenian history is remarkable as much for its
longevity as for its fragility—especially when we consider that the descendants of the "Kings of Arc'ax" played a prominent role in Karabagh during
the period of the Armenian Republic,[95] and even after the establishment of
Soviet Power, when as recently as 1965, a certain Nikolai Semyonovich

Melik-Shakhnazarov—a direct descendant of Antiochus, Prince of Siwnik' of the time of St. Gregory the Illuminator, was First Secretary of the Communist Party of Highland Karabagh and as such, we may be sure, firmly in control of the land of his ancestors.[96]   This so-called "Autonomous" Province of Highland Karabagh, an Armenian-inhabited enclave within the Azerbaidjani Soviet Socialist Republic, is in direct lineal descendant of the medieval Kingdom of Arc'ax.   A loose end in Armenian geopolitical history, its very existence is a testimony to the significance of the medieval kingdom, whose geography and whose rulers together imposed a sense of unity, identity and self-awareness upon its inhabitants, all reflected in the present-day "Karabagh Question" which has yet to be adequately resolved.[97]

NOTES

[*]This paper represents work in progress and was written before the author obtained access to B. Ulubabyan's Xač'ēni išxanut'yunē (Erevan, 1975). The reader is referred to this important work for additional information, greater detail, and for a Soviet Armenian point of view, as well as to the interesting and valuable article by the late S. G. Barxudaryan, "Arc'axi, Šak'i ew P'aṙisosi išxanut'yunnerē ix-x darerum," Patmabanasirakan Handes (1971), 1:52-76; to the latter's Divan hay vimagrut'yan, vol. V. Arc'ax (Erevan, 1982), and to B. Limper's published doctoral dissertation, Die Mongolen und die Christlichen Volker des Kaukasus (Cologne, 1980), pp. 211-20, all three of which came to my attention after this paper was presented.

[1]Thus, for example, Grousset's Histoire de l'Arménie (Paris, 1949) ends in 1071; J. de Morgan in his L'Histoire du peuple arménien (Paris, 1916), Engl. transl. E. Barry (Boston, 1956), devotes exactly twelve pages to the period between 1375 and 1679; V. Kurkjian in his A History of Armenia (New York, 1958) devotes ten to an even longer period (1064-1878), while D. M. Lang in his Armenia Cradle of Civilization ignores the entire five centuries between 1375 and 1878 altogether!

[2]G. Dédéyan (ed.), Histoire des Armeniens (Toulouse, 1982).

[3]R. H. Hewsen, "The Meliks of Eastern Armenia: A Preliminary Study," REArm 9 (1972), 285-329; idem. "II" REArm 10 (1973-74), 281-300 and "III" REArm 11 (1975-76), 219-43.

[4]C. Toumanoff, "Armenia and Georgia" in Cambridge Medieval History IV The Byzantine Empire, Part I (Cambridge, 1966), 612.

[5]V. M. Vardayan, Vaspurakani Arcruneac' T'agavorut'yunĕ (Erevan, 1969).

[6]C. Toumanoff, Manuel de généalogie et de chronologie pour l'histoire de la Caucasie Chretienne (Rome, 1976); idem Supplement (1978), 15.

[7]T. X. Hakobyan, Syunik'i T'agavorut'yunĕ (Erevan, 1966), 3.

[8]Toumanoff, "Arm. amd Geo.," 617.

[9]Ibid.

[10]Ulubabyan, ibid.

[11]Step'annos Ōrbēlean, Patmut'iwn Nahangin Sisakan (ed. K. Sahnazarian; Paris, 1859); Fr. trans. M. F. Brosset, Histoire de la Siounie (St. Petersburg, 1864), LIX.

[12]Atlas Gruzinskoi Sovetskoi Socialisticeskoj Respubliki (Tbilisi-Moscow, 1964), 251-52.

[13]C. Toumanoff, Manuel, 226.

[14]Ibid.

[15]Ibid.

[16]Ibid., 229.

[17]Hewsen, "Meliks II," 282 ff.

[18]Ibid.

[19]Toumanoff, Manuel, 230 ff.

[20]Hewsen, "Meliks II," 282.

[21]Toumanoff, Manuel, 233.

[22]C. Toumanoff, Studies in Christian Caucasian History (Washington, 1963), 219.

[23]Step'annos Ōrbēlean, LIX.   For the date 1072 cf. Toumanoff, Manuel, 235. By the Kingdom of Bałk' we must understand a "greater" Bałk' which included, besides Bałk' itself, the neighboring districts of Jork' (Łap'an or Kapan), Arewik' (Dašton and Mełri), and Kovsakan (Krham, the later

Bargušat), and also, at its height, Cłukk' (Sisakan) and Haband. Bałk', in both its greater and lesser senses, also included the subdistrict of Kašunik' lying east of Lesser Bałk' and sometimes referred to as the "Other" Bałk'. (T'. X. Hakobyan, ibid. map; Toumanoff, Manuel, 241).

[24]SO. LIX.

[25]SO. LXI.

[26]Ibid.

[27]Ibid.

[28]Toumanoff, Manuel, 71-72.

[29]SO, Ibid.; Toumanoff, ibid., 72.

[30]Toumanoff, ibid., 239.

[31]Descendants of Melik houses sprung from the House of Siwnik' are found in all of these cites, all of them aware of their noble descent but none in my experience aware of their descent from the House of Siwnik.

[32]P'awstos (5.12) cites Arc'ax, the Orkhistene of Strabo (11.4.4), but mentions no princes of the region. Eremyan, however, considers it to have been part of the territory of the Princes of Sōdk', Ptolemy's Sodoukene, but cf. Toumanoff, Studies, 182, n. 146.

[33]Toumanoff, Studies, 216-17.

[34]Movsēs Kałankatuac'i (or Dasxuranc'i), Patmut'iwn Ałuanic' asxarhi (ed. M. Emin; Tiflis, 1912); Engl. transl. C. J. F. Dowsett, The History of The Caucasian Albanians by Movsēs Dasxuranc'i (London, 1961), 3.19, 22.

[35]Ibid., 3.22. We do not know how much of northern Arc'ax the Siwnids controlled. There is evidence that an Ařanšahikid branch held Xač'ēn until at least 1000 A.D. (see Barxudaryan supra n. 1).

[36]Ibid.

[37]Hewsen, "Meliks II," 302-03.

[38]MD, 3.22.

[39]Toumanoff, Manuel, 237.

[40]Ibid.

[41]Ibid.

[42]At least a part of the southern half of Arc'ax, known as Dizak, was under Aṙanšahikid rule until the mid-thirteenth century (cf. Toumanoff, Manuel, 71-72).

[43]Cf. the stemma of the Siwnids by Metropolitan Balthasar Hasan-Jalalean published by Raffi in his critique of the Galt'nik' Larabaḷi (infra, n. 46), published as Gaṙt'nik' Ḷarabaḷi K'nnadatec' Raffi (Vienna, 1906).

[44]Hewsen, "Meliks II," 317-18.

[45]Toumanoff, ibid., 238-39.

[46]A. Beknazareanc' (pseud.?), Gaḷtnik Ḷarabaḷi (St. Petersburg, 1886), 180 ff.

[47]Toumanoff, ibid., 239.

[48]MD 3.22. Xoxanaberd (in Persian), having given its Armenian name, Xac'en, to the earlier land of Arc'ax, must have served as its center for a considerable time.

[49]M-F. Brosset, Histoire de la Siounie par Stephannos Orbelian, Introduction (St. Petersburg, 1866), 164.

[50]Ibid., 167.

[51]Ibid., 165. For the locations of Xoxanaberd, Akana and Haterk' cf. Haykakan SSR Atlas (Erevan, 1961), 106.

[52]Haykakan SSR Atlas, 195-97.

[53]Hewsen, "Meliks II," 321-23; idem. "Meliks II," 293-96.

[54]K. Salia, Histoire de la Georgie (Paris, 1980), 222-25.

[55]Toumanoff, Manuel, 238-40.

[56]So heavy were the exactions laid upon Hasan-Jalal by the Mongols that he was unable to satisfy them, and, as a result, he was arrested, tortured, and cruelly executed at Qazvin in Iran in 1261 (Kirakos Ganjakec'i, Patmut'iwn Hayoc', LXIV Fr. transl.). M. F. Brosset, Deux historiens armeniens, St. Petersbourg, 1870).

[57]C. J. F. Dowsett, "The Albanian Chronicle of Mxit'ar Goš," BSOAS XXI Pt. 3 (London, 1958), 483.

[58]Ibid.

[59]A. Sanjian, Colophons of Armenian Manuscripts (Los Angeles, 1969), 139.

[60]Y. Manandyan, O torgovle i gorodax Armenii v svjazi s mirovoj torgovlej drevnix vremen (Erevan, 1945), Engl. transl. N. Garsoian, Trade and Cities of Armenia in Relation to Ancient World Trade (Lisbon, 1965), 161.

For a more detailed account of the economy of Arc'ax in this period the reader is referred to Ulubabyan's study (supra at *). Horsebreeding must have played a major or if not a preponderant role in the local economy but its very ubiquity led to its being virtually ignored by our sources. In his "Caucasica IV," BSOAS, XV/3 (London, 1953), p. 526, Minorsky translates a passage from Ibn-Hauqal's Kitab al-masalik wal-Mamalik (10th century) in which horses, apparently in large numbers, are cited as being a great part of the annual tribute paid by Arc'ax/Xač'ēn to the Arabs. In his commentary on this passage, Minorsky quotes Brosset (Histoire de la Géorgie, I, 441) to the effect that in the thirteenth century David Soslan, consort to Queen T'amar of Georgia, gave the fortress of Jarmanam and an entire village to obtain a particularly fine horse from the Vakhtang of Xač'ēn.

[61]The original jurisdiction of the Catholicos of Albania was, from at least the fifth century, expressed in his intitulatio "Catholicos of Albania, Lp'ink' and Č'olay," (MD 2.15; 3.23) and included all of southeastern Caucasia from the Araxes River to the Caspian Sea at the Fortress of Č'olay lying c. 40 km. south of Darband. In an inscription in the Monastery of K't'iš dated 1248 and recorded by Brosset (Introduction, 165), the jurisdiction of St. Grigoris, i.e. of the Catholicos of Albania, is described as:

> "having for limits the rivers of Hałun and the Erasx, as far as the banks of Gatuhat; Vakunis, on the River Vałazn; Karatnik (in some mss. Karutnik), with that (i.e. the river) of Xozan; Arist and its river; Hakari and the river of Hazar; Krtaget, its river and its limits; Dizak; Belukan with its river."

Although not all of these places are now identifiable, it is clear that we are dealing with a much more restricted area lying entirely in Karabagh and corresponding to the lands of the Vaxt'ankean and Dop'ean families.

[62]Hewsen, "Meliks II," Chart I.

[63]Brosset, Histoire de la Siounie, 144.

[64]M. Hasrat'yan, M. Thierry, "Le Couvent de Ganjasar," REA XV

(Paris, 1981), 195.

[65]J. M. Thierry, M. Hasrat'yan, "Dadivank' en Arc'ax," REA XVI (Paris, 1982), 259-287.

[66]Toumanoff, Manuel, 238-39.

[67]M. Abełyan, Hayoc' hin grakanut'yan patmut'yun, I (Beirut, 1959).

[68]Ibid., II:43-61.

[69]Ibid., 62-63.

[70]Ibid., 142-57.

[71]Ibid., 188.

[72]Ibid., 205.

[73]Ibid., 199.

[74]Ibid., 192.

[75]Ibid., 215-27.

[76]In the reconstruction of Dadi-vank' and in the codification of the laws by Mxit'ar Goš, the first undertaken by Hasan the Great (1142-1182), and the latter by order of his son Vaxt'ang II Tonk'ik (1182-p. 1214), as well as in the construction of the monastery of Ganjasar by the latter's grandson, Hasan-Ĵalal-Dola (c. 1214-1265/6), we see the age-old concept of renovatio at work whereby the restoration of the kingdom is accompanied by the erection of sacred edifices and the promulgation of codes of law. The reign of Justinian is a classic example of this as are those of Augustus before him and of Charlemagne later on.

[77]Cf. Brosset, Introduction; L. Ališan, Sisakan (Venice, 1893); M. Barxudareanc', Arc'ax (Baku, 1895); and S. Barxudaryan's DHV V Arc'ax.

[78]Cf. Brosset, Histoire de la Siounie, but especially L. S. Xač'ikyan's XIV Dari Hayaren Jeṙagreri Hišatakaranner (Erevan, 1950); Xač'ikyan, XV Dari Hayaren Jeṙagreri Hišatakaranner (Erevan, 1958) and Sanjian's Colophons (based on the last two compilations).

[79]Cf. Beknazarean's Gałtnik' Łarabałi, pp. 180-208, and Balt'asar Metropolitan Hasan-Ĵalalean's genealogical table in Raffi's Critique, pp. 687-700, supra n. 43.

[80]G. Ezov, Snošenija Petra Velikogo S Armjanami Dokumenty (St.

Petersburg, 1898), doc. No. 11, pp. 51-52.

[81]Hasrat'yan-Thierry, "Ganjasar," 294.

[82]Toumanoff, Manuel, 231, 236-40.   Cf. also Ulubabyan, Xac'eni Isxanut'yune which includes a discussion of the titles in use by the rulers of Xac'en.

[83]The exact connection of the Avaneans of Dizak with the Vaxt'-ankeank' line is uncertain but its Siwnid descent appears uncontestible (Hewsen, "Meliks I," 321-23; "Meliks II," 293-96).

[84]Ibid.

[85]Ibid.

[86]Raffi, Xamsayi melik'ut'iwnnerĕ (Vienna, 1906), 105.

[87]Šahinšah, as sparapet, is cited in a colophon in Brosset, Introduction, p. 164.

[88]Brosset, Introduction, 155-56.

[89]Bekhnazareanc', 189-91.

[90]Aṙak'el vdpt., Dizaki Melik'ut'iwnĕ (Vaḷarsapat, 1913), Niwt'er hay melik'ut'ean masin, I.10-20; Raffi, Xamsayi Melik'ut'iwnnerĕ, 18-19.

[91]Toumanoff, Manuel.

[92]Hewsen, "Meliks II," 323-24.

[93]Hewsen, "Three Armenian Noble Families of the Russian Empire," Hask (Antilias, 1982).

[94]Hewsen, "The Meliks of Eastern Armenia IV: The Siwnid Origin of Xač'atur Abovyan," REA, XIV (Paris, 1980), 459-70.

[95]R. G. Hovannisian, The Armenian Republic Vol. I: 1918-1919 (Los Angeles, 1971), 85, 86, 169.

[96]Who's Who in the U.S.S.R., 1965, s.v. Melik-Shakhazarov.

[97]Cf. J. H. Tashjian, "The Problem of Karabagh," The Armenian Review, 21 (1968) 1-81, esp. 3-66; R. G. Hovannisian, "The Armeno-Azerbaijani Conflict over Mountainous Karabagh, 1918-1919," The Armenian Review 24 (1971) 2-94, esp. 3-39.

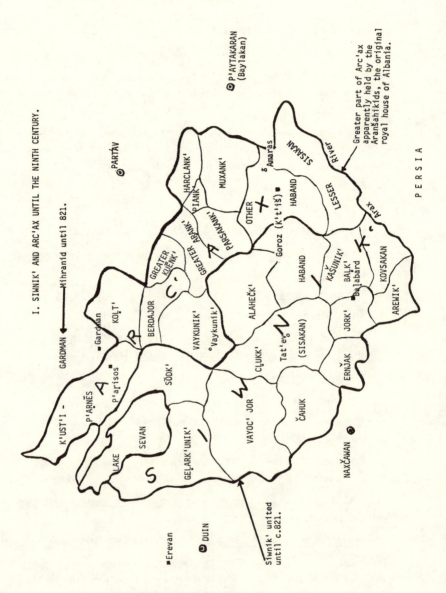

I. SIWNIK' AND ARC'AX UNTIL THE NINTH CENTURY.

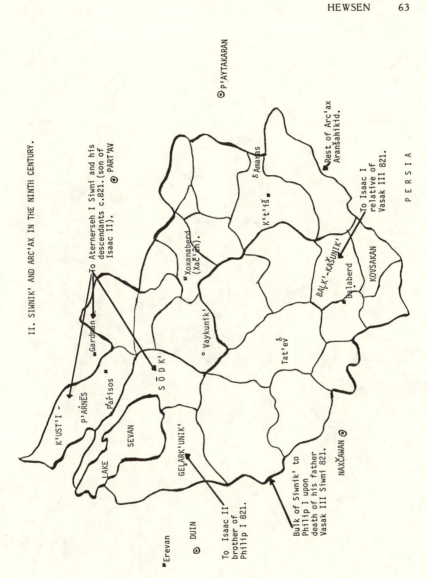

II. SIWNIK' AND ARC'AX IN THE NINTH CENTURY.

To Aternerseh I Siwni and his
descendants c.821.(son of
Isaac II).

⊙ PART'AV

⊙ P'AYTAKARAN

Rest of Arc'ax
Aranšahikid.

To Isaac I
relative of
Vasak III 821.

P E R S I A

δ Amaras

K't'iš

Yoxanaberd
(Xač'ēn).

BAĿK'-KAŠUNIK'

KOVSAKAN

Balaberd

K'UST'I -

P'ARNĒS

Gardman

Pařisos ■

S Ō D K'

° Vaykunik'

Tat'ev δ

LAKE

SEVAN

GEĿARK'UNIK'

Erevan

⊙ DUIN

To Isaac II
brother of
Philip I 821.

Bulk of Siwnik' to
Philip I upon
death of his father
Vasak III Siwni 821.

NAXČAWAN ⊙

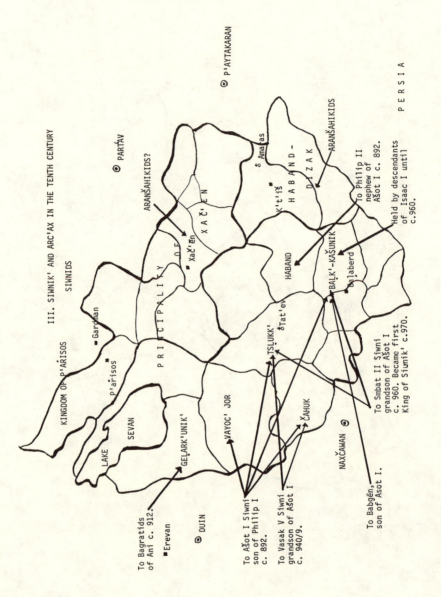

III. SIWNIK' AND ARC'AX IN THE TENTH CENTURY

KINGDOM OF P'ARISOS

SIWNIDS

ARANŠAHIKIDS

PARTAV

P'AYTAKARAN

ARANŠAHIKIDS?

ARANŠAHIKIDS

Amaras

K't'iš

HABAND -

D I Z A K

To Philip II
nephew of
Ašot I c. 892.

Held by descendants
of Isaac I until
c.960.

P E R S I A

XAČ'ĒN

Xač'ēn

PRINCIPALITY

HABAND

BALK'-KAŠUNIK

Gałaberd

Gardman

P'arisos

P R I N C I P A L I T Y

Tat'ev

ŠTat'ew

TSLUKK'

LAKE

SEVAN

GEŁARK'UNIK'

VAYOC' JOR

ČAHUK

NAXČAWAN

Erevan

DUIN

To Bagratids
of Ani c. 912.

To Ašot I Siwni
son of Philip I
c. 892.

To Vasak V Siwni
grandson of Ašot I
c. 940/9.

To Smbat II Siwni
grandson of Ašot I
c. 960. Became first
King of Siwnik' c.970.

To Babgēn,
son of Ašot I.

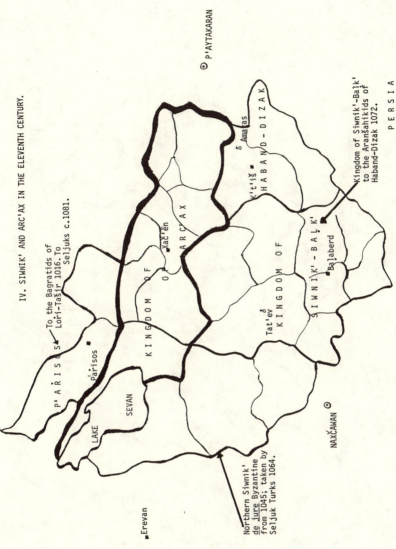

IV. SIWNIK' AND ARC'AX IN THE ELEVENTH CENTURY.

To the Bagratids of
Loṙi-Tašir 1016. To
Seljuks c.1081.

Kingdom of Siwnik'-Baḷk'
to the Aranšahikids of
Haband-Dizak 1072.

Northern Siwnik'
de jure Byzantine
from 1045; taken by
Seljuk Turks 1064.

⊙ P'AYTAKARAN

PERSIA

δ Amaṙas

HABAND - DIZAK

K't'iš

ARC'AX

YaX'ēn

SIWNIK' - BAḶK'

KINGDOM OF

Bałaberd

δ Tat'ev

KINGDOM OF

NAXČAWAN ⊙

LAKE

SEVAN

Pàrisos

P' A R I S O S

Erevan

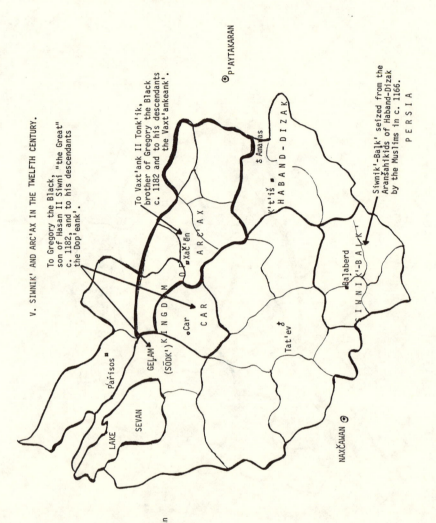

V. SIWNIK' AND ARC'AX IN THE TWELFTH CENTURY.

To Gregory the Black,
son of Hasan II Siwni "the Great"
c. 1182, and to his descendants
the Dop'eank'.

To Vaxt'ank II Tonk'ik,
brother of Gregory the Black
c. 1182 and to his descendants
the Vaxt'ankeank'.

Siwnik'-Baḷk' seized from the
Aranšahikids of Haband-Dizak
by the Muslims in c. 1166.

P'AYTAKARAN

HABAND - DIZAK

K't'iš

ARC'AX

Xač'ēn

CAR

Car

O.D.

KINGDOM

(SŌDK')

GEḶAM

Párisos

LAKE

SEVAN

Erevan

Tat'ev

Balaberd

SIWNIK'-BAḶK'

Amaras

PERSIA

NAXČAWAN

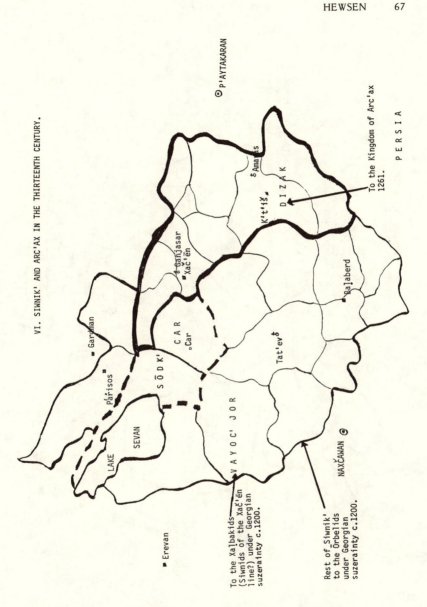

VI. SIWNIK' AND ARC'AX IN THE THIRTEENTH CENTURY.

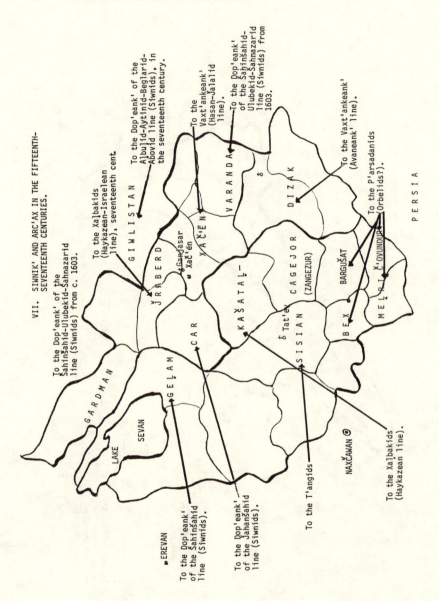

VII. SIWNIK' AND ARC'AX IN THE FIFTEENTH-
SEVENTEENTH CENTURIES.

To the Dop'eank' of the
Šahinšahid-Ulubekid-Šahnazarid
line (Siwnids) from c. 1603.

To the Xaḷbakids
(Haykazean-Israelean
line), seventeenth cent.

To the Dop'eank' of the
Albuḷd-Aytnid-Beḷarid-
Abovid line (Siwnids), in
the seventeenth century.

To the
Vaxt'ankeank'
(Hasan-Jalalid
line).

To the Dop'eank'
of the Šahinšahid-
Ulubekid-Šahnazarid
line (Siwnids) from
1603.

To the Vaxt'ankeank'
(Avaneank' line).

To the P'arsadanids
(Orbelids?).

To the Dop'eank'
of the Šahinšahid
line (Siwnids).

To the Dop'eank'
of the Jahanšahid
line (Siwnids).

To the T'angids.

To the Xaḷbakids
(Haykazean line).

GIWLISTAN

JRABERD

ǴGanjasar
Xaǔ'ēn

XAǓ'ĒN

VARANDA

DIZAK

KAŠATAḶ-

CAGEJOR
(ZANGEZUR)

ǴTat'ev

SISIAN

B E X

C'OVUNDUR

MELŔ'I

BARGUŠAT

CAR

GEḶAM

GARDMAN

SEVAN

LAKE

EREVAN

NAXČAWAN

P E R S I A

T'OVMAY ARCRUNI AS HISTORIAN

Robert W. Thomson

Harvard University

Historical writing is one of the most significant aspects of classical and medieval Armenian literature. And although in modern times the role of so-called "scientific" scholars such as Anania Širakac'i or Dawit' the "Invincible Philosopher" has been emphasized in certain quarters, one may well doubt whether their creative originality was as great as that of a Elise or a Movsēs Xorenac'i. Be that as it may, the popularity and influence of historians in general did not mean that their works were all equally honored. T'ovmay Arcruni is among those writers whose works, significant in themselves, did not have a great impact on later generations. He remains, however, a very interesting example of the influence of earlier Armenian tradition on a tenth century historian. And his History of the Arcruni House articulates in dramatic form the social interests of the Armenian nobility of his own era.[1]

T'ovmay's History has survived in only one manuscript; this was written on the island of Aɫt'amar in the year 752 of the Armenian era, which ran from January 5, 1303 to January 4, 1304. Later copies have been made from this manuscript; there are also some fragments independent of it, the earliest written in 1172.[2]

That an Armenian text should be so little attested is hardly surprising in itself. Physical loss was a grievous fact of life in Armenia. Indeed, it is remarkable that more texts have not disappeared entirely, like the History of Šapuh Bagratuni. Eznik's famous treatise—admittedly, not a popular work—survives in only one manuscript. The earliest surviving whole text of Koriwn's Life of Maštoc' was written 1200 years after Koriwn's death.[3]

T. Samuelian & M. Stone, eds. Medieval Armenian Culture. (University of Pennsylvania Armenian Texts and Studies 6). Chico, CA: Scholars Press, 1983. pp. 69 to 80.

Only one manuscript of Movsēs Xorenac'i's History predates the fifteenth century.   More interestingly, early fragments of Łazar P'arpec'i's History indicate that the text which survives in manuscripts of the seventeenth or later centuries reflects a revised edition.[4]   In other words, much of early Armenian literature has not come down to us in its original form.   To have a manuscript of a complete text written within 400 years of the original date of composition is really quite unusual.

It is, however, important to note that this manuscript of T'ovmay's History written in 1303 contains later additions.   T'ovmay's own work has no proper ending, for a page or pages at the end have been lost; it stops in the first decade of the tenth century.   An anonymous author picked up the thread, repeating in different form certain earlier episodes in order to write a panegyric of the king Gagik Arcruni.   That section also lacks a page or pages at the end.   The text then jumps to the Turkish invasions of the early eleventh century; it mentions the recovery of Jerusalem by the Crusaders in 1099, but concentrates on local events in Vaspurakan down to 1303.   An even later scribe has added a long colophon, which brings us down to 1326.   These later additions are not my present concern.   In what follows I shall deal only with the History written by T'ovmay Arcruni himself.[5]

The person of T'ovmay is entirely unknown.   Apart from later references to him as a "historian,"[6] no source outside his own book refers to "T'ovmay."   He says nothing about himself, only once giving his own name as an unworthy successor of earlier historians, "devoid of wisdom, sense and intelligence," who was forced to this undertaking by his patron.[7]   His initial patron was the Arcruni prince Grigor Deranik (847-887), to whom T'ovmay addresses suitable words of flattery in the Introduction to his History.   But elsewhere T'ovmay refers to his patron as Gagik; that is, the second son of Grigor Deranik, who became the first king of Vaspurakan in 908.   The History proper ends soon after the death of Gagik's elder brother Ašot in 904, before Gagik attained royal status.   T'ovmay claims to have been present at Ašot's death, of which he gives a long, rhetorical description.[8]   He also mentions twice eyewitnesses of events that occurred in 852 or later.[9]   It is therefore quite plausible to suppose that T'ovmay had begun his History by 887; but whether he finished it before 908 is unclear.   The reference to the historian Yovhannēs (who was Catholicos 898-924) as "blessed (eraneli),"[10] has been taken as an indication that Yovhannēs was dead by then.   But the epithet might be a scribal interpolation.   There is no other indication that the book was finished twenty years after the last events described.

T'ovmay makes it perfectly clear what his main purpose is: to give an account of the ancestors of his patron down to the present time. His is a History of the Arcruni House in which the valor and virtue of succeeding generations of nobles will be set forth by name, place, and time. The emphasis will be on genealogy, on the description of great deeds and battles—both victories and defeats. It will also include the story of those who were martyred for their faith, by whose prayers, hopes T'ovmay, the Lord may enable him to write a straight-forward and true account, led by the Holy Spirit with the counsel of Christ, for the pleasure of Grigor Deranik and his kinsmen.[11]

This is very explicit. Unlike some Armenian historians, T'ovmay does not hide his partisan attitude; nor does he claim to be writing a "History of the Armenians" as a whole. Other noble families may have achieved renown; T'ovmay will not rehearse those accomplishments, but neither will he surreptitiously seek to deny them.[12] So if he begins with the genealogy of all mankind from Adam, it is in order to emphasize the lineage of the men who ruled over our land—that is, Vaspurakan, not Armenia—who were descended from the kings of Assyria through Senekerim.[13] In some cases a list of names will suffice; for it is not worthwhile writing about those of whom no striking action or noteworthy valiant deeds are known.[14] T'ovmay will concentrate on the descendents of Senekerim, the great glory of whose stock the prophet Isaiah proclaimed to Israel and whose splendid pre-eminence was recorded in archival documents by Alexander the Great.[15]

Now if this sounds vaguely familiar, we should not be too surprised. For T'ovmay frequently cites as an authority that "world-famous teacher," and "most accurate orator," the "great k'ert'oł Movsēs (Xorenac'i)."[16] If the latter had expounded the Jewish origin of the Bagratids and had averred that Alexander had ordered the translation into Greek of the Ancient History describing Hayk and his descendants,[17] we cannot expect the Arcruni House to have credentials any the less impressive.

T'ovmay's aims, then, are clearly expressed. His History will seek to clarify the glorious ancestry of the Arcrunik'. There is no suggestion that the writing of history serves any moral purpose. T'ovmay mentions Ełišē as a blessed teacher who had composed a History of Saint Vardan and his companions at Vardan's request.[18] But Ełišē's idea that history can teach us moral truths, so that we can avoid evil and choose the good, does not seem to have made any impression on T'ovmay.[19]   One may also doubt whether it had affected T'ovmay's patrons, either.

However, T'ovmay, who calls himself a "truthful historian, <u>ansut patmoł</u>,"[20] knows that the writing of history does have certain rules.   Things have to be set down in order; they should be systematically arranged.   This means putting events in their chronological sequence; the narrative must go forward in a regular fashion, and not be broken by extraneous digressions.[21] To these laudable ideals T'ovmay adheres, except for occasional outbursts of praise or lamentation.

The desire to avoid unnecessary deviations from the main theme is matched by an emphasis on brevity.   Succinctness is not only a virtue when the historian is reminding his reader of what earlier writers have described in greater detail;[22] it is important when reporting events that are so tremendous (for good or ill), that one's natural inclination is to dwell on them at length.   Thus, describing the apostasy of various Armenians to Islam, T'ovmay says:

> I am reluctant to put in writing the perdition of our lords and
> the misfortunes they brought on their souls . . . Nonetheless,
> though unwilling, I am forced to set it out in order, briefly, and
> in short.   I shall summarize in a few words the history of these
> events, for it is impossible to pass over them in silence, or to
> hide the terrible misfortunes which befell us.[23]

These apologies introduce a section of over 2500 words.   Likewise, when it comes to eulogizing a notable Arcruni, in this case Gurgēn Abu Belč, T'ovmay says:

> Do not blame me, O lover of learning, for not including in this
> history all his deeds in detail.   For the deeds accomplished by
> others are one or two or so, whereas his surpass in number the
> activity of many men.   Therefore, for the moment, we have
> abbreviated them into few words.[24]

Not only must events be set down succinctly and in proper order, the reliability of the descriptions must be guaranteed.   For the early period great labor in perusing the written works of antiquarians is required.[25]   What cannot be discovered for certain is not to be put into writing.   So T'ovmay may comment:

> I do not know whether the king really gave way to his
> enticement or not.   And I did not consider it important to write

down what we have not verified.[26]

Or:

> Because none of us was present at the blessed one's responses,
> we did not consider it right to set them down in writing.[27]

Agat'angełos certainly had less restraint in reporting the conversations between Saint Gregory and King Trdat during the course of the twelve tortures inflicted on the Illuminator.[28] Or again T'ovmay:

> But whether this was false or true is not clear to us; and I
> reckoned it better not to write down what is not certain.[29]

T'ovmay may be eloquent in his descriptions of the historian's trade, but he is hardly original. The themes of brevity, veracity, chronological exposition, reliability—these are all taken verbatim from Movsēs Xorenac'i, who in turn was indebted to earlier historians, such as Josephus, or rhetoricians, such as Theon.[30] It is therefore significant for the study of Xorenac'i's influence on later writers that T'ovmay is the first to echo him so explicitly. On the other hand, one has to ask whether T'ovmay was as true to these ideals as was Movsēs. In the latter case, Movsēs often quotes a source as his authority, but in fact added something or changed something in a tendentious fashion. But in the case of T'ovmay such explicit quoting is rare. So when a story appears that is unattested elsewhere, we cannot tell whether T'ovmay himself is responsible for the wording or whether his source—often oral, one suspects—had already cast the tale into its surviving form.

Armenian historians were agreed that the Arcrunik' descended from the Assyrian king Senekerim, whose two sons Adramelēk' and Sanasar had fled to Armenia after murdering their father.[31] So although T'ovmay begins his History with a recapitulation of the early history of mankind—adding to Xorenac'i's account further details from Movsēs' own source, Eusebius—he does not begin to expatiate in detail on the prowess of his patrons' ancestors until he reaches the time of the Assyrian kingdom. Here we do get new information. For example: The struggle of Tigran and Aždahak was well known from the account in Xorenac'i.[32] But according to T'ovmay Adramelēk' and Sanasar played no small role in ensuring the victory for Tigran.[33] More interesting is the attempt to link the Arcrunik' with Jerusalem and the Jews at the time of the return from the Babylonian exile. For according to T'ovmay, their troops—led by Aršēz and K'serk'sēs, grandson and son of king Cyrus, who had received lands in Tmorik' to the south of Lake Van—actually escorted the sons of Israel back to the city of Jerusalem and entrusted the leadership of the Jews to Zorobabel.[34] Presumably, this counters the claim found in Movsēs that the Bagratids descended from a Jewish chieftain who was brought to Armenia at the time that Nebuchadnezzar took the Jews captive.[35]

After these splendid beginnings, however, there was anarchy and confusion in Armenia until the time of Alexander the Great. After Darius had been killed and the Persian empire exterminated, says T'ovmay, resistance to Alexander's generals was continued by the Armenians under the leadership of Asud, a distant descendant of Tigran. Only to Alexander in person would Asud submit. Descending from his horse Asud greeted the conqueror: "When valiant men meet valiant men, audacious deeds need no excuse."[36] So, despite Alexander's irritation at all who opposed his sole rule, Asud was spared and sent to Egypt, where he died. His descendants were eventually resettled in Armenia, and from these derive the Arcrunik'. Outside T'ovmay the name Asud is only attested in Movsēs Xorenac'i. The latter makes Asud a Bagratid Jew, whose tongue was cut off by Tigran since he would not worship images.[37] The name "Asud" provides Movsēs with a convenient etymology for the common Bagratid name Ašot. But for T'ovmay, Asud is a descendant of Sanasar. Is this curious story an invention by T'ovmay to provide an honorable rival to the Bagratid hero? Certainly the Arcruni Asud is not heard of again; he left no mark on later Armenian history.

The resettlement of Asud's descendants in Armenia gives T'ovmay an opportunity to explain the origin of the name Arcruni. He suggests three possibilities:

a)   They were called Arcruni because they were settled in the plain called Arcuik' (in Tarōn), and the first Arcruni had an aquiline nose: arcrungn.

b)   They were so called because their ancestors Adramelēk' and Sanasar were settled in Arzn.

c)   Because of their eagle-like audacity they were compared to eagles: arcuik'.

T'ovmay places his confidence in the first explanation.[38] But it is interesting that, although his methods of reasoning are similar to those of Movsēs Xorenac'i, he has not mentioned the latter's argument that name derives from function. Movsēs offers many etymologies derived from place-names, and some from physical characteristics; but most of the noble families' names he derived from their function. Thus the Arcrunik' were those who carried the eagle-standards: arcui-uni.[39]

As T'ovmay reaches periods for which there is a greater wealth of historical detail, so his own account becomes patently more tendentious. He desires to show that the Arcrunik' played a role second to none—and certainly not second to the Bagratids. For example: King Abgar's father was called Arǰam—an interesting example of T'ovmay going back to Xorenac'i's source, Eusebius, rather than following Movsēs exactly.[40] Arǰam greatly maltreated the Bagratids, and had strung Enanos up on a gibbet for not renouncing his Jewish religion. Now according to Movsēs, Enanos did adore idols when the king threatened to execute his sons before his eyes. Following the apostasy, Enanos was banished to Armenia. But according to T'ovmay, an Arcruni prince, J̌aǰuř, saved Enanos from the gibbet; and when Enanos came to Armenia, J̌aǰuř arranged the marriage of his own son Sahak with Smbatuhi the daughter of Enanos. This was the first marriage alliance between the Bagratids and the Arcrunik', says T'ovmay.[41] J̌aǰuř—and indeed this whole tale—is unattested elsewhere. But it may not be irrelevant that T'ovmay's patron Grigor Deranik was the grandson of an alliance between an Arcruni father and a Bagratid mother.

As is well known, Abgar was the first of the heathen kings to believe in Christ. Movsēs had elaborated on the Abgar story, and made Tobias the Jew—in whose house the missionary Thaddaeus had stayed—a Bagratid; so it was a Bagratid who was the first Armenian to be baptised.[42] However, Movsēs had earlier mentioned a Xosran Arcruni; he was supposedly an Armenian general who had been sent by Abgar to Aretas of Petra in the latter's war against king Herod.[43] According to T'ovmay, this Arcruni, being with Abgar when Christ's letter and portrait arrived in Edessa, was the first to be baptised by Thaddaeus. This Xosran, or Xuran, Arcruni ended his days in Jerusalem with queen Helena, distributing his wealth to the poor. Indeed it was he who took Helena's gold to Egypt in order to buy wheat[44]—the first Armenian entrepreneur!

On occasion the Arcrunik' are mentioned in Armenian sources before T'ovmay, but not as playing a particularly prominent role. For example: When Saint Gregory went to Caesarea for consecration as the first bishop of Armenia, he was escorted by an imposing retinue. This is not mentioned by Xorenac'i, but Agat'angełos lists the nobles—and the Arcrunik' come in last place as number 16.[45]   According to T'ovmay, this was because the prince Tiroc' (not named by Agat'angełos) was a pious man; he strove to make himself recognized by a single person—that is, Christ—rather than by the multitude. Being a studious reader of the gospel which enjoins us not to sit in the first rank, he never claimed superior position among the Armenian nobles. This leads T'ovmay to his references to Isaiah and Alexander quoted above.[46]

So T'ovmay has improved on Movsēs Xorenac'i and has explained away a reference in Agat'angełos. What about Ełišē? Ełišē's hero is Vardan Mamikonean, who died a martyr's death on the battlefield at Avarayr in 451. By the time of T'ovmay several historians had already confused this Vardan with the Vardan who led a revolt in 572. That T'ovmay brings together episodes from the two occasions as part of the same story is therefore not particularly surprising.   More interesting is his introduction of the Arcruni prince Vahan as the original focus of Armenian patriotism in the revolt against Yazkert. T'ovmay assures us that after the extinction of the Arsacid monarchy, when the Persians occupied Armenia and attempted to impose fire-worship (more usually called "ash-worship" by T'ovmay),[47] the Armenian nobles first rallied around Vahan Arcruni, planning to make him king. But for unexplained reasons, the Armenians went over to Vardan Mamikonean; so Vahan Arcruni (who is unattested elsewhere) threw in his lot with Vardan. Together they were killed attempting to reach the impious Vasak, who had taken refuge among the Persian elephants at Avarayr.[48]

These interesting details are unknown to Ełišē, so T'ovmay explains the discrepancy by a strange story. Passing over the parallel account in Łazar without a word, T'ovmay avers that Ełišē's History was doctored by the impious Nestorian Barsauma.[49]   The latter's activity on the confines of Armenia is known to both Syrian and Armenian authors.[50] But no one else indicates that Barsauma got hold of Ełišē's History before it had been published and, in a fit of pique, expunged all references to the deeds of the House of the Arcrunik', including the martyrdom of Vahan. Curiously, these important omissions went unnoticed after Ełišē's death when the text was published. So the History of Ełišē that has come down to us does less than justice to the ancestors of T'ovmay's patrons.

Should we then condemn T'ovmay for betraying the high ideals he had set himself as a historian? Clearly, many histories must have disappeared if the stories T'ovmay is reporting are merely succinct rewritings of previous the stories T'ovmay is reporting are merely succinct rewritings of previous accounts. Or perhaps T'ovmay is simply giving written expression to well known tales that had come down by word of mouth? Although neither possibility—or a combination of both—should be excluded a priori, we may well wonder whether the discrepancy between professed ideals and reported history is due rather to the influence of rhetoric on the former than to deliberate fraud on the latter. T'ovmay produced what was expected of him. More important than the accuracy of the letter was the general spirit of his History. It expressed the ideals of a hereditary aristocracy, where each noble family was in perpetual rivalry with the others. In that rivalry the pen was as mighty a weapon as the sword. Court historians were no more expected to be dispassionate then, than party historians are today.

NOTES

[1]All references to the History of T'ovmay are to T'ovmayi Vardapeti Arcrunwoy Patmut'iwn Tann Arcruneac' (ed. K. Patkanian, St. Petersburg, 1887; reprinted Tiflis 1917). This edition contains certain passages omitted from the first edition (Constantinople 1852), which contained material concerning Islam inappropriate for publication within the Ottoman empire. That first edition was used by M. F. Brosset for his French translation Histoire des Ardzrouni, in his Collection d'historiens arméniens I (St. Petersbourg, 1874). The translation in modern Armenian by V. Vardanyan, T'ovma Arcruni ev Ananun, Patmut'yun Arcrunyac' Tan (Erevan, 1978) is based on Patkanian's edition.

[2]For details of the manuscript (now in the Matenadaran, Erevan, but not listed in the two-volume Catalog of the Matenadaran's holdings) see the Preface to Patkanian's edition. Fragments of the History are found in the following MSS in the Matenadaran:
    1404 (1664 A.D.),
    1882 (1619 A.D.),
    1889 (1675 A.D.),
    1890 (1172 A.D.), and
    2559 (16th century).

[3]Matenadaran 2639 (1672 A.D.).

[4]See C. Sanspeur, "A travers la tradition textuelle de l'Histoire des Arméniens de Lazare de P'arpi," REArm 12 (1977) 85-99; "Note sur l'édition du fragment de l'Histoire de Lazare de P'arpi decouvert dans le MS A82 de Leningrad," Handēs Amsōreay 94 (1980), 13-22.

[5]T'ovmay's own work is on pp. 1-262 of Patkanian's edition; the anonymous additions run from p. 262 to p. 326.

[6]See Kirakos Ganjakec'i, Patmut'iwn Hayoc' (ed. K. A. Melik'-Ohanjanyan; Erevan, 1961) 7, 79.

It is noteworthy that other medieval historians who usually mention their predecessors (e.g. Step'anos Asołik, Vardan, Step'anos Ōrbelean) have no reference to T'ovmay. Particularly striking is his position in the list of Mxit'ar Ayrivanec'i, Patmut'iwn (ed. K. Patkanov, Trudi vostočkago otdelenija imperatorskago russkago arxeologičeskago obščestva, 14, St. Petersburg 1869), 261: T'ovmay vardapet is listed after Koriwn but before Movsēs Xorenac'i, Łazar P'arpec'i and Ełišē. Does this imply that Mxit'ar knew only of the first book of T'ovmay's History (which ends with the abolition of the Arsacid monarchy in Armenia) and therefore supposed him to be a fifth century author? It is certainly evidence that T'ovmay's History was not well known in later scholarly circles.

[7]T'ovmay, 76.

[8]Ibid., 248-251.

[9]Ibid., 120, 168.

[10]Ibid., 243.

[11]Ibid., 3-4.

[12]Ibid., 58.

[13]Ibid., 20.

[14]Ibid., 40.

[15]Ibid., 58.

[16]Ibid., 6, 24, 58.

[17]Movsēs Xorenac'i, Patmut'iwn Hayoc' (ed. M. Abełian and S. Yarut'iwnean; Tiflis, 1913). For the origin of the Bagratids see I 22, II 3; for Alexander and the Ancient History see I 9.

[18]T'ovmay, 27, 81.

[19]Ełišē, Vasn Vardanay ew Hayoc' Paterazmin (ed. E. Ter-Minasian, Erevan 1957), 140.

[20]T'ovmay, 153.

[21]Ibid., 5, 45, 47, 124.

[22]Ibid., 45, 76.

[23]Ibid., 153.

[24]Ibid., 193.

[25]Ibid., 5.

[26]Ibid., 61.

[27]Ibid., 130.

[28]Agat'angełos, Patmut'iwn Hayoc' (ed. G. Ter-Mkrtčian and St. Kanayeanc'; Tiflis, 1909), paragraphs 49-122.

[29]T'ovmay, 224.

[30]See the Introduction to R. W. Thomson, Moses Khorenats'i, History of the Armenians (Harvard Armenian Texts and Studies, 4; Cambridge, Mass., 1978), for a discussion of Movsēs' attitude to history and his sources.

[31]T'ovmay, 8, 37, 121; Movsēs Xorenac'i, I 23.

[32]Xorenac'i, I 25-29.

[33]T'ovmay, 37.

[34]Ibid., 38-40.

[35]Xorenac'i, I 22.

[36]T'ovmay, 41.

[37]Xorenac'i, II 14.

[38]T'ovmay, 44.

[39]Xorenac'i, II 7.

[40]Xorenac'i, II 24, changes the Arǰam of Eusebius to the more Armenian sounding Arsham. See the discussion in Thomson, Moses Khorenats'i, II 24 n. 1.

[41] T'ovmay, 45-46.

[42] Xorenac'i, II 33.

[43] Ibid., II 29.

[44] T'ovmay, 47-49.

[45] Agat'angełos, #795.

[46] T'ovmay, 58.

[47] Ibid., 31, 62, 77. See further R. W. Thomson, Ełishē, History of Vardan and the Armenian War (Harvard Armenian Texts and Studies, 5; Cambridge, Mass., 1982), 66.

[48] T'ovmay, 77-80.

[49] Ibid., 80-81.

[50] See S. Gero, Barṣauma of Nisibis and Persian Christianity in the Fifth Century (Corpus Scriptorum Christianorum Orientalium 426, Subsidia 63, Louvain 1981), 112.

THE HISTORICAL GEOGRAPHY OF THE PAULICIAN
AND T'ONDRAKIAN HERESIES

George Huxley

Queen's University of Belfast (Northern Ireland)

From Byzantine sources alone a coherent, but sadly incomplete, picture of Paulician geography in Asia Minor emerges. From the middle of the seventh century until the Fall of Tephrikē to the imperial armies in the reign of Basil I the heresy was mainly a phenomenon of the eastern frontier lands. In the time of Constans II the first of the series of heresiarchs, Constantine, who took the Pauline name Silvanus, came from Mananalis (Arm: Mananałi) in Armenia to Kibossa, an unidentified place near the kastron of Koloneia.[1] The successor of Constantine-Silvanus, Symeon-Titos, also taught at Kibossa.[2] Later there were Paulicians at a place called Episparis, somewhere between Kibossa and Mananalis.[3] From there some of them were led by their teacher Gegnesios-Timothy, the son of an Armenian called Paul, back to Mananalis. In Mananalis Gegnesios died of plague;[4] almost certainly this was the great plague of 748.[5]

In the next generation Zacharias, the son of Gegnesios, was killed by Arab frontier-guards, with his followers, while attempting to cross back into East Roman territory. His rival Joseph, who took the Pauline name Epaphroditos, was more fortunate: he turned his party's wagons round and persuaded the Arab interceptors that he and his followers were on the way to Syria for pasturage and to make milk.[6] Thus some of the Paulicians were transhumant pastoralists; for such persons, it was natural to move frequently to the highland meadows in summer and, if need be, through No-Man's-land to the Arab or Byzantine territories. Joseph-Epaphroditos, having been left alone by the Arab guards, slipped across with his followers to Episparis. We

T. Samuelian & M. Stone, eds. Medieval Armenian Culture. (University of Pennsylvania Armenian Texts and Studies 6). Chico, CA: Scholars Press, 1983. pp. 81 to 95.

hear that a successor of Joseph, the Paulician leader Sergios-Tychikos, who was an energetic missionary, also spent some time in Pontus, that is, in the Armeniak thema. Later he and his disciples settled at Argaoun within the domain of the Emir of Melitene.[7] Not long after his death there, Argaoun became a redoubt of Paulician soldiers who had escaped about 844 from persecution under the empress Theodora.[8] From Argaoun the Paulicians under their military leader Karbeas moved to Tephrikē, which became the base of their distant and devastating attacks on Byzantine territory. The raids continued under the successor of Karbeas, Chrysocheir, until his death in the battle with the Byzantines at Bathyrhyax in 872.[9] When Tephrikē fell to the Byzantines six years later, some of the surviving Paulicians may well have fled to Mananalis, but the Greek sources are not explicit.

What they do make clear is the strong Armenian connection of the heresy. Constantine from Mananalis is said to have been an Armenian; Paul and his son Gegnesios were Armenians; and one of the leaders of the heretics Baanes, a contemporary and rival of Sergios-Tychikos, reveals by his name (Vahan) his Armenian origins. The close ties of the heresy with Pontus fit the Armenian connection well; for many Armenian troops were among the forces withdrawn from Armenia during the Arab invasion in the mid-seventh century, and they were stationed in Pontus and other parts of northeastern Asia Minor to form the new Armeniak thema. In Asia Minor the connections of the heresy were military as well as pastoral: the great Paulician leader Karbeas himself had been a protomandator in the imperial army.[10] Wise emperors had valued the fighting qualities of the Paulicians instead of alienating them; Constantine V had transferred Paulicians from Melitene and Theodosioupolis (Karin or Erzerum) to defend Thrace,[11] but when the heretics under Karbeas allied themselves with Omar of Melitene they provided a formidable threat to the security of Byzantine Asia Minor.

The historical outlines given in the Byzantine sources become much more complicated when an attempt is made to combine them with the Armenian evidence. First, there is a theological problem about the character of the heresy: in Peter of Sicily it is presented as being both dualist and docetic, but in Armenia, if the eighteenth-century text called the Key of Truth is, as Conybeare[12] and, more recently, Garsoian[13] have supposed, a witness to medieval Paulicianism in Armenia, the Paulicians, and the T'ondrakians, with whom it is customary to link them, were Adoptionists. There is, secondly, a chronological problem about the date when Paulicianism

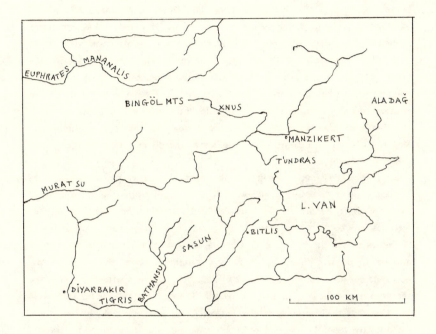

Paulician and T'ondrakian Heresies

arose as a definable and distinct heresy in Armenia. Finally, and this is our main concern here, there is the fact that the only territory agreed to be a home of heresy by the Greek and Armenian sources is Mananalis. Even here we face a problem, because the main account of heresy in Mananalis in Armenia comes from Aristakēs Lastivertc'i,[14] who wrote soon after 1072, some two centuries after the fall of Tephrikē and three centuries after the escape of Joseph-Epaphroditos from Mananalis to Episparis. Thus it is by no means certain that the heretics who were there in the eighth century were akin by ancestry or in doctrine to the eleventh-century T'ondrakian heretics of Mananalis described by Aristakēs. However, though continuity in Mananalis is not documented, it is clear that the district was for a long time a nurse of heresy.

There has been disagreement about the geographical position of Mananalis. The difficulty begins with Peter of Sicily in his report on his visit to Tephrikē on behalf of the emperor Basil I. He stated that Constantine-Silvanus was born in Samosaton of Armenia, in a village called Mananalis.[15] Samosata beside the Euphrates in Commagene is not in Armenia and can have nothing to do with Mananalis. Peter's statement about the origin of the heresy is due to a confused attempt to link the Paulicians with the Paulinists, sectaries who followed Paul of Samosata. The connection between Samosata and Constantine-Silvanus can be rejected; it rests on a theological mistake. Accordingly there is no need to suppose a confusion between Samosata and Arsamosata (Arabic Šimšat), a city beside the Arsanias or Murad Su branch of the upper Euphrates in Armenia.[16] Conybeare[17] thought that Mananalis was a district around Xnus in the valley of the Kinis Çay, a southeasterly-flowing feeder of the Arsanias. This is the canton from which Armenian sectaries brought the Key of Truth when they came to settle at Akhaltzik in Tsarist Armenia in 1828. It is true that Gregory Magistros, who died in 1058, in his letter to the heretics called T'ulaili (who were a branch of the T'ondrakec'i) connects Xnus with their heresy: Xnus he wrote, "recalls a hole stopped up in which the deepest darkness reigns."[18] It is also true that downstream from Xnus lies the district of Hark' in Turuberan, where there were also T'ondrakians according to Aristakēs of Lastivert.[19] So we can be sure that there were T'ondrakians settled in and near Xnus in the eleventh century; it may even be true that those who were still clinging to heresy in the same canton in the early nineteenth century were descendents of them. But the source of Byzantine Paulicianism cannot have been at Xnus, because

Mananalis lay elsewhere. This can be seen in the account of the T'ondrakians in Aristakēs Lastivertc'i.

Aristakes shows that there were T'ondrakians living beside a river, which he calls Mananali,[20] not far from its confluence with the Euphrates. On the other side of the Euphrates, near the confluence, was the awan called Kot'ēr. This awan adjoined the province of Ekełeac', whose position is known: it extended along the upper Euphrates from east to west on either side of modern Erzincan. Ekełeac'/ (Akisilene) reached eastward to the confluence of the Euphrates with its left-bank tributary the Tuzla Suyu, a river that rises in the Bingöl mountains some fifty miles to the east of the meeting of the waters. Thus, as Juzbašjan[21] and others have argued, the Mananali river is the Tuzla Suyu; the river gave its name to the district where the Paulician Constantine-Silvanus was born. Here too the heresiarch of the Paulicians Gegnesios-Timothy settled for a time before dying of plague. Hence also Joseph-Epaphroditos escaped back with his followers and herds to Episparis in East Roman territory. Hereabouts too lived in the lifetime of Aristakēs the local magnates the ladies Axni and Kamara, who were hereditary possessors of two villages. They were joined in their T'ondrakianism by the išxan Vrver, another magnate of Mananali.[22] The spreading of the heresy among the gentry explains why, possibly in the time of John Tzimiskes, the Byzantine authorities had set up a bishopric of Mananalis subordinate to Trebizond.[23] It must have been a lonely posting for a Chalcedonian.

The principal fort in Mananalis was Smbat on Smbatay (berd), a mountain of the same name. According to Aristakes the fort was used as a place of refuge during the early Seljuk incursions;[24] indeed it is likely to have been the main redoubt of the T'ondrakians of Mananali. We do not know who the eponymous Smbat was; but there is a possibility that he too was a T'ondrakian heretic. For a prominent ninth-century leader of the T'ondrakians was called Smbat.

About 987 Grigor Narekac'i wrote a letter to the convent of Kčaw about the doctrine of the T'ondrakians 'Ianes' and 'Iamres.' In the epistle it said that Smbat declared communion bread to be ordinary bread; Grigor also states that Smbat allowed himself to be worshipped by his disciples.[25] But the text provides no chronological evidence A date for Smbat is given by Grigor Magistros, who in his letter concerning the T'ulaili remarked that during 170 years, equivalent to thirteen patriarchates, the heretics had flourished since the time of Smbat.[26]   In another letter Grigor, an active persecutor of the T'ondrakians, wrote that they had infested the land for more than two hundred years.[27]   Since Grigor was writing in the middle of the eleventh century, he dates Smbat in the middle of the ninth.

According to Grigor Magistros, Smbat came forth from the village of Zarehavan in the district of Całkotn.[28]   This is a territory on the northerly slopes of the Ala Dağ (Niphates, Npat) to the northeast of Lake Van.[29]   From Zarehavan he moved to T'ondrak and began to teach there.   The position of T'ontraks, or T'ondrak, which gave its name to the heresy, is known: it lay some three hours to the south of Manzikert and was later called T'undras. The identification was made long ago by the geographer Inčičian.[30]   It is supported by a detail in Grigor Narekac'i, to which A. G. Ioannisjan drew attention in an article in the Soviet periodical Voprosy Istorii.[31]

Grigor admonished the Abbot and monks of the convent of Kčaw by writing that they desired to share the lot of those who had been cut off by the sword of the avenging heathen emir Aplvard.   The emir is Abu'l Bard I, the Muslim ruler of Manzikert in the middle of the ninth century, who according to Constantine Porphyrogenitus had received from Ašot the Great Prince of Princes (r. 862 to 890) the gift of Xliat, Arzes and Perkri.[32]   It is likely that the gift was a reward for support in suppression of the heretics in T'ontraks, since the temptation to ally with them, as Omar of Melitene had done with the Paulicians of Argaoun, would have been strong.   Instead Aplvard massacred them.   It is not clear from Grigor Narekac'i whether Smbat died in the massacre; possibly he escaped to Mananalis to join the heretics there and to give his name to the fortress at Smbatay berd.

But these matters remain obscure; what is clear is that Ioannisjan's identification of Aplvard fits the dating of Smbat to the mid-ninth century and the fixing of the home of the T'ondrakians to the country between Manzikert and Lake Van, in remote terrain near the watershed where northward flowing feeders of the Arsanias rise.   After the massacre some of the heretics survived there or were able to come back later; for Grigor Magistros states that after he had put down T'ondrakian heresy in "Mesopotamia"[33] (that is, the Byzantine thema, formerly an Armenian principality, between the Arsanias and the Çimişgezek-su),[34] he went up to the "well-head, in which the viper and scorpion and dragon of wickedness had nestled. I demolished it, as my ancestors did Aštišat. Then I named the village after the chapel of St. George, which had been taken possession of by the hound Smbat."[35] However, not even the violence of Grigor Magistros could wipe out all trace of the T'ondrakians there, because, as we have seen, a form of the name T'ontraks or T'ondrak survived until the nineteenth century. The very name of the heretics was a constant reminder elsewhere of the geographical origin of their doctrine and of their leader Smbat. Grigor's claim that his ancestors destroyed Aštišat should not be taken as evidence that there had once been Paulicians or similar heretics at that place; he may simply be asserting that his ancestors assisted in the overthrow of pagan cults (such as that of Aštē or Astarte)[36] there, when Christianity was being established in Armenia.

If Smbat initiated heresy at T'ondrak, then we should not expect to find the term T'ondrakec'i applied to heretics of any description in Armenia before the mid-ninth century. The name Paulikianoi or Polikeank' is encountered much earlier: we have already followed Constantine-Silvanus in the Byzantine sources from Mananalis to Kibossa near Koloneia in Pontus, in the third quarter of the seventh century. In Armenian texts too there is proof of the presence of Paulicians in Armenia (whether or not they may have been dualists or docetists or adoptionists) before the mid-ninth century. The reference to Polikean in the fifth-century Call to Repentance of the Catholicos Yovhannēs I Mandakuni may be an interpolation; so it is best left aside. Slightly less dubious, though not much can be inferred from the text, is the reference to Paulicians in connection with 'Nestorians' in the Oath of Union imposed at the Council of Dvin assembled by the Catholicos Nersēs II in 555. Here the laity are said, among both 'Nestorians' and Paulicians, to have brought bread to their teachers in order to receive communion.[37]

We are on firmer ground when we come to the Catholicos Yovhannēs Ōjnec'i, who about 719 summoned another Council to Dvin. Canon 32 of the synod is aimed at the Paulicians, and in his sermon against the same sectaries Yovhannes declares that they had already been rebuked by Catholicos Nersēs. After the death of Nersēs they had fled into hiding somewhere in 'our land' and they were joined by certain Iconoclasts who had been reproved by the Catholicoi of the Albanians.[38] Scholars have differed over the identity of the Nersēs mentioned here by Ōjnec'i. The neatest explanation is that he is Nersēs III (641-661), the Builder;[39] for he was a contemporary of the Emperor Constans II. The persecution of Paulicians by Nersēs would account for the move of Constantine-Silvanus into Pontus from Mananalis, which was then being settled by refugees from Armenia and was, therefore, from the point of view of Nerses III "somewhere in our land." Thus the Armenian and Greek sources agree in taking the origins of the Paulician heresy back at least as far as the mid-seventh century; it is significant that even then the heresy appears as a phenomenon of the frontier.

Evidence exists that there were heretics called Polikeank' in the highlands rising to the southwest of Lake Van on the southern limits of Armenia. In the Catalogue of Heresies in Matenadaran manuscript No. 3681 of 1313, and in the later manuscript No. 687,[40] Heresy No. 153 is that of the K'alert'akan 'the bloodthirsty.' Here we are told that a certain king of the Greeks chanced on the filthy sect of the Pōlikeank' and was not able to turn them from their heresy. "He pursued them beyond the mountains of Caucasus." In the same Catalogue Heresy No. 154 refers to a woman named Šet'i, who is said in the earlier text to be an Arab, in the later to be a Turk. She came to the Armenians and was seduced by a certain Pōl, who is said to have come from Ayrarat and to have been a disciple of St. Ephrem. The significance of the names K'alert'akan and Šet'i has been admirably clarified by R. M. Bartikyan.[41] The river K'alirt is now the Batman Suyu, a left bank tributary of the Tigris. By the Greeks it was called the Nymphios. It rises to the west of Lake Van and flows in a southerly direction between Arzanene (Arcn) on the east and Martyropolis (Np'rkert) on the west. Today travellers from Diyarbekir to Bitlis can still admire the fine Ortakid bridge across the Batman Su close to the point where the river leaves the mountains of Sasun.

Bartikyan corrected Šet'i to Sidma and Sit'it'ma, the Arabic names of the Batman Suyu.[42] He also adduced a passage of the Geography of Pseudo-Movsēs Xorenac'i in confirmation of the link between Paulicians and the country through which the Batman river runs: "The Kalirt, which comes out of the mountains of Salin and Sanasun (or Sasun), separates Np'kert and K'limar; therefore it separates the Romans and the Persians and it is now called Sit'it'ma which is bloodthirsty."[43] The Kalirt river cannot have formed the East Roman frontier at any time between the reign of Heraclius and the tenth century. The political circumstances envisaged by the Geography antedate 641. In the vague reference in the Catalogue of Heresies to the Greek emperor driving the heretics 'beyond the Caucasus' there may be a recollection of heretics being driven out of Byzantine territory from the district of Sanasun, but the "king of the Greeks" is not named. In Georgios Kyprios the people of Sanasun are the Sanasounitai;[44] they were akin to the Chothaitai on the other side of the Tauros range. The same Chothaitai are also found in T'ovmay Arcruni.[45] He describes them as remote mountaineers who had lost the use of their mother-tongue; they lived in the mountains separating Tarōn from Aljnik' and were called adventurers and Xout' owing to their strange language (possibly they had originally not spoken Armenian; T'ovmay thought of them as Assyrian immigrants). Their mountain was called Xoit'. They recited psalms translated by the ancient Armenian translators. They were, declared T'ovmay, Assyrian peasants whose ancestors had come with Adrametek and Sanasar,[46] and they called themselves Sanasnaik.

The district of Sanasun was of great interest to Thomas because the Arcruni family claimed descent from Sennacherib, whose sons fled to Armenia. Moreover the family appropriated the name Senekerim. The mountaineers of Xoyt' may well have been, together with those of Sanasun to the south of the watershed, nominal dependants of the Arcruni in lands claimed by the family. For among the territories alleged to have been given by Senekerim of Vaspurakan to the Byzantine empire are mentioned the mountains of Sasun and Julamerk[47] (Sasun is the later form of the name Sanasun). The psalm-reciting Sanasnaik can be regarded as a branch of the Paulicians of Heresy No. 153, but living on the other side of the mountains. Both groups could threaten the passes or kleisourai through which the roads linking Tarōn with Arcn (Arzanene) ran. Here is the mountain range called Šim by the Armenians, and here occurred some of the most terrible massacres of Armenians in 1894.[48]

The Paulicians of Sanasun and Xoyt' were well placed to ally themselves with the Arabs, as were those of Argaoun and Tephrikē. That they took advantage of their strategic position near the kleisourai to the southwest of Lake Van is suggested in two remarks by Yovhannēs Ōjnec'i. He stated that Paulicians had an alliance with the "circumcised tyrants," that is, the Arabs.[49] He also said that they had spread out from their original home in the district of Jrkay.[50] According to the geographer Inčičian Jrkay was the neighborhood of the Bitlis river,[51] a southward-flowing tributary of the Tigris forming the main pass next to the valley of the Batman Suyu. Here the road still passes by way of Bitlis to Tatvan; this was the Kleisoura Balaleisōn of the Greeks and the Dharb Badlīs of the Arabs.[52] Inčičian's identification of Jrkay can be combined with Bartikian's explanation of the Paulician K'aṭert'akan to show that there had been at certain times Paulicians based in the country extending from the Batman river to the Bitlis river. They are likely to have persisted in these remote highlands for a long time, reciting their old Armenian psalms and uttering their strange speech.

Aristakēs provides evidence for the wide extension of the Paulician and T'ondrakian heresies in the eleventh century in his account of the career of Jacob, who had been a bishop in Hark'.[53] In the time of Catholicos Sargis Sevanc'i (992-1019) he was deprived of office because he had turned T'ondrakian. Having escaped from prison he went to Constantinople, and he later returned to Armenia to settle at T'ondrak. But he was not acceptable to the T'ondrakians of T'ondrak; so he joined the heretics among the remote peasantry in the highlands of Xliat to the northwest of Lake Van. His last days were spent at Muharkin (Martyropolis or Np'rkert), where he would have been within reach of, or among, the Paulicians of Sanasun and the Batman Suyu valley. The heretical career of Jacob links T'ondrakians with Paulicians: Hark' is adjacent to Xnus; T'ondrak is an eponymous center of heresy; and Np'rkert is within the domain of the K'aḷert'akan. A generation earlier the T'ondrakian heresy had been present at Kčaw in the province of Mokk', to the northwest of Bitlis. Here, as the letter by Grigor Narekac'i shows, even the monks had become infected with unorthodox doctrine. At Kčaw the monks were living not far from the heretics of Xoyt' and may well have been affected by them.

Apart from the wide distribution of the heresies in Armenia and beyond, two geographical factors should be emphasized in conclusion. The first is the mobility of the heretics. It was not only the teachers and heresiarchs who travelled far; their flocks migrated too. Nor in the high country of Armenia and Pontus is such mobility strange. Many of the heretics belonged to the pastoral population of the countryside. They were used to transhumant movement to new grazing grounds and to seasonal changes of abode. Secondly, there is the factor of persistence in the heresies.[54] Part of the explanation for the continuity of heretical belief is to be found in the cantonal character of the Armenian terrain. The life of a remote mountain canton can become historically fossilized: armies may pass by at the foot of the valley; proponents of centralized orthodoxies may never penetrate into harsh and unwelcoming gorges leading to a plateaux where shepherds live. There was heresy in Mananalis in the seventh century and in the eleventh. There was heresy in the valley of Xnus in the eleventh and still heresy (though not necessarily the very same one) in Xnus in the late eighteenth century. Thus the doctrines of the Key of Truth, when considered in the light of historical geography, are likely to be much more ancient than the time (1782) when the text as we have it was written; but how much more ancient is mainly a question of theology and philology, not of historical geography.[55]

NOTES

Shortened references to the following works will be found:

Conybeare   Fred. C. Conybeare, The Key of Truth. A Manual of the Paulician Church of Armenia (Oxford, 1898).

Garsoîan   Nina G. Garsoîan, The Paulician Heresy (The Hague and Paris: Mouton, 1967).

Hübschmann   Heinrich Hübschmann, Die Altarmenischen Ortsnamen (Amsterdam 1969, reprinted from Indogermanische Forschungen 16 (1904) 197-490).

Lemerle   'L'histoire des Pauliciens d'Asie Mineure d'après les sources grecques,' Travaux et Mémoires 5 (Paris, 1973) 1-142, reprinted in Essais sur le monde byzantin (London, 1980).

Markwart   Jos. Markwart, Sudarmenien und die Tigris-quellen nach griechischen und arabischen Geographen (Vienna, 1930).

Sources   Ch. Astruc, W. Conus-Wolska, J. Goillard, P. Lemerle, D. Papachryssanthou, J. Para-melle, "Les sources grecques pour l'histoire des Pauliciens d'Asie Mineure," Travaux et Mémoires 4 (1970) 1-227.

[1]Peter of Sicily, History, 94, 101. (Sources, pp. 41, 43.)

[2]Peter of Sicily, History, 107. (Sources, p. 45.)

[3]Peter of Sicily, History, 112, 121, 127. (Sources, pp. 47, 49, 51.) For a likely position of Episparis (near the Upper Euphrates in the frontier zone)

see Lemerle, 78.

[4]Peter of Sicily, History, 121-122. (Sources, p. 49.)

[5]See Lemerle, 65, note 43 on Theophanes 1.422-424 (ed. de Boor, repr. Olms: Hildesheim, 1963).

[6]Peter of Sicily, History, 125-126. (Sources pp. 49, 51.)

[7]Peter of Sicily, History, 177-179. (Sources, p. 65.)

[8]For the chronology see Lemerle, 88-90.

[9]Lemerle, 92-103.

[10]Theophanes Continuatus 4.16, p. 166 (ed. I. Bekker; Bonn: Weber, 1838).

[11]Theophanes 1.429, 19-22 (ed. de Boor).

[12]Conybeare, xxxv, lxxvii.

[13]Garsoïan, 211-213.

[14]Aristakēs Lastivertc'i, Patmutiwn, 119-133. [pp. 118-127 in K. N. Jusbašjan, (ed. & trans.), Moscow: Nauka, 1968; pp. 108-120 in M. Canard and H. Bérbérian, (ed. & trans. of Jusbašjan) Bibliotèque de Byzantion No. 5; Brussels, 1973].

[15]Peter of Sicily, History, 94. (Sources, p. 41.)

[16]Concerning Arsamosata see now Anthony Bryer in A. Bryer and Judith Herrin (eds.) Iconoclasm (Birmingham: Centre for Byzantine Studies, 1977) 84.

[17]Conybeare, lxix.

[18]Ibid., p. 142. For a description of the plain of Khinis see H. F. B. Lynch, Armenia. Travels and Studies (London, 1901) 2.255-258; also 184 & 187 for sheep-fairs held there.

[19]Aristakēs Lastivertc'i, 119.

[20]Ibid., 130.

[21]Ibid., 170. See also Bryer, Iconoclasm, 83.

[22]Aristakēs Lastivertc'i, 119.

[23]Jean Darrouzès, Notitiae Episcopatuum Ecclesiae Constantinop-

olitanae (Paris, 1981) No. 424, p. 303.

[24]Aristakēs Lastivertc'i, 66, 71.

[25]Conybeare, 126, 128. Cf. Garsoïan, p. 143, n. 137.

[26]Conybeare, 142-143 and 145.

[27]Conybeare, 151.

[28]Conybeare, 144. Garsoïan, 141.

[29]Hübschmann, 361 and 363.

[30]See Ł. Inčičian, Storagrut'iwn Hin Hayastani (Venice, 1822), 130; Hübschmann, 330.

[31]A. G. Ioannisjan, "Dviženie Tondrakov v Armenii IX-XI vv.," Voprosy Istorii 10 (1954) 10:103. See also R. M. Bartikyan, Konstantin Ciranacin (Erevan, 1970) 225, n. 17.

[32]De Administrando Imperio 44, 17-21 (ed. Moravcsik and Jenkins). Concerning the Ašot's diplomacy toward the Arabs see S. Runciman in De Administrando Imperio 2 Commentary (London, 1962) 158, 169-70.

[33]Conybeare, 146.

[34]Nicolas Oikonomidès, Les Listes de Préséance byzantines des IXe et Xe Siècles (Paris, 1972) 349.

[35]Conybeare, 143.

[36]For Aštišat = 'Aštē's delight' see Markwart, 288. For pagan cults at Astisat see R. W. Thomson (ed. & trans.), Agathangelos' History of the Armenians (Albany, NY: SUNY, 1976) 347, para. 809.

[37]Garsoïan, 88-90, who provides a translation of part of the oath.

[38]Yovhannēs Ōjnec'i, Contra Paulicianos 88-89, trans. in Garsoian, 132.

[39]S. Runciman, The Medieval Manichee (Cambridge: University Press, 1947; reprt. 1955) 37-38; cf. Lemerle, 55.

[40]Catalogue of Heresies as cited and translated by Garsoian, 112-113.

[41]R. M. Bartikyan, "Pavlikyan šaržman mi k'ani albyurnerc šurĵē," IAN ArmSSR (1957) 6:85-97, esp. 95. See also Garsoïan, 130-31.

[42]See also Markwart, 270, 279.

[43]Ašxarhac'oyc' Movsisi Xorenac'woc' (ed. H. A. Siwk'rian; Venice, 1881) as cited and translated in Garsoĩan, 130, n. 77. See also the improved edition by J. Marquart (ed.) "Ērānšahr nach der Geographie des Ps. Moses Xorenac'i." (Abh. Gött. Akad. Wiss. Phil.-hist. kl. N. F. 3, 3 (Berlin, 1901) part 2, chap. 26. (text on 14, 17-20; trans. on 141-142).

[44]Georgios Kyprios (ed. H. Gelzer; Leipzig, 1890) para. 945-947. See also discussion in Markwart, 220; W. Tomaschek, "Sasun und das Queliengebeit des Tigris," S. B. Akad. Wien phil.-hist. kl. 133 (1896) No. 4 p. 8; R. H. Hewsen, "Armenia according to the Ašxarhac'oyc'," REArm 2 (1965) 327-328 relates that Sanasunk' in Aljnik' is No. 28 and Xoyt' in Tawuberan is No. 29 in Eremyan's list of Cantons.

[45]Tovmay Arcruni, Patmut'iwn [(trans. Brosset, Collection d'historiens arméniennes; St. Petersburg: Academy, 1874-1876) 2. 106] as quoted in Garsoĩan, 227; see also Tomaschek, "Sasun," 13. Markwart, 209.

[46]Compare 2 Kings 19: 37 "And it came to pass, as he [Sennacherib] was worshipping in the house of Nisroch his god, that Adrammelech and Sharezer his sons smote him with the sword; and they escaped into the land of Armenia [v. 1 Ararat]. And Esarhaddon, his son, reigned in his stead." For alleged descendants of Sanasar in the mountains of Šim in Sanasun see R. W. Thomson (ed. & trans.) Moses Khorenats'i. History of the Armenians (Cambridge, MA & London: Harvard, 1978) 112.

[47]Ms. Vienna Arm. Mekh. N. 10 B1.478a. noted by Markwart, 465-66. For Arcruni claims to Sanasun, see Markwart, 473.

[48]J. Bryce, Transcaucasia and Ararat (London, 1896) 486-89.

[49]Contra Paulicianos 78-79, as quoted in Garsoian, 135.

[50]Contra Paulicianos 88-89.

[51]Garsoĩan, 135 n. 100. referring to Inčičian, Geography of Armenia (Venice, 1822). In the Library of the Mekhitaristes in Vienna P. Generalabt Grigoris Manian (to whom Dr. W. Seibt kindly conducted me on November 19, 1982) generously sought out reference to J̌rkay. In the printed text of Yovhannēs Ōjnec'i Matenagrut'iwn (Venice, 1833) 39. it is not clear that J̌rkay is a proper noun; but M. Č'amč'ian, in his Patmut'iwn Hayoc' (Venice, 1785) 2.386, treated the word as a toponym, as did Ł. Inčičian—in the edition

of the Ašxarhac'oyc' published at Venice in 1835 (I.166). Inčičian lists J̌rkay
as a lake. The name is cognate with √j̄rg and so means 'the watery place';
the meaning is appropriate to a headwater of the Tigris but the position of
J̌rkay is still problematical. A new, and penetrating, study of tributaries of
the Tigris to the south of Lake Van is by J. M. Thierry, "Les Sources du Tigre
oriental selon la tradition hellénistique," in Geographica Byzantina (ed. H.
Ahrweiler, Sorbonne, Paris 1981) 131-138.

[52]Tomaschek, "Sasun," 8.

[53]Aristakēs Lastivertc'i, Patmut'iwn, 119-125.

[54]Note also the Paulinstai near tenth-century Euchaita in Pontus who
may have been Paulicians; on them see J. Darrouzès, Epitoliers byzantins du
Xe Siècle (Paris, 1960) 275, 28. Other persistent heretics, to be compared
to the 'Assyrians' of Sanasun and Xoyt', were the 'perfect ones' still to be
found less than a century ago among the Syriac-speaking shepherds on the
hills to the north of Mardin: "These have their christs and Dr. Wallis Budge,
to whom the present writer owes his information, was shown the stream in
which their last christ had been baptized." (F. C. Conybeare, "Paulicians,"
Encyclopedia Britannica (11th ed.; 1911) 20. 962).

[55]Conybeare, xxiii, xxvii. For the connection between the T'ondrakians (*Θονδραγῖται) and the eleventh-century Byzantine heresy
of Φουνδαγῖται see R. Bartikjan, Lraber HG (1980) 9.58-68, esp. 63-64.

ARMENIAN SCULPTURAL IMAGES PART II:
SEVENTH TO FOURTEENTH CENTURIES

Lucy Der Manuelian

Armenian Architectural Archives
Rensselaer Polytechnic Institute

The architectural sculpture of medieval Armenia is a rich and important source of information not only for her art but also for a fuller understanding of her history, religion and culture. The study of these little-known carved images on religious structures and commemorative stelae will amplify appreciably the fragmentary knowledge available at present through Armenian historians' accounts, inscriptions and colophons.

Since the tradition of carving figural images in stone on the exterior of churches begins in Armenian at least as early as the fifth century[1] and extends into the fourteenth, this corpus of sculpture is particularly significant for gaining a fuller understanding of the history of Christian art in the West. In the West, the tradition was not established essentially until the late eleventh century. Thus, Armenian sculpture is relevant to Western art in general with regard to the haunting and as-yet-unanswered question of why the practice did not begin earlier in the West, and is particular with regard to how it did originate and eventually lead to the richly carved portals of Romanesque and Gothic churches.

In addition, Armenian sculptural reliefs are more directly relevant since there is much evidence of the presence of Armenians in various parts of Europe from the sixth to the fourteenth century including bishops, monks, saints, merchants and craftsmen.[2] Whether or not this "Armenian presence" is in some way an "Armenian connection" with the sculptural revival in Europe is an open question which deserves further study.[3] In view of these

T. Samuelian & M. Stone, eds. Medieval Armenian Culture. (University of Pennsylvania Armenian Texts and Studies 6). Chico, CA: Scholars Press, 1983. pp. 96 to 119.

considerations, Armenian architectural sculpture is an important part of the history of art, and not a pariochial subject.

Despite the importance of this corpus, it has not yet been described and catalogued systematically.[4] For this reason, my paper, presented at the First Markarian Conference on Classical Armenian Culture, took the form of a survey of figural images in the sculpture from the fifth to the seventh century.[5] These images were also compared to those in other Christian cultures of the same period. Evidence was presented showing that Armenian sculpture shares some figural compositions in common with other cultures. It was also shown how Armenian sculptors produced original works, the elaboration and transformations of traditional Christian scenes, and by the creation of entirely new compositions not found elsewhere in Christian art. Armenian sculptural reliefs were found to be carved not only on portals, as in the West, but also over windows (Ōjun, seventh century; Mren, 631-639), on cornices (Sisawan, second half of the seventh century), on facade niches, and on the interiors of buildings (Sisawan).

The images as a whole demonstrate a direct emphasis on salvation as espoused by primitive Christianity, as well as a particular interest in the individual. The latter concern is expressed by the practice of including historical Armenian personages in sacred compositions. These characteristics reflect what is contained in important Armenian religious texts and historians' accounts such as Agat'angełos' History, The Teaching of Gregory, and Movsēs Xorenac'i.[6]

The present paper is a sequel to my previous study and is concerned with the corpus of figural stone images carved on Armenian churches and stelae between the seventh and the fourteenth century. Like the earlier paper, it is also in the form of a brief survey. Because the sculpture has been so little studied both in Armenia and in the West, this format has been chosen to provide an introduction and some general remarks which may serve as a guide for future lines of research.

In addition to providing a description of the types of figural images, this paper will (1) point out the strong threads of continuity from the preceding, classical period; (2) examine whether there are interrelationships with the medieval West; (3) touch on the kinds of creativity displayed by Armenian sculptors; and (4) comment on what all of this reveals about medieval Armenian Christianity.

The Armenian reliefs of Classical times are, as our survey has shown, predominated by images of Christ, the Virgin, saints, angels, ecclesiastics, apostles, and biblical scenes, almost all of them from the Old Testament. Representations of secular personages such as kings, princes, stonemasons and praying figures are also found.   It is interesting to note that the Old Testament scenes of Daniel in the Lions' Den, an image of salvation, is the single most popular one next to images of Christ and the Virgin.   Another point of significance is that there are examples of four different types of donor scenes representing patrons of churches who were contemporary princes or ecclesiastics.

A preliminary survey of the sculpture of the later period reveals that there is not much difference in the choice of images. Of course there is a risk of oversimplification in discussing a period of seven centuries in such general terms, particularly when the information available is so incomplete. However, judging by the published material and the fieldwork carried out in Soviet Armenia by the author,[7] the same types of figures and compositions are used during both periods.   Some Old Testament scenes such as the Sacrifice of Abraham and the Three Worthies in the Fierny Furnace are essentially dropped from the repertoire but the Daniel scenes still appear. There are some group compositions new to the corpus which will be discussed below but there are no dramatic shifts in iconography or focus, and no deviations from the course set in the classical period.

For example, images of the Virgin and Child in the Classical period do not appear to include those of the Adoration of the Magi with its overtones of kingly homage, and the same is true of our period.   This is particularly striking when compared with the many examples on Western European churches of the period, at Germigny l'Exempt (1215-1220) for example. Moreover, there are not to my knowledge any scenes on Armenian churches showing the Coronation of the Virgin, a composition which became extremely important in the great cathedrals of the West at Chartres (north transept, 1205-1210), Paris (shortly after 1160) and elsewhere.[8]

That Armenia does not show interest in representing the frightening apocalyptic images of the Last Judgment which are so popular in the West, demonstrates further the continuity of religious focus in Armenia and, at the same time, its contrast with Western architectural sculpture.   The gloomy tympana of Romanesque Europe with images of the suffering of the damned (Autun, 1125-1135, Plates 1 and 2), for example, are warnings to the viewers about a potentially terrible fate on the Day of Judgment.

These European tympana emphasize the kingly aspect of Christ with hieratic and hierarchic imagery to a degree not found in Armenian sculpture. Moreover, whenever historical personages are included in Western compositions, they are primarily drawn from centuries past, as is the case at St.-Denis (before 1140) and Chartres (1145-1155) with their representations of Old Testament kings. In contrast to many Armenian compositions, contemporary figures are hardly used. By including their own historical personages, the Armenians seem to be emphasizing through visual means their belief that Christ was ever-present, living among them in their own time. The reliefs on the lintel of the west portal of the Cathedral at Mren (631-639), discussed in the earlier paper[9] and again as below, is a good example.

During the medieval period, there are a few tympana in Armenia, which, by composition, look like Last Judgment scenes found in the West, but which do not have grim scenes portraying the damned. One is on the interior of the gawit' (1038) of the eleventh century church of S. Yovhannēs at the Monastery of Horomos (Plate 3) in present-day Turkey.[10] It is carved on the eastern side of the central lantern.

The scene shows Christ at the top with symbols of the Evangelists carved on either side. Below him, there are two rows of ecclesiastical personages. The upper four are identified by inscriptions as the first patriarchs of the Armenian church. The early date (1038) of this composition is of particular interest when one considers that one of the earliest carved representations of the four symbols of the Evangelists on a Western church is at Moissac in c. 1115-1120.

Another example of an Armenian tympanum similar in its general apparance to Western scenes of Judgment is found on the west portal of the Church of S. Karapet (between 1216 and 1221) of the Monastery named Yovhannavank' (Plate 4).[11] Christ is shown enthroned at the center flanked by two groups of figures as in traditional compositions, and the scene appears to represent the parable of the Wise and Foolish Virgins as seen in Western tympana. However, there is a distinctly new element introduced into the image because the figures are all bearded, those to the right of Christ holding candles and also those on His left looking distressed.

Male figures may have been represented here because Yovhannavank' was a monastery and, at the same time, well-known for its school. The message may have thus been aimed specifically at the monastic community.

The scene may also be related to the present-day liturgical practice in Armenian churches of having young boys enact the story of the Wise and Foolish Virgins on Holy Thursday during the reading of the Gospel. This may in turn go back to an earlier tradition of having monks take those roles.[12] If so, this tympanum would be an example of the Armenians referring to their own particular religious customs in their art even while creating a traditional composition.[13]

Another Armenian tympanal composition, again with groups of figures, is at the monastery named Noravank' at Amału (Plates 5 and 6). It is carved above the window of the gawit' (1223, and restored in 1321)[14] on the west side of the Church of S. Karapet. This scene is a creation unique in Christian art. It expresses theological concepts in an extremely lucid and striking manner. The composition provides another example of how salvation is emphasized in Armenian sculpture without resorting to terrifying images.

At Noravank', God the Father very tenderly holds the head of Adam cradled in His hand (Plate 6). The Dove hovers above Adam's head, and another appears in the beard of God. There is a Crucifixion scene on the left with images of the Virgin and St. John. The right hand of God is raised above them in a sign of blessing. The composition is a very reassuring image for the faithful. It states graphically that a forgiving God created Adam and gave him the breath of life. Although mankind was lost through Adam's sin, it will certainly be saved by the new Adam-Christ.

This composition is very different from the spirit of the apocalyptic imagery in the West in which the relation between God and man is represented in very different emotional terms. In some ways, the Noravank' scene is an Armenian summa sculptura because it restates in a more complete and detailed way the concepts which seem to have governed the choice of images in Armenia from the fifth century on.

As already mentioned, one of the most striking ways Armenian sculptural compositions differ from those of the West is their portrayal of contemporary Armenians in facade compositions, either accompanying saintly figures or appearing by themselves as patrons of the church. This practice also indicates the independent development of Armenian religious art which in turn is an expression of the independence of Armenian Christianity. These donor portraits proclaim to the viewer the message of personal commitment to the Church; they are images of Christians practicing their faith. The word "proclaim" is appropriate since the images are carved in such prominent places, not only on the portal but often just under the eastern gable of the church as though heralding the action to the faithful. The donor portrait is used so often on Armenian churches that it emerges from the survey of both periods as one of the most important motifs in the history of Armenian architectural sculpture, a remarkable continuity for a motif in any culture.

There are four types of donor scenes found in Classical Armenia and they continue to be represented in the medieval period. They are as follows, with an example given for each: 1) the donor shown with Christ at the center of the composition (Cathedral of Mren); 2) the donor shown alone with no accompanying saintly figures (Sisawan); 3) the donor shown in a hunting scene mounted on horseback fighting a lion or boar (Church of Ptlni, seventh century) (Plate 7); 4) the donor or pair of donors presenting a model of the church (Church of S. Nšan, Ałt'amar, 915-921; Church of S. Nšan, 971-991, of Hałbat Monastery, Plate 8).

All of these types of compositions appear in the West as well but much more sporadically than in Armenia. An example of the first type in Armenia, the Cathedral at Mren,[15] shows Christ on the lintel of the west portal flanked by the Saints Peter and Paul and by contemporary Armenian personages and donors. Standing next to St. Peter are the Armenian Bishop Theophilus and Prince David Saharuni. Another Armenian prince, Nerseh Kamsarakan, is shown to the right of St. Paul. According to an interpretation of the inscription,[16] Prince David Saharuni commissioned the church to be built but Prince Nerseh was the founder.

All the Armenian personages are in local attire and the entire spirit of the scene contrasts with that of a similar composition shown on the apse of the Church of San Vitale (c. 526-546/48) in Ravenna.[17] In the latter example, Christ is enthroned on the orb of heaven, and is flanked by angels. St. Vitalis is on His right and Bishop Ecclesius on His left presenting a model of the church. Christ is represented as the universal sovereign with his attendants, and holds his crown and a cross. This is very much an imperial image whereas āt Mren, Christ holds in His hand His robe, not a crown, and has no orb. Moreover, David Saharuni is shown in a more informal pose than the Ravenna dignitaries and presents Christ to the faithful in a lively and spontaneous way. Christ Himself is not represented as a timeless figure. On the contrary, he is shown as participating in a contemporary seventh-century scene in Armenia, in which donors wear Caucasian robes.

A similar comparison can be made between the tympanum of the gawit' (by 1270) (Plate 9) of the Monastery of Arates and the Porte Sainte-Anne (after 1160) (Plate 10) of Notre Dame Cathedral in Paris. At Arates, the two donors, Prince Smbat Ōrbēlean and Princess R̊uzuk'an, leaning towards the Virgin and Child, seem not so much to be conforming to the curve of the tympanum as to be spontaneously drawn together out of affection or for protection. In contrast, the figure of the donor at Notre Dame kneels ceremoniously in the corner of the composition at quite a distance from the Virgin. The effect is entirely different from the Arates tympanum. Moreover, both R̊uzuk'an and the Virgin wear similar, contemporary garb.

At the Monastery of Hałarcin (thirteenth century) in Armenia, on a tympanum fallen from an unidentified church, the donors are carved in the same expressive way as at Arates. But at the Armenian church of Barjrak'aš S. Grigor at Dseł (1221) (Plate 11), now completely destroyed, Christ, who is at the center of the composition, lays his hands very reassuringly on the heads of the kneeling donors. How very different these scenes are from the awesome Last Judgments in the West, such as at Autun (Plates 1 and 2) and St.-Denis (Plate 12). At Dseł, salvation is shown being attained, not in some judgment scene in the distant future, but at that very moment.

The second type of donor scene, the hunting image (Plate 7), also has a long history in Armenian sculpture but is most common in the thirteenth century. It is carved on different parts of the church as well as on the face of xac'k'ars (Plate 13). For example, it appears on the west portal tympanum of the Church of S. Nšan (Thirteenth century) at the Monastery of T'anahat (Plate 14), on the interior of the monastery church of Spitakawor (1320-1321), and on the gawit' interior, carved in 1261 (Plate 15) of Noravank', whose window sculpture was described above. One of the xac'k'ars is that of Prince Grigor Proš (1233) (Plate 13) who is shown in a hunting scene below the large cross, and that of Christ with saints.

In one of the earliest examples of the scene, on the seventh-century Church of Pt̊ni (Plate 7), it is associated with martyrdom. The donor figure on the left of the window arch is securely identified by inscription as the Armenian martyr-prince Manuēl Amatuni who perished at the hands of the Persians.

The hunting image is traditionally one of personal courage. It is an ancient motif used in the Near East to show the rider-hero triumphing over the enemy. As Garsoīan has pointed out, in Sasanian times, it was also a symbolic image of the heroic apotheosis.[18]   At the same time, in Christian art, the composition is used to depict Christian warrior-saints triumphing over evil.   In Armenian sculpture, it is used as a personalized image of Christian triumph which is the triumph over death through eternal salvation. Moreover, since the rider-hero being commemorated in Armenian sculpture is a champion of the faith, he serves as an exemplar for the members of the congregation.   They are thus exhorted to be courageous, unwavering in the moral struggle with evil, and steadfast in their faith in order to have a triumphant passage into the next world.

In the West, a number of medieval churches in the French province of Aquitaine contain similar equestrian images carved on their facades.[19]   One of the examples is on the west portal of the twelfth century Church of Saint-Pierre at Partheny-le-Vieux (Plate 16).   Seidel explains them in much the same terms except that in the French examples, the impetus for the sculpture appears to be the Crusades.   The equestrian motif, according to Seidel, was chosen as an elite image to please local noblemen who had social aspirations.[20]   Unlike the equestrian motifs used at Noravank', Spitakawor, and on the xač'k'ars, in Aquitaine, the images are not identified specifically as martyred individuals.

The last donor type shows the donor on the exterior of the church presenting a model of the church (Plate 8).   The earliest reported example is a sixth- or seventh-century stele at Agarak (Plate 17) in which the standing female figure holds the model of a basilica directly in front of her.

The next example of importance is at the Church of S. Nšan (915-921) on the island of Ałt'amar.   The figure of King Gagik, the founder of the church, is shown on the western facade standing to the left of the central window.   The image of Christ is carved on the other side of the window. More commonly, this type of donor scene appears without accompanying figures and consists either of one donor with a model or a pair, holding the model between them.   It is interesting to note that the figure of Christ, instead of being a larger, more authoritative figure, is actually smaller in size than that of Gagik.

Other notable examples of this motif include those at the monasteries of Sanahin (Church of S. Amenap'rkič, 966), Halbat (Church of S. Nšan (Plate 8), Haričavank' (Church of S. Astuacacin, 1201), Dadivank' (the Kat'ołike, 1214), Ganjasar (church of S. Yovhannēs, 1216-1238) (Plate 18), Halarcin (S. Astuacacin, 1281) and Noravank' at Amału (S. Astuacacin, 1339) (plate 19).

Although the motif itself is repeated, Armenian sculptors display their creativity through the different styles in which each is carved as well as in the variety of locations in which it appears. For example, at Haḱbat (Plate 8) and Sanahin, the pair of donor princes holding the church model are placed in a niche just under the eastern gable. At Hařičavank', the figures appear further down the east elevation below th outline of a large cross, while at Dadivank', the unframed figures are placed on either side of the central window of the south and the east elevations looking as though they were treading on air. The donors at Ganjasar (Plate 18) are shown individually on the drum, each on panels which flank the figures of Adam and Eve at the west end. The donor figure is shown standing with arms stretched upwards, holding the platform on which the church model, different in each case, rests. The sculptor shows them very effectively supporting the church literally as well as figuratively, i.e. physically as well as financially. At Noravank' (Plate 19), the representation is even more innovative. The figure of Prince Burt'el forms part of a column of the central rotunda of the upper part of the mausoleum-church of S. Astuacacin. The Virgin appears nearby on another column.

In Western medieval art, this motif of a donor holding the church model seems to appear very seldom in any media, and carved examples analogous to the Armenian ones do not seem to exist. It is interesting to note that the only other culture in which this scene is as popular is in the neighboring country of Georgia,[21] whose history is closely intertwined with Armenia's.

Some examples in the West during this period include the figure in the fresco of the ninth-century church of San Benedetto in Malles Venosta, and that of Abbot Desiderius in the apse of St. Angelo in Formis (1085) (Plate 20), both in Italy.

What is the explanation for the popularity of these images in Armenia? Are they simply images of self-aggrandizement proclaiming the wealth and power of these princes by showing that they were able to commission impressive churches? This may be the case in some instances since the donor or donors were alive at the time of the church's construction. In others, the patrons were already dead and are being commemorated by family members, as at Dadivank' and Ganjasar which were erected by the widows of both princes.

According to the texts of donors' building inscriptions and literary sources, the donor would erect the church to gain salvation for his family. He often included the names of his parents, siblings, children and spouse as well as other relatives, either living or dead. In some cases, he would add his own to the list. Consequently, the church structure became a kind of intercessor for them all. Also, the inscriptions document the commissioning of the church as an act of giving, a pious deed which was an expression of love for his God, family and fellow Christians.[22]

It is interesting to note at this point that the impetus for carving inscriptions on churches and adding descriptive colophons to manuscripts is explained in religious texts as the desire to have one's name inscribed in the Register of Life for having erected the church or commissioned the manuscript. In the passage from Luke (20:10) reading "you should rejoice that your names are enrolled in Heaven," Armenian texts change the phrase "register of heaven," yerkins, to "register of life," i dprut'ean kenac', as Maksoudian has pointed out.[23] The phrase is found in the 36th article of the seventh-century canons attributed to Sahak Part'ew and in Grigor Narekac'i's Book of Lamentations. In view of this, it is possible to suggest that besides putting one's name in an inscription, having the image of the deed would have been another way of recording one's name in the register, not for earthly but for spiritual glory.

By the same token, as suggested above, these figures would have served as exemplars for the faithful as they did in the hunting scenes. According to St. Gregory the Illuminator in his Teaching "the whole universe is a school of types,"[24] so that not only Old Testament personages but also contemporary Armenians could serve as "types." As Thomson pointed out, medieval Armenians often thought in terms of exemplars. For example, Armenian historians recounted the deeds of Armenian heroes as much to instruct by example as to narrate.[25] Consequently, the impetus for these images could be to show that one could become a champion of the faith through this kind of pious act as well as through martyrdom.

The focus on the church model itself may also be significant. According to literary sources, the model, representing the church physical, was, for the Armenians, not only a structure in which they worshipped but also a representation of the church metaphysical. It is the indestructible church as expounded by Agat'angełos, and it is the church as heaven on earth, as described by Yovhannes Ōjnec'i and Nersēs Šnorhali in their writings. Just as the Armenians fighting and dying for their faith could look up to the mountains and see the church structure and be reassured, knowing they would triumph in the end whether or not they survived the battle, the same would be true of these models which would be viewed in the same way, with the same strong sense of symbolism.

In these general remarks on the nature of Armenian architectural sculpture in both Classical and Medieval Armenia, the corpus emerges as a coherent, consistent set of carefully selected images, which reflect the essentially unchanging focus of Armenian Christianity in both thought and practice through the centuries. The images are clear and direct expressions of the message about salvation without the references to the imperial nature of Christ or the awesome Day of Judgment to come, found in Western imagery. The emphasis is on positive action, and the scenes are accordingly very compressed yet highly creative in a variety of ways.

The Armenian corpus is also strikingly different in spirit from what is represented in the Christian art of Western Europe during this period. As a result, it is possible to propose that in many ways, the corpus is the Gospel according to the Armenians, recorded in stone.

NOTES

[1]At the Cathedral of Ējmiacin, the basilicas of Ereroyk' and K'asał, and the church of Tekor, for example. Prior to the fifth century, figural reliefs are carved on the interior of the mausoleal chamber at Ałc' dated 364 which represent Daniel in the Lions' Den and a hunter in combat with a wild boar. For illustrations of these and other examples described in this paper, see the following publications: J. Strzygowski, Die baukunst der Armenier und Europa 2 vols. (Vienna: A. Schroll, 1918); T'. T'oramanyan, Nyut'er haykakan čartarapetut'yan patmut'yan, 2 vols. (Erevan: HSSH GA, 1942-1948); G. Hovsepian, "Sepulchral Steles and their Archeological Value for the History of Armenian Art," Materials for the Study of Armenian Art and Culture (fasc. 3; New York: No publisher cited, 1944) (In Armenian and English); B. Arak'elyan, Haykakan patkerak'andaknerě IV-VII darerum (Erevan: HSSH GA, 1949); Architettura medievale armena, Roma-Palazzo Venezia 10-30 giugno, 1968 (Rome: De Luca Editore, 1968); S. Der Nersessian, The Armenians (Praeger Series Ancient Peoples and Places 68; New York: Praeger, 1969); N. Stepanian and A. Tchakmaktchian, L'art décoratif de

l'arménie médiévale (Leningrad: Editions Aurore, 1971); L. Azaryan, Vał
miĵnadaryan haykakan k'andakě (Erevan: HSSH GA, 1975); V. Harouthiounian
and M. Hasrathian, Monuments of Armenia (Beirut: Société Techno-Presse
Moderne, S.A.L., 1975); S. Mnac'akanyan, Haykakan ašxarhik patkerak'andakě
IX-XIV darerum (Erevan: HSSH GA, 1976); S. Der Nersessian, Armenian Art
(Paris: Thames and Hudson, 1977).

[2]See M. Brosset, Les ruines d'Ani, 2 vols. (St. Petersbourg: Imprimerie de l'Académie Imperiale des Sciences, 1860) 1.138-143; J. Baltrušaitis,
Le problème de l'ogive et l'arménie (Paris: Librairie Ernest Leroux, 1936),
63-70; A. Alpoyačian, Patmut'yun hay gałt'akanut'yan, 3 vols. (Erevan: HSSH
GA, 1941-1961); S. Der Nersessian, Etudes byzantines et arméniennes, 2 vols.
(Louvain: Editions Peeters, 1973), 592-593; and L. Zekiyan, "Le colonie
armene del medio evo in Italia e le relazioni culturali italo-armene (Materiale
per la storia degli armeni in Italia)," in Atti del primo simposio internazionale
di arte armena (Bergamo, 28-30 Giugno 1975 (San Lazzaro-Venice: Tipo-
Litografia Armena di Venezia, 1978), 803-929.

[3]Baltrušaitis laid some groundwork through his study of scriptural
motifs shared in common between Armenia and Europe.   J. Baltrušaitis,
Etudes sur l'art médiéval en Géorgie et en Arménie (Paris: Librairie Ernest
Leroux, 1929).

[4]Relatively little work has been done on the subject in general,
particularly in comparison to the attention given to medieval Armenian
architecture and manuscript painting.   The sculptured stelae of Classical
Armenia have been studied to some extent by Hovsepian, "Sepulchral Stelas,"
Ařak'elyan, Haykakan patkerak'andaknerě, and Azaryan, Vał k'andakě, Ařak'-
elyan has also included in his discussion some sculptural reliefs on the early
churches.   Mnac'akanyan, Ašxarhik patkerak'andagě, deals primarily with the
representations of secular personages on churches from the ninth to the
fourteenth century.   There is no comprehensive survey of the corpus as a
whole including the particularly interesting animal motifs.   However, in a
comparative study of thirteenth-century Armenian architectural sculpture by
the author, some of the motifs were traced back through the centuries to the
Classical period, and were also related to Byzantine and Islamic examples.
See L. Der Manuelian, "The Monastery of Geghard: A Study of Armenian
Architectural Sculpture in the 13th Century" (Diss. Boston University, 1980).
See also, L. Der Manuelian, "Some observations on the carved images of

classical and medieval Armenia," <u>Aarhus Armeniaca Acta Jutlandica LVI</u> (Humanities Series 56; Aarhus; Learned Society of the University of Aarhus, 1982) 83-102.

[5]L. Der Manuelian, "Armenian Sculptural Images, Fifth to Eighth Centuries," <u>Classical Armenian Culture</u> (ed. T. J. Samuelian, University of Pennsylvania Armenian Texts and Studies 4; Chico, CA: Scholars Press, 1982) 176-207.

[6]Ibid., 179 n. 18; 180, n. 21; 181, n. 33.

[7]Research carried out in 1977-1978, under the auspices of the International Research and Exchanges Board and the Societ Ministry of Higher Education. Approximately forty churches and monasteries form the fifth to the fourteenth centuries were studied and photographed <u>in situ</u> by the author. More recently, the limited visual documentation of medieval Armenian architecture available heretofore has been amplified enormously with the publication of <u>Armenian Architecture</u> (proj. dir. V. L. Parseghian; Zug: Inter Documentation Company A.G., 1981), a micro-fiche volume prepared by the Armenian Architectural Archives Project. The first volume contains about 6,000 photographs of more than forty churches and monasteries accompanied by a history, description, art historical discussion and bibliography for each by L. Der Manuelian. Volume II, text by the same author, is in press to be followed by several volumes on other Armenian churches, monasteries, castles, and other structures in the Soviet Union, Iran and present-day Turkey.

[8]For photographs of these and scenes of the Adoration of the Magi, see W. Sauerlander, <u>Gothic Sculpture in France 1140-1270</u> (London: Thames and Hudson, 1970).

[9]Der Manuelian, "Images," 183-184 and Plates 5 and 6.

[10]For further information and photographs, see the recent monograph by J. M. Thierry, <u>Le couvent arménien d'Horomos</u> (Matériaux pour l'archéologie arménienne II; Louvain-Paris: Editions Peeters, 1980).

[11]Volume II (in press) of the Armenian Architectural Archives Project's series entitled <u>Armenian Architecture</u> (supra, n. 7) includes information and photographs on Yovhannavank'.

[12]Private communication with Dr. Krikor Maksoudian.

[13]Another example which can be considered to illustrate a liturgical practice is at the seventh-century Church of Pṛni, as described in Der Manuelian, "Images," 181.

[14]There is some controversy regarding the exact date of this composition. S. A. Avagyan, "Noravank'i Gavt'i Baravori Arjanagrut'yunĕ," HSSH GA Lraber HG (1975) 8: 106-113, believes it to be contemporary with thge construction of the gawit' in 1261 while S. Der Nersessian, "Deux tympans sculptés arméniens datant de 1321," Cahiers archéologique 25 (1976) 109-122, considers it to be 1321.

[15]Plates 5 and 6 in Der Manuelian, "Images."

[16]See M. Sargsyan, "Mreni tačari himnadirneri patkerak'andaknerĕ," P-BH (1966) 4: 241-250, and A. Mnuc'aryan, K'nnut'yan hayastani IV-XI dareri šinararakan vkayagreri (Erevan: HSSH GA, 1977) 63-69.

[17]For an illustration, see Der Manuelian, "Images," Plate 7.

[18]N. Garsoïan, "The Locus of the Death of Kings: Iranian Armenia—The Inverted Image," in The Armenian Image in History and Literature (ed. R. Hovannisian; Malibu: Undena Publications, 1981) 47-54.

[19]They are the subject of a recent study by L. Seidel, Songs of Glory (Chicago and London: University of Chicago, 1981).

[20]Ibid., 70-80.

[21]For illustrations, see R. Mepisashvili and V. Tsintsadze, The Arts of Ancient Georgia (n.p.: Thames and Hudson, 1977).

[22]K. Maksoudian, "Armenian Building Inscriptions as a Source for the Study of Armenian Civilization," paper presented on August 8, 1981 at the Armenian Architectural Exhibition," Watertown, MA.

[23]Ibid.

[24]R. Thomson (trans.), The teachings of Saint Gregory: An Early Christian Catechism (Harvard Armenian Texts and Studies 3; Cambridge: Harvard, 1970) 16.

[25]Łazar P'arpec'i, for example. R. Thomson, "The Fathers in Early Armenian Literature," in Studia Patristica (ed. E. Livingstone; Berlin: Akademie-Verlag, 1975) 468-469.

Photographs by author unless otherwise specified.

1.   Autun. Cathedral, c. 1125-1135. West portal tympanum and lintel.
Last Judgment. (After G. Zarnecki, Art of the Medieval World.)

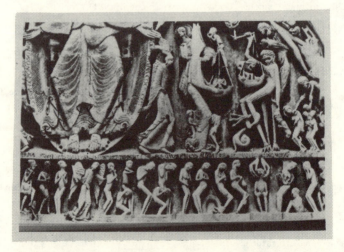

2.   Autun.   Cathedral.   Detail of west portal tympanum and lintel.
Damned souls. (After G. Zarnecki.)

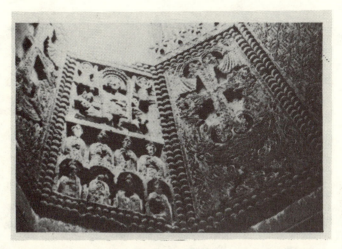

3.   Horomos.   Gawit', 1038, Church of S. Yovhannes, Monastery of
Horomos.   Interior of central lantern, east and southeast panels.
Christ, symbols of evangelists and patriarchs of the Armenian Church.
(After J. M. Thierry, Le couvent armenien d'Horomos.)

4.   Yovhannavank'.   Church of S. Karapet, between 1216 and 1221,
Monastery of Yovhannavank'.   West portal tympanum.   Christ with
bearded figures.

5.   Amału. Gawit', 1223 and 1321. Monastery of Noravank'. Sculpture
over west portal window. The Ancient of Days and the Crucifixion,
probably fourteenth century.

6.   Amału. Gawit'. Detail of window sculpture of west portal.

7.   Ptłni.   Church, early seventh century.   Sculpture over south facade
window.   Detail showing Prince Manuēl Amatuni with Christ and
Apostles.

8.   Hałbat.   Church of S. Nšan, 971-991, Monastery of Hałbat.   Donor
portrait under east gable.   Princes Gurgen and Smbat.

Figure 9. Arates. Gawit', by 1270,
Monastery of Arates. West portal
tympanum, now missing. Virgin and
Child, Prince Smbat Orbelean and
his wife Ruzuk'an. (After
S. Mnac'akanyan, Haykakan asxarhik
patkerak'andagĕ IX-XIV darerum.)

Figure 10. Paris. Cathedral of
Notre Dame. West portal, right
doorway. Porte Sainte-Anne,
shortly after 1160. Virgin enthroned
with angels, king, bishop and scribe.
(After W. Sauerlander, Gothic
Sculpture in France 1140-1270.)

Figure 11.   Dsel. Church of Barjrak'as
S. Grigor, 1221, now completely
destroyed.   Probably west portal
tympanum.   Christ with donors,
possibly Prince Marcpan Mamikonean
and wife.   (After Mnac'akanyan,
Ašxarhik patkerak'andagĕ.)

Figure 12.   St.-Denis. Abbey church,
before 1140.   West portal tympanum,
center doorway.   Last Judgement.
(After W. Sauerlander, Gothic Sculpture.)

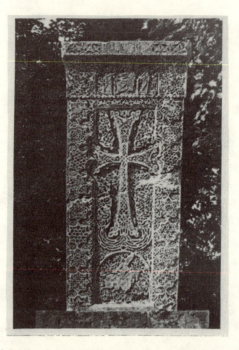

13.   Xač'k'ar of Prince Grigor Proš, 1233. From Imirzek, now at Ējmiacin. Christ and saints above cross.

14.   T'anahat.   Church of S. Nšan, thirteenth century, Monastery of T'anahat.   West portal tympanum.

15.   Amału.   Gawit'.   Monastery of Noravank'.   Interior sculpture, 1261.
Probably Prince Smbat Ōrbēlean.

16.   Parthenay-le-vieux.   Church of Saint-Pierre, twelfth century.   Facade
sculpture.   Equestrian figure.   (After L. Seidel, Songs of Glory.)

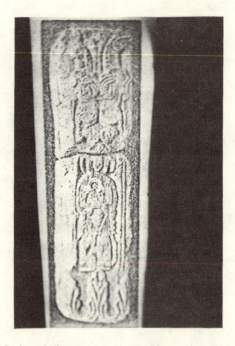

17.   Agarak.   Stele, sixth or seventh century.   (After B. Aṙak'elyan, Haykakan patkerak'andaknerĕ IV-VII darerum.)   Woman with church model.

18.   Ganjasar.   Church of S. Yovhannēs, 1216-1238.   West side of drum. (After M. Hasratyan and M. Thierry, "Le couvent de Ganjasar." REArm 15 (1981).

Figure 19. Amalu. Church of
S. Astuacacin, 1339, Monastery of
Noravank'. Column of central rotunda.
Prince Burt'el with church model.
(After S. Mnac'akanyan, Ašxarhik
patkerak'andakě.)

Figure 20. Sant' Angelo in Formis.
Apse wall painting c. 1080. Detail.
Abbot Desiderius with model of his
church.

A MEDIEVAL PALACE IN AVAN*

Mario D'Onofrio

Università di Roma (Italy)

In the city of Avan, six kilometers north of Erevan, rises a famous basilica dating between the sixth and seventh century (fig. 1). The basilica has never been studied in detail by scholars of Armenian architecture. Moreover, flanking this church are the ruins of an ancient palace, whose existence was completely unknown up until a few years ago. In 1972, on our first expedition to Armenia, the vague outlines of the groundplan were determined from sparse traces of the wall which emerged from the massive stones and rubble spread along the adjoining area to the north of the church. A few survey photographs taken ten years ago record the condition of the area surrounding the basilica (fig. 2). The provisional plan which was drawn based on the few walls still standing suggested at first glance the existence of a neat organization of spaces, all rather regular and all parallel to the major axis of the nearby church.

Under the auspices of the qualified Armenian authorities an archaeological excavation of the area in question was carried out recently, during which new structures came to light, indicating that the development of the design of the ancient palace was far more complex than had been previously thought (fig. 3). These structures were found about 1 meter lower with respect to the level of the pavement of the nearby basilica. The disparity can directly be explained by the topography of the site. On the north side, the terrain presents today, as it already had in antiquity, a rather steep slope, thus the chambers of the palace, which have already been uncovered on the extreme north end, now lie on an even lower plane than the rooms towards the center (fig. 4).

T. Samuelian & M. Stone, eds. <u>Medieval Armenian Culture</u>. (University of Pennsylvania Armenian Texts and Studies 6). Chico, CA: Scholars Press, 1983. pp. 120 to 130.

The most sensational discovery during the excavation was the chimney located inside the central chamber, which we will call for the sake of convenience the "room of the chimney" (fig. 5). In this room the excavations revealed an interesting chimney circumscribed by a platform running along the sides of the same chamber and ornamented with a peculiar sculpture in the form of a primeval animal (perhaps a lion?). The lower portion of the chimney is composed of a circular tub in stone. The upper part is connected to two small partitions, rising to enclose the back wall, which follows the same curvature of the braziers lying underneath (fig. 6). The platform which interlocks around these elements, including a bench, is decorated with a beautifully molded cornice (fig. 7) and terminates at the top of the chimney itself with the sculpture which I mentioned previously. The sculpture is worked only on the front: here two feet turned inward can be observed (fig. 8). On the legs of the animal rests a large chubby head with flattened forehead, two bulbous egg-shaped eyeballs, the ridge of the nose wide and flat, and the mouth rather small, roughly scratched with a few ferrows by a stylus. This "lion" holds little verisimilitude to nature; most likely its function is not merely decorative, but apotropaeic: perhaps it is a symbol of the great Mher (called ariwcajew, 'lion-shaped') of the Armenian epic, who, through his identification with Mithra, is associated with fire.

The most probable hypothesis concerning the function and origin of the complex which has been unearthed is that it may be identified as the private residence of the anti-Catholic Yovhannēs Sinuagan (591-611 A.D.). Historical sources inform us that Sinuagan, during the reign of the Persian king Xosrov, contended for the Patriarchal seat with Movsēs II (576-604) and that the residence chosen by him was precisely the village of Avan in the region of Kotaik (Sebēos, XXIII). Here, before Yovhannēs came to Karin, where he fell prisoner to the same Persian king, he had the splendid church constructed (fig. 1). Despite the fact that no direct textual references have been found, it is nonetheless probable that together with the church, or immediately thereafter, Yovhannēs Sinuagan had a palace built for himself and his community.

It can be determined, based on a careful analysis of the wall construction, that the building or the history of the palace had two distinct phases. To the first period can be assigned all of the courses of walling which were executed with large blocks of stone carefully squared off according to a technique which is encountered again in the wall fabric of the adjacent church (fig. 9). Structural affinities between the two buildings do indeed exist. Nevertheless, further observation may show that they were built at slightly different times.

When observing the points of contact between the two constructions, it might be noted that the building erected for the purpose of habitation is juxtaposed to the church in such a way to utilize in part the podium which runs along their common border, though at the same time the palace is set just far enough from the church to provide a sort of corridor or open portico (fig. 3). Even if we take into account a different chronology for the construction of the two buildings, it is entirely plausible that the palace may have been erected immediately after the church, not only because of the affinity of the wall technique already pointed out, but also on account of the presence of two spurs emerging from the podium on the north side of the church itself (one in correspondence with the entrance and another on the east edge) (fig. 3, c-d).

These similarities would indicate, beyond the continuity and homogeneity of the construction, an intentional coupling with the residential building, almost in the modern sense of 'contextual' planning. The dating, therefore, of the oldest parts of the palace can be placed at the beginning of the seventh century, a period during which in Armenia the custom of constructing buildings based on the models established by the two palaces of the quarter of Duin (fifth to sixth century) became consolidated. Following the residence at Avan, two more monumental palaces were shortly later realized: the palace of the Catholicos Nersēs III at Zuartnoc' (641-661) and the palace of the Prince (iškan) Grigor Mamikonian at Aruč (661-682). The dating of the palace at Avan is supported furthermore by the style of the molded cornices which we have seen in the "room of the chimney." Its classicizing style reminds us of a few bases in the cathedral of Ējmiacin, in the church of Ełvard and in several other cases, all dated between the fifth and seventh century.

The "lion" adjoining the chimney confronts us with a puzzling question. Sculptural production in Armenia during the seventh century is not yet known well enough. Armenian sculpture, in this period, seems to show us two different trends: on the one hand, the formal scrolls and elegant capitals of Duin and Zuartnoc' and on the other, sculptural pieces and other artifacts of more modest workmanship, such as the stele of Aruč from the sixth-seventh century, characterized by rather summary and archaizing facial traits, tending to stress more immediate effects. The piece from Avan seems to link up precisely with this type of expression through a certain correspondence in taste and execution. The stele of Aruč and the amulet of Avan reveal in fact a common tendency to accentuate the eyeballs emerging from the sockets and to flatten the superficial contours on the face into receding and assymetric planes.

To the second phase of construction, instead, can be traced all those interventions which we can see in the presence of crude walling using stones of deformed and small sizes (figs. 9 and 10). In some cases, these stretches of walling are laid directly over the older courses, while in other areas new rooms were formed, thereby altering the original layout of the palace. The precise date of these modifications which altered the previous structures confronts us with a difficult task. The date of 1285, which is recorded in an inscription placed on the exterior foundations of the nearby church, may suggest a terminus for the restructuring of the palace itself. For this second period of building activity, however, we have no definite art-historical basis to rely on, except for a few crude ornamental details, which are attempts to emulate the antique. One example can be recognized in a stone carved in the manner of a fluted column conserved in situ in a chamber adjoining the "room of the chimney" (fig. 11). An indication of the architectural revival in Armenia during this same period may be noted in the construction of the palace and gardens of Mren of the Bagratid Sahmadin, dated precisely between the years 1276 and 1286. Unfortunately, no other evidence is available to us.

In conclusion, the palace of Avan, is not only a monument of particular interest in itself, but also contributes to our understanding of the larger chapter in the history of the residential architecture in medieval Armenia. Until now, little has been written on the subject, obviously in part due to the scant documentation of surviving buildings of residential type, in comparison to the many examples known from religious architecture. In Soviet Armenia, six or seven medieval palaces have been brought to light so far. But the historical evidence relating to the establishment of such buildings is more considerable. We need only to refer, for a moment, to the tenth-century historian T'ovmay Arcruni. After recounting the revolts of the Armenians against the Persians around 450 A.D., he states explicitly that the Armenian leaders constructed regal houses, splendid cities, etc. Probably even more remains are still underground, awaiting patient investigation by archaeologists in the future. If other similar evidence should eventually emerge, it will complete our sketchy understanding of the role played by architecture in the cultural and political life of Armenia in the Middle Ages.

Translation into English: Philip Jacks

*This research represents part of a larger project on medieval Armenian architecture financed by the Italian Consiglio Nazionale delle Ricerche.

Figure 1.   Avan: the basilica (7-8th cent.)

Figure 2.   Avan: the zone surrounding the basilica (1972)

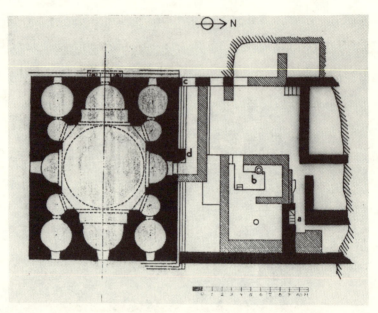

Figure 3.   Avan: plan of the basilica and palace (a: stairs; b: "room of the chimney"; c-d: abutments). Drawing: P. Cunes, M. Hasratian.

Figure 4.   Avan, palace: stairs on the north side of the palace

Figure 5.   Avan, palace: the "room of the chimney."

Figure 6.   Avan, palace: chimney.

Figure 7.   Avan, palace: molded cornice in the "room of the chimney."

Figure 8.   Avan, palace: sculpture in the "room of the chimney."

Figure 9.   Avan, palace: two different techniques of masonry.

Figure 10.   Avan: structures of the medieval palace.

Figure 11.   Avan, palace: fluted stone.

GRIGOR TAT'EWAC'I:
A GREAT SCHOLASTIC THEOLOGIAN AND
NOMINALIST PHILOSOPHER

Mesrob K. Krikorian

University of Vienna

Introduction

Vardapet Grigor Tat'ewac'i has been a dominant figure in fourteenth-
and fifteenth-century Armenian Church history. An eminent theologian and
teacher, he shaped the events and orientation of the Armenian Church in the
following centuries. His pupils and later Armenian authors generously and of
course rightly call him "the great Vardapet" [teacher], "heavenly champion,"
"the brilliant torch of Tat'ew," "eternally shining sun," "a source propagating
the teachings of Christ," "Second Enlightener" (the first being Grigor Part'ew,
the first official Patriarch of Armenia), "Second John Chrysostom" and many
other high appellations.

The second half of the fourteenth century was a very difficult time
for the Armenians. From the East the Mongol-Tartar hordes, under the
leadership of Timur Lang (1336-1405) were raiding, plundering and destroying
Greater Armenia; from the South the Mameluks of Egypt continuously
attacked the Lesser Armenia or Cilicia, which finally lost its independence
in 1375. The Armenian Church also suffered due internal and external
conflicts and struggles: the local Patriarchal See of Ałt'amar near Lake Van
(the present Ahtamar/Akdamar in Turkey) had revolted against the Mother
See whose center was still located at Sis, in Lesser Armenia. At the
beginning of the fourteenth century, according to a missionary program,
Rome endeavored persistently to win over the Orthodox Armenians and
Syrians and to bring them under its authority. The Franciscan fathers

T. Samuelian & M. Stone, eds. Medieval Armenian Culture. (University of
Pennsylvania Armenian Texts and Studies 6). Chico, CA: Scholars Press,
1983. pp. 131 to 141.

preached and taught in Cilicia, Northern Armenia and Georgia, and the Dominicans, in greater Armenia and Persia. The leaders of the Armenian Church were very disturbed by this challenge and sought a solution.

A Short Biography

Grigor was born about 1346 in the province of Vayoc' Jor at the village T'mkaberd. His father Sargis, originally from Arčeš, had married a girl from P'arpi and settled down in Vayoc' Jor, in the country of Siwnik'. After his elementary education, he entered the monastery of Aprakunik' to study with the famous vardapet Yovhannēs Orotnec'i. According to reliable historical sources, he studied for 28 years with his teacher. Presumably this would mean that after completing the Seminary, he continued as assistant lecturer in the monastery. He was ordained a priest in Jerusalem during a visit; in Erzinka he received the title of vardapet (Church doctor), and in 1387 the degree of higher vardapet at the same monastery of Aprakunik'. Upon the death of his teacher Yovhannēs on January 13, 1388, Grigor was elected rector of the Theological School. He remained in the Seminary of Aprakunik' only two years, then because of financial difficulties he was compelled to move to Tat'ew where he enjoyed the support of his uncle, prince Smbat Ōrbelean, (son of Iwanē and grandson of Burt'ēl), and his sister's son, Archbishop Aŕak'el Siwnec'i. In the Seminary of Tat'ew he gathered numerous pupils around him, taught and trained them, propagated education among the people and promoted cultural activities. In his syllabus, besides the main biblical and theological studies, he gave a prominent place to philosophy, thus emphasizing the importance of Greek philosophers for Christian doctrine. The writings of Aristotle, Porphyry and Philo provided the fundamental philosophical material for the students. Yovhannēs Orotnec'i and Grigor of Tat'ew themselves wrote commentaries on the books of these philosophers in order to facilitate and deepen the study of theology. In 1408, Grigor moved to the monastery of Mecop' in the province of Arces, this time forced by political circumstances. He lectured on biblical and philosophical commentaries and taught the doctrine of the Armenian Church to nearly one hundred monks and vardapets. He also attempted to contribute to the unity of the Church. Although the central See or the General Catholicossate in Cilicia was failing in authority and reputation, the local Catholicossate of Aŕt'amar which also included the region of Arčeš was growing in power and position. In fact, the catholicoi of Sis had officially condemned Aht'amar as a disobedient and disloyal See. Grigor assembled a synod in Mecop' with the agreement and participation of vardapets and bishops, dethroned the Catholicos Dawit' and freed Aht'amar from the bonds of anathema. Then all the members of the Synod wrote to the General Catholicos Yakob in Sis and asked for his confirmation and blessings. Naturally, Grigor's ultimate aim was first to strengthen the internal unity of the Church and then to remove the center from Sis back to its original place in Ējmiacin (Etchmiadzin), Armenia. Unfortunately he did not live long enough to see the realization of his plan. The deposed Catholicos Dawit' gaining the assistance of political rulers, chased his adversaries from Arčeš. In 1410 Grigor returned home and shortly after his arrival in Tat'ew fell sick and died on December 25 at the age of 64.[1]

The Literary Works of Grigor

The literary works of Grigor are numerous and varied in their subjects and can be characterized as erudite, scholarly and comprehensive writings. On the one hand, he admired and utilized the books of Greek philosophers and theologians; on the other, he profited from the logical art and methodological system of the western scholastic theologians whose works were brought, translated, and spread in Armenia by the Dominican and Franciscan friars. He quotes extensively from the classical Greek fathers: Dionysius of Alexandria, Gregory Thaumaturgus of Neo Caesarea, Athanasius of Alexandria, Gregory of Nazianzus, Basil of Caesarea, John Chrysostom, Epiphanius of Salamis/Cyprus, Cyril of Alexandria and Dionysius the Areopagite. Of the Latin authors he is acquainted with: Augustin of Hippo, Albertus Magnus, Isidorus of Sevilla and especially Thomas Aquinas. Like the scholastics of Europe, Tat'ewac'i also made every effort to interpret the mysteries of the Christian faith through formal logic and rational dialectic. Of course the theology of Tat'ewac'i was the theology of the Armenian Church, but following the way and example of the scholastics, he composed systematic works, exposing syllogistic arguments and always paying attention to exactitude. "Question and Answer" is his normal art of inquiry and demonstration: the replies present categorical syllogisms and the disputations are reinforced by rich quotations from the Bible, the early Greek Byzantine theologians and Aristotle. Occasionally he calls as witness the Arab philosopher Averroes/Ibn Rushd (1126-1198) and the Armenian theologian Grigor Lusaworič' (Gregory the Enlightener).

The literary works of Tat'ewac'i can be divided into four main groups: theological, philosophical, pastoral-liturgical and biblical commentaries.

Theological Writings

1. Grigor's best known work Girk' Harc'manc' (The Book of Questions) is in fact an encyclopedia which covers different branches of theology, written in 1397 in ten volumes or books. He starts with luck and destiny, examines the dualistic doctrine of the Good and Evil (vol. 1), and refutes the teachings of the Manicheans and Jews, Arians, Theopaschites and of the Chalcedonians (vol. 2). Then he introduces the theology of Dionysius, discusses about God and godly nature, angels and demons (vol. 3), the Creation in general (vol. 4) and the creation of man in particular (vol. 5). In the next two volumes he recounts the books of Pentateuch, of Joshua and Judges and the four books of Kings (vols. 6 and 7). Volume 8 is devoted wholly to the Incarnation of Christ (32 chapters), and the following book provides rich information and discussion concerning the Church and clergy, national-ecclesiastical synods of the Armenians, the formation of various Churches, sacraments and worship (vol. 9). He regards the main Apostolic Sees as the centers of the four Evangelists: Antioch, Alexandria, Rome and Ephesus (later replaced by Constantinople) and adds to those three autocephalous Churches: Jerusalem because of the Holy Sepulchre, Cyprus because of the tomb of Lazarus and Armenia because of St. Gregory the Illuminator. In the concluding part (vol. 10) the author presents the faith and doctrine of the Armenian Church regarding human and eternal life, agony and death, 'abodes' or 'stations' of the souls, purgatory, resurrection and the Last Judgment. In this last book the influence of Thomas Aquinas is evident.

2. Girk' P'ok'r Harc'manc' (A Short Book of Questions)

A similar writing completed in 1387 upon the request and questions of Vardapet Georg from Erzinka.

3. Oskep'orik (The Book of Golden Content)

This is Grigor's main theological work, really of 'golden content,' written in 1407 and divided into four books.

Book 1: About faith and theology, the existence of God, the Holy Trinity, refutation of the teachings of Arius, Macedonius, Sabellius and of other gnostic heretics (14 chapters).   Chapter 13 is addressed against the doctrine of Filioque.

Book 2: On the Incarnation of Christ (chap. 15 to 23).

Book 3: Attestation and quotations concerning the Incarnation of the Word
from the Holy Scriptures and Greek Byzantine Church fathers (chap.
24 to 33).

Book 4: About the birth, circumcision, baptism, passion, death and resurrection of Jesus Christ (chap. 34 to 45). The last four chapters are
disputations with Dyophysites.

Book 5: This book was compiled at a later date and added to the main work;
a collection from the writings of Vahram Rabuni, an Armenian
theologian of the thirteenth century, and of Grigor Tat'ewac'i (chap.
46 to 50).

4. Commentary on the Scholia of Cyril of Alexandria

5. The Creed of the Armenian Church

The Nicene-Constantinopolitan Creed is the official confession of faith
of the Armenian Apostolic Church.   In the fourteenth century Grigor
Tat'ewac'i perhaps together with his pupils, formulated afresh the doctrine of
the Armenian Church on the text and in terms of the Nicene Creed, but
additionally utilizing the Armenian theological literature, such as "The
Teaching of St. Gregory" in Agat'angelos and the Book of Letters (theological). The Nicene Creed is recited at the beginning of the Holy Mass,
after the reading of the Gospel lesson.   The Creed compiled by Grigor
Tat'ewac'i is used at the beginning of festival celebrations of the Holy
Liturgy and during ordinations. This shows the importance attached to it by
the Church. In fact it forms a part of chap. 47 of the fifth volume of the
Book of Golden Content, but it can be found in every Service-Book or in the
Ritual of Ordination, entitled "Profession of the Orthodox Faith."   Here, in
this Creed, the Christology of the Armenian Church has been summarized in
an exact and clear formulation:

We believe that one of three Persons, God the Word, was
born from the Father before all eternity; in time descending
into the Virgin Mary, and taking of her blood, he united it with
his Godhead. Nine months he patiently remained in the womb
of the spotless Virgin, and the perfect God became perfect man,
with soul, mind and body; one person, one countenance (Arm.
dēm) and one united nature. God became man without any
change or transformation; conceived without sperm and having
an incorruptible birth. As his Godhead has no beginning,
likewise, there is no end for his Manhood, for as Jesus Christ

was yesterday and (is) today, so he will be the same for ever.

6. Summa contra Gentiles

The original title of this theological book was Against the Taciks. The name 'Taǯik' derives from Pahlavi and means 'Arab,' but it is generally applied for Muslim peoples, Arabs, Persians and Turks, and consequently signifies also 'Muslim.' In fact this theological tract forms a part of Grigor's larger Book of Questions (vol. 1, chap. 3), but beginning with the edition of 1729/30, printed in Istanbul, the publishers cut it out in order not to excite the anger of the Sultan or of the Muslim faithful. It was later edited in Vienna in 1930. The treatise itself is divided into 16 sub-chapters or questions as follows: (1) They deny the Holy Trinity. (2) They think the Good and Evil come from God. (3) They deny the Incarnation of the Word. (4) They do not confess Christ as God, but only as man and prophet. (5) They do not admit the Holy Scriptures. (6) They accept Muhammad as prophet. (7) They believe in bodily resurrection. (8) They regard the angels and souls as mortal. (9) They do not venerate the Holy Cross and the pictures of the saints. (10) They do not differentiate between 'holy' and 'unholy' animals, eating the meat of the horse and camel. (11) For them the wine is unlawful and forbidden. (12) They wash themselves with water and consider this as expiation from sins. (13) Concerning circumcision. (14) About fastings of the Muslims. (15) They do not eat the flesh of animals slaughtered by Christians. (16) They regard themselves (only) to be lawful! Interestingly in this last part the author cites a quotation from the 'Platonic Political Law' that "Fornicators and adulterers known (to the public) should sit in the streets and at broadways so that others might be separated from them and become abhorrent of the Evil"! In general this polemical writing is a valuable work not only in a theological sense, but also as a source for the historical study of the Muslim rituals and laws.

Philosophical Writings

The main philosophical writings of Grigor are:

1. Brief Commentary of the Isagoge of Porphyry
2. Brief Commentary of the Philosophy ('Definitions of Philosophy') of David (Invincible)
3. Brief Commentary on the Virtues of Aristotle

He has also collected and compiled two books by his teacher Yovhannēs Orotnec'i, namely:

4. Commentary on the Categories of Aristotle
5. Brief Commentary on Interpretations of Aristotle

Pastoral-Liturgical Writings
1. The Books of Homilies
       Two large volumes, one entitled Amaran 'Of Summer' and the other
Jmeran 'Of Winter.'
2. Fundamentals of Pedagogy
3. Commentary on the Prayers of Grigor of Narek
4. On Worship-Service
5. Order of the Installment of Vardapets
6. Prayer of Myron
7. Prayer of Dismissal
8. Letter to the Bishops of Ałt'amar
       In manuscript some other pastoral or liturgical short writings are to
be found, mostly extracted from his larger Book of Questions.

Biblical Commentaries
       For the course of exegesis at the School of Tat'ew, Grigor needed
comprehensive Biblical commentaries on the whole Scriptures. Of course, the
Armenian literature since the fifth century had produced numerous exegetical
works, original or in translation from the Greek or Syriac. Yet with
emergence of a new period through theological, philosophical and educational
activities of Latin intellectuals in Armenia, a great demand for new Biblical
commentaries was strongly felt. Apparently Grigor completed a systematic
exegesis of all the books of the Bible; as mentioned above, he has devoted
the sixth and seventh volumes of his Book of Questions to the study of the
Pentateuch, of Joshua, Judges, and the four books of Kings. The rest of the
commentaries too, have survived for the most part, but they are still
unedited.   The following expository writings are to be found in the
Matenadaran (Library of Manuscripts) of Erevan: Job, Psalms, Proverbs, Song
of Solomon, Isaiah; the Gospels of Matthew and John and the Epistles of Paul.

Scholastic Theologian and Nominalist Philosopher
       The heritage of the neoplatonist David the Invincible (sixth century)
has influenced the philosophical thought and tendency of Armenian writers
throughout the centuries.   In the tenth century a new interest in ancient

Greek philosophy began with the writings of Grigor Magistros (c. 990-1058) and was continued by Yovhannēs Sarkawag, the Philosopher (eleventh century) and patriarch Nersēs Clajensis Šnorhali (1048-1173). Vahram Vardapet Rabuni (fourteenth century), a contemporary of Thomas Aquinas (c. 1225- 1274), studied the Aristotelian philosophy and wrote several treatises:

1. Commentary on the Categories of Aristotle
2. Commentary on the Isagoge of Porphyry
3. Commentary about Aristotle's Book on Cosmos

Esayi Vardapet of Nič' (1338), from the country of Sasun, developed a movement of learning and theology and founded the School of Glajor on the level and program of a university, gathering around him about 350 students. At that time the Dominican friars had already arrived in Armenia and started strong missionary-educational and literary activity. From 1320 to 1350 most of the works of Thomas Aquinas, Bartholomew of Bologna and of Peter of Aragon were translated into Armenian, especially through the efforts of Yovhannēs Corcorec'i and Yakob and Yovhannēs K'řnec'i. Naturally, discussions and disputations between the Latin missionaries and the leaders of the Armenian Church were inevitable, as it was in the case of the Byzantines. Yovhannēs Vardapet Orotnec'i (1315-1386), a pupil of Esayi, settled down in the monastery of Tat'ew and continued the School of Glajor there (his main philosophical treatises are mentioned above). Under Yovhannēs, and his student and successor Grigor, a renaissance in education and learning spread through Armenia, and the confrontation with the Latins in the end, produced a positive result. In this long-lasting and critical process, Grigor of Tat'ew together with his numerous pupils, played the most important role—teaching, preaching and writing erudite studies. Between the devoted followers of Dominican Fathers, and those who were faithful to the national Church tradition, Grigor succeeded in balancing the situation and skillfully brought about an "Armenian Reception" of Latin Scholastic theology. His Book of Golden Content together with the Book of Questions corresponds to the Summa Theologica of Aquinas, and the treatise Against the Tačiks, to Summa contra Gentiles. Without exaggeration, he can be regarded 'Thomas Aquinas of the Armenians' and at the same time may be compared to the Byzantine Neilos Kabasilas (†1363).

I would like to introduce here as an example the arguments of Grigor concerning the existence of God which are very similar to those of Thomas Aquinas. In his Book of Golden Content[2] he presents the following theological discussion. He speaks first against those who say: "The thinking (Intellect) can not prove the existence of God; only by Faith can we attest that God exists." Plato and Aristotle were not believers, but by rational examination they showed that God existed! Then he brings forward the argument from cause; from the caused things and phenomena one can conclude the existence of a cause or the First Cause; that is, from the creatures we can understand that there is a Creator. The next argument runs as follows: according to Aristotle "whatever moves is moved by someone else." Going infinitely from movement to mover, we arrive at the First Mover who does not move; that is, God. Continuing this line of reasoning, Grigor quotes Averroes, "the commentator of Aristotle," that "it is impossible for contrary and disorderly things to come into correlation (co-existence), if there were no ordering power." Now we see in this world the corporeal (material) and the incorporeal are contrary to each other, just as the four elements, yet they are correlated in nature and do not corrupt each other. Then Tat'ewac'i returns to the characteristics of substances or existences: the created have both beginning and end; consequently there should be a Reason/Cause without beginning and without end. Likewise, other natures are relative or imperfect: Goodness, Righteousness, etc. Moreover, "all the created who have the good and righteousness, do not possess these by nature, but have received them from somebody else. Consequently, there should be such One who possesses Righteousness and Goodness in full; that is, God."

Grigor Tat'ewac'i as a nominalist philosopher emphasizes the importance and value of the individual (anhat = 'individuum'). For him the general ideas (ĕndhanur imac'ut'iwn 'universalis') are only names (anun = 'nomina'). "The individual, above all, forms the real and first existence," he says.[3] Universals do not exist in the external world like the particulars. Rather they come into existence in our thinking and continue to exist. They are not even like our thoughts—since they have no analogy in the external world, as do the former. In fact we deduce the general from external individual existences. He criticizes the Stoic philosophers, who, according to him, considered everything physical and claimed that in the universal resides the form and the nature of the particular. He also criticizes Plato, who again, according to him—like the Stoics regarded the universal as "changeable." He adheres to Aristotle, declaring that only the special is physical, and therefore changeable, and that the general can not be substantiated and/or separated from the sensible (zgalik' = 'sensualis') or from the tangible.[4] Such of

Grigor's arguments incidentally, have been misinterpreted by some scholars who make him out to be a philosopher of materialist tendency. As to the relation of the genus and species to the individuum, Grigor explains that "the individual is the primary existence and then come species ('tesak') and the genus ('seṙ')." Genus and species exist by the power/energy (of the individual), and actually the individual operates on them. Then he adds: "And the individuum is better, for when individuals gather together, species and genus come into existence, but when individuals disappear, they also cease to exist."[5]

Let me conclude this study with a pedagogic-philosophical view of Tat'ewac'i. It was the English philosopher John Locke (1632-1704) who accepted 'sensation' and 'reflection' as sources of knowledge and perception. The soul or the mind of a new-born child is intact and plain like a tabula rasa which later receives impressions and perceptions from the external world and accumulates experience. Interestingly, Grigor also expresses the same opinion. In his Book of Homilies he writes: "The thinking/rational soul of man is like an unwritten tabula or a washed parchment—whatever is written, is impressed on it."[6]

Unfortunately, the life and writings of Tat'ewac'i are virtually unknown in the West. Larger studies in European languages will without doubt earn him international recognition.

NOTES

[1]On the life and literary works of Grigor Tat'ewac'i see M. Ormanian, Azgapatum (3 vols.; Constantinople, 1912-14; Jerusalem, 1927) paras. 1366-67, 1397-1404; H. Acaryan, Hayoc' Anjnanunneri Baṙaran (5 vols: Erevan, 1942-62) 1.599-695; S. Arewsatyan, "Grigor Tat'ewac'i," Hay Mšakuyt'i Nšanavor Gorcič'nerě (Erevan, 1976) 406-416; Haykakan Sovetakan Hanragitaran (Erevan: HSSH GA, 1977) 3.221-23; S. Arewšatyan, "Tat'ewi p'ilisop'ayakan dproc'e ev Grigor Tat'ewac'u ašxarhahayeac'k'ě," Banber Matenadarani 4 (1958) 121-137; S. Arewšatyan, "Nominalizmi aṙajac'umn u zargac'umě mijnadaryan Hayastanum," Banber Matanadarani 6 (1962) 75-92.

[2]Grigor Tat'ewac'i, Oskep'orik (Constantinople, 1746) pt. 1, chap. 4.

[3]Grigor Tat'ewac'i, Girk' Harc'manc' (Constantinople, 1729) 550.

[4]Grigor Tat'ewac'i, <u>Hamaŕot Tesut'iwn i Girs Porp'iwri</u> (Madras, 1793) 327-34.

[5]Grigor Tat'ewac'i, <u>Lucumn hamaŕot i tesut'iwnn Dawt'i</u> (Anyaŕt'i), Matenadaran Ms., No. 1695, 47a.

[6]Grigor Tat'ewac'i, <u>Girk' K'arozut'ean: Amaran</u> (Constantinople, 1741) 454.

AN IMPORTANT TEXT PRESERVED IN MS VEN. MEKH. NO. 873,
DATED A.D. 1299 (EUSEBIUS OF EMESA'S COMMENTARY
ON HISTORICAL WRITINGS OF THE OLD TESTAMENT)

Henning J. Lehmann

University of Aarhus (Denmark)

The collection of texts contained in MS No. 873 of the Mekhitarist library of San Lazzaro, Venice (dated A.D. 1299),[1] is clearly intended as a tool for the study of the historical writings of the Old Testament. The commentaries found in the manuscript fall into four groups. First come Ephraem's commentaries on the books of Joshua, Judges, Samuel, Kingdoms, and Chronicles (pp. 3-137). Then follows a commentary on the Pentateuch plus the historical writings mentioned, except Chronicles (pp. 137-235), in the manuscript ascribed to Cyril of Alexandria. Ephraem's commentary on the Pentateuch makes up the third section (pp. 235-433); and finally follows a catena on Leviticus (quoting such authors as Origen, Apollinarius, Eusebius of Emesa, Cyril of Alexandria, Severus of Antioch, et al.) (pp. 434-507).

For a comprehensive description—in Italian—of the manuscript one must turn to Zanolli's book (of 1938) on the Leviticus catena. The full title of Zanolli's book runs as follows in English translation: About an old catena on Leviticus, which is lost in Greek, but preserved in Armenian; about its close relation to Procopius of Gaza's commentary; and about the three codices of S. Lazzaro containing the text.[2] In the Mekhitarist edition of 1980,[3] to which we shall return, a description of the manuscript is given in Armenian.

As appears from the title of Zanolli's book, he was particularly concerned with the assistance that can be gained from our manuscript, especially its fourth part, the Leviticus catena, for the study of Procopius'

T. Samuelian & M. Stone, eds. Medieval Armenian Culture. (University of Pennsylvania Armenian Texts and Studies 6). Chico, CA: Scholars Press, 1983. pp. 142 to 160.

commentary on the first books of the Old Testament and other Greek catenae of the early Middle Ages.

We shall here be concerned with the second text—or group of texts—to be found in the MS, the pseudo-Cyrillic commentary on historical writings of the Old Testament.

The honor of having demonstrated that the Armenian translator or copyist—or his Vorlage—is not justified in attributing the text to Cyril of Alexandria, belongs to Father Vahan Hovhannessian of San Lazzaro; it was done in an article in Bazmavēp in 1923;[4] and through a lifetime, Father Vahan was concerned with the text, so, undoubtedly, the Venice edition of the text, which—as mentioned already—did not appear until 1980, i.e. after Hovhannessian's death, rightly bears his name on the title page.

In his first article concerned with our text (also in Bazmavēp 1923)[5] Hovhannessian already questioned Cyril's authorship. He considered the possibility of Eznik being the author, but finally—in his second and following articles[6]—on the basis of catena quotations, he reached the right conclusion: that the commentary is by Eusebius of Emesa.

Almo Zanolli still voiced some doubts as to the question whether the text could be attributed to Eusebius in its entirety.[7] In my view, however, the arguments on the basis of correspondence with catena fragments are quite definitive. The fragments can with certainty be attributed to Eusebius and the correspondences can to-day be expanded and substantiated much more coherently and comprehensively than Hovhannessian and Zanolli were able to do, so that the extent of possibly non-authentic material is very limited—if existent at all.

The circumstances and events of Eusebius of Emesa's life and the contents of his work are not too well-known.[8] He was born in Edessa, presumably around A.D. 300. He was educated both in Antioch and Alexandria, and it is related in particular that he was trained in biblical studies by Patrophilus of Scythopolis and Eusebius of Caesarea, presumably around 325. Some sources say that Eusebius was not too well received as a bishop of Emesa (a town in Phoenicia, to-day Homs); the precise reasons for the upheavals are difficult to decipher. Eusebius is said to have accompanied the Emperor Constantius during one—or more—of his campaigns against the Persians, but whether this should apply to the campaigns before 350 or those of the years 357-360, is hard to tell. According to Jerome[9] Eusebius died under Constantius, which would take us to a year before 361; in 359 Emesa is represented by another bishop at the Council of Seleucia, so maybe Eusebius' death should be dated even earlier than that.

On the basis of a piece of information given by Jerome[10] he is remembered as Arian—or at least semi-Arian—in theology, and this theological reputation of being semi-heretical may have earned Eusebius the ill fate of his writings encountered in the history of transmission. Today we know of only one single text preserved in its entirety in Greek, for which Eusebian authorship is claimed: a homily "on repentence,"[11] but even here there are reasons to doubt that he is in fact the author. I shall return to the indirect Greek transmission—in catenae; otherwise we have to turn to translations. Apart from a few fragments in Syriac and a couple of texts in Georgian, it is the Latin and the Armenian branches of transmission to which we owe most of our knowledge of Eusebius. A number of homilies now form the core of Eusebius' literary production as known to us.[12]

I took as my starting point MS Ven. Mekh. No. 873. This, indeed, is by far the most important witness for the Armenian translation; only one other manuscript is known to contain the text in its entirety, namely MS No. 231 of the Mekhitarist library of Vienna, and this manuscript is a nineteenth-century copy of the manuscript of San Lazzaro. For about the last third of the text there is one further witness: a fifteenth-century manuscript of the Matenadaran in Yerevan (MS No. 1267). Here also the author is given as Cyril; I have not had the opportunity to examine the Yerevan manuscript myself, but judging from the Venice edition, its variant readings do not show many important differences from the manuscript of San Lazzaro.

The Venice edition does not list indirect Armenian witnesses—such as the quotations in the Leviticus catena of the very same manuscript as that containing the commentary, so it may be true that a certain amount of editorial work still remains to be done. However, the most important thing to be said about the Venice edition is that it has made this important text available to patristic scholars, church historians and other readers.

Parts of the Armenian translation have in fact been available for a number of years, namely in T'. T'ofnian's anthology of classical Armenian texts—here of course under the name of Cyril of Alexandria.[13] As no translation has been available and the number of patristic scholars who know Armenian is rather limited, the impact of the editions has so far been very modest. A translation into a language more widely known than Armenian may very well be the most urgent desideratum as regards this text.

In this paper I shall be concerned with an attempt to list and explain what other tasks seem to me to be the most important to be undertaken in the wake of the Armenian edition of Eusebius of Emesa's commentary on historical writings of the Old Testament.

Within the framework of a conference on Medieval Armenian Culture it might be natural to give prominence to the question of the use of the text in medieval Armenian literature. Since the text as described above has only been known to a modest extent even where Armenologists are concerned, very little has been done in the direction of searching through the works of medieval Armenian exegetes for this purpose.

I have not myself gone into that question so far, so I would like to round off this paragraph of my paper with an appeal to experts on medieval Armenian exegesis to be aware of the possibility of finding quotations or allusions to the text in Armenian authors. I should be most graceful for hints about such findings.

For the Greek transmission of the text undoubtedly the most important field to be examined is that of the catenae. The Latin word catena—meaning 'chain'—was chosen to designate commentaries consisting of quotations from earlier authors strung together as links of a chain. One of the first examples of this genre, dating to the early sixth century, was Procopius of Gaza's commentary on the first books of the Old Testament. A number of others followed, and as could be guessed, this traditionalist type of literature was in later centuries often despised because of the lack of originality and spiritual activity inherent in its making.

For one purpose, however, scholars of later centuries found the catenae highly useful; namely, for identifying fragments of earlier exegetic works, a number of them no longer extant in their entirety. It could be added that exegetes seemed more liberal than other theologians in using and including quotations of heretical authors in their works. Thus, the image of Apollinarius might have been still more blurred, had it not been for the catenae.

Usually, from the outset, the catenist would quote the author's name with each quotation, and when linking fragments from the same author, he would say "by the same." This technique, of course, when abbreviations and additions took place in the course of transmission, might lead to wrong attributions. Identifying the authors used by Procopius in his catenae is a particularly intricate process since the names of authors are never given. Instead the quotations have been combined into a continuous commentatorial text.

What has been said here may have been common knowledge; I have included these basic facts, among other reasons, because modern catena research has in fact had to re-evaluate a number of basic and elementary theories and assumptions.

This re-evaluation—concerning the distribution of manuscripts in families and branches of tradition, the attribution of fragments to their right authors, the preferable technique of edition, etc.—is particularly the outcome of years of meticulous work by Françoise Petit of Louvain. It must be hoped that she can accomplish the huge task of edition; so far only one volume has been published, namely the Sinaiticus Catena on Genesis and Exodus (published 1977).[14]

An impression of the mutual benefit of the study of the Armenian Eusebius translation and research into the Greek catenae can be gained from the surveys given in appendices I-III.

In the first survey (appendix I) are listed—in the third column—the identifications of passages in the Armenian text with passages in the Catena Sinaitica in Françoise Petit's edition. It should be noted that the first passage of this catena comments upon Gen 12, 17, the last one upon Ex 2, 18-22; hence the limit of our survey.

Column 4 shows further identifications in Procopius as edited in Migne's Patrologia. This edition, however, is very unsatisfactory, even if it is better for Genesis than for the rest of the books commented upon. In any case, identifications on the basis of this edition cannot be expected to be exhaustive, but they can give a first hint of possibilities. A full examination of Procopius must be done on the basis of the Greek manuscripts available.

After the first survey, there follows a tally of fragments published under Eusebius of Emesa's name in the Catena Sinaitica edition, with an indication of what passages find parallels in the Armenian translation (appendix II). The numbers are: 14 out of 26 passages for Genesis, and 2 out of 10 passages for Exodus. This register, of course, raises the question whether the Armenian text is a translation of a complete Eusebius text. If it is, the surplus Greek passages must either be inauthentic or derived from other works by Eusebius.

In the last list (appendix III) are recorded those fragments which are not published under Eusebius' name in the Greek edition, but do find parallels in the Armenian text. In a number of cases, Françoise Petit's notes are quoted, from which it appears that hints occur in the Greek material pointing towards Eusebian authorship. On the whole, this list of course illustrates the possibilities of using the Armenian translation to identify anonymous passages and passages falsely attributed to other authors in the Greek tradition.

From what has been adduced so far, I hope the usefulness of the Armenian translation for the important task of determining what is in fact left of the Greek original of Eusebius' commentary on historical writings of the Old Testament has become sufficiently evident. It may have appeared as well that much of the work still remains to be done.

The next question to be considered is what material might be found in Armenian catenae. As far as I know, research into such collections of texts and editorial work lag behind the study of related collections such as dogmatic florilegia, collections of canonical rules and writings, etc. Of course, a few things have been done. As was mentioned by way of introduction, Zanolli, for instance, was primarily concerned with the Leviticus catena to be found in the same manuscript as the Eusebian commentary.

In the library of San Lazzaro this catena is contained in three manuscripts; apart from No. 873: No. 352, a manuscript of the second half of the twelfth century, and No. 740, dated 1835, in which can be found both the catena as such (even if in a mutilated shape) and, separately, a collection of fragments of the catena. This late manuscript also contains a catena on the Gospel of Luke and parts of a Genesis catena.

The three manuscripts are mutually independent, it seems,[15] even if there are a number of corresponding features. The translation represented by the three witnesses must for linguistic reasons be dated rather late; Zanolli, from a piece of information in MS 873, assumes the translation to have been made in Constantinople in 716 A.D. The name of the translator is given as David, counsellor and butler (?) of the royal table, son of the priest Elia; the scribe is Step'anos, priest and doctor of the province of Siunik.[16] As to the Vorlage of this catena, Zanolli assumes a very close connection to Procopius's catena.

Of course, a thorough-going investigation into the Armenian translation and transmission of Greek catenae, and the question whether the Procopius branch is the only one to be transmitted or the predominant one should be pursued on a much broader scale than Zanolli's, comprising only three manuscripts and a few probings in supplementary material in the library of San Lazzaro; and due regard should be given to the new achievements hinted at above, as far as research into the Greek catenae is concerned.

Let me just add one further observation concerning forthcoming catena research on the Armenian tradition so far neglected: this field of research can hardly be isolated from the field mentioned above, that of the use of exegetic literature of the Old Church in medieval Armenian literature, here exemplified through Eusebius of Emesa.

To illustrate this point let me refer to Vardan Arewelc'i, the famous historian, traveller and exegete of the thirteenth century, whose commentaries on writings of the Old Testament are characterized by Vahan Inglisian as "florilegia,"[17] used by B. Outtier under the designation "chaîne scripturaire,"[18] and compared by A. Zanolli with the Leviticus catena, esp. quotations from Ephraem.[19] A commentary such as that compiled by Vardan raises the question whether he uses earlier authors directly, or indirectly through catenae, and in the latter case, whether these have been taken over directly from Greek Vorlagen or have been elaborated on Armenian ground.

What has been adduced so far can to some extent be said to belong to the technicalities of the process of drawing as full a picture as possible of the transmission of the text, of establishing the best text possible, and of finding such portions of the original behind the version or versions, as can be identified. It will have appeared that a number of questions still wait for their answer.

These answers are important and must necessarily have a prominent place on the agenda. But of course, the text historian must admit in modesty that considerations of this kind can only rank as prolegomena to an analysis of the contents of the text.

What, then, does the text contain? I cannot, of course, describe that in any detail, but I hope, through a few illustrations, to be able to demonstrate that in the title of this paper, I was right in applying the adjective "important" to this text, primarily preserved through the efforts of medieval Armenian scribes.

Above all, an analysis of the text will give us an improved understanding of Eusebius' profile as an exegete. Church historians usually divide exegetes of the fourth and fifth centuries into "schools," primarily the allegorists of Alexandria and their opponents and critics in Antioch, to which may be added the Syriac-speaking schools of Edessa and Nisibis, and, of course, Latin exegetes, more often than not dependent on the school of Alexandria. From contemporary sources it is known that one of the central figures of the school of Antioch, Diodorus of Tarsus, was considered to be a pupil of Eusebius of Emesa.[20] This can now be substantiated more broadly than before, and we can, therefore, say that we are better informed of the early phase of the school of Antioch, which has in the past to some extent been clouded in mists of darkness.

The roads of tradition and spiritual and scholarly interdependence were not so narrow, however, as to exclude influence and inspiration from one school onto another. Before I turn to a couple of considerations of that topic, it may be natural to point out in the first place, that Eusebius' approach to the Scriptures is very linguistic. Thus, in the commentary he is very much aware of the problems of translation. He knows that the Hebrew language has a number of characteristics, which make it difficult to render the meaning of a passage or a word into Greek in a very literal and verbatim translation, and he often discusses the translational choices of the various Greek versions of the Old Testament, and the Syriac renderings as well. In fact, in one of the examples in the list of anonymous quotations from the Greek catenae[21] the "author" is cited as "the Syrian." This is an identification which can already be found in Eusebius' text. "The Syrian" is, in fact, the name of a Bible translation, which is usually assumed, despite its name, to be a Greek version; there are, however, indications in Eusebius, which to my mind necessitate the re-opening of the discussion, whether this designation does instead cover an early pre-Peshitta Syriac version. In order to illustrate the importance of the Armenian testimony, I have chosen an instance where the Armenian deviates at a crucial point from a Greek fragment known already.

It is to be found in a comment on Ex 4:25 (and 26), i.e. an element of the dramatic tale of the Lord meeting Moses "by the way in the inn," seeking to kill him, which is avoided by the circumcision of Moses' son through the hand of Zipporah, his wife, who then says: "Surely a bridegroom of blood are you to me" (v. 25), "a bridegroom of blood for the circumcision" (v. 26). Instead of these phrases the Septuagint has a reading which can be translated: "The blood of circumcision of my son 'stood' (maybe = 'is staunched')."[22]

In a Greek catena fragment attributed to Eusebius of Emesa we are given the information that instead of the Septuagint rendering Aquila reads: "I have a bridegroom of blood," and "the Hebrew": "He (or she) sealed the blood of circumcision."[23]

This fragment is now found in the Armenian translation with one interesting deviation from the Greek, insofar as it reads "the Syrian" instead of Aquila.[24] In fact, the reading attributed to Aquila in the Greek, and to "the Syrian" in the Armenian, corresponds to the reading of the Peshitta; and it might be worthwhile noting that the Peshitta reading has been challenged and discussed, since the change of one single letter would make it conform to the Hebrew text ('nt instead of 'yt).[25]

I have found no further comment on the reading attributed to "the Hebrew," apart from Field's note[26] that the reading is due to a change between an m and an n (htm, 'to seal' instead of htn, 'bridegroom'). At any rate, it should by now be apparent that the Eusebian readings cannot be classified as trivial.

I shall not venture to give any final verdict on how much new information can be gained from our text about the history of the versions of the Old Testament, but I should like to add that besides references to Bible versions such as Aquila and Theodotion, the Syrian and the Hebrew, we also come across source references such as: "A certain Hebrew says." This, of course, means that Eusebius had some knowledge of Jewish exegesis of his own age or of earlier periods. The lines of tradition connecting Jewish and Christian exegesis have been known and studied before, not least for the school of Edessa, which was, as will be remembered, Eusebius' birthplace; and if we consider Philo, the Christian school to be mentioned would, of course, be that of Alexandria. However, certain traditions of rabbinical exegesis have not been as well-known as Philo; nor has it been possible to judge their impact on Christian interpretation of the Old Testament. Research into these lines of connection is currently in progress, so here again our text will be welcomed for its contributions.

After these few references to fields and topics where the contents of Eusebius' commentary are of special interest and to one of the directions into which considerations of his sources will take us, let me conclude this paper with a consideration taking us the other way; namely, to a use of Eusebius, which has hitherto appeared enigmatic to researchers and led to a number of wrong conclusions.

I am referring to a crux in Augustine[27] that has for centuries puzzled scholars.   In a number of Augustine's exegetic works he discusses what the right understanding of <u>Gen</u> 1:2c is.   Does the clause refer to the Holy Ghost? Should it be translated: "And the Spirit of God moved upon the face of the waters" (with the RSV) or "a mighty wind swept over the surface of the waters" (to quote the NEB)?   In his <u>De genesi ad litteram</u> Augustine refers to a source for his final considerations as being "a certain learned Christian Syrian."   Now, it is easy to demonstrate that Augustine has taken this reference from Basil the Great.   But to which text and which author, then, does Basil refer?   Through the centuries a number of answers have been given to this question.   To my mind, there is no doubt that the right answer is: Eusebius of Emesa's Commentary on <u>Genesis,</u> and so, through Basil's characterization of the Syrian author as being orthodox[28] it could be maintained that the Armenian scribes have helped not only to solve the literary crux here sketched and answer the question of Augustine's and Basil's ultimate source, but also to relieve Eusebius' reputation of being semi-heretical, as Basil's testimony should be considered as weighty, at least, as that of Jerome.

APPENDIX I

Correspondences between Greek catena fragments in Francoise Petit's edition of the Catena Sinaitica and the Armenian translation of Eusebius of Emesa's Commentary on Historical Writings of the Old Testament.

Column 1:   MS Ven. Mekh. No. 873, page, line.
Column 2:   Quotations of Biblical texts.
Column 3:   Identifications in the edition of the Catena Sinaitica (F. Petit's numbering).
Column 4:   Further identifications in Procopius (PG 87, column, paragraph, line).
Column 5:   Non-identified elements.
Column 6:   Remarks.

1	2	3	4	5 6
162,29-31	Gen 12:17			
162,31-35		G 2		
162,35-38		G 1,1-3		
162,38-163,4			329,D2-7	
163,4-7			329,D10-13	
163,7		G 1,4		
163,7-8			329,D14-332,A1	
163,8		G 1,4-5		
163,8-11		G 9,2-4		
163,11-14				x Conc. Gen 14:18.20
163,14-16	Gen 15:2			
163,16-17		G 16:2-3		
163,17-19	Gen 15:8-9			
163,19-31		G 22		
163,31-164,7		G 20,2-12		Arm. a little amplified
164,7-9	Gen 15:15f			
164,9-11		G 37		
164,11-18			341,D4-10	Cf. G 37, note b
164,18-22		G 31a		
164,23-25			344,B1-4	Cf. G 31, note *.

164,25-31		G 31b	Arm. a little amplified
164,31-32	Gen 17:5		
164,32-34			x Conc. Gen 17:5
164,34-37	Gen 17:17-19		
164,37-165,8			Parallels with G 83
165,8-10	Gen 17:14		
165,10-12		G 64,1-3	Arm. a little amplified
165,12-14	Gen 18:19		
165,15-20			x Conc. Gen 18:19
165,21	Gen 18:21		
165,22-26			x Conc. Gen 18:21 (not G 87)
165,26-27	Gen 18:27		
165,27-29			x Conc. Gen 18:27 (not G 93)
165,29-38		369,D1-371/372,A6	
165,38-166,8		G 116	Arm. a little amplified
166,8-9	Gen 20:2		
166,9-15		G 129	
166,15-28			x Conc. Gen 20:3ff (cit. 6.16a)
166,28-31		G 139	
166,31-167,2			x
167,2-6	Gen 20:17f		
167,6-12			x
167,12-14	Gen 21:14		
167,14-23		G 151	
167,23-24		G 150,1-2	
167,24-26			x (Cf. G 147,1)
167,26-29		G 147,3-6	
167,30-31			x Cf. PG 87,384,21
167,31-32		G 150,2-4	
167,32-35			x Cf. PG 87,386,8f
167,36-37			x Cf. PG 87,388,A9-12

167,38	Gen 21:22			
167,38-168,2			x	
168,2-8			388,C16-D7	
168,9-12			x	
168,13-16		G 177		
168,16-21		G 189		= Proc. 1.1-6
168,22				x Conc. Gen 22:1
168,22-24	Gen 22:12			
168,24-29		G 183		
168,29-32				x (Cf. G 185—not identical!)
168,32-34	Gen 23:4			
168,34-169,3				x Conc. Gen 23:4.6 (cf. 194)
169,3-5	Gen 23:15			
169,5-9				x Conc. Gen 23:15
169,9-10	Gen 24:2			
169,11-13		G 209		
169,13-14			x	
169,14-16			x	
169,16-21		G 211		
169,21-32			395/396,A27-34	
169,32-33	Gen 24:5			
169,33-35				x Conc. Gen 24:5
169,35-37			403/404,C9-10	
169,37-38	Gen 24:49			
169,38				x Conc. Gen 24:49
170,1-2	Gen 24:50			
170,2-3		G 233		
170,3	Gen 24:63			
170,3-6			401/402,B12-17	
170,6-8				x (Cf. G 16)
170,8	Gen 25:22			
170,8-9			407/408,A14-16	(Devreesse, p. 75)
170,9-10	Gen 25:26			
170,10-16			407/408,C10-15	(Devreesse, p. 75)
170,16-17	Gen 25:27			

170,17-20			409/410,A1-5	
170,20-21	Gen 25:28			
170,21-28		G 261		= Proc.
170,28-33			409/410,A21-28(31)	(Cf. G 262, note a)
170,33-34	Gen 25:31			
170,34-171,4			411/412,A3-13	
171,4-6		G 266		Arm. a little amplified
171,7	Gen 26:31			
180,21	Ex 1:12			
180,22-24		E 11		
180,24-26	Ex 1:20f			
180,26-29		E 16		= Proc.
180,30-38			513/514,B17-21	
180,38-181,2	Ex 1,20f			
181,2				x Conc. Ex 1:20f
181,2-4				x Conc. Ex 1:22
181,5-25				x Conc. Ex 2:1ff
181,25	Ex 2:14			
181,26-28		E 34		= Proc.
181,28-31				x Conc. Ex 2:14
181,31	Ex 2:24f			

APPENDIX II

Passages published in the Catena Sinaitica under Eusebius of Emesa's name.
Parallels in the Armenian translation marked with *. Numbering of Greek
fragments according to Francoise Petit's edition.

Genesis Fragment No.		Exodus Fragment No.	
2	*	11	*
9	*	15	
20	*	16	*
22	*	21	
64	*	22	
87		23	
91		33	
92		36	
93		43	
99		44	
100			
116	*		
118			
119			
139	*		
150	*		
151	*		
153			
177	*		
183	*		
185			
189	*		
192			
209	*		
210			
211	*		
Total 26	14	10	2

APPENDIX III

Passages published in the Catena Sinaitica edition under other names than
Eusebius of Emesa, for which parallels are found in the Armenian translation.

Greek Fragment No.   Attributions in Greek Catenae

G   1   The same; Anonymous; Eusebius (Bs) (1)
G   16   Anonymous; Eusebius (Len); Diodorus (2)
G   31   Origen; Anonymous (3)
G   37   Anonymous; Philo
G 129   Anonymous; Didymus
G 147   Anonymous; Eusebius (Len); Diodorus (4)
G 233   The Syrian
G 261   The same; Eusebius (Len); Anonymous
G 266   Anonymous

E   34   Anonymous

Notes (quotations of relevant passages from Françoise Petit's notes).

1: p. 3f, note (a)   Ce morceau n'est intelligible que si l'on tient compe
                      te du précédent . . . Les deux sont distincts dans
                      Sin, Mosq et Procope; ils sont liés dans Len et Bs
                      (avec, dans ce dernier, attributions à Eusèbe d'Em-
                      èse) . . .
2: p. 19, note *   . . . La rédaction des chaînes du premier groupe
                      pourrait bien revenir à Eusèbe d'Emèse . . .
3: p. 36, note (a)   Dans Len, soudé à G 30, attribué à Eusèbe d'Emèse.
4: p. 141, note *   . . . Comme pour G 16, nous pensons que la rédaction
                      de Sin Len Mosq[1] Bs revient à Eusèbe d'Emèse . . .

NOTES

[1]According to Almo Zanolli: Di una vetusta catena sul Levitico, perduta in greco e conservata in armeno, della sua stretta relazione col commentario di Procopio di Gaza e dei tre codici di S. Lazzaro, che la contengono (Venezia: Prem. Tipografia Armena, 1938) 78; 98, the last part (pp. 434-507: the Leviticus catena) may have been copied a few years later.

[2]Cf. note 1.

[3]Eusèbe d'Emèse: Commentaire de l'Octateuque, préparé par P. Vahan Hovhannessian (Venise: St. Lazare, 1980).

[4]V. Hovhannessian, "Commentarium in Genesim d'Eusebe d'Emese," Bazmavēp 81 (1923) 353-358 (in Armenian); cf. Henning, J. Lehmann: Per Piscatores. Studies in the Armenian version of a collection of homilies by Eusebius of Emesa and Severian of Gabala (Aarhus, 1975) 17, 31-33.

[5]V. Hovhannessian: "Commentarius in Genesim de S. Cyrille patriarche d'Alexandrie," Bazmavēp (1923) 225-228 (in Armenian).

[6]Cf. note 4. The article is continued in: Bazmavēp 82 (1924) 3-6, 33-36, 65-68, 225-228, and a summary is given and a few pages of the text published in: Bazmavēp 93 (1935) 345-352 (in Armenian).

[7]Zanolli, Catena sul Levitico, 17, 83-86.

[8]A biographical sketch, where the sources are exploited to their utmost capacity, can be found in: E. M. Buytaert: L'héritage littéraire d'Eusèbe d'Emèse (Bibliothèque du Muséon 24; Louvain: Bureaux du Muséon, 1949) 43-96.

[9]Hieronymus: De viris illustribus (ed. W. Herding; London, 1924) 54; cf. Buytaert, L'héritage littéraire, 6, 94.

[10]Hieronymus: Chronicon (ed. R. Helm, in: Eusebius: Werke, 7, Die griechischen christlichen Schriftsteller 24; Leipzig: J. C. Hinrichs, 1913) 236; cf. Buytaert, L'héritage littéraire, 7, n. 9.

[11]Buytaert, L'héritage littéraire, 150-156, 16*-29*.

[12]See especially Eusèbe d'Emèse: Discours conservés en latin 1-2 (ed. E. M. Buytaert, Spicilegium Sacrum Lovaniense 26-27; Louvain, 1953-1957), and N. Akinian, "Die Reden des Bischofs Eusebius von Emesa," Handēs

Amsōreay, 1956, 291-300, 385-416; 1957, 101-130, 257-267, 357-380, 513-524; 1958, 1-18, 19-22. Cf. Lehmann, Per Piscatores, 37-272.

[13]T'adēos T'ornian: Hatĕntir ĕnterc'owack' i matenagrut'eanc' naxneac' (Vienna, 1866) 386-423.

[14]Catenae graecae in Genesim et in Exodum. I. Catena Sinaitica (ed. Françoise Petit, Corpus Christianorum, Series Graeca 2; Turnhout: Brepols, 1977). For articles and reports by Françoise Petit prior to 1977 reference may be made to this edition, XI. From the years after 1977 the following articles can be mentioned from her pen: "L'édition des chaînes exégétiques grecques sur la Genèse et l'Exode," Le Muséon 91 (1978) 189-194; "La tradition de Théodoret de Cyr dans les chaînes sur la Genèse," Le Muséon 92 (1979) 281-286.   In Buytaert, L'héritage littéraire, 95*-143*, the Greek catena fragments of Eusebius' commentary as known in 1949 are published. For a better edition see: Robert Devreesse: Les anciens commentateurs de l'Octateuque et des Rois (Studi e Testi 201, Citta del Vaticano, 1959) 55-103; This, of course, is not the place for a full discussion of modern research on OT catenae including important works by such authors as E. Muhlenberg and G. Dorival and others.

[15]Zanolli, Catena sul Levitico, 128.

[16]Ibid., 2, 97.

[17]Vahan Inglisian: Die armenische Literatur (Handbuch der Orientalistik, hrsg, v. B. Spuler, 1. Abt., 7. Bd., 156-254; Leiden, Köln 1963).   Cf. esp. p. 200: Seine (Vardan's) Kommentare zur Genesis, Jesua, zu den Büchern der Richter, der Vier Könige, zu Psalmen und Hohenlied kann man als Florilegium bezeichnen.

[18]B. Outtier, "La version arménienne du commentaire des Psaumes de Théodoret. Premier bilan," REArm 12 (1977) 169-180. Cf. esp. 174: Les chaînes scripturaires ont utilisé notre texte, en premier lieu Vardan l'Oriental.

[19]Zanolli, Catena sul Levitico, 102.

[20]Hieronymus, De virus illustribus, ed. Herding 62; cf. Buytaert, L'héritage littéraire, 9.   For Diodorus's contribution to the exegesis of the historical writings of the Old Testament, cf. esp. J. Deconinck: Essai sur la chaîne de l'Octateuque avec une édition des commentaires de Diodore de

Tarse qui s'y trouvent contenus (Paris: Librairie Ancienne Honore Champion, 1912). A fuller picture of Diodorus as an éxegete is emerging with the edition of his commentary on the Psalms: Diodorus Tarsensis: Commentarius in Psalmos, 1 (ed. J. Olivier; Corpus Christianorum, Series Graeca 6, Turnhout: Brepols, 1980). For B. Outtier's identification of Armenian evidence for this text cf. the article mentioned above (note 18).

[21]See Appendix III, item G 233.

[22]Cf. G. Vermes, "Baptism and Jewish Exegesis: New Light from Ancient Sources," New Testament Studies 4 (1957-58) 308-319, see esp. 310-311.

[23]Devreesse, Anciens commentateurs, 90-91.

[24]MS Ven. Mekh. No. 873, 185, 30-33, ed. Hovhannessian, 108, 434-437.

[25]Cf. the note in A. E. Brooke and N. McLean: The Old Testament in Greek (Cambridge: University Press, 1917) 167. In the new Peshitta edition (The Old Testament in Syriac according to the Peshitta Version 1, [The Peshitta Institute; Leiden: Brill 1977] 125) no variants to the 'yt ly ('I have,' lit. 'there is for me') are quoted, and it is interesting to note that Field, in his Hexapla-edition (Origenis Hexaplorum quae supersunt, ed. J. Field [Oxford: Clarendon Press, 1875] 87-88), on the basis of his assumption that Aquila besides his knowledge of Hebrew was well acquainted with traditions behind the Syriac Bible versions (Prolegomena XXIV) already refused to correct a Syro-Hexaplaric 'yt into 'nt, because he saw the ἔχω, presumed to belong to Aquila, as a support for the reading 'yt.

[26]Origenis Hexaplorum, 88.

[27]For a fuller discussion of Augustine's interpretation of Gen 1:2c, referred to in the following, with references to sources and secondary literature cf. Henning J. Lehmann, "El Espíritu de Dios sobre las aguas. Fuentes de los comentarios de Basilio y Agustín sobre el Génesis 1,2," Augustinus 26 (1981) 127*-139*.

[28]Basil's exact phrasing is: Έρῶ σοι οὐκ ἐμαυτοῦ λόγον,ἀλλὰ Σύρου ἀνδρὸς σοφίας κοσμικῆς τοσοῦτον ἀφεστηκότος, ὅσον ἐγγύς ἦν τῆς τῶν ἀληθινῶν ἐπιστήμης.
Cf. Basile de Césarée: Homélies sur l'Hexaéméron (ed. Stanislas Giet; Sources Chrétiennes, 26; Paris: Les éditions du Cerf, 1949) 168.

THE RISE OF SAINT BARTHOLOMEW'S CULT IN ARMENIA
FROM THE SEVENTH TO THE THIRTEENTH CENTURIES

Michel van Esbroeck

Bollandist Fathers (Belgium)

Between the seventh and thirteenth centuries, a most remarkable phenomenon, provoking our reflection on Armenian history and society, is the introduction of a new claim to Apostolicity within the Armenian Church. The name of the apostle Bartholomew had first been introduced into Armenian historiography at the beginning of the seventh century. The last vestige of the legend is to be found in the thirteenth century in the History of Siwnik by Step'anos Ōrbelian.

The story of the cult of Bartholomew in Armenia is riddled by a puzzling placename: Urbanopolis of Great Armenia.[1] That name appears everywhere in the Armenian sources as the place where the apostle died and was buried. It was first mentioned, however, as is often the case, in the History of Movsēs Xorenac'i. This work is once again at the center of the problem. We will not discuss here the age of Movsēs's History, but we will show that his source, in the passage where he quotes the apostles Bartholomew and Jude, is a Greek one from the seventh or eighth century. Whether that passage may be considered as an interpolation is another question which would require separate treatment.

Various hypotheses were proposed by J. Markwart and R. Lipsius to explain Urbanopolis, but without convincing arguments. The most recent legend, it is true, declares ingenuously that Urbanopolis is no other than Ałbak[2] at the sources of the Tigris. But the ruins of the convent of Saint Bartholomew of Ałbak are from the thirteenth century,[3] and an earlier legend on the apostle does not mention Ałbak at all.[4]

T. Samuelian & M. Stone, eds. Medieval Armenian Culture. (University of Pennsylvania Armenian Texts and Studies 6). Chico, CA: Scholars Press, 1983. pp. 161 to 178.

Our purpose in the present paper is to demonstrate that "Urbanopolis of Great Armenia" is a Greek designation for Nikopolis of Pontus, and that all the various legends of Bartholomew can be easily explained and understood if the Latin and Parthian legends of Bartholomew were originally located in Nikopolis of Pontus.

The first step will be to show how perfectly the expression "Great Armenia" fits the Greek sources at the end of the sixth century in reference to a place name in the region of Nikopolis; the second step will be to give evidence from a Georgian source which clearly writes "Urbanopolis" as a second name for Nikopolis; the third point will be to demonstrate that Movsēs's History depends on the Greek Lists of the Apostles, where Bartholomew's name is found in Armenia only in the seventh century.

In another part of our argument, we will show how the southern house of the Ŕštuni dynasty enhanced the cult of Bartholomew, with the oldest Armenian legend in the eighth century, and how it became central to the conflicts with the Byzantine Church during the reign of Maurice. Finally, we will say a few words about the last group of legends in Siwnik, and their revision of the older traditions.

In their oldest historical accounts, the Armenian historians omitted Bartholomew. P'awstos and Agat'angełos do not say a word about Bartholomew. However P'awstos, in his prologue, gives an exact report of the works of other writers who spoke about the events "from the time of Thaddeus's preaching until the death of Gregory, from the martyrdom of that apostle to the reception of the faith."[5] Movsēs Xorenac'i, or his interpolator, adds the following words: "However, the apostle Bartholomew, who brought his life to a close in the town of Arebanos (var. Aresbanos, Arbanos, Arevbanos) received Armenia also in his apostolic field." As to Simon who received Persia as his own field, I cannot tell precisely what he has done, nor where he died, even if some people say that a certain Simon died in Veriosphor (var. Veriophora, Veriophober, Verin Sophor, Verios Phor). I do not know if it is true that that was his reason for his coming in this region, but I mentioned it merely to make you aware that I did not spare any effort to give you any possible tradition."[6]

Those are the words of Movsēs. They fit perfectly if he had before him the Greek Lists of the Apostles, which appeared at the end of the sixth century. The form in -os indicates already the probability of a Greek original. There we find that the apostle Jude died in the Bosphorus, which is certainly to be connected with Veriosphor. Movsēs's hesitation about Simon can easily be understood by looking at the complex reports of the various Lists of the Apostles.

Let us read some of them. The Breviarium Apostolorum, attested already c. 600 A.D., writes: "Iudas qui interpretatur confessor, Iacobi frater, in Mesopotamiam praedicavit: sepultus est in Nerito Armeniae urbe,"[7] But that Jude is already somewhat confused with Simon the Zealot, whose feast day is the same, and whose name appears immediately before that of Judas. Judas is listed as the successor to James the Just in Jerusalem, and the notice concludes: "Post annos CXX meruit sub Adriano per crucem sustinere martyrii passionem. Iacet in Portoforo (var. Porro foro, porto photo)."[8] The list of the pseudo-Hippolytus sends Jude to Edessa, and has him buried en Beryto, which is the key to Nerito. That entry gives evidence of a confusion between Jude and Addeus/Thaddeus, which in turn makes the paradoxal "Nerito in Armenia" of the Latin tradition understandable.[9]

Finally, a third List of Apostles, this one Anonymous, gives Simon the Zealot of Cana in Galilea (thus identified with Nathanael), as having died en Bospero tes Iberias, that is, in the Crimea.[10] The destination of his mission field was reinforced in the ninth century by the Greek monk Epiphanius.[11]

If Movsēs had before him the Lists of the Apostles, with entries of both Bartholomew and Jude, then clearly he checked the two entries with the name "Armenia": Bartholomew in Urbanopolis from Great Armenia, and Simon the Zealot in a puzzling "Beyrouth of Armenia," already transformed into Veriosphorus and Bosphoros by assimilation with the other Jude. His hesitation stems from the fact that he did not recognize the place name. Latin Nerito from Beryto as a place in Armenia, and that he mentioned Simon and not Jude in the Bosphoros, rejecting the widespread assimilation of Simon-Jude. Note also that Movsēs tried to say everything he knew about apostolic traditions. His laconic mention of Urbanopolis shows how little he was able to present to his readers, having only the Greek lists before his eyes.

More recent historians do not say much more than Movsēs. Step'anos Asołik who writes his History up to 1004 gives the following brief account: "However the apostle Thomas [That is Jude-Thomas] received Armenia by lot, as well as Bartholomew who ended his life in our region in the town of Arabion."[12] Step'anos is native of Tarōn and writes for the house of the Bagratids just as Movsēs Xorenac'i does. Zenob of Glak, whose History is to be placed in the tenth century, quotes a letter supposed to be from Leontios of Caesarea to Gregory the Illuminator. There we read: Thou wast chosen in the election place of the holy apostles Bartholomew and Thaddeus, remember their works."[13] Pseudo-Zenob already places Bartholomew before Thaddeus, even if he writes in the Turuberan, at the convent of the Nine Sources.

As a matter of fact, in the beginning of the tenth century, the apostolic claim through Bartholomew is used by all the Catholicoi. The first one is Yovhannēs V Drasxanakertc'i, who cites Bartholomew before Thaddeus. Not long after, Anania Mokac'i (943-965) speaks in the same manner, and Xač'ik Anec'i (972-992) also includes both of the apostles in the title of the letter he sent to the metropolitan of Melitene Theodore.[14]

Other legendary accounts also speak about Bartholomew. The Letter of Movsēs, the Wise Rhetor, to Sahak Arcruni, about the founding of the convent of Hogeac' Vank' by the apostle Bartholomew, is from the end of the eleventh century, for it mentions the death of Atom, the son of Sennekerim.[15] Moreover, that legend already implies the existence of the Armenian Passion of the Apostle, and of the Finding of his body in Barm, near Urbanopolis.

The oldest testimony about Bartholomew has come to us through Greek sources. It is the well-known Narratio de Rebus Armeniae, which was published and commented on by G. Garitte in 1952. The original, lost model was certainly written in Armenian. One paragraph of that chronicle directly concerns Saint Bartholomew:

> In the time of Aršak, Armenia was divided; at that time Theodosiopolis was also founded. That place was originally called Kalè Archè. The great apostle Bartholomew, who went among the Parthians, baptized the cousin of the King of Persia, and with him 3000 people in the river Euphrates. In that place, he founded a church with the name of the holy Theotokos. A citadel having been erected, he called it Kalè Archè. Theodosius saw that the water was good at that spot, and he built a city there and changed its name to Theodosiopolis. To him was subordinated Aršak prince of Great Armenia; Xosrov, however, the king of Armenia, was subordinated to the king of Persia who reigned in the Armenian region.[16]

This is the first example of the title "Great Armenia" used for the western part, while to the east, after the peace of Jovian, which was so favorable to the Persians, Xosrov is said to only reign over "Armenia." The Parthian legend referred to by the Chronicle exists in Latin, Greek and Armenian, but is still unedited in the two later versions.[17] Those texts never speak about Urbanopolis. The tradition of the founding of a church devoted to the holy Theotokos has two parallels in the East. In the legend of Hogeac' Vank', Bartholomew, after having driven out the devs, built the church of the Virgin and brought there the Icon of Our Lady which he received at the moment of the Dormition of the Virgin. And in the History of Siwnik Step'anos Ōrbelian says how the church of the Presentation of the Virgin was erected by Bartholomew in the district of Gołtn just at the frontier of Arevik'. This is the last account in the thirteenth century.[18]

Let us look first at the role of Saint Bartholomew on the western frontier. The Parthian legend of Bartholomew was analyzed by von Gutschmid. He showed that the Pontus region is the proper context for the legend. The king Polemon II, client of Rome, converted to Judaism and married Berenikē, the widow of Herod of Chalkis. Polemon reigned from 54 A.D. and ended his career in Cilicia in 74.[19] Nikopolis was the most important city of the old kingdom of Pontus. It received its Greek name when Pompey in 66 B.C. was victorious over Mithridates VI Eupator, King of Pontus, who took refuge in the kingdom of Tigran, his brother-in-law."[20] Nikopolis was included in the "Little Armenia" while eleven other cities of Pontus were assigned to the province of Bithynia. Strabo says, about 25 A.D., that Nikopolis was an important city near the Lykos in Armenia which is not to be confused with the Lykos in Cilicia, the Lycaonia mentioned in a more recent legend, as the mission field of Bartholomew, together with Philip and Mariamne.[21]

At that time, "Lesser Armenia" was under Roman rule, while Great Armenia was ruled by Tigran with its capital in Tigranocerta, today Mayafariqīn.[22] About 34 B.C. Anthony succeeded in capturing the Tigran's son, Artavazd III; therefore he first attacked Nikopolis.[23] In 54 A.D., the Hasmonian Jew Aristobulos was made governor of Lesser Armenia, that is Nikopolis and Satala, in northwest Cappadocia.[24] At that moment, the future Theodosiopolis was under the rule of the Arsacid Trdat, the brother of the Parthian king. This is exactly the context which fits the Narratio de retus Armeniae and the Parthian Passion.[25]

In 63, Trdat was king of Armenia under Roman protection. Under

Hadrian's rule, the imperial province Armenia minor receives a garrison in Satala.[26]   At the same time, in East Armenia, we find the inscription Aurelios Pacorus basileus megales Armenias.[27] When Diocletian restored the Roman hegemony in Armenia, the Laterculus of Verona, in 297, records the military presence with the designation Armenia minor nunc et maior addita.[28] And in 387, Ammianus Marcellinus only knows one Armenia minor in which Melitene is included, but in which Satala and Nikopolis are to be added, for Epiphanius speaks of Sebastia as a town of Pontus, the so-called Lesser Armenia.[29]

A new division appears in 386.   An edict of Theodosius places Ariarathos and Comana in Armenia secunda.[30] In 457, in the answers sent by the bishops to the questions of emperor Leo, we find an Armenia prima with Nikopolis, Sebaste, Sebastopolis, Koloneia, Dazina and Satala, and an Armenia secunda with Melitine, Arca and Arabissos.[31] That division dates from 384. The same division appears in the Synekdemos of Hierokles in 527-528.[32] Thus from 384 to 527-528, there is no question of Western Great Armenia.

From Justinian himself, there is a law dated 528, where the expression Great Armenia is used:

> Elegimus certasque provincias, id est magnam Armeniam quae
> interior dicebatur, et gentes, et primam et secundum Arme-
> niam, et Pontum Polemoniacum tuae curae commisimus comite
> Armeniae penitus sublato.[33]

In 536, another text of Justinian makes it clear that the part of Great Armenia which was known as inner Armenia is the region of Bazanis, previously Leontopolis, and subsequently Justinianopolis.   The fourfold division of Justinian includes following cities:[34] Armenia 1a: Theodosiopolis, Baberd, Satala, Nicopolis, Trebizond and Karasunt. Armenia 2a: Sebaste, Comana and Zela. Armenia 3a: Melitene, Arca, Arabissos, Cucusa, Comana Chryse. Armenia 4a: Martyropolis and the five satrapies which were named gentes in 528, that is Sophene, Anzitene, Balabitene, Ashtianene and Sophanene.

Nikopolis was thus separated from Sebaste and was a part of eastern Greek Armenia. What must be examined is whether the expression Greater Inner Armenia for Theodosiopolis and Bazanis means that the first Armenia is in reality the whole Great Armenia. In 553, this is explicitly done in the subscription of the bishops to the Acts of the Council: there is one Gregorius misericordiae Dei episcopus Iustinianiopolitanorum civitatis Magnae Armeniae provinciae.   In 681, we find the Greek equivalent Ioustinianopoleos tes megales Armeniae, and Coloniae civitatis magnae Armeniae provinciae[35], and last but not least, in the subscription of the Council in Trullo, 691 A.D., we find "Photios chariti Theou episkopos tes Nikopoliton philochristou poleos tes megales ton Armenion eparchias."[36]

Procopius the historian uses the same terminology when he writes the Peri Ktismaton between 553 and 555.[37]   The demonstration of this point would require too much space.   It is thus absolutely clear that 536 onwards, Nikopolis could be referred to as Nikopolis of Great Armenia.

Of course Nikopolis has another name before Pompey's conquest.   The Georgian calendar of John Zosime, written in the tenth century, has for July 10: "The feast of the 40 martyrs who suffered martyrdom in the town Urban of Armenia."[38]   The date shows beyond doubt that the group is identical with the well known Greek martyrdom of the 40 martyrs of Nikopolis.

There is thus no difficulty in explaining the appearance (in Greek sources from 600 A.D.), of an entry about Bartholomew being murdered in Urbanopolis of Great Armenia.   That entry made its way into the History of Movsēs Xorenac'i among other apostolic fields of Simon-Jude.   The hypothesis of Markwart: Arewân in Syria, or of Lipsius Ervandashat in central Armenia, are pure phonetical guesses.[39]

One should note that Bartholomew was promoted to the role of palladium or symbol of divine protection for the East limes from the time of Theodosius I to that of Justinian.   An accurate study of various sources—The Armenian Chronicle (published by G. Garitte).   Malalas, Procopius and Theodorus Anagnostes—which cannot be presented here in detail, reveals the following facts.   Theodosius I (379-395) built two towns called by his name, one in the North, and the other in the South, in accordance with a bilateral agreement with the Persians to leave the 300 km which separated the two citadels free of any fortification.[40]   The Theodosiopolis in the North claimed the favor of the apostle Bartholomew.

Between 506 and 509, Emperor Anastasius (491-518) also built a town in the South, Dara, and Theodorus Anagnostes tells us that Anastasius received a vision of Bartholomew who instructed him to put his relics in the new fortress which was rebaptised Anastasiopolis.[41]   But Anastasius rebuilt, on the same site, the old citadel of Theodosiopolis, which had opened its door to the enemy in 502, and gave the citadel the name Anastasiopolis.

Lastly, emperor Justinian (527-565) built many citadels, but in the North he made a new Justinianopolis from the old Bazanis, the Armenian Bašean, and he also gave his name to Martyropolis in the South. There is no report about Bartholomew in the sources of Justinian's reign,[42] but the Armenian Finding of the relics of Bartholomew is placed at the time of Marutha in Martyropolis,[43] which is certainly a more recent construction. Marutha's time is in the beginning of the fifth century.

The matter of the relics of Bartholomew in Dara is well known. In 573, on November 11 or 15, Dara was captured by Xosru Anushirvan.[44] An anonymous Syriac chronicle from 724 describes the catastrophe as follows:

> In the year 824, Xosru came against Dara with his troops and captured it. He sent the marzpan Adharmahan who reached Antioch, burned Amos and the church of Saint Julian. . . .When he came back to his Shah, he took Dara, made the population prisoner, the emptied town, and introduced a new Persian population.[45]

The echo of the catastrophe was so great that it was alluded to by Gregory of Tours in the fourth book of his Historia Francorum, before 593.[46] The first real opponent to the Persian winners was the future emperor Maurice. In the summer 578, the emperor Tiberius transported all the Christians of the region of Martyropolis, 10,090 people, to the island of Cyprus.[47]

In Cyprus the feast of Saint Bartholomew had been associated with that of their own apostle Barnabas. But a dozen years later, the bishop Agathon of Lipari, alerted by a revelation, discovered the relics of Saint Bartholomew which were contained in lead coffins.[48] The new relics then made their way to the West, first to Benevento then to Rome and to other places. At the same time, the eastern and southern part of Armenia made a new claim to apostolicity.

There are two general causes that provoked the Armenians to claim the new apostolicity. One is purely political, the other is essentially religious.

From 908 onwards, the house of Arcrunis became kings of Vaspurakan, and T'ovma Arcruni wrote the History of Armenia from the viewpoint of the new dynasty. In 925, the Catholicos Yovhannēs V Drasxanakertc'i takes refuge in the Joroc' Vank', in Vaspurakan under king Gagik's protection. The three successors of Yovhannēs were R̆štuni princes, and before his death in 936, Gagik built the splendid cathedral of Aħt'amar for T'ēodoros R̆štuni. The legend of Hogeac' Vank' is addressed to the successors of Gagik. There are four legends about Bartholomew in Armenia. (1) the <u>Finding</u> of the relics by Marutha in Urbanopolis at a place named Barm and their deposit in Martyropolis, (2) the Armenian <u>Passion</u> under Sanatruk, (3) the legend of Bartholomew and Jude which is the source of Step'anos Ōrbelian, and (4) the legend of the founding of Hogeac' Vank' in Ałbak. They are all located in the bounds of the house of Vaspurakan, with a slight excursion into Siwnik, in Her, Gołtn and Zarewand.

In the history of the numerous apostolicities claimed by various churches from east to west, no better explanation has been given than that which Yovhannēs V proposed himself. Let us first follow his argumentation; afterwards we will analyze how deeply his reasoning was rooted in the beginning of the eighth century.

The program of Yovhannēs V is apparent from the very beginning of his <u>History</u>. He wishes to explain how, at the time of Vałaršak of the house of T'orgom,

> the establishment of the holy Christian faith spread all over the
> earth, and above all among the Armenian people, thanks to
> Bartholomew, who is one of the twelve, and Thaddeus who is
> one of the seventy, who received by lot of Our Lord Jesus
> Christ the responsibility foir evangelizing and spreading the
> doctrine in our Land.[49]

In order to substantiate his thesis, Yovhannēs could have followed Movsēs Xorenac'i's <u>History</u>. Movsēs attributes the division of the four Armenias to the eponymous hero Aram, and adds: "What some people say about Greek Armenia does not appeal to me. Let the others work in their own way!"[50] Yovhannēs quotes manifestly from Movsēs, but instead of the four figures, he explains further:

> The so-called Armenia as far as the boundary with Pontus was
> named first Armenia; from the Pontos to the frontiers of the
> town of Melitene second Armenia; from Melitene to the
> frontiers of Sophene, third Armenia; and from Sophene to
> Martyropolis and the land of Alcnik in the west, fourth
> Armenia. The fourth one extended its territory to the frontier
> of Armenia itself. But its own natural and sovereign territory
> was called <u>Great Armenia</u>.[51]

The fundamental divergence from Movsēs touches directly the Great Armenia near Martyropolis. That interpretation is obviously contrary to the Greek sources we mentioned first.

> Yovhannēs's motives are clearer when he speaks about Maurice. The emperor Maurice arrogantly changed the names of the land which had been fixed by Aram. . . He named fourth Armenia the land whose capital is Martyropolis, that is Np'rkert or Justinianopolis, and he inscribed all those definitions in the archives of the kingdom. And consequently, he named the land of Karin, whose capital is Theodosiopolis, part of great Armenia. . . . Having changed everything in that way, he inscribed this in the archives of the kingdom. I write this to you, in order to escape the accusation of ignorance about what I said first on the first, second, third and fourth Armenia, while the first designation is from our valiant Aram, the second, however, is from Maurice the emperor of the Greeks.[52]

This paragraph is most interesting. We already saw that the division attributed to Maurice is in fact that of Justinian. Yovhannēs, however, makes explicit the reasons which were alluded to by Movsēs Xorenac'i. He adds, moreover, the name of Great Armenia to the region of Theodosiopolis. One should remember that from 604 to 610, there was a brief period during which the legend of Agat'angełos was interpreted with a local seat in that region under Yovhannēs Bagaranec'i's pastoral rule.[53] This could be an additional reason for rejecting Maurice's division of Armenia. On the other hand, one cannot understand why Pontus was called part of Great Armenia after Maurice's victories, if it had not already been considered part of Great Armenia before, as we saw in the subscriptions of the bishops.

To return to the argumentation of Yovhannēs V. In the seventeenth year of Trdat's reign, Saint Gregory the Illuminator was enthroned on the see of the holy apostles Bartholomew and Thaddeus.[54] We will see that the Finding of the relics of Bartholomew on the Roman limes is intended to introduce one of the twelve apostles in the real Great Armenia, and the reasons which led the Catholicos to make this new claim of apostolicity are quite clear.

In relating the pontificate of Nersēs the Great, Yovhannēs tells us of his reception of the pontificate (hayrapetut'iwn) in Caesarea, and the success of his evangelization under Pap's reign. He adds:

> Not long before, Constans, the son of Constantine the Great,

transferred the precious relics of Saint John the evangelist from Ephesus to Constantinople.[55] For the same reason, Jerusalem became bold and attributed to itself the rank of patriarchate, justifying this by the fact that the Word of the Father had been born there, was seen and lived among human people, was baptized by John, crucified, buried, and resurrected the third day. Until that time, there were only four patriarchates on earth, corresponding to the four evangelists. Matthew in Antioch, Mark in Alexandria, Luke in Rome and John in Ephesus. But now, there were in fact six. Therefore our King Aršak and the naxarars of Armenia were also emboldened, and they elevated to patriarchate of the house of T'orgom, the great Nersēs, citing as evidence the presence of our apostles Bartholomew and Thaddeus, who received from the Lord the mission to preach and to evangelize the region of Ashkenaz. Their precious relics are among us, and the living martyr Gregory obtained their See. When they thus achieved their aim, the number of the patriarchates stood at seven, and it continued as such for all eternity. Thus in our land, the primacy of ecclesiastical authority has its fulfillment with only nine hierarchical orders: the chiefs of archbishops in Iberia and Albania by whom the archbishops are ordained; in Sebaste they settled metropolitans as in Melitene and Martyropolis the bishops according to their functions ordained the priests, the deacons, the subdeacons, the lectors and the cantors. Thus everywhere in the majority of the Armenian churches they were harmoniously placed for the glory of God.[56]

That theme is central for Yovhannēs V. He says in the same way speaking about Sahak:

They placed with him (Nersēs) on the throne Sahak, of the race of Albianos, an estimable man adorned with apostolic and religious qualities. He was not sent, according to previous tradition, to Caesarea, but putting aside the previous law, they ordained him according to the law of the patriarchs who receive their mission from the episcopal assembly, as it is in Antioch, Alexandria, Rome, Ephesus, Constantinople and Jerusalem, so that the autonomous patriarchate could not fall into the hands

172 MEDIEVAL ARMENIAN CULTURE

of foreigners.[57]

The role of Saint Bartholomew in the history of Yovhannēs VI Catholicos is quite central. The presence of one of the Twelve and note merely one of the seventy—that is, Thaddeus—is required for a theology of ecclesiastical hierarchy in the east. That theory, replaced by Yovhannēs V under the patriarch Nersēs the Great, serves as a justification of Armenian autonomy under Sahak's Patriarchate. According to that view, Yovhannēs modifies the translation made by Constans in 356, which in reality concerned Timothy and not John the Evangelist whose body was never found.[58] But he needed a precedent of acquiring the rank of patriarchate through the translation of the relics of one of the Twelve.

Was it, however, Yovhannēs V himself who first elaborated the whole theory? There is strong evidence that he is transmitting older reports and if we wish to discover at what time Bartholomew first figured in on Armenian legend implying that he died in Armenia itself, ancient testimonies must be sought. In fact the theory of the nine hierarchical orders can be traced to the beginning of the seventh century.

The argument concerning the four patriarchates and the nine orders of the church is set forth by Step'anos Ōrbelian (+1305) who quotes the three sources he uses. That is the History of the Caucasian Albanians by Movsēs Dasxuranc'i (tenth century), the History of the Secession of the Iberians by Uxtanēs of Edessa (tenth century), and the Epistle by the Catholicos Maštoc' (+896), Yovhannēs's predecessor. Those three sources are available, and the most complete is that of Maštoc', the spiritual master of Yovhannēs V. The letter of Maštoc' is an answer to a consultation of the Catholicos Gēorg (876-897) on the ecclesiastical rank of the primacy of Siwnik.[59] The demonstration of the association of the four patriarchates with the evangelists is found at the same time in the letter of Patriarch Photius to the Catholicos Zak'arias (+875).[60]

Even if we do not know the real author of that letter, it explains the point of view of the Greeks, and it is noteworthy that it does not mention Bartholomew together with Thaddeus in the title of the address. The canons of Sirakavan which are appended to the letter of Photius testify that the Greeks did not succeed in persuading the Armenians. This is a good indication that the discussions are taking place between 862 and 875. On the other hand, the patriarch Ignatius of Constantinople, the adversary of Photius, makes use of the theory of the four evangelists in the presence of the Roman apocrisiars. Yovhannēs V did not originate the apostolic claim of Constantinople, even if he adds the translation of the relics of John of Ephesus.

The controversy with the Byzantines was even older. Both Movsēs Dasxuranc'i and the letter of Maštoc' used a document which unfortunately has disappeared: the letter addressed by Solomon Mak'enoc'ac'i circa 735 to the future patriarch Salomon (+791).[61] That document was based on the discussions which set the Greeks and Yovhannēs Mayragomec'i in opposition at the Council of Karin in 632 under Esdras's Catholicossate. More than the Council of Chalcedon, as Nersēs Akinian wrote back in 1910, the constitution of the hierarchical church was the center of the discussion, already in the time of Catholicos Abraham in 610.[62] Uxtanēs also underlines the apostolic pretention upon which the Greeks founded their theories at the time of Maurice. It is at that moment, he says, that the Albanians began to claim that their land was converted by the apostle Eliseus, disciple of James of Jerusalem.[63]

If, before Yovhannēs Catholicos, there is no attempt to send the apostle Bartholomew to east Armenia, this is due to the fact that, on the Chalcedonian side, the apostle Bartholomew was already the symbol of a well-established and very old tradition, as we can read in the Narratio de Rebus Armeniae. The relics of Bartholomew were well-known to Anastasius when he built the church of Saint Bartholomew in Dara, where the relics were preserved until the catastrophe of 573. Note that some time after Kiwrion, it is a bishop named Bartholomew who is the head of the Iberian Chalcedonian Church.

This is the general context in which the appearance of the four Armenian legends of Bartholomew can be explained. The old Armenian Passion with the translation by Marutha are inserted in the Tonakan of Muš, the great parchment Ms. Matenadaran 7729.[64] After a long analysis of the whole repertoire of that prestigious collection, I think it very probable that Sołomon Mak'enoc'ac'i introduced the two pieces into his collection, dated 747, accoording to the original title, which was recopied in 1200.

We suggest that on the east facade of the church of Ałt'amar the apostle pictured facing Elias, is not Thomas as was proposed by Sirarpie Der Nersessian, but Bartholomew.[65] The equation of the east facade has to be read in the following scheme: John the Baptist is to Gregory Illuminator what Elias is to Bartholomew for the founding of the Armenian church.

NOTES

[1]For different realizations of that place name, see M. van Esbroeck, "Chronique Armenienne," Analecta Bollandiana, 80(1962) 425-428.

[2]K. Č'erakian, Ankanon girk' arak-elakank' (Venice, 1904) 358-364.

[3]J. M. Thierry, "Monastères arméniens du Vaspourakan III," REArm 6(1969) 162-180; Date proposed on pp. 178-179.

[4]Edited by Č'erakian, Ankanon Girk' 333-357. That text will be referred to as the Armenian Passion of Bartholomew.

[5]P'awstos Biwzandac'i, Patmut'iwn Hayoc', (Tiflis, 1912) 9-10.

[6]Movsēs Xorenac'i, Patmut'iwn Hayoc' (ed. M. Abełian and S. Yarut'iwnian, Tiflis, 1913) II. 38 (p. 158); Cf. R. W. Thomson, Moses Khorenats'i. History of the Armenians (Harvard Armenian Texts and Studies 4; Cambridge: Harvard, 1978) 174-176.

[7]B. de Gaiffier, "Le 'Breviarium apostolorum,'" Analecta Bollandiana, 81(1963) 105.   Th. Schermann, Prophetarum Vitae fabulosae, Leipzig (1907) 211.

[8]Th. Schermann, Prophetarum, 210-211.

[9]Ibid., 166.

[10]Ibid., 172.

[11]Cf. Patrologia Graeca 120, col. 221.

[12]Step'anos Asołik, Patmut'iwn Tiezerakan (ed. S. Malxaseanc'; St. Petersburg, 1885) 46.

[13]Zenob Glak, Patmut'iwn Tarōnay, (Venice, 1889) 302.

[14]Girk' Tłt'oc', Tiflis 1901, 302.

[15]Srboyn Hōrn Meroy Movsēsi Xorenac'woy Matenagrut'iwnk' (Venice, S. Lazzaro, 1865) 282-296.

[16]G. Garitte, La narratio de rebus Armeniae (Louvain, 1952) 382-395.

[17]Cf. M. Bonnet, Acta Apostolorum Apocrypha, 2.1 (Leipzig, 1898) 128-150.   The Greek text is a translation from the Latin model.   For the unpublished Greek legend, see J. Noret, "Manuscripts grecs à Weimar," Analecta Bollandiana, 87(1969) 82, n. 12.   The unpublished Armenian Parthian

legend is to be found in the codex Matenadaran 7853 (1366), ff. 374v-380r. I hope to publish soon the entire dossier of Bartholomew.

[18]Step'anos Ōrbelian, Patmut'iwn Nahangi Sisakan (Tiflis, 1911).

[19]W. Hoffman, "Polemon II," Pauly's Realencyclopadie, (Stuttgart, 1952), 22.2, col. 1285-1287.

[20]J. van Ootegham, Pompée le Grand: bâtisseur d'Empire, (Bruxelles, 1954), 209.

[21]J. Sturm, "Nikopolis" Pauly's Realencyclopädie (Stuttgart, 1936), sv. col. 536. For the Greek legend, see F. Halkin, Bibliotheca Hagiographica Graeca, Bruxelles, 1957, s.v.

[22]R. Grousset, Histoire d'Arménie, (Paris, 1947) 87-89.

[23]Sturm, "Nikopolis," col. 536.

[24]R. Grousset, Histoire, 107.

[25]On the Latin names of the Parthian Passion see von Gutschmid, Kleine Schriften (Leipzig, 1891) 2.351-52, who also recognized some persons as Polemon II of Pontus and Zenon Artaxias, and also some local divinities.

[26]R. Grousset, Histoire, 111.

[27]Ibid.

[28]O. Seeck, Notita dignitatum (Berlin, 1876) 248.

[29]Epiphanius of Cyprus, Panarion 75, 1, 5 (ed. K. Holl; Leipzig, 1933) 333; Ammianus Marcellinus, Rerum gestarum libri, 19, 8, 12, and 20, 11, 4.

[30]Codex Iustinianus recognovit P. Krueger (Berlin, 1912) 11, 48, p. 441.

[31]E. Kuhn, Die städtische und burgerliche Verfassung des Römischen Reichs bis auf die Zeiten Justinians, (Leipzig, 1865) 2.243-50.

[32]E. Hönigmann, Le Synekdemos d'Hierokles (Bruxelles, 1939), 37.

[33]Codex Iustinianus 1, 5. Cf. K. Güterbock, Römische Armenien und Römische Satrapien, (Königsberg, 1900) 40-51.

[34]Justinian, novelle 31 (ed. Z. Lingenthal; Leipzig, 1881) 277.

[35]Hardouin, Acta conciliorum et epistolae decretales 3(1714) col. 204,

1392 and 1434.

[36]Ibid., col. 1705.

[37]R. Rubin, "Prokopeios von Kaisareia," in Pauly's Realencyclopedie, (Stuttgart, 1957), 23.1 col. 574.

[38]G. Garitte, Le calendrier palestino georgien du Sinaiticus 34, (Brussels, 1958) 77 for July 10.

[39]J. Markwart, Untersuchungen zur Geschichte von Eran, Leipzig 1905, p. 232-235. R. Lipsius, Die apokryphen Apostelgeschichten, (Braunschweig, 1884). 2.2 p. 100.

[40]Procopius of Caesarea, De Aedificiis (ed. J. Haury; Leipzig, 1913) 2, 1, 5 on p. 46. This probably is a condition derived from Theodosius I, not from Theodosius II. For the conditions 422, cf. E. Stein, Histoire du Bas-Empire, (Bruges: Desclée de Brouwer, 1959) 1.281 and notes on p. 564. The war took place at Nisibis and Theodosiopolis to the North, because there were no other fortifications. However, B. Rubin, Das Zeitalter Justinians (Berlin, 1966) 256-257, appears to attribute this condition to Theodosius II in view of the peace of 442.

[41]The text is traced back to John Diakrinomenos in the most recent edition, Theodorus Anagnostes. Kirchengeschichte (ed. G. Ch. Hansen; Berlin, 1971) 157, 9-11.

[42]Procopius of Caesarea, De Aedificiis, 2, 3, 4, on pp. 53-54, and 2, 3, 26.

[43]see Bibliotheca Hagiographica Orientalis 159, for the translation of the relics by Marutha.

[44]Michael the Syrian, Chronique (ed. J. B. Chabot; Paris, 1901) 2. 312.

[45]John of Ephesus, Histoire Ecclesiastique (ed. E. W. Brooks; Louvain, 1936) 3, 6, 6 on pp. 221-222; [text (Paris, 1935) 292-293]. Also Chronica minora (ed. I. Guidi; (Paris, 1903) p. 42 = text p. 145.

[46]Gregory of Tours, Historia Francorum (ed. W. Arendt, Monumenta Germaniae Historica; Hannover, 1885) 4, 4 on p. 174.

[47]Theophylacte Simocatta, Historiae (ed. De Boor; Lipsiae, 1887) 143.

[48]Gregorius I Papa, Registrum epistolarum (ed. P. Ewald and L.

Hartmann; Berlin, 1891) 3, 53 on p. 210 and letter II, 19; p. 116 and II, 51.

[49] Patmut'iwn Yovhannu Kat'ołikosi (Jerusalem, 1867) "Introduction," p. 8.

[50] Movsēs Xorenac'i, 1.14 (Abełian p. 47).

[51] Yovhannu Patmut'iwn, 24. [Trans. M. J. Saint-Martin; Paris, 1841 p. 12].

[52] Ibid., p. 88-89 [Saint-Martin, p. 57-58.]

[53] M. van Esbroeck, "Un nouveau témoin de l'Agathange," REArm, (1971) 152-153.

[54] Yovhannu Patmut'iwn, p. 51 [Saint-Martin, p. 32.]

[55] This detail is obviously wrong since Constans did not find the body of John the Evangelist.   However, the removal of Timothy's body from Ephesus as well as those of Andrew—one of the twelve—and of Luke the evangelist, made it difficult to desire to follow in the footsteps of Ephesus. Yovhannēs pleaded his own case by making the translation of John the basis of the Patriarchate of Constantinople. He proceeded no differently in the case of the translation of Bartholomew whose original existence (on the Western border) he did not deny.

[56] Yovhannu Patmut'iwn, 61-63 [Saint-Martin, 39-40.]

[57] Ibid, 67-68 [Saint-Martin, 43].

[58] U. H. Delehaye, Melanges d'hagiographie grecque et latine (Bruxelles, 1966) 407-13.

[59] Step'anos Ōrbelian, Histoire de la Siounie, (ed. M. Brosset; St. Petersburg, 1864) Ch. 25 on pp. 62-63 and Ch. 27 on p. 69. In Movsēs Dasxuranc'i, Ch. 48; Giulxandanian, "Toułt' eraneloyn Maštoc'i, Ararat 35 (1902) 748-749.

[60] Girk Tłtoc' (Tiflis, 1901) 279-281.

[61] M. van Esbroeck, "Salomon de Makhenots: vardapet of the eighth century," Armeniaca. Melanges d'Etudes Arméniennes (Venice, 1969) 40-41.

[62] N. Akinian, Kiwrion Kat'ołikos Vrac' (Vienna, 1910) 254.

[63] Ukhtanes d'Edesse, in Deux historiens arméniens [Translated by M. Brosset; St. Petersburg, 1871] 343.

[64]The structure of that manuscript was the subject of a paper delivered at the Conference on Linguistics in Yerevan in September 1982, to appear in the Acts of that Congress.

[65]S. Der Nersessian, Aght'amar: Church of the Holy Cross, (Cambridge, Mass., 1965) 16 and Plate 33.   It is possible that the apostle is not named so as to satisfy the ambivalence of Thomas-Bartholomew.

THE MOTIF OF THE BIRD IN ARMENIAN EPIC LITERATURE
AND ITS RELATIONS WITH IRANIAN TRADITION

Francine Mawet

Université Libre de Bruxelles (Belgium)

Traditionally Arm. hawat(k') 'faith, believe' is related to the word for bird Arm. haw, Lat. avis, Umbr. auif, auef 'bird, presage,' Ved., Av. vi-, Gr. οἰωνός, αἰετός 'eagle, presage.'[1] The semantic development from 'bird, presage' to 'faith believe' which is implicit in this etymology rests on a mythic representation, attested in Greek, Latin, Indian and especially Avestan traditions. The bird (always a big and lonely bird: an eagle or falcon) is the intermediary between men and gods in the process of reciprocity, of do ut des, which is established between them, the god being pledged to a gift (fides) in return for the prayers or the offerings of the faithful. This divine favor may consist of material richness, welfare, moral protection, superiority or ardor in war.[2] A few examples of this motif are attested in the remnants of Armenian epic, principally in the fragments given by Movsēs Xorenac'i.[3] But this motif seems to have lost its specific mythic character, inherited from Indo-European, and appears to be only a vestige of a legend. We intend to show how this bird-motif evolved in Iran up to the Middle-Iranian period and how this reshuffled version from Pahlavi literature seems to have been borrowed into Armenian literature.

In the Avesta, the bird (or any part of the bird) has the power of giving the faithful xvar nah, divine favor (yana), strength and superiority before enemies as well as material wealth and health. This is amply attested in the passage of the Avesta[4] in which the xvarənah of Yima escapes in the form of a bird vārəɣna 'falcon,' when Yima commits the sin of lying. The warlike god Vərəθraɣna himself either appears personified in the form

T. Samuelian & M. Stone, eds. Medieval Armenian Culture. (University of Pennsylvania Armenian Texts and Studies 6). Chico, CA: Scholars Press, 1983. pp. 179 to 193.

a bird vārəγna[5] or is compared with saēna 'the eagle' when he surrounds the faithful's house with xvarənah and wealth of cows (gaosurābiiō).[6]   The karšipta bird ('the falcon'?) propagates Mazdaism on the Yima's var.[7] It is in the shape of a bird that the frauuašis honored by the righteous help him.[8] Finally, the tree of the eagle (saēna) grants remedies (ərəδβō.bīš 'having highest remedies,' vispō.biš 'having all remedies').[9]

In each of these examples we have a very accurate and coherent representation of the bird acting as an intermediary in the relations between men and gods and not merely as a miraculous appearance. Although Old-Iranian the shape of the bird is only the external appearance under which the xvarənah comes to light, this association of the xvarənah with the bird is an important point in the further evolution of this motif, as we shall see. Perhaps it is not out of place to mention again the debate about the significance of xvarənah in Avestan.   One passage of the Avesta[10] in particular enables us to give a more accurate definition of it.[11] In that passage xvarənah is closely linked to the notion of both wealth and light; it manifests itself thanks to the light of the sun; indeed when the sun warms up, the divinities gather together the xvarənah in order to distribue it on earth. On the other hand, it is itself the basis of wealth. Thus in Old-Iranian there are two distinct notions which join together in some contexts and which directly depend on religious concepts: the bird, in the mutual relations between gods and the faithful, is one of the shapes under which xvarənah appears;   xvarənah is itself one of the manifestations of divine goodwill: It is closely connected to light, and it secures the welfare of the righteous (ašahe gaēeā). As we shall see, this connection develops markedly during the Middle-Iranian period, the bird being merely a miraculous sign and xvarənah becoming the 'royal glory,' i.e. the mark of sovereignty.   Failure to distinguish clearly between the various chronological stages in the use of this term account for the confusion.

ARMENIAN CONTEXT

Before going on with the examination of Middle-Iranian data, let us have a look at the Armenian records which we shall be able to examine further in the light of Pahlavi tradition.

What remains of the Armenian epic is but a fraction of what it must have been. Many explanations may be put forward for its near disappearance.

First among them is the importance of Christian literature. But the Armenian authors' fastidiousness toward the fabulous pagan motifs certainly took its toll. The apparent concern for verisimilitude that Movses Xorenac'i expressed, often with considerable insistence, is an example of this attitude:

> k'anzi antełi ē mez ayžm erkrordel zaṙaspelsn yałags erazoyn p'ap'agoy . . . ayl mek' asasc'uk' miayn zstoygn, or inč' čšmartut'eann vayelē patmut'iwn 'As it is not advisable for us now to repeat the fables about P'ap'ag's dream' . . . but we shall only tell the truth, all that belongs to the true history.'[12]

Child protected by a bird:

The first and most important type of context, is one in which a child is protected and saved by a bird.

About Artašēs' birth:

> na ew aycin diec'umn mankann ěnd hovaneaw arcuoyn, ew gušakumn agṙawun, ew gerapancin pahpanut'iwn aṙiwcun handerj arbanekut'eamb gaylun 'and this, the goat's suckling of the child under the protection of the eagle and the presage of the crow and the warding of the illustrious lion with the service of the wolf.'[13]

The motif of an animal's suckling of a child belongs to I.-E. legends (Romulus and Remus suckled by the she-wolf).[14] As for the wondrous reference to the eagle protecting the baby, it is, as we shall see, probably the distortion of a properly Iranian myth.

Some pseudo-etymological explanations are given to the names of various of Vałaršak's officers. So the Arcruni are those who carry the eagles before Vałaršak (*arciw-uni).[15]   In connection with this etymology a reference is made to fables published at Hadamakert. One of those is the following:

> mankan nirheloy anjrew ew arew hakaṙakeal ew hovani t'ṙč'noy patanwoyn t'alkac'eloy 'the rain and the sun were tormenting a sleeping boy. The protection of the youth fallen down in a faint was assumed by the bird.'[16]

Although less obvious, another passage can be explained in the same way as the previous ones. The name of Sanatruk is decomposed by Movsēs Xorenac'i into Sanot, the name of a nurse, and turk' "gift."[17] On this etymology, it is related that during a journey in winter in Armenia, Abgar's sister, Awte, was caught in a snow-storm. The prince's nurse saved the child, keeping him on her breast under the snow for three days and three nights and a marvelous animal protected the child. About this animal, Movsēs Xorenac'i says:

> zormē aṫaspelabanen, et'ē kendani imn norahraš spitak yas-
> tuacoc'n aṫak'eal pahēr zmanukn. bayc' orc'ap' eḷak' verahasu,
> ayspēs ē: šun spitak ĕnd xndraksn leal, pataheac' mankann ew
> dayekin. 'about him (Sanatruk) they tell the following fable: a
> marvelous white animal, sent by the gods, protected the child,
> but as far as we have understood, it happened like this: a white
> dog, among those who were searching for the child and the
> nurse, discovered both of them.'[18]

The last sentence, as it seems to us, is only a rationalization of the miraculous phenomenon which has been previously told.   Indeed, the marvelous, white (spitak) animal would be a bird. Spitak, as it is known, has been borrowed from Iranian: M.-Ir. spētak, spēt, from a root indicating the brilliant whiteness, the light.[19] Let us remember that the I.-Ir. name of the 'eagle,' Skr. ṛjipya-, Av. ərəzifiia-, O.-P. *ardufya- or *ṛdufya-[20] is connected with a root meaning 'brilliant, white' and 'swift' together (Gr. ἀργικέραυνος   'with bright lightning,'   ἀργίποδας κύνας 'swift dogs,' HSCH. ἀργός·   λευκός, ταχύς   Av. ərəzifiiō.parəna-, Skr. ṛjra- 'swift, brilliant,' epithet of an arrow, probably involving a comparison between the swiftness of the arrow and that of the eagle).[21] Arm. spitak could thus evoke a big bird, an eagle, without naming it, by the combination of the swiftness of its flight and the sparkling whiteness of its feathers.   The terms yastuacoc'n arak'eal 'sent by the gods' also evoke the formula of the passages already examined in the Avesta, although the reference to divine intervention here is cautious and oblique.

Dreams:

The second type of context involves dreams. In Movsēs Xorenac'i, the Median Aždahak (Astyage) saw, in a dream, a woman giving birth to three heroes in Armenia.   The first one, mounted on a lion, was dashing to the west, the second one, on a leopard, to the north; and the third one, on a dragon, was rushing upon the Median empire.   Suddenly the last dashed upwards on wings, fighting fiercely against Aždahak.   This dream portends that the ruin of the Median empire will come from the country of the

Armenian Tigran:

> ew yankarc i ver nayec'eal zayn or i veray višapin heceal kayr,
> arcuanman slac'eal t'ewawk' tesi yarjakeal, or mawt haseal
> xohēr korcanel zdisn. isk es ašdahak xtroc ĕnd mēỹ ankeal, ew
> yis zaynpisi ełeal yarjakumn ĕnkalay, mart ĕnd sk'anč'elwoyn
> arnelov diwc'azann 'and suddenly I looked up to this one who
> went mounted on the dragon and who was flying with the wings
> of an eagle, and I saw him attacking and getting nearer,
> intending to throw the gods to the ground. But I myself,
> Ašdahak, in interposing, received such an attack upon myself
> and had to fight against the prodigious hero.'[22]

In both types of context, the bird has nothing in common with the mythic representation already seen in many I.-E. traditions. It is merely the mark, the external sign of a miraculous event, belonging to the realm of legend; moreover, the religious significance, in particular the notion of reciprocity in the intercourse of devotion, is completely missing in those contexts. Now a similar development can be observed, in Iran, particularly from the Sasanian period on, and the parallelism of evolution can most probably be explained either as an Armenian loan from Middle-Iranian traditions or as their continuation through Armenian culture.

Parallels to this motif are found in Middle-Iranian literature. The theme of the child protected by a bird (always royal children as in Armenian tradition), is used by Aelianus, the Greek author of the second and third centuries AD, who relates to us a legend concerning Achaimenes

> Ἀχαιμένη ⟨γε⟩ μὴν τὸν Πέρσην, ἀφ' οὖ καὶ κάτεισιν ἡ
> τῶν Περσῶν εὐγένεια ἀετοῦ τρόφιμον ἀκούω γενέσθαι

'The Persian Achaimenes, to whom the Persian aristocracy goes back, was, as I understand, brought up by an eagle.'[23]

An identical theme is found in the Šah-Nāmeh,[24] when Zāl, abandoned by his father Sam, was carried away to the mountain where the mythic bird, Simūrγ roosted, and was brought up by it. It is also thanks to Simūrγ that Roubabe gave birth to her very strong child, Rostam.[25]

Although no trace of child-protector motif has been found in the parts of the Avesta which have reached us, this passage from Aelianus provides evidence of an ancient association of this theme with Achaimenes.

The motif of the bird attending a princely birth, belongs to what G.

Widengren called the royal legend of Iran.[26]   The set of circumstances surrounding the king's birth and childhood are the sign of his peculiar character: light, presages and miraculous visions occurring at his birth, his education among animals and shephards and the revelation of his royal descent thanks to the nobleness of his behavior, and so on. This tradition persisted in Iran, from antiquity, with Zaraӫuštra's legend, the Zarā-tuštnāmak, and the Pahlavi Zand i Vahman Yašt, which itself arises from the lost Avestan Vahman Yašt,[27] up to the Šāh-Nāmeh, through such Middle-Iranian works as the Kārnāmak i Artašir i Pāpākān and similar Armenian traditions. The persistence of Old-Iranian myths even up to Islamic times has been pointed out by A. Christensen

This theme ought certainly to be related to the illustrious births and nursing of children by animals common in Indo-European mythology. It seems to us that the references to an eagle (or another big bird), have a special origin in Iranian tradition. As we have seen, the eagle is one of the Iranian representations of xvarǝnah, which itself seems to have a particular affinity with the first function, the royal and sovereign one. In spite of Yima's myth in which his xvarǝnah was recovered by representatives of the three functions, Miӫra, Ӫraetaona and Kǝrǝsāspa, successively. It was Miӫra, who first recovered the xvarǝnah. Moreover, the fire farnbāg (or Ātur Xvarr) belongs to the priests. In the interpretation of Papak's dream, Ātur farnbāg is the great men's religious knowledge: u ātur farnbāγ dēn dānātīk i mas martān i moγ-martān u ātur gušnasp artēštar u spāhpatān u ātur burzīn mihr vāstryōšān u varz-kartārān i gēhān 'and the fire farnbāg is the science of the higher men and the magi, and the fire gušnasp is the warrior and the army-chief, and the fire burzīn mihr is the peasants and the cultivators of the world.'[28]

A clear confirmation of the close connections among xvarǝnah, the eagle and the royal being in Middle-Iranian literature is given in the Dēnkart's[29] account of Zaraӫuštra's creation. Zaraӫuštra was created thanks to Vahuman and Asvahišt's Hōm which was set down in the nest of two birds and was gathered by Purušāsp, Zaraӫustra's father. Besides the relation between the preacher and the birds, we find here once again the Avestan connection between birds and haoma. For instance:

10 aruuaṇtǝm ӫβā dāmišātǝm baγō nidaӫaṯ huuāpā haraiӫiio paiti barǝzaiiā̊

11 āaṯ ӫβā aӫra spǝnta fradaxšta mǝrǝγa vīžuuaṇca vībarǝn auui

škata upāiri. saēna. . .

'Thou valiant, wise, a god well-doing set you down (haoma) on
the height of haraiti and from there, beneficient learned birds,
flying over and over, brought you on the škata upāiri. saēna (=
which is over the eagle').[30]

In the Dēnkart the story follows thus:[31]

ō hān i ōyšān mānišn apar šūt hend vahuman ašvahišt u hān
murv hampursīt hend kū: franāmišn amāh hač-mān hān hōm
xvādišn

'Vahuman and Ašvahišt came down in their nest and said to the
birds: We are ordered to go and ask this hom.'[32]

The hōm passed from Purušāsp and his wife's bodies to Zaraθustra's. While
drinking hōm with milk, the parents created Zaraθustra, who was formed from
the union of his xvarrah, his fravahr and his substance.[33]

So the eagle, the sign of the xvarənah and of the royal person of the
king or the preacher, would also be the mark of his special place in the first
function.   The ancient association between the shape of the bird and the
royal person gives proof in itself for the origin of this theme of royal birth
under the protection of the bird.[34] It should be noted that, according to this
hypothesis, the rescue of Yima's xvarənah by representatives of the three
functions would agree with the first function and the two others riding one
on top of the other, just as in Miθra's complex character.

Miraculous appearances of birds are also able to save kings.   The
Kārnāmak i Artašir i Pāpākān[35] tells us Artašir's story who was nearly
poisoned by his wife, Ardavan's daughter.   Just when Artašir grasps the
poisoned cup, the fire farnbāg, appearing in the form of an eagle, casts it
away and saves the king.

Taxmoruv descends from the Avestan hero, Taxma Urupi, who during
his 30 years reign subdued devils and men and mounted Aŋra Mainiiu changed
into a horse.[36]   In Mīrxond,[37] a Persian author from the fifteenth century,
Taxmōruv was taken away by the fabulous bird Simūrγ to the land of the
devils, to the Činnistān, and received a few feathers of the bird for
protection. This protecting function of the feathers of the bird goes back to
the Avestan period.[38] In the Šāh-Nāmeh, when Kavous intended to conquer
the sky, he rose up to the skies on a throne carried by four eagles.[39] A more
or less identical representation is to be found in St. Gregory's vision,[40] in the
shape of the big and awful man who flies down from the sky as an eagle:[41]

ew mi ahawor tesil mardoy barjr ew aheł, or zaṙajn unēr ew
zējsn i verust minč'ew i xonarh aṙajapah yaṙajeal . . ew ink'n
slac'sal xoyac'eal gayr ĕst nmanut'ean aragat'ew arcuoy

'and there was the frightful vision of a big and dreadful man
who goes on ahead and comes down from upon to below, leading
the advanced guard . . . and himself flying away, whipping off,
was coming alike to a fleet-winged eagle.'

It is Simūṙ which tends Rostam and his mount Raxš after the duel between
Esfandiyār and Rostam.[42]   The healing function of the bird is already
attested, as we saw, in the Avesta.[43]   Finally we ought to remember that,
following the Bundahišn,[44] the eagle was the first created bird, which shows
the mythic importance ascribed to this bird.   A reshuffled version of this
tradition appears in Eznik's De Deo.[45]   It is told that Ahriman, not wishing
to create a good being, created the peacock:

ard zinč' paycaṙagoyn k'an zloys kayc'ē orum Arhmnn hnaragiwt
elew, kam zinč' gełec'kagoyn k'an zsiramarg zor aṙ i c'uc'-
aneloy zgełec'kagorcut'iwnn arar.

'But what can be more shining than light, of which Ahriman was
inventor, or what more beautiful than the peacock, which he
made in order to demonstrate his ability to create beautiful
things?'[46]

There is thus a noteworthy continuity, within the Iranian tradition
beginning in Avestan times, concerning the representation of the bird.
Nevertheless, the function of this representation has completely changed in
Pahlavi texts: the religious context, with reference to a divinity, the notions
of reciprocity and pledging in the intercourse of men and gods have
completely vanished.   The bird has lost its mythic function, but remains
nonetheless merely a miraculous sign.   Accordingly, there was a shift from
myth to legend.   This same evolution is just what is involved in the
transformation of the royal legend, as described by A. Christensen.[47]   A new
stage takes form in the legendary history of Iran from Sasanian times on.   A
national tradition takes shape beside the religious one.   It is a national
tradition in which eschatalogical notions and certain religious legends have
faded.   The myths, for instance, are rationalized in comparison with the
Avestan našks.   This transformation might have taken place beginning with
the great royal chronicle, the Xvaδyāynāmaγ, the source of the Šāh-Nāmeh.
Now, as can be seen, the Armenian examples of this theme agree with this

miraculous, extraordinary vision of the bird, typical of Middle-Iranian texts.

In the beginning of this paper, we emphasized the relation between the Avestan notion of xvarənah and light. Now, the representation of light in Armenian and Middle-Iranian, according to a recent study of A. Hultgård,[48] confirms our hypothesis of a thematic continuity from Middle-Iranian to Armenian. In Old-Iranian, there is a natural confluence between the notions of light and wealth. Moreover, light takes on, through its purifying value, an eschatological connotation in the designation of paradise (anaɣra raocå) and in the association of light with good and darkness with evil and the abode of the daēvas—an association which was transformed into doctrine in the course of the development of Madzaism. But nowhere in the Avesta do we observe the representation of light as the miraculous sign of a royal or divine revelation.[49] Even when the light is associated with the description of a divinity (Anāhitā, for instance),[50] it is always in connection with notions of wealth, health, youth or beauty, and indirectly to the notion of justice. In ancient Iran, Miθra is the only divine personage portrayed as luminous (huuā. raoxšnō 'having his own light')[51] and he is compared to the moon; the association of Miθra with the sun is, of course, later than the Avesta. In the later evolution of Iranian religion, the symbolism of light undergoes a special development, in cults such as that of Miθra. Fire itself became the symbol of the divinity.[52] The Armenian tradition transmits to us a whole symbolism of light which can be most exactly explained through pre-Christian traditions, which themselves have a direct parallel in Pahlavi texts, and show the deep influence of Middle-Iranian religion on pre-Christian Armenia and even later. According to A. Hultgård's analysis,[53] notwithstanding its Christian context, the picture of fire or light in St. Gregory's vision displays close connections with the Iranian symbolism of light related to birth or advent of a divine personage or messenger (Miθra, Zaraθuštra), of a saviour (Saošiiant), or a king. Some connections can even be dated exactly to Sasanian times, thanks to the testimony of archeology among other things (for instance, the Sasanian fire altars correspond to the description of fire-columns in Agat'angełos).[54]

In our opinion, the motif of the bird in the remnants of Armenian epic literature seems thus to be an accurate testimony of the continuity of literary and religious tradition, from Pahlavi to Armenian, even after the coming of Christianity to Armenia.

NOTES

[1]A. Meillet, "Notes sur la declinaison arménienne," MSL 8 (1892) 165 (= Etudes de linguistique et de philologie arméniennes [ed. M. Mokri; Bibliothèque Arménienne de la Fondation Calouste Gulbenkian; Lisbonne, Louvain, 1977] 2. 20); H. Hübschmann, Armenische grammatik (2 ed.; Hildesheim, 1962 Leipzig, 1897) 1. 465, no 236, 237; A. Ernout and A. Meillet, Dictionnaire étymologique de la langue latine (4th ed.; Paris: Klincksieck, 1959) 1. 58; P. Chantraine, Dictionnaire étymologique de la langue grecque. Histoire des mots (Paris: Klincksieck, 1974) 3. 789; R. Solta, Die Stellung der Armenischen im Kreise der indogermanischen Sprachen (Vienna, 1960) 173; J. Pokorny, Indogermanisches etymologisches Wörterbuch (Bern, Munchen, 1959-1969) 1.86.

Another etymology has been proposed: the word for 'egg' ὠόν would be cognate with that for 'bird': H. Schmeja, "Die Verwandschaftnamen auf -ως und die Nomina auf -ωνός, -ωνή im Griechischen," IF 68 (1963) 34-36 and "Der Vogel—das eigenborene Wesen," Die Sprache 17 (1971), 180-182; J. Schindler, "Die idg. Wurter fur 'Vogel' und 'Ei'," Die Sprache 15 (1969) 144-167. Criticism in R. S. P. Beekes, "H₂O," Die Sprache, 18 (1972) 121, n. 5-6 (οἰωνός can be easily explained as a thematization of οἰών < *ₔouị-on-). See also Beekes, "The Nominative of the Hysterodynamic Noun Inflection," KZ, 86 (1972) 30-63.

[2]"Armenien hawat(k') 'foi, croyance'" in AIPHO (forthcoming).

[3]A survey in Step'anos Tarōnec'i Asołik and in Sebēos's Patmut'iwn Hayoc' did not provide any other example of this theme. The main remnants of the Armenian epic literature were gathered by F. Feydit, 'Cahiers de literature armenienne. 3, L'épopee populaire arménienne," Pazmavēb 115 (1957) 3-39. See also H. Grégoire, "Héros épiques Méconnus," AIPHO 2 (1934) 1:451-463.

[4]Yt. 19. 34-35.

[5]Yt. 14.19

[6]Yt. 14.41

[7]V. 2.42

[8]Yt. 13.70

[9]Yt. 12.17

[10]Yt. 6.1.

[11]F. Mawet, "'Light' in ancient Iranian" JIES 10 (1982) 3-4:283-299.

[12]Movses Xorenac'i (ed. LeVaillant de Florival; Venice, 1841), 2.70.

[13]Ibid.

[14]G. Widengren, Les religions de l'Iran (Transl. L. Jospin; Bibliotheque Historique; Collection Les religions de l'Humanite; Paris: Payot, 1968) 346.

[15]See R. W. Thomson's commentary in Moses Khorenats'i History of the Armenians (Harvard Armenian Texts and Studies, 4; Cambridge: Harvard University Press, 1980), 138, n. 10; Arcui, arcat' is probably directly borrowed from Iranian (Av. ərazifiia- and O.-P. *ṛdifya-): R. Schmitt, "Der 'Adler' im Alten Iran," Die Sprache, 16 (1970) 63-77; R. Schmitt, Dichtung und Dichtersprache in Indogermanischer Sprache (Wiesbaden: Harrassowitz, 1967) §537; M. Mayrhofer, Aus dem Namenwelt Alt-Irans. Die zentrale Rolle der Namenforschung in der Linguistik des Alt-Iranischen (Innsbrucker Beiträge zur Sprachwissenschaft, 3: Innsbruck, 1971) 6-7; Ch. De Lamberterrie, "Armeniaca I-VIII: Études lexicales," BSL 73 (1978) 1:251-262.

[16]Movsēs Xorenac'i, 2.7. Movsēs Xorenac'i found his narration about P'ap'ag on Xoṙohbut's Greek translation of the "History of the first (Kings)," the latter book being written by the so-called Barsum, or Ṙastsohun in Iranian. Barsauma is a frequent Syriac name in Sasanian times and there are many known Barsauma. Thomson (note 5, page 217) assumes that this Ṙastsohun-Barsuma might be Barsauma of Nisibis, the Nestorian bishop at the Council of Dvin. But the details of Barsauma of Nisibis' life do not fit in with Movsēs' story. The other Barsaumas, Barsauma the monophysite archimandrite (fifth century) and the bishop of Karkā de Laden (seventh century) do not seem to fit either. The important point is that this narration concerns an Iranian king and is typically Iranian. Thomson himself, in his introduction (pages 13-17) points out that the sources given by Movsēs are often not reliable and sometimes simply products of his imagination (for 2. 70, Movsēs probably founds his narration on Agat'angeḷos, cf. Thomson, Khorenats'i, 16). Moreover, it is not surprising that an Iranian tradition comes to an Armenian author through the Greek translation of a Syriac story. It is also plausible that, following the custom of the time, Barsauma is only the Syriac pseudonym of an Iranian character. In any case, the Persian origin of this fable seems obvious (see also Thomson, Khorenats'i, 16 about Movsēs Xorenac'i, 2. 70) and confirms our following conclusions.

F. Justi, Iranisches Namenbuch (Hildesheim, 1963) (= Marburg, 1895), 172-173, 258; I. Ortiz de Urbina, S.I., Patrologia Syriaca (Pont. Institutum Orientalium Studiorum, Roma, 1958), 110-111, 133, 187; P. Duval, Anciennes littératures chrétiennes, 2. La littérature syriaque (Bibliotèque de l'Enseignement de l'Histoire Ecclésiastique: Paris, 1899), 345-346, 352, 13-15. Professor J. Hadot kindly gave me bibliographical information about Syriac literature.

[17]This is of course merely a pseudo-etymology, cf. Justi, Iranisches Namenbuch, 282-283.

[18]Movsēs Xorenac'i, 2. 36.

[19]H. Ačaṙyan, Hayeren armatakan baṙaran, (Erevan, 1979) 4. 264-265; M. Mayrhofer, Kurzgefasstes etymologisches Wörterbuch des Altindischen (Indogermanische Bibliothek, 2. R.; Heidelberg: Carl Winter, 1976) 3. 406: Skr. śvetāḥ, Av. spaēta-, O.-Sl. svĕtŭ 'Licht.'

[20]See the discussion by R. Schmitt, "Der 'Adler,'" Die Sprache 16 (1970) 63-77 and Ch. De Lamberterrie, "Armeniaca I-VIII," BSL 73 (1978) 253-262.

[21]R. Schmitt, "Der 'Adler,'" Die Sprache, 16 (1970) 67, n. 22.

[22]Movsēs Xorenac'i 1.26.

[23]De Natura animalium, 12, 21.

[24]J. Mohl (Paris: Maisonneuve, 1976) (1838), 1, 31.

[25]Mohl, 1, 353.

[26]G. Widengren, "La legende royale de l'Iran antique," pp-pp, in Hommages à G. Dumézil (Collection Latomus, 45; Bruxelles, 1960) 225-237; Widengren, Les religions de l'Iran, 343-353.

[27]E. Benveniste, "Une apocalypse pehlevie: le Žāmāsp-Nāmak," RHR 106 (1932) 337-380; A. Christensen, Les gestes des rois dans les traditions de l'Iran antique (Paris, 1936) in particular 33-41, 107-140; Christensen, Les types du premier homme et du premier roi dans l'histoire légendaire des Iraniens (Stockholm, 1918, 1; Leiden, 1934, 2); A. Zajączowski, "La composition et la formation historique de l'épopée iranienne (le Šāh-Nāmeh de Firdausi)," La Poesia epica e la sua formazione (Academia Nazionale dei Lincei, 139; Rome, 1970) 679-690: M. Boyce in Handbuch der Orientalistik

(4 B. Iranistik, 2, Absch. Literatur, 1, Lief.:   Leiden, 1968), 57-60; E.
Benveniste, "Le texte du Draxt Asūrīk et la versification pehlevie," JA,
(1930) 193-225 and Benveniste, "Le mémorial de Zarēr.   Poème pehlevi
mazdéen," JA, (1932) 245-293.

Indeed, a popular Iranian epic literature must have existed since
ancient times, but no direct trace of it has reached us.   One reason for this
is that Old-Persian cuneiform was only used for official inscriptions.   This
Medo-Persian folk-literature must have been kept in Aramean script,
according to the general practice of that time, or orally, but in any case it
is attested by ancient Greek authors, as Xenophon (Cyropaedia, 1, 2, 1).
Moreover, there is, from the Avestan Yašts up to the Šāh-Nāmeh, a
homogeneity in the transmission of epic themes, which implies the existence
of Middle-Iranian epic.   In Sasanian times, as far as we know, there was a
royal chronicle, the Xvađyāynāmaγ 'The Book of Kings,' of which the Pahlavi
original and the Arabic versions are lost, but which survive in a summary in
various Arabic and Persian versions, ultimately leading to Firdausi's epic.
The Šāh-Nāmeh, as well as the Pahlavi Zamāsp Nāmak, undoubtedly have
close connections with the Zand i Vahman Yast, which is the summary of a
Pahlavi version of the lost Avestan Vahman Yast and, in spite of its recent
date, it must proceed from the same Avestan pattern.

[28]G. Widengren, Les religions de l'Iran, 301.   Widengren, "La légende
royale de l'Iran antique," 237, shows the close relation between the king and
the third function through his rustic education, the second one in his activity
as, for instance, a victorious fighter of the dragon.   However, Widengren
points out, the association of the king with the first function does not seem
to have received such a marked mythic expression.   The xvarənah and its
representation under the form of an eagle would thus fill this empty post.
Nevertheless, G. Widengren himself, Les religions de l'Iran, 123,
referring to K. Barr, Fs. Hammerich, 30-36, points out that the xvarənah is
related to the first function.   As mentioned above, in the legend of
Zaraθuštra's birth, it is said that his xvarənah his fravahr (frauuaṣ̌i) and his
gōhr i tan or tan gōhr (gavaθra) are put together to constitute his personality:
among these, the fravahr corresponds to the second function, the gōhr i tan
to the third one and the xvarr, naturally, to the first one.   About gōhr, see
H. W. Bailey, Zoroastrian Problems in the Ninth- Century Books (Ratanbai
Katrak Lectures; Oxford: Clarendon Press, 1971), 83; G. Gnoli, "Un
particolare aspetto del simbolismo della luce nel Mazdeismo e nel Mani-

cheismo," AION 12 (1962) n. 86.

[29]Dēnkart, 2, 24-34.

[30]Y. 10. 10111.

[31]Dēnkart, 7. 25.

[32]Dēnkart, 7. 24-34. M. Molé, La légende de Zoroastre selon les textes pehlevis (Travaux de l'Institut d'Etudes Iraniennes de l'Université de Paris, 3; Paris: Klincksieck, 1967).

[33]Dēnkart, 7. 47-52.

[34]M. Mokri, Le chasseur de Dieu et le mythe du Roi-Aigle (Dawra-y Dāmyārī) (Wiesbaden, 1967), 36, relates many traditions about the eagle. Among them, the custom of the bāz-paranī 'throwing of an eagle' when a king died without children, the people let a bird fly away and the person on the head of whom the bird settled three times was chosen to be the new king.

[35]A. Christensen, Les gestes des rois, 78-83.

[36]Yt. 19. 28-29.

[37]A. Christensen, Les types du premier homme, 1. 213-215.

[38]Yt. 14. 36, 38.

[39]Mohl, 2, 45.

[40]Agat'angełos, §735.

[41]A. Hultgård, "Change and Continuity in the Religion of Ancient Armenia with particular reference to the Vision of St. Gregory (Agathangelos §§731-755)", Classical Armenian Culture (ed. T. J. Samuelian; Univ. of PA Armenian Texts and Studies, 4; Chico, CA: Scholars Press, 1982) 15.

[42]Mohl, 4, 665.

[43]Yt. 12. 17.

[44]Bundahišn, 12.20.

[45]Eznik, De Deo (ed. L. Mariès; Patrologia Orientalis, 28. 3-4; Paris, 1959) 2, 8, §188.

[46]The etymology of siramarg is much disputed, but the second term of the compound certainly is the correspondent of Av. marəya, M.-Ir. mur : H. F. J. Junker, "Mittelpers. frašēmurv 'Pfau'," in Wörter und Sachen

(Heidelbergh, 1929) 150, §12; Hübschmann, Armenische Grammatik, 237, no. 576; E. Liden, Armenische Studien (Goteborg, 1966) 49-50; H. W. Bailey, "Iranian in Armenian," REArm 2 (1965) 1; M. Leroy, 'Les emprunts iraniens dans les composés nominaux de l'arménien classique' REArm (forthcoming).

[47]Christensen, Gestes des rois, 33-41; Christensen, Les types du premier homme, 2.54-55.

[48]Hultgård, "Change and Continuity."   The same conclusions are reached by J. Haudry for the Armenian epic, "La religion de la verité dans l'épopée armenienne," Etudes Indo-Européennes 2 (1982) 1-21, and more accurately by B. L. Tchukasizian, "Echos de légendes épiques iraniennes dans les 'Lettres' de Grigor Magistros," REArm 1 (1964) 321-329.

[49]F. Mawet, "'Light' in ancient Iranian," JIES 10 (1982).

[50]Yt. 5.64.

[51]Yt. 10. 142.

[52]G. Widengren, Les religions de l'Iran, 303.

[53]Agat'angełos, §§ 731-755.

[54]Agat'angełos, §735.

THE GREEK BACKGROUND OF SOME ARMENIAN PILGRIMS
TO THE SINAI AND SOME OTHER OBSERVATIONS

Michael E. Stone

Jerusalem and Philadelphia

I

The Armenian pilgrim graffiti from the Sinai Peninsula have cast light on various aspects of the history of pilgrimage in general and of Armenian pilgrimage in particular.[1] Since the publication of these inscriptions, a number more have come to light—one of unknown provenance and a few from A-Tor (ancient Raithou), as well as a further two-line Georgian inscription from a site near Jebel Ashka, in the eastern Sinai.[2] The purpose of the present paper, however, is not to publish these new inscriptions, nor to study the overall importance of the corpus. Instead, a specific problem will be addressed: what evidence can be culled from them about the non-Armenian, particularly Greek, elements in the cultural background of the pilgrims?

The first, striking fact to be considered is that all the inscriptions are in Armenian script, with nothing integral to them written in any other letters. It is possible, of course, that as the Greek graffiti of the Sinai are studied, it will turn out that some of them were written by Armenians, but nothing is known of this now.[3] Our evidence here, however, will be non-Armenian elements in the Armenian inscriptions.

The chief non-Armenian influence that can be detected is Greek, and the most striking witness to this is S Arm 9.[4] This inscription is situated on the rock over the Grotto of Moses, underneath the mosque on the peak of Mount Sinai.[5] The inscription cannot be dated precisely on paleographic grounds, and all that can be remarked here is that it is in uncial script that

T. Samuelian & M. Stone, eds. Medieval Armenian Culture. (University of Pennsylvania Armenian Texts and Studies 6). Chico, CA: Scholars Press, 1983. pp. 194 to 202.

would not be incompatible with an eleventh or twelfth century date, or perhaps slightly older. The text of the inscription is:

S(ŕ)ſ ՈՂՈՐ ՄՒՆՁ
Գ ՄՄԵՂԻ ԵՒ ԽՈՂՀ Է ԳՈՄԻ

"Lord have mercy
on the camel and on the guide."

In this inscription, the two words "camel" and "guide" are trans-literated from Greek.[6] The word for "camel" is <u>gamēli</u>. The first letter is almost completely destroyed, but it would be difficult to read the remaining signs as կ , which might be expected as a transliteration of Greek <u>kappa</u>.[7] Yet, the vowel ē corresponds to Greek <u>ēta</u>.   The Greek word is, of course, κάμηλος .   The Armenian seems likely to be derived from this Greek word rather than the Arabic <u>gamal</u>, both because of its vocalization and because of the next word.[8]   In any case, there is no case ending taken over from Greek and the Armenian oblique case is added directly onto the last stem consonant.

This is not the case with the second Greek word in this inscription. Armenian <u>xodēgosi</u> is an obvious transliteration of Greek ὁδηγός "guide," with the Greek case ending of the nominative to which, somewhat anomalously, the Armenian oblique case ending has been added. The <u>spiritus asper</u> of Greek is represented in Armenian by the guttural <u>x</u>. The shift from <u>h</u> to <u>x</u> occurs also in an Armenian word in H Arm 61. There the form <u>vanxayr</u> appears; it goes back to *<u>vanaxayr</u>, deriving from <u>vanahayr</u> 'abbot.'[9]

The content of the inscription is not paralleled in the other Armenian inscriptions from the Sinai but, nonetheless, it is not particularly surprising. The use of camels, sometimes together with donkeys, is well attested for pilgrims from the time of the Nessana papyri down to modern days.[10] What is striking is the use of two Greek words in Armenian transcription. These do not belong to that element of old Armenian vocabulary that was borrowed from Greek in ancient times.[11] Moreover, the transcriptions were probably made by someone well versed in Greek, for the ētas are faithfully represented in Armenian, in spite of the phonetic shifts that had taken place in Greek, which often led Greek scribes of the middle ages to itacism in spelling.

Some other instances of Greek influence on the Armenian inscriptions of the Sinai have been observed. H Arm 48 contains the name **ՒՈԱՆՆԷՍ [Ս]** 'Ioannēs[s].' This is, of course, a transliteration of the Greek Ιωάννης. The name has not been transliterated by the norms used in Classical Armenian, in which the consonantal iota is rendered by Armenian y- (which was presumably already pronounced [h] in initial position at the time the inscription was written). Nor is the omega transliterated ov as is the Classical Armenian convention. Observe, however, that ēta is transliterated ē. The normal Armenian form of this very common name is Yovhannēs, of which numerous variants exist. Among the Sinai inscriptions alone, the variants Yohan (H Arm 42, H Arm 44), Yohnik (H Arm 61), Yovannēs (H Arm 55) and Vanik (H Arm 64) are encountered. Ačaṙyan lists others in his Dictionary of Armenian Proper Names, s.v. But neither Ačaṙyan's Dictionary, nor any of the other sources consulted, listed the form Ioannēs.[12] The closest analogies known to me are some post-Classical transliterations of names mediated to Armenian through Greek or Latin.[13] The form Ioannēs in Armenian, therefore, was transliterated from Greek. Moreover, the person who did this actually called himself Ioannēs, the Greek form, and not Yovhannēs as in Armenian. Otherwise, why should he have written it?

In another of the Wadi Haggag inscriptions, H Arm 37, the name Menas appears. This is a variant of the quite common Armenian name Minas. In Greek, the older form of the name, which indeed gave rise to the ordinary Armenian, is Minas, but by the age of the Sinai inscriptions, the name was customarily written Menas in Greek. The form Menas is unparalleled in Armenian and its occurrence in H Arm 37 is probably the result of Greek influence. It does not seem likely just to be the result of inner-Armenian phonetic change.[14]

One final piece of evidence may be the name Adrinē. The name does not occur in any Armenian source that we have found, but it does occur in H Arm 70, a regular uncial writing deeply engraved on the rock. The name is not simply to be identified with any well-known Greek name, but the final long vowel, the ē which corresponds to ēta suggests that it is a woman's name probably derived from Greek.[15]

The implications of these facts should be explored a little. The use of the words 'camel' and 'guide' in Greek, when there are perfectly good Armenian words for them, is suggestive. The guides through the Sinai desert were usually Beduin or other Arabs. This is clear from an extensive range of sources from ancient, medieval and modern times. It is also a reasonable

Figure 1.   Wadi Haggag Inscription H Arm 71

Figure 2.   Mount Sinai S Arm 9

conclusion in view of the exigencies of desert travel and the special skills required safely to pilot pilgrim caravans through the wilderness. Thus it does not seem plausible to suggest that the author of the inscription annexed some local colouring by using Greek words, for they were probably not part of the local colouring.

What seems far more likely is that the inscription was written by a bilingual Armenian, a speaker of Armenian and Greek. This is also surely the case in the instance of Ioannēs. The person so recording himself must have come from a Greek-speaking environment. The same conclusion might have also fit the person who wrote his name Menas, and perhaps also the woman Adrinē. This fact, of course, still leaves a large range of chronological and geographical possibilities open, but if we take a date after 1000 C.E., the possibilities are somewhat reduced—the primary area involved would be the Byzantine realm. There is no point in documenting here the role of the Armenians in the Byzantine empire; it is well-known indeed. The Greek elements in the inscriptions, however, seem to imply that the pilgrims to the Sinai included Armenians from the Greek-speaking areas, and perhaps then some orthodox, pro-Chalcedonian Armenians.

II

Certain of the inscriptions indicate the route taken by the pilgrims. L Arm 3, in Wadi Leja which separates Jebel Musa (Mt. Sinai) from Jebel Katarina reads: tesa ēƚ, 'I have seen Jerusalem.' The form tesa is taken as an aorist active of tesanem.[16] Ēƚ is taken as an abbreviation of 'Jerusalem' which was the centre from which pilgrimage to the south set forth.

In the area of Jebel Musa (Mt. Sinai) inscriptions are to be found which were written by people who also left inscriptions elsewhere en route. Thus a certain Kaspar left his very distinctive signature carved on one of the panels of the right-hand valve of the Justinian door of St. Catherine's church (S Arm 28). The same Kaspar also left his signature in Wadi Mukatab, a number of days' travel to the west of St. Catherine's monastery, on one of the main thoroughfares frequented by travellers crossing the southern Sinai.

Other inscriptions, found on the peak of Mt. Sinai, were written by people who travelled by way of the eastern Sinai routes. These routes have come to the attention of researchers lately, chiefly as a result of the discovery of the Armenian inscriptions,[17] as well as of Nabatean, Greek and

other inscriptions in Wadi Haggag.[18] So Petros wrote his name on the rock
over the grotto on Mt. Sinai (S Arm 13) and on Rock III in Wadi Haggag (H
Arm 22). So also, at an earlier date, the person named Vasak inscribed S Arm
17 and H Arm 24.

Perhaps the most controversial of the inscriptions touching on the
route travelled is H Arm 71. The text of this inscription is:

ՄՈՒՍ /Հ ԱՆ ՊԱՏԱՑԻ

"I circumvented/Moses"

The material reading is quite beyond doubt, but my interpretation of
the inscription has been queried by as redoubtable authorities as Archbishop
Norayr Bogharian and Dr. O. Yeganian. Consequently, it is worthwhile to
review the matter once more. The chief difficulty in my interpretation is
that the word patac'i is taken as an aorist, 1 pers. sing. of a verb formed
from the stem pat- meaning 'to encircle, circumvent.' The usual aorist form
from this stem is patec'i, i.e. it is an -e- class verb. To accept my
interpretation we must posit an otherwise unattested -a- class derivation,
with -an- infix or without. This would be *patam/patanam which would
alternate with patem. There are a number of instances of this happening in
Armenian, so e.g. tenč'im/tenč'am, yamem/yamenam,[19] karem/karenam,
k'ahanayem/k'ahanayanam, and tṙp'im/tṙp'am/tṙp'anam just to name a few.
There are also cases of manuscript variants that show -e- class / -a- class
alternations.[20] In view of this phenomenon, which is broader in scope than
could have been initially expected, the reading of patac'i as a form of
*patam or *patanam in a graffito in the Sinai peninsula, does not seem in the
slightest measure implausible.

Materially, there seems to be a more distinct gap between the nu and
the pe than between the other letters. Given the irregularity of word
division in old Armenian inscriptions, this may serve only as corroborative
evidence, not more.

The reading Mowsēsn 'Moses' refers, by our interpretation, to Jebel
Musa, i.e. 'Mount Moses' (Mt. Sinai). The use of Moses in this sense is also
to be observed in the History by Sebēos. In an epistle addressed to Modestus,
Primate of Jerusalem, Komitas, Catholicos of the Armenians speaks of
pilgrims who prayed and says sp'ṙein zanjuk srti zastuacamerj Sinēakan
lerambn aṙ Movsisiw 'they poured forth the desire of (their) hearts around the
Sinaitic mountain, close to God, beside Moses.'[21] Incidentally, it should be

noted that -ov- in names like this is predominantly spelt -ow- in the Sinai inscriptions, as in many medieval manuscripts.

There remain, therefore, no severe objections to the reading which I have proposed. That which N. Bogharian and O. Yeganian would support is reached by setting the word division after the second s, thus reading: Mowses Npatac'i, i.e. 'Moses of Npat.' Npat, a mountain on the Euprates, is mentioned from ancient times, cf. Agat'angełos, para. 818.[22] This interpretation of the inscription avoids the difficulty of patac'i. It would be the most obvious one in the normal make-up of groups of Armenian inscriptions. In the case of the Sinai inscriptions, however, there are two considerations that weigh against it. The first is that, in all the nearly 120 inscriptions from the Sinai known to date, there is not a single gentilic or local denominator, nor any surname. It is not impossible, of course, that H Arm 71 is the one exception to that rule, but the probability is not particularly high. However, even this probability recedes when it is taken into account that Npatac'i is a rather rare local denominator. If the view of Bogharian and Yeganian is accepted, therefore, then the only local denominator found would also be a rather rare one. This becomes very unlikely.

An additional consideration in favour of our view is that the pilgrims delighted, so it seems, to mention the places to which they had made pilgrimage. Not only in L Arm 3 does Jerusalem appear, but also apparently in H Arm 41, H Arm 42, and H Arm 64.[23] Saint Catherine, perhaps the monastery or the mountain, appears in the fragmentary H Arm 42. In this context the mention of Jebel Musa in H Arm 71 is not strange.

If our interpretation is accepted, therefore, it shows nicely that the author of this inscription travelled to Wadi Haggag after circumventing Mt. Sinai. This, of course, serves as a neat confirmation of what we had already surmised, that the route ran from Jerusalem to Mt. Sinai and that, for most Armenian pilgrims, Wadi Haggag was on it.

Thus the inscriptions do teach us about the pilgrim routes and even more about the pilgrims' pride and joy in their achievement. These led them to record their exploits on the rocks of the Sinai and so, indirectly, to open for us a window onto their world.

NOTES

[1]The chief publications of the inscriptions are: M. E. Stone, Armenian Inscriptions from Sinai: Intermediate Report (Sydney: Maitland, 1979); Stone, "Sinai Armenian Inscriptions," BA (1981) 27-31; Stone, The Armenian Inscriptions from the Sinai with Appendixes on the Georgian and Latin Inscriptions by M. van Esbroeck and W. Adler (Harvard Armenian Series; Cambridge, MA: Harvard, 1982) referred to henceforth as Inscriptions. A first study, based in its preliminary parts on Stone, Armenian Inscriptions 1979 is P. Mayerson, "The Pilgrim Routes to Mt. Sinai and the Armenians," IEJ 32 (1982) 44-57.

[2]On the A-Tor area see Stone, Inscriptions, 4-5. Copies of some inscriptions there were made by Y. Tsafrir. The inscription of unknown provenance was photographed by B. Rothenberg, whose photograph I examined. The Georgian inscription near Jebel Ashka was sighted by U. Avner at co-ordinates 62811893.

[3]None such are known to the writer, either from personal examination or from published or unpublished texts.

[4]All the sigla conform with those used in Stone, Inscriptions.

[5]See ibid., 73; this inscription is visible in Plates 13-14, following p. 264, of I. Ševčenko, "The Early Period of the Sinai Monastery in the Light of its Inscriptions," DOP 20 (1966).

[6]The interpretation of the word for guide was first suggested by M. van Esbroeck.

[7]This might be dialectal, but compare the use of դ and գ in the next word, corresponding to Greek delta and gamma.

[8]This is so, even if an Arabic dialect is presumed in which the letter is pronounced hard g.

[9]Compare variation between h and x in the manuscripts of 4 Ezra at 6:44, 7:41 and conjecturally at 6:43. Unfortunately it is impossible, from the situation of the manuscripts, to draw conclusions about the geographic provenance of the variant.

[10]Compare C. J. Kraemer, Jr., Excavations at Nessana: Vol. III, The Papyri (Princeton: 1958) papyrus 72 (684 C.E.) and 73 (683 C.E.) and

W. M. F. Petrie, Researches in Sinai (London: Murray, 1901), passim for the nineteenth and twentieth centuries.

[11]They are not listed, for example, in H. Hübschmann, Armenische Grammatik I, Armenische Etymologie (Leipzig: 1897); nor in H. Ačaŕyan, Hayeren Armatakan Baŕaran (Erevan: University, 1971-9).

[12]The indexes of H. A. Ōrbeli et al., Corpus Inscriptionum Armenicarum, Vols. 1-4, 6 (Erevan: Academy, 1966-) were also consulted, to no avail.

[13]See M. E. Stone, Armenian Apocrypha Relating to Patriarchs and Prophets (Jerusalem: Academy, 1982) 161, 174-5.

[14]The vowel shift from i to e is not paralleled in the Sinai inscriptions, but H Arm 34 does show a shift of e to i.

[15]There are, of course, in Armenian many names of Greek origin, or of Semitic origin mediated through Greek. These are part of the Christian and classical heritage of the Armenians and cannot serve as evidence for our discussion, which must centre on uniquely Greek elements that are not part of Armenian culture in general. The name is found among some present day Armenians (information from Prof. D. Kouymjian).

[16]On the form, compare J. Karst, Historiche Grammatik des Kilikisch-Armenischen (Strassburg: Trubner, 1901) 324-7; see also A. Awetik'ian, et al., Nor Baŕgirk Haykazean Lezui (Venice: Mechitarists, 1873) 2.867c.

[17]Stone, Inscriptions, 36-39; cf. Mayerson, "Pilgrim Routes."

[18]See A. Negev, The Inscriptions of Wadi Haggag, Sinai (Qedem, 6; Jerusalem: Hebrew University, 1977).

[19]These two examples pointed out by J. J. S. Weitenberg and S. P. Cowe.

[20]Note the variants kataral (4 Ezra 14:25) and halacal (4 Ezra 8:53).

[21]G. V. Abgaryan, Patmut'iwn Sebēosi (Erevan: Academy, 1979) 119, lines 19-20.

[22]See also H. Hübschmann, Die altarmenischen Ortsnamen (repr.; Amsterdam: Oriental, 1969) p. 457.

[23]Certain of these are problematic: see the discussion in Inscriptions concerning these inscriptions.

ANOTHER LOOK AT MARR: THE NEW THEORY OF LANGUAGE
AND HIS EARLY WORK ON ARMENIAN

Thomas J. Samuelian

University of Pennsylvania

Medieval Armenian culture was the touchstone of Marr's thought about language. It was the field of his apprenticeship and much of his later theorizing can be tied to problems he first encountered while studying Armenian culture, which was for him preeminently the culture of the middle ages—of Ani and Vardan Aygekc'i. Indeed in every revision of his Japhetic or New Theory of Language the analysis of Armenian was the focal point or at least a crucial part of his presentation and evidence.

The linguistic controversy of 1950, Marr's own exaggerations and follies, and the seemingly unattainable goal of a Marxist linguistics have obscured not only Marr's theories, but also his early philological and archeological work. Recently, Marr's work has been the object of renewed interest in the Soviet Union and abroad. A number of ideas Marr incorporated into his New Theory—notably, language mixture as a major process of language creation, and gesture as a precursor of spoken language—are, without reference to Marr, attracting many adherents in linguistics and anthropology.[1] Inasmuch as most of his work dealt explicitly or implicitly with Armenian, Armenian scholars, particularly those of the medieval period, are in an especially good position to understand his theory, its sources and its development.

Nikolaj Jakolevič Marr (1864-1934) is best remembered as the leading Soviet linguist of the twenties and thirties, whose New Theory of Language, raised to dogma during the anti-cosmopolitan reaction after World War II, was denounced by Stalin in _Pravda_ in 1950. Marr was of course a scholar;

T. Samuelian & M. Stone, eds. Medieval Armenian Culture. (University of Pennsylvania Armenian Texts and Studies 6). Chico, CA: Scholars Press, 1983. pp. 203 to 217.

but he was also an academic and political leader. He served as Dean of the Faculty of Social Sciences at Leningrad University, member of the Leningrad City Council, Director of the Leningrad Public Library, Founder and President of the State Academy of the History of Material Culture (GAIMK), Vice-President of the Academy of Sciences and member of the All-Russian Central Executive Committee, to name but a few of the most prominent posts he held during the early years of Soviet rule.

The "linguistic discussion" of 1950, during which Marr was denounced sixteen years after his death, was the culmination of years of turmoil in linguistics. During the anti-cosmopolitan repression after World War II, Marr's "New Theory" was forcibly imposed by Stalinist authorities as part of the campaign for ideological purity. Opponents were reviled at academic meetings and in the press; many, including full members of the Academy of Sciences, were removed from their posts. Beginning on May 9, 1950 some two dozen linguists contributed articles to Pravda defending and denouncing Marr's theory on linguistic and Marxist grounds. The Pravda discussion reached its climax on June 20th with Stalin's "Concerning Marxism in Linguistics." In this article he exposed Marr's distortion of the Marxist category of class and put forth his own formulation of Marxist linguistics, which in turn was raised to dogma in all social sciences until well after his death in 1953.[2]

In the aftermath of the discussion, two volumes appeared under the title Against the Vulgarization and Distortion of Marxism in Linguistics. Among the forty some odd articles was one by I.K. Kusikjan. In the course of his refutation of Marrism, Kusikjan dropped a very suggestive line, which he chose not to pursue, since his purpose was not so much to explain Marr's theory as to point out his deviations in the treatment of Armenian. It read:

> One could say without fearing exaggeration, that a significant
> part of his [Marr's—T.S.] general linguistic theory is founded,
> along with Georgian, on Armenian material.[3]

While I am loath to say that the material led the man, there are many questions to be answered about a theory which ran counter to the scientific consensus of its time. During the twenties and thirties many Western analysts pinned Marr's excesses on the distorting influence of ideology. But even if the influence of ideology goes a long way to explain the conditions that made Marr's ascendancy possible, it does not explain why Marr believed what he did long before he or Russia were Marxist. A close examination shows that, as Kusikjan hinted, the hunches, intuitions and impressions crucial to the full-blown New Theory of Language date to his early work on Armenian beginning in the 1890s.

Japhetidology, later the New Theory of Language, never had a formal or final formulation; therefore, in all fairness to Marr any systematic exposition of his ideas should be prefaced with at least a mention of his own consistently undogmatic stance.

Marr's theory, as it stood at his death, can be derived from two not totally independent theses on language set against the background of historical materialism:

1. language is a superstructural phenomenon,
2. there is a unified process of language origin and growth; in Marr's own words, a single glottogonistic process

Marr held that man first communicated by hand language and that spoken language is a later acquisition overlaid on it, as modern gestures vestigially show. Spoken language at first had a special magical or religious function in primitive society and was the possession of a special social group, as Grabar (Classical Armenian), had been the language of the church. Still later, national norms or standard national languages were the possession of the ruling elite in society. Marr concluded that from the very beginning language had been a class phenomenon.

Class differentiation is the hallmark of superstructural categories. Marx and Engels wrote in The German Ideology, which it should be noted, was not published until 1932, that "Language is the immediate actuality of thought."[4]   And just as thought or consciousness is a superstructural category, so too must language, its embodiment, be. Marx and Engels had shown that ultimately, superstructural phenomena change in response to the course of socioeconomic development, which they organized into a scheme of stages.

Language as a superstructural phenomenon must also develop through a corresponding course of stages: Marr's single glottogonistic process. In principle, linguistic change was the response to social change as reflected in thought and thereby in linguistic structure. On this basis he distinguished three fundamental morphological types with a variety of transitional types: (1) amorphic, (2) agglutinative, (3) inflectional. The method of study was linguistic paleontology or the four-element analysis (SAL, ION, BER, ROŠ), the most notorious of Marr's creations. The elements were supposed to have arisen from the first diffuse syllables of magical spoken speech incanted to the tribal totem. The process of language change was mixture, which Marr understood to be the free intermingling of elements from various languages. The transition from stage to stage, as with the socioeconomic stages of historical materialism, was by way of revolutionary leaps.

At the time of Marr's death, a leading Marxist theorist, A. M. Deborin found in Marr's theory a number of features which commended it as Marxist: (1) its all-embracing scheme of linguistic development, (2) the union of language and thought and their mutual dependence on social change, (3) the union of opposites in the meaning of primitive words, (4) the denial of any scientific basis for Fascism or racism and finally, (5) the treatment of language as a superstructural category. In all, he wrote "Marr's Theory of Language confirms the correctness of Marxism-Leninism in all its parts."[5]

According to Academician Jahukian, a Soviet Armenian historian of linguistics currently serving as the director of the Institute of Language in Erevan, whatever else linguistics may have believed about Marr's theory, the thesis that language was a superstructural phenomenon was virtually unquestioned during the period from 1934-50.[6] This is worth remembering since this thesis was the central issue of the controversy in 1950 and the pretext for Stalin's intervention in the role of the leading authority on Marxism-Leninism in the Soviet Union.

As Deborin's comments indicate, Marr's ideas had an independent source; the theory was a Marxist doublet. Marr's success lay in coming upon ideas which coincided with Marxism and in so doing provided independent proof of Marxism's truth.

Long before the revolution Marr had formed very strong opinions about the unified study of language and culture. This unified approach provided the basis for his conclusion that language is a superstructural phenomenon. As a graduate student Marr had been a philologist of Veselovskian persuasion. In a retrospective address at his alma mater, renamed Leningrad State University, he credited Veselovskij, the central figure in Russia's journey into universal and holistic cultural and literary history, with having imbued the "atmosphere" with the ideas which inspired the New Theory. Nevertheless, as Marr's biographer Mixankova relates, Marr, who on his appointment was seen as Veselovskij's representative in Eastern languages and literatures, came to reject Veselovskij's theory of wandering themes because "tracing the varied and multifaceted ties of themes with fables of other languages failed to explain their meaning in the history of Armenian literature as such, and by this type of analysis the themes are made anonymous and torn from their concrete historical circumstances."[7]

Marr used similar argumentation in his contributions to several Armenian controversies of his day. To the literary critics who questioned the authenticity of the classical historian Xorenac'i, he responded that all considerations of Xorenac'i's priority aside, his word had to be considered not only in relation to other texts, but also in its "real," "living," national context.[8] Similarly, Marr rejected Strzygowski's claims for the influence of Armenian architecture on the West because "in basing his claims on formal analysis" Strzygowski had "failed to take into account the immediate sources and ties of Armenian architecture to its neighbors and historical-cultural context."[9] Another reason Marr is said to have reacted to Strzygowski in this way was that he saw European interest in Armenian things as patronizing, and he openly disliked anything which would fuel Armenian national pride or aggravate Armenian-Georgian relations. Throughout his life, Marr was the target of much national prejudice both from Georgians who found their compatriot's interest in Armenian things unseemly and from Armenians who resented his Georgian descent.[10]

As these two instances show, Marr had a penchant for abstract, methodological refutation, which would serve him well in promoting and defending his own theory in the Soviet period. More importantly, they show his commitment to the unified study of all aspects of culture, which was recognized in a grand gesture by Lenin, who entrusted Marr with the trailblazing Academy of the History of Material Culture in 1919.[11]

Advocacy of the unified study of culture is still a step away from the thesis that language is a superstructural phenomenon. What was missing is the notion that class struggle is reflected in culture. Marr first stated this belief in two of his best known Armenian studies. In his Master's thesis on Vardan Aygekc'i's parables, published in 1899, Marr wrote of the struggle between the feudal classes and the new bourgeois trading class as depicted in the parables.[12] Similarly, in explaining the fall of Ani, he emphasized the role of internal struggle, not external foes.[13] In 1933, looking back over his early research, Marr made the following link between material culture as a class phenomenon and language as a class phenomenon:

I studied the medieval Armenian language of Vardan's

Parables, which is a combination of two diverging and opposed social tendencies—the feudal and the bourgeois. This opposition finds its expression in architecture and literature of the corresponding social class, but their seeming juncture responds directly to the demands of the petit bourgeois class of the urban population with its guild organization, which on the whole constituted the makeup of any city of this period, especially Ani in the thirteenth and fourteenth centuries.[14]

During his excavations at Ani Marr came into contact with spoken Armenian. He later construed the difference between Modern and Classical Armenian to be one of class struggle as well. Some say that Marr was misled into this belief under the influence of the nineteenth-century populist movement to replace Classical Armenian—by then a language used predominantly by the clergy—with the vernacular or Modern Armenian language.[15]   Marr projected the classical-vernacular struggle back into the middle ages and earlier:

It warrants repeating that at one time the vernacular and now living Armenian language, which lies at the base of the modern Armenian literary language is a special language, distinguished from the other Armenian, the princely language, the living language of the Armenian feudal lords, which lies at the foundation of the literary language of Ancient Armenia.[16]

He called Classical Armenian k̲-Armenian and Modern Armenian r̲-Armenian after the predominant plural marker in each language.

Thus he came to the conclusion that language reflected class distinctions or more generally that language was a class phenomenon.

Had Marr at this point been a historical materialist, this thesis would have been a self-sufficient source for the New Theory. What his belief in linguistic class struggle lacked was a principle of progress or a scheme of developmental stages such as historical materialism provides. Marr was by his own admission not a historical materialist even as late as 1927.[17] But in time he did come upon a unifying principle for his observations on the development of Armenian and other languages.

One of the first things that struck Marr about Armenian and his native Georgian was that

Armenian in its significant, most characteristic part, especially in phonetics, lexicon and wordbuilding, belongs to one common language family with Georgian, provisionally called Japhetic, and since the Japhetic family is related to the Semitic, the aforementioned most ancient part of the Armenian language is related to Semitic. Popular forms preserved for us in Vardan's parables, provide a good many facts supporting this idea.[18]

Next he turned to literary ties moving freely from literature to language. "The layering in literature could not but be reflected in language," he writes.[19] Having established much that was common between Armenian and Georgian folklore, Marr wanted to explain these similarities not merely by the proximity of Armenians and Georgians. "The linguistic tie between the Georgian and the pre-Aryan layer of Armenian, has become clearer and clearer to me. It gives us the basis to propose that the shared motifs in oral literatures of these peoples dates to an era, when the Armenians and Georgians composed related nationalities . . ."[20]

In search of a cause for the similarities he found, Marr chose the most widely accepted linguistic explanation—genetic relation. By casting his account in terms of a common source instead of borrowing or cultural diffusion, Marr made a fateful choice. When he was accused of misusing the historical comparative method, which is based on genetic relations,[21] he stood by his observations and retorted that any method which failed to account for his observations was flawed and should either be revised to include them as he had done or totally abandoned, as he later would do. Marr's European critics were adamant that revision was out of the question because Marr's observations were of a kind unsuited to the comparative method.   Their criticism was translated to mean that Marr's observations were unscientific or false. Marr's break with the historical comparative method was further abetted by a sense of stagnation in historical linguistics at the turn of the century and Marr's animosity toward such figures as Hubschmann which dated to his student days in Strassburg.[22] From this point on Marr was more expansive in his theorizing. In his 1903 Grammar of Classical Armenian he stated definitively that Armenian was bigenetic.

> The Armenian language is even now an unsolved riddle
> for scholars. One thing is clear, it is a highly characteristic
> example of a mixed language. Of course I am not speaking here
> of the rich admixture of obviously borrowed words, easily

distinguished and to a significant extent already separated out. I have in mind the core of the real Armenian language, which arose on the soil of historical Armenia. This core itself is bigenetic.[23]

Japhetic, that tie between Armenian and Georgian, was gradually transformed from an ancient source to a product of similar social conditions. The crucial step came when Marr declared that "architectural monuments, arising in different class environments of the Armenian nation, exhibit fewer traits in common than monuments arising in the same social conditions of different people, such as the Georgians and Armenians."[24]

He had by then rejected the possibility of a common source as an explanation for the similarities he found. What remained was explanation by independent invention; similarities being attributable to the similarity in the conditions which engendered them.

This statement about architecture he gradually extended to other aspects of culture in the form of a principle that cultures arising from the same social conditions or standing at the same stage of social development have more in common than any single culture has with its predecessors or successors. Twenty years later this idea would find forceful expression in the Stalinist formula, "National in form, socialist in content."

Thus Marr the Armenian philologist, had in his own uncanny way stumbled upon a position which came very close to Marxism some twenty years before Marx and Engels' most explicit statements on the nature of language.[25]   The central theses of Japhetidology, later called the New Theory of Language, were, therefore, present and operating some twenty years before the revolution.

In due course Marr embellished his theory with many of the concepts current in nineteenth- and early twentieth-century linguistics. Early in the nineteenth century Humboldt, the Schlegel's, Bopp and others believed that languages develop through three stages distinguished by morphological type. Each stage is to reflect a stage in man's mental development.[26] Marr, under the influence of this concept and more current work on primitive thought and language by Lévy-Bruhl, consolidated his grand theory of cultural, mental, and linguistic development.[27]   Extending the theory to yet earlier times, Marr proposed a period of gestural or hand language, which was gradually supplanted, but never totally replaced by spoken language. In the late nineteenth century, the hand-language hypothesis had been put forth by several anthropologists, most prominently, Ludwig Noiré and Frank Cushing, on whom Marr relied.[28]

In the Soviet period the transformation of Japhetidology into the New Theory of Language was not so much a reworking of his ideas in the Marxist framework as a recognition of their kinship with certain Marxist categories and values. The New Theory, announced in 1924, was in no way new. It was simply the continuation of the Japhetic theory. In fact Marr did not adopt a consciously Marxist idiom until his Baku course of 1927.[29]

His opposition to Western linguistics did, however, grow more and more strident until on November 23, 1923 he made his final break with Indo-European linguistics. At the meeting of the Academy of Sciences he reported that

The Indo-European languages of the Mediterranean never were a special racial family of languages nor did they (the Indo-Europeans) come from any place with some special linguistic material. Even less do they go back to any racially special proto-language. In fact, in the beginning, there was not one, but a plurality of tribal languages; a single proto-language is a scientific fiction which has outlived its usefulness.[30]

The Indo-European languages had become for Marr little more than a stage of greater linguistic complexity. This complexity was the result of the linguistic mixture which had taken place during the revolution in social conditions associated with certain new forms of production. These new forms of production were, in turn, called forth by the discovery of metals and their widespread use in the economy. "The Indo-European family of languages typologically is the creation of new economic conditions, but its material is vestigial and its inner construction shows it to be the later stage of all the Japhetic languages of the Mediterranean."[31]

This new conception of the relation of the Indo-European languages to the Japhetic languages called for revisions in the treatment of Armenian as well.

The Armenian and, to an extent, the Albanian languages are not mixtures of the Indo-European languages and Japhetic languages [which are in fact different stages of the same language] but are in transition between Japhetic and completely

Indo-European.[32]

By 1925 Marr's theory was well on its way to governmental endorsement. Marr himself had emerged as a trusted public servant and an academician with an institutional domain extending from Leningrad to Baku. There were by then two institutions—the Japhetic Institute of the Academy of Sciences and the State Academy of the History of Material Culture (GAIMK)—inspired by his theory and devoted to his line of research on a large scale. Marr, cast out by Western linguistics, had gained influence and even acclaim at home. By 1925 Lunačarskij, the Commissar of Education, could write in Izvestija, "The idea of the Academy of Material Culture arose in the fecund mind of the great philologist of our Union, and perhaps the greatest living philologist of our time, N. Ja. Marr."[33]

In the last ten years of his life Marr turned from the study of particular languages to Language in general. His work on Armenian never really ended, but it became less significant in its relative volume and impact. The call for Marxist science was sounded louder and more frequently in those years, and Marr from his position of prominence in Soviet scientific and political life was naturally looked to for leadership in the search for a Marxist linguistics. A struggle ensued, which was as much a part of the bolshevization of the Academy of Sciences and the terror of the late twenties as the scientific ferment in linguistics. Marr, being in a position of power, was not easily discredited or displaced. Just when Marr, ailing and tired of being under fire, was ready to withdraw from the linguistics scene, he was reaffirmed by the Communist Academy as the undisputed authority on Marxism in Linguistics. As a conversation, recorded in the memoirs of one of his students, I. A. Orbeli, shows, it was an accolade Marr would rather not have received.[34] What resulted was a theory, never meant to be adopted as doctrine, being confirmed as a nearly final truth over the qualms of its creator.

Marr's theory was not nearly so unique as it was made out to be by either his supporters or his critics. His programs echoed those of many of his contemporaries and predecessors—a fact which lent support and credibility to his criticism of the West. His image as a dissenter, an underdog, and a renegade all captivated his Soviet audience. That image combined with his Georgian descent contributed greatly to the favor he enjoyed in the eyes of political leaders who found in him a suitable appointment, symbolic of a new regime pledged to the eradication of Great Russian oppression.

As for the concrete linguistic work itself, while it may be intriguing to unravel the intricate web Marr spun out of the languages he saved from obscurity, the beliefs themselves should not be so readily dismissed. One has to pause, in light of recent developments in socioand ethno-linguistics to appreciate how enlightening such perspectives on language could be if used with measure and skill. Current interest in the social stratification of language, creolization, the study of language in context and language policy touch upon some of the beliefs and directions of Marr's work. Notable among those encountered in his early work on Armenian are:

1. language mixture as a major process of language change and genesis
2. and conversely, the rejection of the supremacy of genetic relations
3. differentiation of language by function and class
4. attraction to universal schemes of linguistic development, especially typological

That the concrete analyses did not in any way correspond to reality was beside the point. They provided an account of the material which supported the desired conclusions, and the spinning of the web gives the appearance of science in the viewing and the pleasure of puzzling together linguistic data in the making. If it had matched reality, so much the better, or as Marr would say in 1925,

My students tell me (and for that matter non-students acquainted with Japhetic linguistics as well), that in fact I confirm the premises of Marxism. I will not argue if this is so; but Japhetic linguistics is not Marxism any more than it is a theoretical construct. Now if in it there are premises which support the Marxist doctrine, then, from my point of view, so much the better for it and the worse for its opponents, since in reality linguistic facts do not permit the questioning of the premises of Japhetic linguistics.[35]

Those facts, by and large, were Armenian facts.

NOTES

[1]V. V. Ivanov, Očerki po Istorii Semiotiki v SSSR (Moscow: Nauka, 1976) brought to light a number of recent studies which adopt Marr's positions without reference to him. See K. Hill, ed. The Genesis of Language (Ann Arbor: Karoma Publishers, 1979); J. Hill, "On the Evolutionary Foundations of Language," American Anthropologist 74(1972) 3:308-317; G. Hewes, "Primate Communication and the Gestural Origin of Language," Current Anthropology 14(1973) 1-2:5-24. On another of Marr's pet ideas—the development of articulated language from amorphous religious chant—see Bruce Richman, "Did Human Speech Originate in Coordinated Vocal Music?" Semiotica 32(1982) 3-4. Western reaction to Ivanov's book is a good gauge of how deep a scar Marrism left on linguistics around the world, see A. V. Isačenko, "Marr—Redivivus?" Russian Linguistics 4(1978) 1:83-87; D. Laferriere, "Semiotica sub Specie Sovietica: Anti-Freudianism, Pro-Marrism and other Disturbing Matters," PTL 3(1978) 437-54.

[2]For English translations of the articles which appeared as part of the Linguistic Discussion see the collection by V. Murra, M. Hankin & F. Holling, The Soviet Linguistic Controversy (NY: King's Crown Press, 1951). See also the June 1977 issue of Langages (ed. J. B. Marcellesi). The entire issue is devoted to "Langage et classes sociales: le Marrisme" and includes a chronicle of events.

[3]I. K. Kusikjan, "Ošibki N. Ja. Marra v osveščenii istorii armjanskogo jazyka," 2:426-446 in V. V. Vinogradov & B. A. Serebrennikov (eds.), Protiv Vul'garizacii i Izvraščenija Marksizma v Jazykoznanii (2 vols., Moscow: AN SSSR, 1951-52) 429.

[4]K. Marx & F. Engels, The German Ideology, Pt. I (ed. C. J. Arthur; NY: International Publishing, 1978) 118.

[5]A. M. Deborin, "Marksizm i Učenie Marra o Jazyke i Myšlenii," Vestnik Akademii Nauk (1935) 4:25-40; Deborin, "Novoe Učenie o Jazyke i Dialektičeskij Materializm," 21-75 in XLX Akademiku N. Ja. Marru (Moscow-Leningrad: AN SSSR, 1938) 21; Deborin, "Genial'nyj Lingvist," Izvestija CIK SSSR 21 Dec. 1934 [Reprinted in Problemy Istorii Dokapitalističeskogo Obščestva (1935) 3-4:200-201.

[6]G. Jahukyan, Lezvabanut'yan Patmut'yun (2 vols. Erevan: Erevan

Hamalsarani Hrat., 1960-62) 2:434.

[7]On Marr and Veselovskij see N. Ja. Marr, "Jafetidologija v Lenin gradskom Universitete," 1:254-272 in his Izbrannye Raboty (Leningrad: GAIMK, 1933) 271; V. F. Šišmarev, "N. Ja. Marr i A. N. Veselovskij," Jazyk i Myšlenie 8(1937) 321-339; V. A. Mixankova, Nikolaj Jakovlevič Marr (Moscow-Leningrad: AN SSSR, 1948), 62.

[8]Mixankova, Marr, 67.

[9]Ibid., 143.

[10]Marr, Ani: Knižnaja istorija goroda i raskopki na meste gorodišča (Izv. GAIMK 105; Moscow-Leningrad, 1935). Although published post-humously, this book is composed of Marr's course notes on Ani dating to 1910-1912 and represents, with the exception of the introduction which was written shortly before his death, his thinking in the pre-revolutionary period. See also A. Movsisyan, N. Ya. Mari Kyank'ē ev Stelcagorcut'yunē (Erevan: HSSR GA Hrat, 1946) 8.

[11]Mixankova, Marr, 249.

[12]Marr, Sborniki Pritč Vardana (St. Petersburg, 1899) as quoted in Mixankova, Marr, 90-91, 186. See also M. Abełyan, Hayoc' Hin Grakanutyan Patmut'yun (2 vols.; Erevan: HSSR GA Hrat., 1946) 2:169-172.

[13]Marr, Ani, vi.

[14]Marr, "Doistorija, Preistorija, Istorija i Myšlenie," Izv. GAIMK 74(1933) 19.

[15]Kusikyan, "Ošibki Marra," 429; L. Thomas, The Linguistic Theories of N. Ja. Marr (Berkeley & Los Angeles: U. of CA, 1957) 25.

[16]Marr, "O Čanskom Jazyke" (1910) 1:39-49 in his Izbrannye Raboty (Moscow-Leningrad, 1933) 39. It is generally held that Modern Armenian is a descendant of the classical language, which was first committed to writing in the fifth century. Marr, on the contrary, believed that the two languages had distinct sources or at least a different proportion of these sources in their makeup. In Modern Armenian, the Japhetic elements native to Eastern Anatolia and the Caucasus were predominant and in Classical Armenian, the Indo-European or Aryan elements. Later, when Marr rejected the notion of the Indo-European family altogether, the mixture hypothesis became mean-ingless and he proposed that Armenian was caught between the Japhetic and

the Indo-European stages of linguistic development.   Modern Armenian, therefore, was more archaic than Classical Armenian.   On Marr's interest in archaism in living languages see Mixankova, Marr, 104.

[17]Mixankova, Marr, 338.

[18]Marr as quoted in ibid., 83.

[19]Ibid., 255.

[20]Ibid., 91.

[21]The central premise of the comparative method is that recurrent correspondences of comparable linguistic units (usually phonemes) in two or more languages indicate that those languages have a common source.   To attribute these either to coincidence or massive, identical borrowing defies the laws of probability, on which see E. D. Polivanov, "Even Mathematics can be Useful," 226-272 in his Selected Works (ed. A. Leontiev; trans. D. Armstrong; The Hague: Mouton, 1974).   Conversely, languages which are related display recurrent correspondences.   Marr's correspondences are by comparison sporadic and idiosyncratic for each word.   It is not that languages could not in some possible world develop as Marr portrayed it in his work, but that they do not is the great empirical finding of nineteenth-century linguistics.

[22]Mixankova, Marr, 37.   On the sense of stagnation in historical linguistics at the turn of the century see Hans Aarsleff, "Bréal vs. Schleicher: Linguistics and philology during the latter half of the nineteenth century," 62-106 in H. Hoenigswald, ed., The European Background of American Linguistics, Dordrecht, Holland: Foris Publications, 1979.

[23]Marr, Grammatika Drevnearmjanskogo Jazyka (St. Petersburg: Imperatorskaja Akademija Nauk, 1903) xxxi.

[24]Marr, Ani, 123.

[25]The German Ideology, in which Marx and Engels expounded the unity of language and thought, the cornerstone of Marxist linguistics, was not published until 1932 by the Institute of Marxism-Leninism in Moscow, two years before Marr died.

[26]Wilhelm von Humboldt, Linguistic Variability and Intellectual Development (trans. G. Buck & F. Raven; Philadelphia: U. of PA, 1972) 5, 131.

27Marr refers to Lévy-Bruhl for his ideas on pre-logical thought and polysematicity of primitive language. Relevant passages from Lévy-Bruhl's work can be found in J. Cazeneuve, Lucien Lévy-Bruhl (Paris: Presses Universitaires de France, 1963) 30, 34, 56.

28Marr, "O Proisxoždenii Jazyka," 286-337 in Po Ètapam Razvitii Jafetičeskoj Teorii [PERJT] (Moscow-Leningrad: Naučno-Issledovatel'skij Institut Ètničeskix i Nacional'nyx Kul'tur Narodov Vostoka SSSR, 1926) 320; L. Noiré, On the Origin of Language (2nd ed.; Chicago: Open Court Publishing, 1898); F. H. Cushing, "Manual Concepts: a study of the influences of hand-language on culture growth," American Anthropologist 5(1892) 4:289-317. For recent interest in this hypothesis see n. 1 above.

29Marr, "Jafetičeskaja Teorija" (1927) 2:3-135 in his Izbrannye Raboty (Moscow-Leningrad: Gos. Soc-Ekonomičeskoe Izd., 1936).

30Marr, Indoevropejskie Jayzki Sredizemnemor'ja (1924) 244-245 in Po Ètapam Razvitii Jafetičeskoj Teorii [PERJT] (Moscow-Leningrad, 1926), 244-245.

31Ibid.

32Ibid.

33A. Lunačarskij, "Materializm i Filologija," Izvestija CIK SSSR 12 Apr. 1925.

34I. A. Orbeli as quoted in A. Leontiev, L. I. Rojzenzon & A. D. Xajutin, "The Life and Activities of E. D. Polivanov," 11-31 in E. D. Polivanov, Selected Works (trans. D. Armstrong; The Hague: Mouton, 1974).

35Marr, "Osnovnye Dostiženija Jafetičeskoj Teorii," 246-257 in PERJT 249.

CRITICAL REMARKS ON THE NEWLY EDITED EXCERPTS
FROM SEBĒOS

Jean-Pierre Mahé

Sorbonne Nouvelle (France)

In 1831, when Yovhannes Šahxatuneanc' found, in a manuscript of Ējmiacin (which has now become Yerevan No. 2639 of the year 1672),[1] an Anonymous Chronicle relating the history of Armenia in the sixth and in the seventh centuries, he tried to identify it with "The History of Heraclius and the Holy Cross," which was referred to by ancient chroniclers[2] as the work of Bishop Sebēos.[3] His opinion was generally accepted by modern scholars.[4]

Nevertheless, Gevorg Abgarian, who prepared a new critical edition of the text, has striven for some twenty years now to show that the Anonymous Chronicle can in no way be ascribed to Sebēos.[5] In the preface to his edition, which was published in 1979, he gathers and partly corrects his former views on the problem and restates the relevant data.[6]

In the first stage of his research, Abgarian had pointed to the fact that this chronicle is ordinarily referred to by ancient authors as the "History of Xosrov." For this reason he supposed Xosrov was the name of the author; but this opinion proved to be erroneous, since we have no clear indications about the existence of a Xosrov patmič' in the Armenian sources.

In fact, as Ananian eventually suggested to Abgarian, Xosrov is not the name of the author, but of the central character of the chronicle, that is, King Xosrov Apruez (Xusru II Abarwez) of Persia who led the last Persian war in Armenia before the coming of Arab conquerors. Xosrov's important role is described even in the first words of the book, that is, after the interpolation of the chapters 1 to 9:[7] "Book of the chronicle, / royal

---

T. Samuelian & M. Stone, eds. Medieval Armenian Culture. (University of Pennsylvania Armenian Texts and Studies 6). Chico, CA: Scholars Press, 1983. pp. 218 to 239.

history, / heroic tale,/ universal assault / of the Sasanian plunderer, / Xosrov Apruez, / who set on fire and burned out / everything on earth, / shaking the sea and the land, / calling forth devastation / all over the earth."[8]

Further, all events before the Arab invasions are dated in the book from the years of Xosrov's reign.   Now if we consider that none of the ancient chroniclers who had known this text (i.e. T'ovma Arcruni, Yovhannēs Drasxanakertc'i, Step'anos Asołik, Vardan Arewelc'i, Simēon Aparanec'i and Vardan Bałišec'i) names its exact title and its author, we must conclude, as Abgarian finally did, that it has been anonymous at least since the tenth century[9] so that they were compelled to call the book by the name of its main hero "History of Xosrov," which is quite another book from Sebēos' "History of Heraclius." It is most remarkable that all the authors who refer to Heraclius do not know Xosrov. Such is the case for Samuēl Anec'i, Mxit'ar Anec'i, Kirakos Ganjakec'i and Mxit'ar Ayrivanec'i.   There is only one exception, Step'anos Asołik who borrows important data both from Sebēos and from the Anonymous Chronicle but never presents us both of them as one and the same work.[10]

G. Abgarian has proved the lost history of Sebēos to be a distinct document by publishing, as an annex to his critical edition of the Anonymous Chronicle, the three excerpts from Sebēos which have reached us by indirect tradition.[11]

The first excerpt has been preserved in Uxtanēs[12]who writes as follows about Smbat Bagratuni, the marzpan of Vrkan:[13]

> He is of our nation, of the race of our kings the Bagratids.
> He is dear to us as a true and loyal brother of our Kings and
> he has been made marzpan in the [border] province of Vrkan by
> order of Xosrov Apruez the King of Kings of Persia during the
> reign of King Maurice of the Greeks. He drove back and
> overthrew many attacking armies among the Armenians the
> Greeks and the Persians as you can read in the History of
> Heraclius. And now for the present times, submitting himself
> to the faith of his ancestors, accepting willingly the orthodox
> creed of the holy Fathers and Doctors, he is most helpful and
> he shares all the needs of those who are in need, he supplies
> with his assistance our [people] of Armenia. He is strengthened
> by God and he is strong with God. So in that time of anarchy

in Armenia he replaced our absent kings and patriarchs . . .[14]

It is clear that the first part of the text cannot have been written before the reign of the Bagratids because it contains Uxtanēs's own remarks about the royal origin of Smbat, his career and military successes. These, on the contrary, are explicitly presented as a rapid glance at Sebēos chronicle. Finally the last sentences of this text "And now, for the present time, etc." are a direct quotation of an author who wrote when Smbat was still alive.[15] This author must have been quoted by Sebēos and we can only state with Abgarian that this quotation is not included in the Anonymous Chronicle which Šahxat'uneanc' thought to be Sebēos.

Two other excerpts from Sebēos have reached us in liturgical collections, as readings for the feasts of the Holy Cross.

Excerpt A, which is more ancient, is to be found in the Ms. Yerevan No. 7729, i.e. the famous Čaŕēntir of Muš, which was written in Awag-Vank' during the years 1200-1202, after the model of a Tōnakan compiled in the eighth century by Sołomon Mak'enoc'ac'i.[16] Due to the loss of one page of the manuscript this text is incomplete. It was published for the first time by Abgarian.

Excerpt B is somewhat longer and more recent. It was published for the first time by N. Marr in his edition of Antioches Strategos' chronicle about The Taking of Jerusalem by the Persians in 614.[17] It has reached us in the ms. Yerevan No. 993 of the year 1456.[18]

The titles of both texts explicitly present them as excerpts from the History of Heraclius.[19] Furthermore Movsēs Kałankatuac'i gives a shorter account of this History, which coincides with our excerpts.[20] So it is difficult to challenge their authenticity.[21] Nevertheless none of these two excerpts can be considered a literal quotation of Sebēos. Both of them relate the same facts but not always with the same words. N. Marr thought that fragment B had been altered in the ninth or tenth centuries by a Chalcedonian writer.[22]

It would be very difficult to reconstruct a synthetic text on the basis of A and B. One can only make a summary of their contents, pointing out the different topics Sebēos had included in his History.

1.   Exchange of letters between Xosrov and Heraclius. Boasting his strength, the Pagan King insults the Christian Emperor. The latter answers by warning him of divine punishment (only in B).

2. Brief account of the campaign of Xorian,[23] the Persian general, from Antioch to Palestine (A and B).

3. Theological speculations about the taking of Jerusalem. How did the Lord allow impious nations to take and to plunder the Holy City? This happened four times because of the infidelity of its inhabitants and this fourfold manifestation of the divine wrath had been predicted in Daniel's vision of the four beasts: the first one is Nabuchadnezzar, the second one is Antiochos, the third one, Vespasian and the fourth and apparently the last one,[24] more terrible than the preceding, is Xosrov (quite developed in A but also some indications in B.)[25]

4. After a long and rather unfruitful siege, the Persian general Xorian takes Jerusalem thanks to the help of the Jews. Then the Persians desecrate the churches and steal the wood of the Holy Cross, which they carry away in captivity (A and B).

5. Naturally all these calamities have been planned and ordered by Providence for the punishment and the instruction of the Christians. For this reason King Xosrov is unconsciously forced to pay homage to the Holy Cross by going out to meet it with his whole court when it arrives in his capital. Then he takes it and puts it with great respect in a chest of aloes wood which he keeps in his treasury (A and B).

6. Xorian's campaign against Constantinople. Heraclius has been betrayed by his ally "the king of the Čenk', the great Xak'an." Consequently he is defeated by the two armies of King Xosrov, which contain not only Pagan nations but also some "Sons of T'orgom" (that is, Armenian soldiers) as well as other nations of the Caucasus (A has only the first part of this episode; the second one was in the lost page of the codex).

7. Penance of the Christian Emperor. For three days Heraclius prays continuously imploring the help of the Theotokos. The fourth day he sees in a vision the fall of his enemy. Immediately he exhorts his troops who defeat the Persians and kill King Xosrov (B).

8. Xosrov's successor, Child Artašīr, unjustly charges Xorian with treason. The latter is compelled to flee and to propose his help to the Christian Emperor. At the head of the Byzantine army, he then kills his former sovereign (B).

9. Epilogue. After this victory Xorian gives back the Holy Cross which arrives in Constantinople "through the highway of Georgia." Then they commemorate the feast of the Holy Cross which is celebrated September 13

and 14 in the churches of the Holy Sion and the Ayia Sophia (B).

At first sight this story is rather enigmatic. How is it possible that a chronicler has written such an inexact report as to suppose that Xosrov has been killed in a battle against Heraclius or to name Artašīr as his direct successor on the throne of Persia? On the other hand, external evidence certifies the authenticity of the title, [Excerpt] "from the History of Heraclius" (A and B). We know, for instance, that the tōnakan on the basis of which the manuscript of our first fragment was written, was compiled in Mak'enoc' during the years 701 to 747.[26] On September 14 of the year 736 Prince Vahan Goɫt'nac'i visited the monastery for the feast of the Holy Cross. He was received by Soɫomon the compiler of the tōnakan who gave him "homiletic advice and comfort in the Christ."[27] So we may conclude that less than a hundred years after Bishop Sebēos participated in the synod of Duin in 645, Soɫomon confirms the authenticity of this chronicle.

We, therefore, should take into account the fact that the compiler of a liturgical collection often modifies the texts he includes in his book. Being much more concerned with edification than with chronology, he may abridge the story and insist only on significant details with hagiographic interest rather than preserve the logical order of the events. In the present case, without any date or explanation, our excerpt juxtapose—as if they were closely related to one another—three different episodes of Heraclius's war against the Persians which took place during the years 610 to 630. If we restore a correct chronology,[28] the story contains far fewer mistakes than one might expect on first reading.

1. From 610 to 615

Among other historians the so-called Sebēos i.e. the author of the Anonymous Chronicle of Šahxatuneanc' tells us that Heraclius sent an ambassador to Xosrov as early as 610, or in any case before the fall of Jerusalem.[29] Our text merely inverts the situation: Xosrov sends a letter to the Emperor and begins the war.

The description of the campaign is correct. The Persians first take Antioch and Caesarea in 613. While the army of Šahen marches toward Constantinople, the troops of Šahrvaraz go to the south and arrive in Jerusalem.[30] Our author knows only Šahrvaraz, whom he names Xorian, as the so-called Sebēos. We read in excerpt A that "an order which had come from the celestial court did not allow the [inhabitants] to surrender willingly the city into the hands of the [enemies]." We know in fact that patriarch Zachariah, who wanted to capitulate, was charged with treason and threatened with death.[31] Monks organized the defense of the city. They are described in our text as "saints fighting the battle, [who] delivered themselves to death for the sake of the life-giving Holy Sign of Christ." (A). Thanks to their efforts the town held out more than two weeks and was taken only after its walls had collapsed.

Like all other descriptions of this event, our text lays great stress upon the number of the casualties, 34,000 according to Antiochos and 90,000 according to Theophanes.[32]   He reckons that the Jews contributed to provoking this slaughter. In fact we know that, after many Jews of Jerusalem had been killed by the Christians, the survivors and Jews of Palestine joined the Persian army and that they created a special fund, in order to buy Christian prisoners and to slay them.[33] During several months the Christian fugitives who had escaped the slaughter were hunted down by Jewish soldiers striving to free the city of the Christian yoke: "Even if someone was fleeing and hiding himself from the Infidels, he could not escape from the hands of the Jews." (A, see also B)

The treasures of the various churches were plundered by the invaders and the Holy Cross was taken away in captivity. Certainly this booty had great value, both material and psychological. Our author imagines somewhat naively that Xosrov was forced by the Providence to pay homage to the Holy Sign of Christ, which he kept with great honor in his treasury (cf. Dan 1,2). This affirmation may correspond to two historical facts. First, after having accepted the support of the Jews,[34] Xosrov soon found it much more advantageous to flatter the Christian populations, who were for the major part Monophysites and for this reason rather hostile to the Byzantines.[35] Second, granting the request of some Persian Christians, he kept the Holy Cross in Tabriz in a church, the ruins of which still existed in the seventeenth century and were visited by Chardin.[36]

So far, our author offers us an account of the events which is not complete but contains authentic features and gives a good idea of what happened during the years 610 to 615. The difficulties we meet in the following text result only from the fact that, without any explanation, the excerptor suddenly abridges the story, excluding from his text the victorious campaigns of the Byzantines which took place between 615 and 625, and thus he jumps to one episode of the siege of Constantinople during the summer

626.

2. The siege of Constantinople in 626

In order to fight the Persians more energetically, Heraclius had been forced to buy the peace from the Xak'an of the Avars who had invaded Thracia in 623. This treatise had been concluded during the winter 623-624.[37] During the year 625 the Persians persuaded the Avars to join them by offering more money than the Greeks, so that in spite of the victorious campaigns of Heraclius in Persia they were able in 626 to threaten the security of Constantinople.[38] Xosrov had gathered a large cavalry from all the nations of his empire.[39] One part of this cavalry being commanded by Xorian Šahrvaraz joined the Avars and besieged the capital from the European side; the second part arrived in the Asiatic side of the town.[40]

Our Armenian excerpt describes adequately the cosmopolitanism of the Persian troops by saying that they included "a multitude of Infidel nations" as well as "sons of T'orgom," "people from Atrpatakan" and "pagans from the mountains (B)." His account of the deeds of the Avars and of the situation of the Byzantine armies however, is fairly inexact. The most serious error of the author is to think that Xosrov and Heraclius are personally fighting each other under the walls of Constantinople. The reality is quite different. During the siege of his capital, Heraclius was in the East. As to Xosrov, he never took a direct part in any campaign and he was not killed by the soldiers of Heraclius but murdered in Ctesiphon.

Nevertheless the Armenian chronicler agrees with a Byzantine tradition in explaining the delivery of the town by a miracle of the Theotokos.[41] Byzantine authors give various accounts of the nature of this miracle. According to the Pascal Chronicle the Theotokos appeared to the Xak'an of the Avars as a soberly dressed woman walking around the walls alone.[42] According to Theodore Syncellos, Mary herself fought personally with the Byzantines and terrified their enemies.[43] George Pisides,[44] Theophanes, Nicephoros, Constantine Manasses, Cedrenos and others tell us about such traditions, which were subsequently included in the Greek homiliars.[45]

So it is not surprising that our Armenian Čaṙĕntir borrows from Bishop Sebēos the story of such a miracle. But he is indeed very original in making Heraclius the center of this story while the Emperor was in fact very far from Constantinople.[46] According to Armenian text, the Theotokos appears to Heraclius in a dream and gives him an unsheathed fiery sword, promising him that he would defeat his enemies.   After waking up, the Emperor recounts his vision to his troops and concludes: "By the intercession of the Holy Mother of God, Christ is with us and we have been granted victory (B)." All this is obviously most similar to the miracle of Constantine.   One should notice that the official propaganda drew such a parallel.   The bronze coins which were minted in 620 show the Emperor with a globe in his left hand a cross in his right hand and the motto of Constantine ʿ Εν τούτῳ νίκα.[47]

3. 628-630

After the siege of Constantinople, the Armenian fragment relates the events which took place from the murder of Xosrov in 628 up to the rebellion of Šahrvaraz and the peace of 629-630.   This report is confused by the fact—which may have resulted from an awkward abridgment by the excerptor—that the successor of Xosrov is supposed to be Artašīr.   In fact after the revolt of 628 the new king was Kavad,[48] who reigned only one year and left as his successor, his seven year old son Artašīr.[49]   The Armenian author is right in naming the latter manuk Artašīr, i.e. Child Artašīr. Nevertheless, since he places the death of Xosrov two years too early and reckons the reign of his grandson three years before it really was, he is compelled to suppose that Xorian Šahrvaraz has revolted against this child.

In reality, as easrly as 627-628 the Persian general began to betray Xosrov[50] and finally he met with Heraclius in Arabyssos, a town of Cappadocia, already under the reign of Artašīr as the Armenian writer correctly states.   During this meeting they probably decided (a) That the Persians should withdraw from all the occupied territories and give back the Holy Cross, (b) That the emperor would help Šahrvaraz to overthrow Artašīr, which did happen in 630.[51]

Our Armenian čařĕntir reproduces quite exactly the terms of this treatise but in a more dramatic way.   According to the author, Xorian Šahrvaraz falls at the feet of the Holy Emperor beseeching him: "Give me troops, stand by me and help me and I will do all that your soul desires (B)." Heraclius grants this request and orders him to go to Persia and to bring back the Holy Cross.

Now we do not know exactly the way this precious relic came back in the Byzantine Empire.[52]   According to our Armenian author Šahrvaraz overthrew Artašīr with the help of four Byzantine armies commanded by several generals who have Armenian names: Gēorg, Dawit', Vahan, and

Smbat. Two of these might be well known personalities. Michael the Syrian and the Chronicle of Seert tell us that Dawit' was the name of the Byzantine general who accompanied Sahrvaraz into Persia and brought back the Holy Cross, which he gave to Heraclius in Hierapolis on the beginning of the year 630.[53] As for Vahan, he might be the unfortunate Vaanes who commanded the Byzantine troops in Yermuk in 636.[54]

The idea of associating Armenians in the reconquest of the Holy Cross certainly corresponds to one of the political advantages Heraclius could expect from such a glorious action. Only the possession of this symbol which was acknowledged by all the Christians could help the Byzantines to be reconciled with the Monophysites of their Empire and to confirm the Monothelist compromise of 624.[55]

Many chroniclers affirm, as does our text, that the Holy Cross was given back by Šahrvaraz. Such are Antiochos Strategos, the Anonymous Chronicle of Guidi, the so-called Sebēos of Šahxat'uneanc', Nicephoros and Michael the Syrian. Other sources point to the date of 628 under the reign of Kavad, which is not very likely.[56]

As to the return of the Holy Cross, the Armenian excerpt concords with Theophanes in writing that the precious relic was first transferred in Constantinople and then in Jerusalem.[57] Other chroniclers as Nicephoros state, on the contrary, it was first brought back to Jerusalem and then taken to the capital.[58]

There, it was put by patriarch Sergios in the church of the Theotokos in Blachernae, then in the Ayia Sophia. The Armenian excerpt tells us in the same way that the Holy Cross was welcome by a crowd of patriarches and nobles who put it in the little church of the Holy Sion and one day later in the Ayia Sophia.[59] The author remarks that the date of this ceremony i.e. September 13 and 14 corresponds to the feast of the dedication—the nawakatik'—which naturally was already celebrated before the return of the Holy Cross. Certainly this feast has no direct link with the glorious deed of Heraclius.[60]

The examination of these excerpts confirms their authenticity which may be proved both by internal and external evidence. They must have belonged to the lost chronicle of Bishop Sebēos. Though the text has been shortened for liturgical needs, its historical content turns out, after close examination, to be more consistent than one might expect on first reading. Of course it is difficult to draw general conclusions from the comparison of these scarce excerpts with the Anonymous Chronicle which has been hitherto considered as Sebēos. We would need to see other excerpts from the true Sebēos in order to know if, actually, contrary to the Anonymous Chronicle, the central character of which is Xosrov, the bishop of the Bagratids celebrated the praise of the Greek emperor as the title of his work and the story about the miracle of the Theotokos may suggest.   Anyhow, a hellenophilic orientation would provide a good reason for the fact that the chronicle has been lost, except the short excerpts edited by G. V. Abgarian.

Translations
(See the list of biblical references below)

Excerpt A: Ms. Yerevan No. 7729 (Carentir of Mus) 1200-1202[61]
From the History of Heraclius concerning the ruin of Jerusalem and the taking to captivity of the holy wood of the Cross to Persia.

Then the general of the Persians, Xorian, who held the whole country of Syria and the great metropolis of Antioch, also took Caesarea and all the towns of Palestine. Thus did the wrath come by heavenly order [in the form of] a steel sword[a] which had been carried there, under the sky, and now came here, on earth. The wrath which had taken its origin from the House of the Lord was coming upon the Holy City of Jerusalem. And surrounding it, the general of the Persians, Xorian besieged it so that the word might be fulfilled which says: "When ye shall see Jerusalem compassed with troops know that the day (awr, reads awer "desolation") thereof is nigh" (Luke 21, 20). And having besieged it for many days, he captured the city.

That was the fourth wrath which had come upon Jerusalem. The first one [was] Nabuchadnezzar's,[b] the second one, that of Antiochos, the third one, Vespasian's,[c] but this fourth one was the heaviest and the worst. And it [was] even more pitiable than the others, as in the example of "the fourth piece of iron which was crushing and grinding everything" in the vision of Nabuchadnezzar (Dan. 2, 40), or in the vision of Daniel, [like] the fourth beast which "devoured and broke in pieces and stamped all the residue with its feet" (Dan. 7, 7). Likewise did this fourth monarchy of the Persian nation stand with a great might, according to the words of the angel, who was speaking to Daniel.[d] And [this monarch] arose against the kingdom of the Greeks and they did [everything] they wanted. Now an order which had come from the celestial court did not allow the [inhabitants] to surrender willingly the city of Jerusalem into the hands of the [enemies], but fighting the battle, the saints delivered themselves to death for the sake of the life-giving Holy Sign of Christ.[e] Therefore Xorian, the general of the Persians, became irritated, not only because of the great difficulty [of the siege], but because many of his troops perished and many were wounded. Now when the sentence of God's wrath arrived and they came by force into the city, General Xorian ordered his troops to put the whole city to the edge of the sword and to kill absolutely everybody. Then the Jews who were living inside, in conformity with the usual revolt of their fathers against God,[f] came to an understanding with the enemies and they helped them even from inside the city. And the wrath was fulfilled: as the general had ordered, they put [the city] to the edge of the sword and they slew [all of them]. Even if someone were fleeing and hiding himself from the Infidels, he could not escape from the hands of the Jews. And the sword of God's wrath, arising thus against all the inhabitants of Jerusalem was drunk with the blood of the saints.[g] There was much weeping, wailing and moaning.[h] Women and children [were] crying, the blood of the victims [was] flowing, the corpses of the dead [were cast] before the evil birds of the sky, and the bodies of the saints to the beasts and of the earth to the reptiles.[i] Blood [was] streaming as water all around Jerusalem.[j] And the city was full [with it] from one extremity to the other[k] and there was no one to bury [the dead].[l] Then [the enemy] entered the sanctuaries of the life-giving Resurrection. And they took the chalices of the beautiful [church of the] Resurrection, made of gold and silver, and the crown of the Kings, and they stole the liturgical vessels decorated with pearls.[m] They also took the precious wood of Christ's Cross. So, having taken all these things they kept them preciously [and] carefully. Then [the general] ordered that the city be set on fire.[n] And after such an accomplishment of [God's] wrath had come upon it, the city of Jerusalem was left to rack and ruin. Then [the general] gathered the vessels of the town with the precious wood of Christ's Cross, all the church vessels of Jerusalem and the vessels from the churches of Palestine and he had all this carried to King Xosrov.[o] Now when the precious Cross of Christ arrived near the doors of the royal city (of Persia), the king ordered his troops to go and meet the Cross with honor, in order to show the valour of his reign. He said: "What never happened in the time of my fathers is happening nowadays in the time of my reign." [All that] did not happen according to his will, but by necessity, so

that willingly or unwillingly the name of Christ might be glorified[p] [by them].
Now the precious wood of Christ's Cross entered the city with such an honor;
King Xosrov of Persia took it and put it in his treasury[q] with great honor,
in a chest made of aloes wood and he kept it carefully. Then after the
overthrow of Jerusalem, the capture and the exile of the Holy Sign of Christ,
did general Xosrov go to the royal city of Constantinople with a great and
heavy crowd. However King Heraclius, having been warned of it before,
called to his aid the great King of the Čenk', the Xak'an. And this latter
agreed to come and help him, [provided that] Heraclius paid him a tribute.
But when General Xorian came, King Xosrov came too and both of the Kings,
i.e. King Xosrov and Xak'an treacherously reached an understanding with
each other. . .

Excerpt B: ms. Yerevan No. 993 (1456)[62]
        Concerning the Holy Cross. From the Histories of Heraclius.

        In the days when Xosrov, the impious king, reigned over Persia, he
began to be envious of the godly-established King Heraclius. Executing a
mean project he wrote to him in the following words: "I, Xosrov, sitting over
the clouds and glorified among the gods, order you, Heraclius, to come [here]
and to assume a position as a slave after my cooks. Now, when my order
reaches you, do not delay your coming, and worship me, otherwise I will bring
upon you terrible disasters." And this [or he?] was like an implacable tumult.

        However [King Heraclius] thus retorted to this arrogance, writing:
"The sword of God[r] and [his] iron rod[s] shall crush you."[t] Then Xosrov
preparing troops gave them into the hands of Xorian, [one of] his nobles. And
Xorian gathering the multitude of his army went to the country of the
Greeks. And he began to burn and plunder the entire country of Palestine.
He took, set on fire and plundered Antioch, the very metropolis, and
Caesarea. Then he came to the Holy City of Jerusalem, in order to take it.
He surrounded and besieged it during many days, so that the word which has
been told might be fulfilled: "when ye shall see Jerusalem compassed with
troops then know that the desolation thereof is nigh" (Luke 21, 20).

        Now the Jews who were living there, in conformity with the usual
revolt of their fathers against God,[f] came to an understanding with the
enemies and one night they opened the doors and let the foreigners inside,
so that their own nation might stay in peace [with them].

        O the disaster which came upon Christian [people]! for there was great flows of blood.   That was the fourth wrath which had come upon Jerusalem.   The first one [was] Nabuchadnezzar's,[b] the second one that of Antiochos,[o] the third one Vespasian's, but this fourth one [was] much heavier and more pitiable than the others.   For they cast their corpses before the evil birds of the sky and their bodies to the beasts of the earth.[i]   They caused the blood [of the victims] to stream like water all around Jerusalem,[j] and there was no one to bury [the dead].[l]   For the sake of Christ's Cross did they fight or undergo individual martyrdom, all those whose names have been written on the Book of Life (Rev. 3, 5; 13, 8; 21, 27).   And if anyone fled from the enemies, he could not escape the Jews.

Now Xorian gathered all the church-vessels with the precious wood of Christ's Cross and he had it carried to the kingdom (i.e. the royal city) of Persia.[o]   And when the Holy Cross was near the kingdom of Persia, did Xosrov himself go and meet it, so that, either willingly or unwillingly, was the wood of the Cross glorified.[p]   Then the [king] took it and put it in the treasury[q] of his palace in a chest and he disposed inextinguishable luminaries before it.   And Xorian departed and he went to the city of Constantinople. Then did Heraclius, the God-loving King of the Greeks, call to his aid the king of the Čenk', the great Xakan.   And Xorian warning Xosrov asked him for troops.   Then King Xosrov gathered the multitude of the Infidel nations, many myriads of Barbarians, as well as people from Atrpatakan, Sons of T'orgom [i.e. Armenians], pagans from the mountains and, [at the head of them], he himself went and met Xorian.

And when they fought the battle againt each other, it happened that King Xakan of the Čenk', the Infidel betrayer, reached an understanding with Xosrov, and the troops of Heraclius were defeated and fled inside the city. And Heraclius casting down his crown and taking off his bright purple coat,[u] put on hair clothes.   Then he threw himself into the ashes[v] and he put his face on his knees.[w]   Bending his neck as a convict, [in] a carean,[x] he offered prayers to [God], the Highest, having as intercessor the glorious Mother of God, the Holy Virgin Mary.   He shed bitter tears and with pitiable voice he begged saying: "We have no intercessor but only Thou, Mary."   And during three days he ate nothing[y] and said nothing else, but unweariedly he offered his prayers till he received the fruit of [his] prayers.[z]   "And on the fourth day, he said, I, Heraclius, saw that there was a high hill and Xosrov on the top of the hill.   And all kinds of nations speaking [all kinds] of languages[aa] were prostrating themselves before Xosrov and they were praising him, but

I, Heraclius, neither prostrated myself nor praised him. And while staying there, I saw the Holy Mother of God holding a bare fiery sword in her hand.[ab] She gave it to me and she said 'strike him and cast him down.' And receiving wings like an eagle,[ac] I took my flight [and I pounced] upon him and crushed his head in front of the whole multitude of the assembly." Then Heraclius standing up said to his soldiers: "By the intercession of the Holy Mother of God, Christ [is] with us and we have been granted victory."

And when dawn was breaking, they went and fought the battle. Now the lads of Heraclius pursued Xosrov, cut off his head and brought it to Heraclius; then they mercilessly slaughtered the pagans. And the survivors withdrew and took flight; they went and seated the child Artašīr, a son of Xosrov, on the throne.

But when the next year came, Heraclius, the God-loving King, assembled a great multitude, came to the East, and went to the country of Persia in order to avenge himself against his enemies. Now, as child Artašīr had begun his reign, he threatened Xorian and sentenced him to death. And all [the courtiers] said he deserved death because of his deeds. But his friends and relations, who were in the house of the king, warned Xorian. Then Xorian went and fell at the feet of the Holy Emperor (Kaysr) and he said: "Give me troops, stand by me and help me and I will do everything your soul desires."

The Great King accepted to give him troops and four generals, whose names were Gēorg, Dawit', Vahan, Smbat, with the Armenian naxarars. Then they went and attacked the infidels. And child Artašīr died and, upon the order of the Holy Emperor, they seated Xorian on the royal throne of Persia. But the Great Emperor was very sad on account of the precious Cross of Christ. He wrote to Xorian: "Order the booty of Jerusalem and the precious wood of Christ's Cross to be brought to me." Now Xosrov thinking that this did not matter much answered: "How can the Great King ask for a miserable piece of wood?"[ad] Then putting magnificent gifts in the hands of the troops and of the generals, he paid a royal homage to the Holy Cross and had it taken to Heraclius. And Heraclius, full of joy, gave thanks to God because of his favours. Then he put it on a cart and he carried it with many troops through the highway of Georgia until he brought it to the kingdom of the Greeks, in Constantinople. And when the Holy Cross was near the kingdom of the Greeks, it happened that the good news reached the town and a multitude went out and met it: patriarchs, nobles and moreover a crowd of men and women, old and young people together, and all of them were praising God as with one voice. Then they took [the Cross] and put it in the small church of Holy Sion and they celebrated the great day of the dedications (nawakatis) on September 13.

Then the next day they held another service in the great cathedral (kat'uɫikē) which was called Ayia Sophia (Surb Sop'i) and they celebrated the feast of the Holy Cross, which was the 14th day of the month of September, with a plenty of oxen (zuarakawk'), sweet-smelling incense and shining luminaries, for they decided to celebrate the feast of the Holy Cross during eight days. Therefore let all of us feast and adore the Holy Cross so that the light of the face of Christ our God may be manifested to us:[ae] glory and honour to Him for ever and ever.

Colophon

Lord, through the return of thy Cross
And the prayers of thy immaculate Mother,
Deliver the soul of the present writer
From the captivity of the Prince of Evil.

LIST OF BIBLICAL REFERENCES (Explicit quotations are noted in the Translation; we use the occidental names of the biblical books)

[a]Wis. 18, 16   [b]Cf. 2Kgs 25, 1f.; Jer. 52, 4f.   [c]Cf. 1 Mac. 1, 20f.; 5, 11f. [d]Dan. 11, 2   [e]Acts 15, 16   [f]Ps. 78 (77), 8; Neh. 9, 26-37; 2 Chr. 29, 6; Acts 7, 51   [g]Rev. 17, 6; Is. 34, 6   [h]Mt. 2, 18   [i]Dt. 28, 16; Jer. 7, 33. 16, 4. 19, 7   [j]Ps. 79 (78), 3   [k]2Kgs 21, 16   [l]Jer. 14, 16   [m]Esther 1, 6 (read endeluzeal margartovk' instead of yeluzeal margartov   [n]1 Ezr. 1, 54-55; 2 Kgs 25, 9   [o]2 Kgs 24, 13. 25, 13; 2 Chr. 36, 18   [P]Cf. Phil. 1, 18   [q]Dan. 1, 2   [r]Cf. Is. 27, 1. 34, 5f. 66, 16; Jer. 12, 12. 47, 6; Ez. 21, 8. 30, 24. 32, 10; Lev. 26, 33   [s]Ps. 2, 9; Rev. 2, 27. 12, 5. 19, 15   [t]Ps. 110 (109), 5   [u]Jon. 3, 6; Ez. 26, 16   [v]Esther 4, 3; Jer. 6, 26; Ez. 27, 30   [w]1 Kgs. 18, 42   [x]Is. 58, 5 (read zanur instead of zanawr   [y]Esther 4, 16   [z]Mt. 3, 8; Luke 3, 8   [aa]Dan. 3, 4. 5, 19. 7, 14 etc.   [ab]Gen. 3, 24; Nb. 22, 23, 31; Jos. 5, 16; 1 Chr. 21, 16   [ac]Cf. Is. 40, 31   [ad]Wis. 10, 4. 15, 5   [ae]Ps. 4, 7.

NOTES

[1]Written in the monastery S. Karapet, in Bałēš (Bitlis), by the scholar Vardan Bałišec'i; cf. G. Abgarian, "Remarques sur l'histoire de Sebēos" REArm 1 (1964) 203-215 (especially p. 209). This article is a French translation from the Armenian text in Banber Matenadarani 4(1958) 61-72.

[2]Cf. M. Krikorian, "Sebēos Historian of the Seventh Century" in T. J. Samuelian (ed.), Classical Armenian Culture (Armenian Texts and Studies 4, University of Pennsylvania, 1982) 52-67 (esp. 52-53); Z. Arzumanian, "A Critique of Sebēos and His History of Heraclius, a Seventh-Century Document," in ibid. 68-78 (esp. 69-70); G. Abgarian, "Remarques" n. 1. takes a critical inventory of these testimonies. One should remark there are in fact two distinct questions: (1) Is the Anonymous Chronicle the same work as the "History of Heraclius and the Holy Cross" ascribed to a certain Bishop Sebēos? (2) Is this alleged author the same person as Bishop Sebēos, who took part on the Synod of Duin in 645?

[3]Brosset's copy of the manuscript No. 2639 comments the text as follows: "The author never names himself in his work but he speaks like a contemporary. Father Jean Chakhatounof thinks it most likely that he is Bishop Sebēos who is referred to more than once in the History of John Catholicos 200 years later. See the Description d'Edchmiadzin . . .by Jean Chakhatounof."

[4]Cf. G. Abgarian, Patmut'iwn Sebēosi, Yerevan 1979, with a full list of the previous editions (13-19) and of the translations (20-25) of the chronicle.

[5]Cf. Abgarian, "Remarques," REArm 2 (1965) 468-470 (a review by H. Berberian of Abgarian's various articles) and M. Krikorian, "Sebēos," 65-66, n. 10. G. Abgarian's works were the occasion of much discussion mainly by P. Ananian, Sebēosi Patmut'ean grk'i masin k'ani mě lusabanut'iwnner (Bibliothèque d'arménologie Bazmavep, (Venice, 1972) and M. Krikorian, Ditołut'iwnner ew srbagrut'iwnner Sebiosi patmagroc' bnagrin veray (Azgayin Matenadaran 214, Vienna, 1972-1973).

[6]Abgarian, Pat'mut'iwn; G. Abgarian has also given a brief account of his work in REArm 14 (1980) 478-480 "A propos de la publication de H. Hübschmann Zur Geschichte Armeniens. . . dans REArm 13."

[7]In spite of the opinion of St. Malxaseanc', P. Ananian (Sebēosi Patmut'iwn) and other scholars, these chapters are generally regarded as an independent source from the end of the fourth or from the fifth century, which is called by C. Toumanoff, "The Third Century Armenian Arsacids," REArm 6 (1969) 233-281, esp. 235, Primary History of Armenia [English translation in R. W. Thomson, Moses Khorenats'i, History of the Armenians, Harvard 1978, 357-368.

[8]According to G. Abgarian, Patmut'iwn 72. 375 these lines could be regarded as some kind of verses: Matean Žamanakean / Patmut'iwn t'agaworakan,/ Vēp ariakan, / Vanumn tiezerakan, /Hen Sasanakan /yApruezn Xosrovean, / or hrdeheal boc'ac'oyc' / zaŕ i nerk'oys amenayn, / dlordeal zcov ew zc'amak' / zart'uc'eal zkorcamumn / i veray amenayn erkri.

[9]G. Abgarian, Patmut'yun, 375.

[10]Ibid., 376-377.

[11]Ibid., 421-433.

[12]See the pertinent observations of P. Peters "Sainte Sousanik, martyre en Arméno-Géorgie," Analecta Bollandiana 53 (1935) 247-260, concerning the very heterogeneous compilation ascribed to Uxtanes, bishop of Edessa or Sebastia.

[13]Cf. R. Grousset, Histoire de l'Arménie, Paris 1947 (pr. 1973) 264.

[14]Uxtanēs Patmut'iwn Hayoc', Vaŀaršapat 1871, 56 (cf. M. Brosset, Deux historiens arméniens. . . St Petersburg, 1870-71, 309). New edition of the Armenian text with a modern Georgian translation and a commentary by Z. Aleksidze, Historia separationis Iberorum ex Armeniis, Tbilisi 1975, 97 (348-358: discussion of Abgarian's works). The last sentence of Abgarian's quotation may belong to Uxtanēs's subsequent narration.

[15]G. Abgarian, Patmut'iwn 422 regards the end of the fragment as a quotation from a memorial (yišatakaran) written by a contemporary of Smbat, who can be neither Uxtanēs nor the author of the History of Heraclius.

[16]Concerning the origin and the history of this manuscript, see A. Mat'ewosian, "Where and when was the Tōnakan / Čaŕēntir from Muš written?" Banber Matenadarani 9 (1969) 137-162; M. van Esbroeck, "Structure du répertoire du Tōnakan de Mush," International Symposium on Armenian Linguistics (Abstracts), Yerevan 1982, 30-31, tries to reconstruct the

primitive structure of Solomon's <u>Tonakan.</u>

[17]Cf. N. Marr, <u>Antiox Stratig. Plenenie Ierusalima Persami v 614 g.</u> (= Teksty i razyskanija po armjano-gruzinskoj filologii, IX), St. Petersburg 1909, 2-59. The Georgian version of Antiochos' Chronicle has been also published with a Latin translation by G. Garitte, "La prise de Jerusalem par les Perses en 614" <u>CSCO</u> 202-203, 1960; Arab versions of the same work in <u>CSCO</u> 340-341. 347-348, 1973-1974.

[18]M. Van Esbroeck and U. Zanetti, "Le manuscrit Erevan 993. Inventaire des pieces," <u>REArm</u> 12 (1977) 123-167, esp. 160 No. 382, suggest comparing this text with the manuscript Venice No. 288, chapter 141. According to Abgarian, <u>Patmut'iwn</u> 429, the manuscript of Venice has been copied from Yerevan No. 993.

[19]Cf. translation, <u>infra.</u>

[20]G. Abgarian, <u>Patmut'iwn</u> 423, quotes Movsēs Kałankatuac'i <u>History of the Albanians</u> II, 10 (ed. V. D. Ałak'elian (Yerevan, 1983, 129), 146; translation in modern Armenian by V. D. Ałak'elian, Yerevan 1969, 98): "He (i. e. Xorian) captured and set fire to the big city of Jerusalem and he took to captivity the wood of Life, the Cross, . . . and the vessels of all the sanctuaries in these regions, (vessels) made of gold and silver . . . and (decorated with) pearls." This text is very close to our fragment.

[21]Abgarian also compares other details with Samuel Anec'i and Yovhannēs Drasxanakertc'i.

[22]Cf. N. Marr, <u>Antiox Stratig</u>, 60, points at the fact that Heraclius is called "the Holy Emperor" (<u>Surb Kaysr</u>) in the ms. Yerevan No. 993. Nevertheless, as Abgarian rightly observes (<u>Patmut'iwn</u>, 425), no parallel to this text as been preserved in Yerevan No. 7729 so that one cannot conclude that this epithet belongs exclusively to the redactor of the manuscript Yerevan No. 993. On the other hand this latter more than once calls the Emperor <u>astuacasēr</u> φιλόθεος an epithet which is not to be found in the parallel developments of the manuscript No. 7729.

[23]G. Abgarian, <u>Patmut'iwn</u>, 276 f. n. 351, explains that Xorian is the same person as the Persian general Šahrvaraz (alias Sarbaraz, Sarbanazas).

[24]One could perhaps argue that the text was written before the Arab invasions since the author does not seem to know of any other Infidel

invaders of the Holy City after the Persians.

[25]Excerpts A and B quote our Lord's prediction in Luke 31, 20 concerning the ruin of Jerusalem. B's developments about Daniel's vision have been inserted after the description of the taking of the Holy City. A and B also quote Jeremy and John's Revelation.

[26]Cf. M. Van Esbroeck, "Salomon de Makenoc, vardapet du VIIIe s.," in Armeniaca ("Melanges d'Etudes Armeniennes publies a l'occasion du 250eme anniversaire de l'entree des Peres Mekhitaristes dans l'ile de Saint-Lazare 1717-1967"), Venice 1969, 33-44.

[27]Ibid., 41 About Vahan Goɫt'nac'i see H. Ačaṙian Anj. B. 5, 14 (Vahan No. 35).

[28]In the following pages we are much indebted for the chronological data to A. N. Stratos, Byzantium in the Seventh Century M. Ogilvie-Grant; Amsterdam, 1968) 1. 602-634. Besides the numerous sources referred to in this fundamental work, one should also mention the Georgian Chronicle about the Sieges of Constantinople which has been preserved in a manuscript of the year 1042 and was compiled certainly much earlier. This chronicle has been translated into French by M. Van Esbroeck, "Une chronique de Maurice a Heraclius dans un recit des sieges de Constantinople," Bedi Kartlisa 34 (1976) 74-96.

[29]Cf. G. Abgarian, Patmut'iwn 113 (chapter 34 lines 3-11) [French translation by F. Macler, Histoire d'Heraclius par l'eveque Sebeos, (Paris, 1904) 46]; compare with T'ovma Arcruni, Patmut'iwn III, 3, (Tiflis, 1917) 152-153 [modern Armenian translation by Vrez Vardanian, (Yerevan, 1978) 107]. See also Theophanes Chronography, ed. De Boor, Leipzig 1883, I, 300-301; Chronicon Pascale (ed. L. Dindorf; Bonn, 1832) 1. 706-709.

[30]Cf. A. N. Stratos, Byzantium 105-106.

[31]Cf. Antiochos Strategos, The Taking of Jerusalem in 614 (ed. Marr) V, 8-15, CSCO 202, 12-13 [Georgian] 203, 8-9 [Garitte's Latin translation).

[32]Ibid., XI, 20, CSCO, 29 [Georgian]. 203, 20 [translation]; Theophanes Chronology, I, 301 n. 29. A. N. Stratos Byzantium, 109 also mentions other sources.

[33]Cf. Theophanes, Chronography, I, 301:

Antioches (ed. Marr) X, 4, CSCO 202, 26 [Georgian], 203, 18 [translation].
The hostility of the Jews is also mentioned by the so-called Sebēos 34
(Abgarian, Patmut'iwn) 115; F. Macler, Histoire d'Heraclius 68.

[34]According to A. N. Stratos, Byzantium, 110, Sahrvaraz had "handed
over the city administration to the Jews as a reward for the services they
had rendered."

[35]Thanks to the intercession of Komitas Catholicos of the Armenians
(617-625), the Christians of Jerusalem were soon granted certain advantages
as we can read in the socalled Sebeos 35 (Abgarian, Patmut'iwn 116; F.
Macler, Histoire d'Heraclius, 70; M. Stone, The Armenian Inscriptions from
the Sinai (Harvard, 1982, 34).

[36]Cf. Chardin, Voyage du chevalier Chardin en Perse. . ., (ed. L.
Langles, Paris, 1811) 2. 326.

[37]Cf. Theophanes, Chronography, 302; Nicephoros, Opuscula (ed. De
Boor; Leipzig, 1880) 17-18; Cedrenos, Summary of History, P G 121, 716.

[38]Cf. A. N. Stratos, Byzantium 173 ff.

[39]Theophanes, Chronography 314: (χοσρόης) νέαν έποιήσατο
στρατείαν στρατεύσας ξένους τε καὶ πολίτας καὶ οἰκέτας,
ἐκ παντὸς γέωους ἐκλογὴν ποιούμενος.

[40]Cf. A. N. Stratos, Byzantium, 177-178.

[41]Cf. Ibid., 195.

[42]Chronicon Pascale (ed. Dindorf) I, 726.

[43]Theodoros the Elder and Synkellos of Ayia Sophia, a member of the
embassy sent by the Byzantines to the Χακ'αν of the Avars seems to be the
author of a poem "Concerning the savage assault of the godless Avars and
Persians against the Divinely protected city and God's mercy in turning it
through the Holy Virgin in a shameful retreat," (ed. Sternbach) in Analecta
Avarica (Cracovia, 1900). [cf. G. Moravsik, Byzantinoturcica I, 294].

[44]George Pisides, Bellum Avaricum, P. G. 92, 1353. 1356. 1364, very
near to the Georgian chronicle edited by M. Van Esbroeck, Bedi Kartlisa 34
80-88. Many of the other accounts of the siege in the Synaxars have been
collected in P G 92.

[45]Examination of the sources in A. N. Stratos Byzantium, 370-371.

[46]The Georgian chronicle edited by M. Van Esbroeck, Bedi Karlisa 34 82, also describes the Heraclius and his prayers to the Theotokos but all these events take place before his campaign in Orient, not during the siege of Constantinople.

[47]Cf. A. N. Stratos, Byzantium, 127; concerning the revival of the cult of the Holy Cross after the VIIth century, see N. Thierry, "Le culte de la croix dans l'empire byzantin du VIIe s. au Xe s. dans ses rapports avec le guerre contre l'infidèle. Nouveaux témoignages archéologiques," Rivista di studi Bizantini e Slavi 1 (1981) 205-228, esp. 207 (picture of a silver coin), 208 (about the military use of the words Ἐν τούτῳ νίκᾳ).

[48]Cf. A. N. Stratos, Byzantium, 228.

[49]Ibid., 246.

[50]Ibid., 233.

[51]Ibid., 246.

[52]Ibid., 249. 384-387.

[53]Chronique de Seert, (ed. Tr. Mgr Addai Scher- J. Perrier - R. Griveau; P O, 4. 13; Paris, 1919). 236. 556; Michel le Syrien, Chronique, (ed. tr. J. B. Chabot; 3 vol.; Paris, 1899-1904) 2. 427.

[54]Cf. H. Ačaṙyan, Anj. B., 5.13 (Vahan No. 26). One could also think of Vahan No. 27, Mamikonian, the grandson of Gayl Vahan, who fought against the Persians together with his father Smbat Mamikonian, then with Prince Smbat of Hastenk', and brought to Caesarea a relic of the Holy Cross.

[55]Cf. D. M. Lang, Armenia, Cradle of Civilization, London 1970, 173-174; F. L. Cross, The Oxford Dictionary of the Christian Church, London 1957, 917.

[56]See the discussion by A. N. Stratos, Byzantium, 385- 386.

[57]Theophanes, Chronography, 327-328.

[58]Nicephoros, Opuscula, 22.

[59]Ibid.

[60]Cf. A. N. Stratos, Byzantium, 254. 388 and the remarks of A.

Renoux, Le codex arménien Jérusalem 121, II (P O 168), Turnhout 1971, 361
n. 1-2.

[61] Abgarian, Patmut'iwn, 429 ff.

[62] Ibid., 431.

LE MANUSCRIT ACTUEL DE L'OUVRAGE D'EZNIK EST-IL CELUI DE LA PREMIERE EDITION?

Martiros Minassian

Université de Genève

De nos jours, arméniste, historien des Chrétientés d'Orient ou de la philosophie et de la religion iraniennes ne sauraient ignorer le petit ouvrage d'Eznik Kołbac'i ou natif du village de Kołb, dans la plaine d'Ararat, —traitant de Dieu, des philosophies grecques, de la religion mazdéenne, des croyances populaires et de l'hérésie marcionite,—c'est pourquoi nous ne le présenterons pas ici. Au monde entier, actuellement on n'en possède qu'un seul manuscrit, Matenadaran 1097, contenant d'ailleurs également des commentaires bibliques d'Ephrem, copié en 1280 AD, en un lieu non indiqué, conservé anciennement à la bibliothèque des manuscrits du couvent d'Ēǰ-miacin, où le philologue Galust Tēr Mkrtč'ian le signale au linguiste Hrač'eay Ačařian en avril 1902.[1] La question posée alors et qui se pose encore, à notre avis, est de savoir avec certitude si ce Ms est celui de la première édition de l'ouvrage en 1763, à Izmir ou Smyrne.[2] Contrairement à l'opinion reçue, nous essayerons de répondre par la négative à travers un bref historique des deux premières éditions et une étude très sommaire du Ms 1097 du Matenadaran.[3]

L'édition princeps de l'ouvrage d'Eznik porte le titre de <u>Girk' ěnddimut'eanc'</u> 'Livre des contestations,' un petit volume de 16,5 x 10,5 cm, 12 pages non numérotées + 293 p. contenant l'avant-propos de l'éditeur Yakob Nalian, Patriarche des Arméniens de Constantinople, l'oeuvre d'Eznik les 'Conseils du même Eznik' (en réalité ceux de Nilus), une table des matières sous forme d'idées principales de l'ouvrage proprement dit, le mémorial non signé de l'imprimeur Markos et la correction de 29 errata en deux pages.

T. Samuelian & M. Stone, eds. <u>Medieval Armenian Culture</u>. (University of Pennsylvania Armenian Texts and Studies 6). Chico, CA: Scholars Press, 1983. pp. 240 to 249.

L'éditeur et l'imprimeur nous apprennent que le possesseur du Ms, l'évêque, Abraham vardapet, de la région d'Izmir, "charmé" par la lecture du livre d'Eznik, le présente au Patriarche et en souhaite une publication avec sa subvention. Celui-ci, "epris" à son tour par ce texte découvert, prépare une édition en "corrigeant" le Ms corrompu, un prêtre recopie le texte ainsi revu, l'imprimeur Markos se met au travail en juillet 1762 et le petit livre sort le 22 mars 1763, date que nous retenons, avec certains philologes avertis, comme étant celle de la première parution de l'ouvrage d'Eznik, à Izmir.

Avant 1763, on connaissait Eznik Kołbac'i, mais pas son ouvrage, bien que l'imprimeur Markos dise dans son memorial: "Ce saint livre n'etait pas tellement répandu dans notre nation, on n'en entendait que le titre;"[4] cependant aucun chroniqeur n'avait signale une production litteraire d'Eznik Kołbac'i. Selon Koriwn, celui-ci avait été un élève de Mesrop et Sahak, les deux piliers des lettres arméniennes, il avait été mandé en Syrie et à Byzance en compagnie de son condisciple Yovsēp', afin de traduire les écrits des Pères de l'Eglise; après avoir effectué cette tâche délicate et envoyé en Arménie leurs traductions, les deux amis étaient rentrés de Byzance avec un exemplaire impérial des Septante, et le catholicos Sahak, alors destitué, avait passé ses derniers jours dans la province de Bagrevand à revoir avec Eznik la première version "hâtive" de la Bible arménienne ou à refaire une nouvelle traduction à partir du grec. L'historien Ełišē (Ve s.) avait mentionné dans son épopée historique un Eznik, évêque de la region de Bagrevand, comme signataire de la fameuse réponse des Arméniens à l'édit de Mihrnerseh exigeant la conversion de l'Arménie entière au mazdéisme. Sans la précision d'Ełišē, on s'accorde à identifier cet évêque de Bagrevand avec Eznik Kołbac'i, d'abord à cause du nom de la région, puis à cause des critiques du mazdéisme qu'on retrouve dans la réponse de la noblesse arménienne et dans l'ouvrage d'Eznik plus largement. A notre avis, l'identité de l'évêque Eznik et de l'auteur Eznik Kołbac'i est plus que probable. Mais revenons à la première édition de son ouvrage.

La langue et le style du "Livre des contestations" ne laissent aucun doute quant à l'appartenance de l'ouvrage à la première moitié du Ve siècle, époque dite classique, quoi qu'on y trouve des irrégularités grammaticales et des mots non classiques.[5] Mais pour ce qui est du manuscrit, on n'en sait absolument rien, l'éditeur et l'imprimeur n'en ayant soufflé mot, le possesseur Abraham n'ayant pas eu de voix au chapitre.[6] En tous cas, pour être pleinement digne de la période classique de l'ancienne littérature arménienne, le texte nécessitait une épuration de formes, qui vint avec la deuxième édition en 1826, à St. Lazare de Venise. Le petit livre de gousset (11,5 x 6,5 cm) du même Eznik de Kołb s'appelle Ełc ałantoc' 'Réfutation des sectes,'[7] sans nom d'éditeur. On apprenait plus tard de bouche en bouche que celui-ci était le célèbre grammairien et écrivain P. Arsēn Bagratuni, qui déclare dans son avant-propos (non signé) que le manuscrit de cette édition date de Č'IT' ou 729 de l'ère arménienne = 1280 AD, qu'il a corrigé certaines fautes de lettres "indésirables" et qu'il a subdivisé en livres et chapitres le texte continu du Ms.[8] Ces déclarations, si brèves et laconiques soient-elles, firent supposer, à tous ceux qui étaient hors du couvent St. Lazare, que les Mekhitaristes de Venise possédaient un manuscrit d'Eznik, surtout que le texte publié était assez différent de celui de 1763.   C'est pourquoi le P. Grigoris Galémk'iarian, Mekhitariste de Vienne, qui projetait une nouvelle édition revue d'Eznik et aidait le chanoine Joh. Michael Schmid dans sa traduction allemande (parue à Vienne en 1900), débarque à St. Lazare en septembre 1897, afin d'étudier le "manuscrit" d'Eznik. Il est profondément déçu: dans une lettre datée du 15 décembre 1898, postée de Constantinople, il apprend au chanoine Schmid que le "manuscrit" supposé n'était autre qu'un exemplaire corrigé de l'édition de 1763, mais corrigé sur le Ms d'Izmir ou de Mgr Abraham.   Le Père bibliothécaire du couvent, P. Mkrtič' Awgerian a inscrit ce qui suit au verso de la feuille de garde de cet exemplaire corrigé: "Ce livre d'Eznik est corrigé par le diacre Gēorg Tēr Yovhannisian sur un manuscrit copié en l'an 729 de l'ère arménienne /1280 AD/; il nous est parvenu en octobre 1784," 21 ans après la première publication.[9]   Le correcteur Gēorg, philologue et lexicologue bien connu, a laisse les lignes suivantes à la fin de l'ouvrage d'Eznik, p. 272, lignes où le P. Grigoris Galémk'iarian a reconnu à juste titre deux mémoriaux: celui du copiste du Ms et celui de Gēorg relatif à sa correction de l'exemplaire imprimé; nous les reproduisons en ouvrant les abréviations: _Šnorhok' ew ołormut'eambn_ _astucoy katarec'i zgirk's eznkay es apikar t'ovma vardapets i vayelumn_ _amenagov vardapetin nersēsi. i t'uis hayoc' Č'IT'_ 'Par la miséricorde de Dieu, j'ai terminé ce livre d'Eznik, moi incapable _vardapet_ T'ovma, pour la jouissance du très louable _vardapet_ Nersēs, en l'an 729 des Arméniens' (1280 AD): ceci doit avoir été considéré par Gēorg comme le mémorial du copiste T'ovma. Voici le sien: _Yor apa ew mek' hayec'eal ullagrec'ak' ztpeals zays._ _ew jeřagir orinakn ayn ēr, yormē ztpealn haneal ēin i t'uakanut'eann hayoc'_ _ŘMŽA yizmir k'ałak'in,_ c'est-à-dire 'Sur lequel ayant regardé nous-même plus tard, nous avons corrigé cet exemplaire imprimé, et le manuscrit etait celui-là d'où l'on avait tiré l'imprimé en 1211 de l'ère arménienne (1762 AD), dans la ville d'Izmir'. Et le P. G. Galēmk'iarian de conclure dans sa lettre à M. Schmid: "Il est donc clair maintenant que le seul manuscrit connu, copié par T'ovma vardapet en 1280, est celui de la première édition de Smyrne en 1762, manuscrit que Gēorg Tēr Yovhannisian a eu plus tard sous la main pour une nouvelle collation, et que cet exemplaire corrigé est parvenu en 1784 à la bibliothèque des Mekhitaristes de Venise. Quant au manuscrit, il est disparu aujourd'hui ou, peut-être, brûlé à Smyrne en 1845," lors du terrible incendie ayant ravagé cette ville, secouée auparavant par des tremblements de terre. Mais qui pourrait certifier que le manuscrit d'Eznik n'avait pas été gardé au patriarcat arménien de Constantinople ou dans la bibliothèque du Patriarche Y. Nalian, érudit et amateur de livres rares?[10] Répondant aimablement à notre question, M. Gēorg Pamboukdjian, l'actuel bibliothécaire du patriarcat arménien d'Istanbul, nous assure que les archives du patriarcat n'ont conservé aucun manuscrit, ni une copie quelconque de l'ouvrage d'Eznik, un incendie ayant tout ravagé au 19e siècle. Et Gēorg n'indique pas son lieu de correction: Constantinople ou Izmir?

Une collation minutieuse lors de la préparation d'une nouvelle édition critique de l'ouvrage d'Eznik nous a montré que le P. A. Bagratuni a reproduit fidèlement le texte corrigé par G. Tēr Yovhannisian, et la date 1280 de la copie du Ms, mentionnée dans son avant-propos, vient du mémorial du copiste T'ovma, reproduit par le correcteur: mais n'aurait-il pas dû éclairer ses lecteurs sur ces détails philologiques importants! Cependant l'histoire du Ms nous réservait d'autres surprises.

Dans le cahier de juin 1902 de la revue Handēs Amsōreay, H. Ačařian annonçait ceci: "L'unique manuscrit d'Eznik, qu'on croyait brûlé dans l'incendie de Smyrne, est retrouvé le 25 avril 1902, dans la bibliothèque des manuscrits d'Ējmiacin."[11] Rien que cette annonce montre que l'on croyait à l'identité du Ms retrouvé avec celui d'Izmir, ce que G. Tēr Mkrtč'ian se proposait de démontrer dans un des chapitres de l'étude mentionnée ci-dessous dans la note 11, mais il n'en a pas eu le loisir, d'après le témoignage de H. Ačařian.[12] Bien plus tard, celui-ci affirme que "L'édition de Venise provient d'un manuscrit de 1280, l'unique manuscrit existant au monde est le même."[13] A l'exception du P. Ełia P'eč'ikian de St. Lazare, les autres philologues et linguistes ont fait le leur cet avis des deux decouvreurs du Ms 1097 qu'il nous fallait étudier, à notre tour, pour en savoir plus.

Le Ms 1097 du Matenadaran (16,5 x 13 x 6,3) contient des commentaires bibliques d'Ephrem (p. 1-187v à la moitié), l'ouvrage d'Eznik (187v moitié - 314v) et un bref commentaire biblique (315r - 320v). L'écriture est en bolorgir bien lisible avec très peu d'abréviations autres que celles de noms en -ut'iwn (abrégés irrégulièrement), dépourvue de miniatures ou d'ornements marginaux, à l'encre noire, à l'exception des titres et de certaines lettres capitales en rouge. L'état du Ms est bon.[14] L'examen de l'écriture montre également que le Ms a eu deux copistes, l'un principal, qui a copié du début à la p. 314v, l'autre secondaire, qui a copié le dernier commentaire biblique. Le Ms contient des mémoriaux et certaines petites notes, soit au début, soit à la fin, mais rien dans l'ouvrage d'Eznik ou relatif à celui-ci. Voici les principaux mémoriaux qui éclairent la question qui nous intéresse ici.

Mémorial du copiste principal Luser: Šnorhawk' ew ołormut'eambn astucoy katarec'i ztaṙs astuacašunč's es p'cun ew apikar groł LUSER. i vayelumn surb ew amenagov. vardapetin nersēsi. ałač'em zdass luseramic' yišel zbazmameł groliks ew zžaṙankord gris zhṙetor zvardapetn ew astuc yišołac't ołormesc'i. i t'uis hayoc' Č'IT' grec'aw. (p. 145 r) 'Par la grâce et la miséricorde de Dieu, j'ai terminé les écritures inspirées par Dieu (il vient de terminer des commentaires bibliques. M. M.) moi, vil et incapable scribe LUSER, pour la jouissance du saint et très louable vardapet Nersēs; je supplie les choeurs des anges de se souvenir de moi, petit scribe grand pêcheur, et de l'héritier de ce livre, le vardapet rhéteur, et que Dieu ait pitié de vous qui vous souviendrez; en l'an 729 des Arméniens (1280 AD) fut écrit.' On voit nettement que le scribe principal du Ms 1097 est Luser, tandis que celui du Ms d'Izmir (vu par G. Tēr Yovhannisian) est T'ovma vardapet. Comparons leurs mémoriaux.

Le mémorial du scribe T'ovma vardapet (recopié par Gēorg) est composé de 23 mots (en arménien), les prépositions étant considérées comme unités et la date Č'IT' (729 de l'ère arménienne) comptant pour trois mots; or, 18 de ces 23 mots se retrouvent littéralement et dans le même ordre syntaxique dans le mémorial du copiste Luser, ce qui est une coincidence eloquente et troublante; les seules divergences essentielles sont, dans le memorial de T'ovma: "moi, incapable T'ovma vardapet," Luser se disant "moi, vil et incapable scribe Luser;" T'ovma déclarant "j'ai terminé ce livre d'Eznik," Luser notant, après des commentaires bibliques, "j'ai terminé des écritures inspirées par Dieu." Il semble que le mémorial du scribe T'ovma vardapet ait été calqué sur celui du copiste Luser; serait-ce Gēorg qui aurait "amalgamé" les deux mémoriaux, comme le pensait L. Mariès: "Ter Hovhannessean parait avoir résumé incorrectement, en les amalgamant . . . Mais les deux noms: Tomas et Nersēs, sont les mêmes, la date de transcription surtout, 729, est la même: l'identité du manuscrit apparaît nettement;"[15] à notre avis, pas si nettement que ça. Dans le cas où Gēorg aurait copié correctement le mémorial du scribe T'ovma vardapet, la mention expresse de celui-ci "ce livre d'Eznik" détruit la supposition du même manuscrit, car, comme on l'a dit, on ne trouve aucun mémorial à l'intérieur ou à la fin du livre d'Eznik concernant celui-ci dans le Ms 1097. Gēorg, qui a consciencieusement corrigé un exemplaire de l'édition de 1763, aurait-il, en effet, "amalgamé" le mémorial du copiste Luser et un mémorial d'un certain T'ovma qu'on retrouve dans le Ms 1097? Notons enfin que le memorial du copiste T'ovma du Ms d'Izmir (selon Georg) contient l'accusatif non classique zgirk's "ce livre," au lieu de zgirs.

Un certain T'ovma vardapet a laissé deux notes dans le Ms 1097. La première est à la p. 108 v, dans la marge inférieure, hors du texte, ajoutée après la copie, en caractères fins et un peu laids, en arménien moderne: Awał ew ełuk ē angēt gragrin: astuacahalac hogi.   inč' karnes.   gitem banakan es. zgirs tołel es mēkimēk yinč' es kc'el 'Hélas et malheur au scribe ignorant! Ame persécutée par Dieu, que fais-tu? Je sais, tu es raisonnable, tu as aligné des livres et pourquoi les as-tu rattachés l'un à l'autre? Cette note sans nom d'auteur, est de la même écriture que la suivante, à la p. 145 r, juste après le mémorial du scribe Luser (voir plus haut): Astuac ołormi nersēs varžapetin ew inj t'ovma vardapetis or zanaruest girs yawart aci. k'ristos astuac ayn ašakertin ołormesc'i or sakaw ink'n ēnd mez tanĵi amēn 'Que Dieu ait pitié du maître Nersēs et de moi, T'ovma vardapet qui ai mené à fin ce livre sans art; que le Christ Dieu ait pitié de cet élève qui lui-même souffre un peu avec nous, amen.' On suppose que le vardapet Nersēs, qu'on retrouve dans ce mémorial et dans celui du copiste Luser, est Nersēs de Muš, fondateur de l'école superieur de Glajor, en Arménie orientale, fondée en 1280 d'après certains philologues, en 1282 d'après d'autres.

Qui est ce T'ovma vardapet du Ms 1097? D'après H. Ačarian il serait un correcteur qui aurait collationné la copie de Luser avec l'original; cette supposition fut partagée par L. Mariès.[16] Selon le philologue Ašot A. Abrahamian et d'autres, ce T'ovma vardapet aurait été l'un des copistes du Ms 1097; supposition absolument fausse, car il n'y a aucune page ecrite de la main de l'auteur des deux mémoriaux. D'après des notes du même genre et de la meme ecriture, laissées dans d'autres manuscrits du Matenadaran, le philologue Artašēs Mat'evosian a su déterminer que ce T'ovma vardapet n'était autre que T'ovma vardapet Mecop'ec'i (1378-1446): celui-ci avait la facheuse habitude de laisser de telles notes dans les manuscrits dont il terminait la lecture ou l'étude avec ses élèves;[17] ceci explique pourquoi ses deux notes sont insérées après coup dans le Ms 1097. T'ovma vardapet Mecop'ec'i aurait-il laissé une copie du livre d'Eznik, qui serait celle d'Izmir, vue par Gēorg? Ceci expliquerait le mémorial rapporte par ce dernier.

Dans une étude parue dans la revue Bazmavēp en 1928-1929,[18] le P. Ełia P'ēč'ikian fut le seul à réjeter l'affirmation de l'identité du Ms 1097 avec celui d'Izmir. Il ne doute ni de l'honnéteté, ni de l'exactitude de Gēorg rapportant le mémorial du scribe T'ovma vardapet, bien que ce dernier ne se soit pas déclare scribe dans son mémorial. Les mémoriaux des scribes T'ovma et Luser confirmeraient, selon lui, que nous avons affaire à deux manuscrits differents; cette divergence est confirmée par ailleurs par des dizaines de variantes textuelles entre l'exemplaire corrigé par Georg et le Ms 1097. Pour justifier la même date de 1280 AD des deux manuscrits et le nom de T'ovma vardapet comme scribe, E. P'ēč'ikian fait une suite de suppositions: Luser aurait terminé sa copie en 1280 pour le vardapet Nersēs, mais elle n'aurait pas plu à T'ovma vardapet, un élève du vardapet Nersēs (ce qui n'est pas prouvé du tout): T'ovma vardapet aurait entrepris et terminé alors, la même année, une autre copie du livre d'Eznik, et qui serait celle de l'édition d'Izmir, celle vue par Gēorg. E. P'ēč'ikian lui-même déclare que ce n'est qu'un essai de justification, son argument principal demeurant les nombreuses variantes textuelles.

Ces réelles variantes textuelles constituent notre deuxième argument, apres les mémoriaux, de la divergence des manuscrits d'Izmir et 1097. Leur nombre considérable ne permet nullement de supposer une identité de manuscrit ou une inadvertance si énorme du correcteur Gēorg. En voici quelques-unes:

Lectures de l'exemplaire corrigé par Georg	Lectures du Ms 1097
amenayn i nmanē (p. 3)	i nmanē
ēut'eann žamanec'uc'anel (p. 3)	ēut'eann
miaynoy sephakaneal (p. 3)	miayno
ink'n mnay anxaxut (p. 4)	ink'n anxaxut

aysink'n zbanawors (p. 4)	zbanawors
oč' miayn ards (p. 21)	oč' ards
linin uremn (p. 24)	linin
pahanǰē (p. 30)	pahanǰic'e
t'ēpēt merjaworut'iwnn (p. 31)	merjaworut'iwnn
miwsoyn (p. 39)	miwsumn
etc.	etc.

Ajoutons aussi ceci: à la page 81 de l'exemplaire corrigé par Gēorg, neuf mots du Ms 1097 font défaut; mais, par contre, à la p. 226, il a 6 lignes de plus que le Ms. Aux pages 255-256 du corrigé ou de l'édition de 1763, une page et demie occupe une autre place dans le Ms. Par contre, lors de la reliure du Ms 1097 quelques folios sont intervertis, et il faut lire, d'apres les mots coupés et la suite des idées, comme le signale H. Ačaṙian,[19] dans l'ordre des pages 299, 301, 300, 302, 303, 305, 304; or, la première édition et le corrigé de Gēorg ont l'ordre correct: était-ce dans leur manuscrit? Ou est-ce l'éditeur Y. Nalian qui aurait effectué le déplacement indispensable? On ne peut supposer que dans le Ms 1097 l'ouvrage d'Eznik ait été détaché d'un autre manuscrit et relié avec 1097, à la suite des commentaires bibliques d'Ephrem, car le dernier commentaire se termine à la moitié de la page, et le livre d'Eznik y commence aussitot, avec la même écriture, celle du scribe Luser.

Notre quatrième argument est que la première édition (ou le manuscrit vu par Gēorg) contient, à la suite de l'oeuvre d'Eznik, les 'Conseils' de Nilus (attribués à Eznik) corrigés également par Gēorg; or, le Ms 1097 ne les a pas, et Gēorg parle d'un seul manuscrit dans sa note: jeragir orinakn ('l'exemplaire manuscrit').

Nous dirons en conclusion: le Ms 1097 du Maténadaran du traité d'Eznik n'est pas celui de l'édition de 1763, vu par Gēorg pour sa correction, celle-ci ayant servi de texte à l'édition de 1826. On a donc deux manuscrits du livre d'Eznik, peut-être issus de la même famille. Les conséquences de cette constation sont importantes pour le rétablissement du texte critique. Notre édition, qui paraîtra à St. Lazare de Venise avec la collaboration du P. Nersēs Tēr Nersēsian, reproduira le texte critique du Ms 1097, l'apparat critique fera connaître les lectures non admises du Ms, des éditions de 1763, 1826, 1850, 1863, 1951 et 1959, ainsi que toutes les corrections textuelles proposées jusqu'à nos jours, le tout étant annoté en détail. Le texte sera suivi de sa concordance dans le même volume.

NOTES

[1]Les deux hommes ont etudié le Ms, collationné le texte avec celui de la 2e édition (St. Lazare, 1826), H. Ačaŕian a décrit le Ms et proposé des corrections textuelles, le tout dans K'nnut'iwn ew hamematut'iwn Eznkay noragiwt jeŕagrin, tiré à part de Handēs Amsōreay, 1904.

[2]Disons tout de suite que la 2e édition, St. Lazare, 1826, a été faite indirectement du Ms de la 1re.

[3]Nous en possédons une photocopie, tirée du microfilm ayant appartenu au P. Louis Mariès, éditeur, avec le P. Charles Mercier, de l'édition critique de l'ouvrage en 1959, Paris.

[4]Girk' ĕnddimut'eanc' (Izmir, 1763) 288.

[5]Dans une étude parue dans la revue Bazmavēp en 1925-1926, l'historien et philologue Nicolas Adontz croyait qu'Eznik Koɫbac'i aurait des pages dans l'ouvrage, mais le tout était l'oeuvre d'un rédacteur ou compilateur. Cependant ce droit entier d'auteur est attesté par la première édition et l'en-tête du Ms 1097.

[6]Son nom n'est mentionné que comme bienfaiteur à la première page du livre. L'imprimateur Markos signale que les dépenses ont été partagées avec un diacre.

[7]Les PP. Mekhitaristes de Vienne ont adopté Ĕnddēm aɫandoc', 'Contre les sectes,' le mot eɫc 'réfutation' n'étant pas classique. Le petit volume contient en supplément les "Conseils du même vardapet Eznik": tout en maintenant le nom d'Eznik, l'éditeur déclare dans son avant-propos (d'une page) que ces "conseils" appartiennent à Nilus, mais il les publie car ils ne se trouvent pas dans les oeuvres en grec de ce Père.

[8]Le P. Arsēn Bagratuni a omis de faire savoir qu'il a donné un nouveau titre à l'ouvrage et des titres à ses subdivisions en quatre "livres." Le 1er et les 2e et 3e tirages du volume sont identiques, à quelques differences près de composition, imperceptibles à première vue; ceci a induit en erreur plusieurs philologues et linguistes. Cette édition fut reproduite plusieurs fois à Paris, Constantinople, Tiflis et Buenos Aires.

[9]G. Galēmk'iarian, Noragoyn aɫberk' Eznkay' Koɫbac'woy Ĕnddēm aɫandoc' matenin (Vienne, 1919) Supplément, 18.—Nous avons vu personnelle-

ment l'exemplaire corrigé par Gĕorg, et deux autres, corrigés défectueuse-
ment sur celui-ci par certains Pères au couvent St. Lazare; il ne faudrait pas
s'y méprendre.   Le P. Grigoris Galĕmk'iarian en a fait une 3e correction—
également défectueuse—conservée au couvent des PP. Mkhitaristes de Vienne,
mis également sur microfilm.

[10]M. Ormanian, Azgapatum, s.v. "Yakob Nalian" dans l'index des noms
(Constantinople, 1913, 1914; Jerusalem, 1916; Beirut, 1959).

[11]La suite fut l'étude Ačařian, K'nnut'iwn ew hamematut'iwn Eznkay
noragiwt jeřagrin; voir ci-dessus note 1.

[12]Ibid. p. VI.

[13]H. Ačařian, Hayoc' lezvi patmut'yun, Erevan, 1951, 2.90.   Notre
étude minutieuse nous a fait découvrir que G. Tĕr Mkrtč'ian et H. Ačařian
se sont servi, pour leur collation du texte du Ms 1097, non pas du premier
tirage 1826 de l'édition de Venise, mais du 2e ou 3e, d'où des "corrections"
proposées par H. Ačařian, qui sont déjà dans le 1er tirage: la bonne lecture
a été corrompue lors de la recomposition.

[14]Nous possédons en photographie tout l'ouvrage d'Eznik, une tren-
taine de pages de commentaires, notamment tous les mémoriaux.   Le
microfilm, que le P. L. Mariès avait obtenu d'Erevan en 1926 par
l'intermédiaire du linguiste et arméniste Nicolas Marr, nous fut prêté par le
P. Ch. Mercier; les pages des commentaires nous furent aimablement fournies
par notre ami l'arméniste Dom Bernard Outtier, que nous remercions, et qui
se propose d'étudier les commentaires d'Ephrem.

[15]L. Mariès, Le De Deo d'Eznik de Kolb (Paris, 1924) 208.

[16]L. Mariès, De Deo, 1924, 108.

[17]A. Mat'evosian, "Hiravi erb? ew orteł? e himnadrvel Glajori
hamalsaranĕ, Garun (Erevan, 1980) juillet.

[18]E. P̕ĕč'ikian, "Ezniki Ełc ałandoc'i bnagri ew tpagrut'eanc' hamematut'iwn," Bazmavĕp (1928-1929).

[19]H. Ačařian, K'nnut'iwn, 2.

THE TALE OF THE BRONZE CITY IN ARMENIAN

James R. Russell

Columbia University

In the seventh century of the Hegira, in the suburb of Bulaq, I transcribed with measured calligraphy, in a language I have forgotten, in an alphabet I do not know, the seven adventures of Sinbad and the history of the City of Bronze, declares the narrator of Borges's tale The Immortal.[1] The attitude toward life expressed in the history of the City of Bronze mirrors the irony of the hero's meaningless and indestructible senescence; the hoary age of its transmission stretches, like his, to the dawn of literature; the babel of Oriental tongues that preserve its name might well defeat his memory; and the place of the City is as elusive and as fearsome as that of the Immortals.

Hesiod, adding a fifth heroic age perhaps of his own devising, relates in Works and Days a legend of four ages corresponding to four metals; the legend, it has been suggested, may be of Iranian origin.[2] The third generation is of brazen men, and between it and Hesiod's own, basest time of iron are interposed the heroes. The people of the age of bronze were warlike, lived in houses of bronze (Gk. khalkoi de te oikoi)[3] and seem to have been the first generation to go down to Hades, having slaughtered each other. In the Theogony, the poet in his description of nethermost, night-encircled Tartarus notes that it has a fence of bronze around it (Gk. ton peri khalkeon herkos eleatai). The earliest bronze city is a place of death, darkness and ancient evil.

Over a millennium later, in the fifth century A.D., the Latin poet Commodianus foretells the eruption of that evil: the anti-Christ is to lead an army of followers—the nations of Gog and Magog, imprisoned by Alexander the Great in the far North.[4] This is the Bronze City, Tartarus in

---

T. Samuelian & M. Stone, eds. Medieval Armenian Culture. (University of Pennsylvania Armenian Texts and Studies 6). Chico, CA: Scholars Press, 1983. pp. 250 to 261.

250

the remotest and darkest corner of the earth, rather than in its tenebrous depths, for the Qur'ān, XVIII.83 ff. relates that Dhū'l-Qarnain, '(he of) the Two Horns,' i.e., Alexander, in the remote East made a wall of iron covered with molten copper between two mountains to confine Gog and Magog, but it will be broken on the last day.   In the Armenian translation of the Romance of Alexander of Ps.-Callisthenes, Alexander visits Areg k'aɫak' 'City of the Sun' (i.e., Heliopolis, in Egypt); there follows a line considered to be a late interpolation: inj ayspēs t'ui t'ē sa ē or asen k'aɫak' pɫnji 'It seems thus to me: that this is that they call the city of bronze.'[5]   This seems to be a supposition based partly on the tradition repeated by Commodianus and Muḥammad, and partly on the association of brass with the Sun, Old Brazen Face to British witches and Brazen Nose to their scholarly compatriots.[6]

There was, it seems, a historical City of Bronze to the northeast of the Classical world. Among the manuscripts found by the Pelliot expedition in 1908 was a scroll containing a copy in Tibetan of a report to the king of the Uighurs by a mission of five men dispatched by him to seek information on the kings of the North. The name of the country from which the mission was sent is called 'in drugu' (i.e., Turkic) Ba-ker-pa-lig; Pelliot suggested this was a rendering of Tk. *Baqīr-balīq 'City of Bronze,' and such an expedition may have been dispatched around 745, when the Uighurs had newly conquered territories which were threatened from the North; their center was then on the Orkhon, east of their later stronghold, and the report mentions places in East Asia.[7]

Naršaxi identifies with Paikand, five parasangs west of Boxārā, the Diž-i Rōyīn 'Brazen Fortress,' capital of Arjāsp and terminus of the seven stations (haft xvān) conquered by the Iranian hero Isfandiyār (Phl. Spandiyād, Av. Spⱥntō.dāṭa-); the heroic exploits of Isfandiyār and the Sasanian Bahrām Čōbīn are similar in many respects, and the latter is said to have captured from the Turks a city called Āvāza (Phl. Nawāzag) which Tha'ālibī likewise identifies with Paikand.[8]   The Phl. Bundahišn mentions a mountain called *Bak(g)ir on which the Turanian Afrasiyab had built a fortress;[9] Darmesteter early suggested that *Bak(g)īr is a rendering of Tk. baqīr 'copper.'[10]   The romance of Bahrām Čōbīn has been shown to be replete with eschatological material: the late sixth-century usurper of the Sasanian throne, perhaps an Arsacid by ancestry, and a fiend who brings chaos upon Iran, is also a hero who shatters the menacing horde of the Turkic Khaqan Šāveh on the eastern frontier of the Empire. Defeated by the combined forces of the Byzantine emperor Maurice and the crown prince Xūsro II (Abarwēz), Bahrām flees east to Balx, where he is assassinated. Half a century later, Pērōz, son of the last Sasanian king Yazdagird III, was to make the same journey—but this time the fugitive was hero, not scoundrel, escaping not the righteous Šāhānšah but the wicked Muslims. The two epic events seem to have been associated in the Zoroastrian texts of vaticinatio ex eventu written after the fall of the Sasanians, in which messianic redemption from the East is longed for by the conquered Zoroastrians.[11] Yet that same East was a source of danger; the pretender had fled there, and it was from there that the Turks, equated with Tūrān—the archetypal enemy in Iranian epic—raided Iran.

Since, as it seems, brazen-walled Tartarus, or the prison of Gog and Magog at the edge of darkness, predate the mention of a historical place called the City of Bronze in Central Asia, the actual place must have been invested with mythological significance by virtue of its name and location. In view of the Turkic form found in the Bundahišn, this process is most likely to have occurred in the late Sasanian period.

The City of Bronze is mentioned in chronicles of the turbulent history of the early 'Abbāsid caliphate. In A.D. 755-6, a year after th murder of Abū Muslim at Baghdād at the order of the Caliph al-Mansur, a man in Xurasan called Sonbād the Mazdakite or the Magian stirred up the followers of the martyr, according to the Siyāsat-nāme of Nizam ul-Mulk, with the startling claim that Abū Muslim had not died, but had pronounced the name of God at his execution, become a dove, and flown to safety in the 'fortress of copper,' where, indeed, lived the Mahdi himself.[12] Abū Muslim himself seems to have been a devout Muslim, and it is not certain that he was even Iranian; but he seems to have united metempsychosis with his Muslim beliefs, and during the uprisings that followed his death and lasted for a score of years, he was believed to have been reincarnated in successive rebel leaders, and their rebellion had a strongly anti-Arab character. There is no belief in metempsychosis in Zoroastrianism. so it has been suggested that Buddhists, who were numerous in eastern Iran, contributed to the hybrid ideology of the revolt.[13] The Bronze Fortress is here a remote place, the home of the occulted twelfth Imam; and a refuge where the souls of the dead live on.

The Iranian fortress of brass, perhaps the subject of a Sasanian tale in the Hazār Afsān, becomes an Arab city of brass in the 1001 Nights, a composite work consisting of Persian tales, or Indian tales transmitted in

Middle Persian, or tales containing Persian elements; tales composed in Baghdād, between the early tenth and twelfth centuries; and tales composed in Egypt from about the twelfth century down to the fourteenth. Borges's grim immortal seems to have lived in the latter place, at the time of the final redaction; the Arabic text was also printed at Bulaq, in 1835.[14]

In the Arabic tale, the place where the dead—or hidden—live becomes a city of death, as will be seen presently. According to Tabarī, King Solomon is said to have built the city by the hands of dīvs, in the outermost desert of al-Andalus (the latter name, in his time, seems to have included the Maghreb with Muslim Spain).[15] The Iranian tradition is united in placing the city in the remote Northeast; Arab sources unanimously locate it in the forthest West. But, just as Hecataeus located fabulous places in India, and Pliny insisted that the same were in Africa,[16] here what is important is that the City of Brass be in a place seen as dark, perilous and remote—for Iranians, the northern wastes of nomad-peopled Central Asia; and for Arabs, the desolate shore of the Western Ocean, associated with death.[17] And instead of Alexander, the imprisoner of demons is that other great figure of magic and power in Near Eastern folklore, King Solomon, although the Dhū'l-Qarnain still figures in many accounts.

The story in the 1001 Nights is, in brief, as follows: the Caliph 'Abd al-Malik ibn Marwān (A.D. 685-705) sends Ṭalib ibn-Sahl to Emīr Mūsa ibn Nusair (who was the historical conqueror of areas of Northwest Africa under this Caliph and his successor), who is to take him to find brass jars in which King Solomon had imprisoned refractory demons. They are accompanied by an old wise man, Sheikh 'Abd al-Samad ibn 'Abd al-Kuddūs al-Samūdī. On the road, the travellers visit various ancient ruined palaces full of treasure and dire inscriptions which only the aged Sheikh is able to read, warning of the imminence of death and against attachment to the illusions of wealth and power. A demon, wedged Ariel-like into a pillar of black stone, tells the tale of his imprisonment by Solomon and is suffered there painfully to remain. They arrive at a huge city with two bronze-sheathed towers that glitter in the sunlight like fires, directed thither by a mechanical equestrian statue of brass in the desert which swivels round at the touch of the hand to indicate the way to the city. Several of the Caliph's men scale the walls, and behold pleasing images, towards which they leap; the water of the mirage vanishes, and they fall to their deaths in the city. Ṭalib himself climbs up, sees the mirages, invokes the name of God, and they disappear. He makes his way inside the town to the gates, which open by the manipulation of another mechanism, and the party enter a town whose inhabitants lie dead at their places of work, amidst their great wealth. All are dead, according to inscriptions, of hunger. The travellers finally arrive at the throne of a dead princess, magnificently bejewelled, and guarded by two robot-soldiers. An inscription warns comers against trying to rob her jewels, but Ṭālib attempts to take them, and the robots cut him to pieces. The others leave the city and arrive eventually at Karkar, a country of Negroes taught Islam by Xiḍr, who live on the flesh of fish in human shape. Here, they find also the jars; when one of these is opened, the demon rushes out, and, thinking Solomon is still alive, cries, "Repentance!" The party return to Damascus, where the Caliph, profoundly moved by the account of their journey, becomes a religious recluse.

The message of the tale is intricate, transcending the simple, even bad Arabic style of the prose and verse passages.[18] The directions to the bronze city, the lock on its gates, and the doom which awaits its robbers, are all mechanical, with the rigid inevitability of judgment and the cycle of life and death. One who becomes a seeker of the things of this world—Ṭālib's name means 'seeker' in Arabic—will be subject to the automatic justice of this world's laws, ultimately to be as frozen and incapable of change as the material objects he cherishes, just like a demon encased in a jar. The people of Karkar, who live in primitive material circumstances and who know Islam from the counsellor of mystics, Xidr, rather than from doctors of theology, seem to provide casually and effortlessly the jars so arduously sought by the travellers, much as another isolated and utopian people, the Phaeacians, transported Odysseus with uncanny swiftness over the same sea that he had toiled over with painful slowness. But here there is no angry Poseidon, only a message of peace requiring that the seeker forsake this life. Life becomes meaningful, in other words, when one ceases to cherish it.

Hesiod's city of bronze was Tartarus, and the dwellers in bronze houses went down to Hades when they died. In Iranian tradition, the bronze fortress was built by Arjāsp, a Turanian enemy; it is in the Northeast; and by the Sasanian period there exists a tradition concerning the imprisonment of an evil and vengeful force there. Vengeance to the defeated is liberation, and in the 'Abbāsid period the fortress of bronze is a place of the dead, but one from which apocalyptic restoration will come, and the soul of Abū Muslim leaves it to live in a new body. The story of the bronze city in the

1001 Nights presents it as a place of death only, where false seekers end their journey, while others continue to enlightenment, and change their lives.

The tale, which unites the hoary city of bronze, an adventure story of travel, and an insistent religious message, became very popular amongst Armenians. The first Armenian translation, according to the title page of a concise version of the tale (Armenian zroyc') written in the early fourteenth century in the Middle Armenian vernacular, was made for David, the Curopalate of Tayk', who died, according to Step'anos Asołik (III.43), on Easter Sunday of the year 1000.[19] [This text was published by Akinian in Handēs Amsōreay 1958.] A translation into Georgian was probably made at the same time.[20] A second Armenian translation was done in the first quarter of the thirteenth century by the vardapet Ařak'el, identified with Ařak'el Anec'i or Širakawanc'i, perhaps with one Mxit'ar Č'eč'kanc' Širakawanc'i; Ařak'el, known as a translator of Arabic and the author of a work on the Zodiac,[21] might have wished to improve on the earlier translation, which is artless and laconic, at least in the manuscript that has survived, or else he did not know of it. Early in the sixteenth century Grigoris I, Catholicos of Ałt'amar, found a manuscript of the History of the Bronze City (Armenian Patmut'iwn Połnjē K'ałak'i), and edited it, making additions and restoring the text where there were lacunae, according to a colophon of 1526 by Margaray vardapet.[22] It is apparent that Ałt'amarc'i was working from a translation rather than making a new one, and that that translation was not the one made for David the Curopalate or the version of it that we have, but another, later and longer, probably that of Anec'i, although whether the latter was the Ařak'el to whom the translation is attributed, is still not certain.[23]

The story of the Bronze City enjoyed wide popularity among Armenians for nearly a millennium. A number of manuscripts, mainly from the sixteenth and seventeenth centuries, are preserved in the West, and the Erevan Matenadaran has 32 manuscripts containing the story, the earliest from 1556.[24] There are manuscripts of the tale in Turkish written with Armenian letters, and in Armenian written with Georgian letters. Often it is found in miscellanies containing other popular works, such as the story of St. Alexianos, the son of a wealthy Roman patrician, who flees on the night of his own wedding to lead a life of wandering and holy poverty. Other tales from the Arabic, such as P'ir P'ahlul, and from the 1001 Nights, such as Harc'munk' Ařjkan "The Questions of the Maiden," Patmut'iwn Eawt'n Imastasirac' "The Story of the Seven Philosophers" and Patmut'iwn Farmani

Asmani "The Story of Farmān-i Asmān," might also be included in such miscellanies, together with works on fortune-telling and astrology; the fourteenth century manuscript published by Akinian contains a number of vičakaxałk',[25] literally 'lot-games': rhymed quatrains, mainly predicting love and marriage. The Romance of Alexander was very popular among Armenians, as among the other peoples of the Near East, and it was seen above how the two narratives were associated—in a Georgian version of the Alexander-Romance, the Macedonian king visits the Bronze City in the company of Solomon himself.[26]

The inscriptions in the Bronze City, and Emīr Mūsa's lamentations following the reading of each one, are in verses called kafas, after an Arabic word qāfiya 'rhyme, meter.' These are mainly monorhymed quatrains with lines of 2+5 or 3+5 syllables, and are usually lamenting and didactic in character.[27] The earliest manuscript has 24 kafas; manuscripts after Grigoris Ałt'amarc'i have 65-75, and Grigoris is known to have composed about 50 kafas to the tale of the Bronze City,[28] and the same number to the Alexander-Romance.[29] In some manuscripts, the kafas to these two texts are found alone, without the connecting prose narrative.[30] The kafas were chanted or sung for entertainment; in some manuscripts, they have musical xaz-notation or instructions on what melody is to be used. One kafa called Asac' matruak ginoys ('My wine-steward said') is to be sung Yisus Ordoy goyn—in the manner of the hymn 'Jesus the Son.'[31]

Č'ōpanian noted that the story of the Bronze City is more fatalistic and world-denying than many of the other tales in the 1001 Nights and suggested that its popularity among the Armenians indicates the tastes and choice of Christian clerics.[32] However grim the message of the Bronze City, the same Grigoris who adorned it with extra kafas also wrote poems of love, as did many other Armenian priests. In this they were not so different from Western European clerics of the same period, men committed to an otherwordly and ascetic path who often turned their Latin eloquence to the praise of love and beauty, as Helen Waddell has shown in The Wandering Scholars, a work as hauntingly lyrical as the poetry it treats. Yet Armenian clerics also condemned literature which was not strictly theological. In the fourteenth century, the scholar Yovhannēs Orotnec'i wrote of various categories of literary composition: isk erkrord, or amenewimb sut, orpēs ałaspelakan girk' ēst patmut'ean Aramazdea ew Herma, ayspēs ew i nors Płnjē K'ałak' ew Šeranšah ew ayl(k') soynpisik', or amenewimb sut en 'and the second (type is that which is) entirely false, such as the mythological writings concerning Zeus and Hermes; similarly, amongst new (writings) the Bronze City and Šērān-šāh, and others of this same type, which are entirely false.'[33]

The Armenian text of the fourteenth century, published by Akinian, anachronistically has Baghdād rather than Damascus as the capital of the Caliphate;[34] this may indicate a late revision, and the presence of Turco-Mongol loan-words such as etč'i 'emissary'[35] proves that the language must be a vernacular later than that of the tenth century translation. Yet there are but scant alterations of the Muslim content of the tale. Although the story ends with an exclamation of glory to Christ, and there is an interpolation on the Second Coming (lines 238 ff.), other Muslim features remain. The Negroes, instructed in astuacapaštut'iwn 'God worship' (if not 'Islam') by a zodiacal animal (not Xiḍr), still explain that yamēn awr hing het aławt's matuc'anemk' 'every day five times we offer prayers,'[36] in keeping with the statutes of Islam. Ṭālib's name is simply transcribed in Akinian's manuscript, but in others it is variously translated as Uznkan 'Desirer' or Xndrak 'Seeker,'[37] indicating that the later translator was perhaps more aware than the first had been of the subtleties of theme in the story.

In the Armenian versions, some of the place-names have been changed; instead of Sicily, manuscripts have Seleuceia, and the Arabic 'sea of Karkar' is given in the Armenian as K(u)rkur,[38] perhaps after the bend in the Euphrates of that name, near Nemrut Dagh, or else for the sake of onomatopoeia: water gurgles. But what is striking about Akinian's manuscript is the location of the Bronze City itself. Ṭālib at the beginning tells the Caliph it is i hiwsisayin dēhn 'to the North' (line 7), and later on the demon (here called K'aj, 'hero,' also one of a race of supernatural giants in Armenian mythology) directs them northward still, towards the dread city (lines 420-1). The k'aj is imprisoned in a mountain rather than a pillar, recalling perhaps the ancient Armenian legend of the captive king Artawazd, chained by the k'ajk' in the cleft of Mt. Ararat. It is significant also that in Akinian's manuscript the jars containing the demons are said at the outset to be near the Bronze City; it becomes associated with the quest, and seems to bear some relationship to the jars themselves that is lost in the Arabic and later Armenian versions.

The first Armenian translation, on which Akinian's text was based, seems to have been made from an Arabic version of the tale, now lost, in which the Bronze City was to the North, not the West; that is, in keeping with Iranian tradition as seen above. The Armenian version may, then, preserve a literary link between the Bronze City or Fortress of Classical, Iranian and early Islamic sources, and the story in the 1001 Nights. It may be suggested further that in the Arabic tale, perhaps itself composed on the basis of an Iranian pre- or early-Islamic sources, the jars were in the City. This would accord with the image of the City as a place of confinement of supernatural powers ultimately to be released, as well as a place of death. With the subsequent elaboration of the tale in successive versions, the two motifs—jars and City—would have been treated more and more as separate themes.

The Armenian texts of the City of Bronze testify to the popularity of Islamic literary forms over the last thousand years in Armenia, and to their integration, particularly the kafas, into Armenian cultural life. The City of Bronze was part of the intellectual baggage of the medieval cleric, even as the Alexander-Romance had been for Movsēs Xorenac'i—and continued to be, indeed, for his descendants. The earliest text known of the story, apparently preserving the link lost in Arabic between ancient and medieval traditions, and between East and West, demonstrates yet again the singular aspect of Armenian culture as intermediary and preserver, spanning the ages and standing exactly between the remote West and the fearsome East, that is, at the farthest remove from Darkness.

NOTES

[1]Jorge Luis Borges, "The Immortal," Labyrinths: Selected Stories and Other Writings (New York: New Directions, 1964) 116.

[2]M. I. Finley, The World of Odysseus (New York: Penguin Books, 1972) 30.

[3]Hesiod, Works and Days, in The Homeric Hymns and Homerica (trans. H. G. Evelyn-White; Loeb Classical Library, No. 57; Cambridge, Mass.: Harvard, 1977) line 150.

[4]N. Cohn, The Pursuit of the Millenium (3rd ed.; New York: Oxford, 1981) 29.

[5]H. Yakovbos vrd. Tašian, Usumnasirut'iwnk' Stoyn-Kalist'eneay (Az-

gayin Matenadaran, Vol. 5, Vienna, 1892) 142-3 n. 3; Text in R. T'reanc', ed., Patmut'iwn Alek'sandri Makedonac'woy (Venice, 1842) para. 258, p. 168.10; A. M. Wolohojian, tr., The Romance of Alexander the Great by Pseudo-Callisthenes (New York: Columbia, 1969) 146, 185 n. 258.6-7.

[6]P. Hughes, Witchcraft (New York: Penguin Books, 1970) 211, 212 & n.; a pre-fourteenth-century brass door-knocker in the shape of a beast's face with radiate grooves around it gave its name to Brasenose College, Oxford (J. Morris, Oxford, London: Faber and Faber, 1965) 211 & pl. opp. 209. The beast presumably represents the Sun.

[7]Jacques Bacot, 'Reconnaisance en Haute Asie Septentrionale par cinq envoyes Ouigours au VII-e siècle,' Journal Asiatique 244 (1956) 137, 139, 145, 151.

[8]J. Markwart, G. Messina, "A Catalogue of the Provincial Capitals of Eranshahr," Analecta Orientalia, 3, Rome, 1931, text, 8; commentary, 34-6.

[9]Indian Bundahišn (ed. F. Justi; Hildesheim: Georg Olms Verlag, 1976) p. 23, line 7; Iranian or Greater Bundahišn (ed. T. D. Anklesaria; Bombay, 1908) p. 79, line 4.

[10]R. von Stackelberg, "Die iranische Schützensage," Zeitschrift der Deutschen Morgenländischen Gesellschaft 58 (1904) 858.

[11]Annette Destrée, "Quelques refléxions sur le héros des récits apocalyptiques persans et sur le mythe de la ville de cuivre," in La Persia nel Medioevo (Rome: Accademia Nazionale dei Lincei, 1971) 641-4; K. Czegledy, "Bahram Cobin and the Persian Apocalyptic Literature," Acta Orientalia Academiae Scientiarum Hungaricae 3 (1958) 1.29.

[12]C. E. Bosworth, "'Abbasid Caliphate," Encyclopaedia Iranica (London: Routledge and Kegan Paul, 1982) 1.1.92; Destrée, "Héros des récits apocalyptiques persans," 639.

[13]R. N. Frye, "The Role of Abū Muslim in the 'Abbasid Revolt," The Moslem World (Hartford, CT) 37 (1947) 1.29-37; R. W. Bulliet, "Naw Bahar and the survival of Iranian Buddhism," Iran 14 (1976) 144.

[14]M. I. Gerhardt, The Art of Story-Telling (Leiden: J. Brill, 1963) 9, 11.

[15]Ibid., 216-9.

[16]Meier in discussion following Destrée, "Héros des récits apocalyp-

tiques persans," 653.

[17]Gerhardt, Story-Telling, 204-5; in the Burhān-i Qāti', the name of Qairawān in the Maghreb is an expression also for the edge of the world. See A. Hamori, "An allegory from the Arabian Nights: The City of Brass," Bulletin of the School of Oriental and African Studies, London, 34 (1971) 18 n. 32).

[18]Gerhardt, Story-Telling, 3.

[19]H. N. Akinian, "Zroyc' Płnjē K'ałak'i," Handēs Amsōreay, Jan.-Apr. (1958) 1-4.22; Paruyr Muradyan, "Patmut'iwn Płnjē K'ałak'i zruyc'i haykakan ev vrac'akan patumneri u nranc' p'oxharaberut'yan šurĵ," Banber Matenadarani, 6 (1962) 250.

[20]Ibid., 258.

[21]Ibid., 250.

[22]H. N. Akinian, Grigoris I Kat'ołikos Ałt'amari keank'n ew kert'uacnerě (Vienna, 1958) lxi.

[23]Ibid., liv.

[24]Ibid., lxiii-iv; H. A. Simonyan, Hay miĵnadaryan kafaner (X-XVI dd.), Erevan: 1975) 142. There are also about a score of printed editions. Tigran Č'it'uni published an ašxarhabar translation in Constantinople, 1919; another modern translation by Y. K'iwrtian appeared in Hayrenik', Boston, 1955.

[25]Akinian, "Zroyc Płnjē K'ałak'i," 23.

[26]Simonyan, Miĵnadaryan kafaner, 139 n. 9.

[27]Ibid., 30-5.

[28]Ibid., 143; text in Akinian, Grigoris, 112-27.

[29]Simonyan, 49.

[30]Aršak Č'opanian, Hay ēĵer (Paris: K. Nersesian, 1912) xl, on kafas to the Alexander-Romance; and Simonyan, Miĵnadaryan kafaner, 142.

[31]Simonyan, Miĵnadaryan kafaner, 37-8.

[32]Č'opanian, Hay ēĵer, xl.

[33]Muradyan, "Patmut'iwn Płnjē K'ałak'i," 260, citing S. Lalafaryan &

S. Arevšatyan (eds.) "Yovhannēs Orotnec'i, 'Hawak'eal i banic' imastasirac','" Banber Matenadarani, 3 (1956) 378-9.

[34]Akinian, "Zroyc' Pʰnjē K'aɫak'i," text, p. 30, line 1.

[35]Ibid., line 360.

[36]Ibid., lines 759-60.

[37]H. Laurentie, "La version arménienne du Conte de la Ville d'Airain," REArm, 1921, 298.

[38]Ibid., 299.

KIRAKOS GANJAKEC'I AND HIS HISTORY
OF ARMENIA

Zaven Arzoumanian

St. Sahag and St. Mesrob Armenian Church, Philadelphia

In the course of its long history, Armenian culture has had several periods of revival and decline. The cultural revival which reached its peak in the tenth century was followed by a decline, due to the wholesale destruction of learning upon the onslaught of Seljuk and Mongol invasions of the Armenian homeland. Eyewitness accounts are given by the historians Aristakēs Lastivertc'i and Kirakos Ganjakec'i.

Although designated as a History of Armenia, the thirteenth-century historiography of Kirakos Ganjakec'i represents an important source for the medieval history of Asia Minor, especially for the Mongol invasions. Interestingly enough the conventional title, History of Armenia,[1] is not warranted by the most important manuscripts of the text. Rather the longer title, a brief history from the time of St. Gregory to the last days, by Kirakos, the worthy vardapet of the well-known monastery of Getik, which is found in at least twenty-five manuscripts[2] and which in fact seems to be a legitimate title, corresponds with the content of the book, since the second half—and the longer part—of the work deals exclusively with the history of Asia Minor, Transcaucasia, Georgia and Albania. Among the four Armenian editions of Kirakos's History the most complete edition is of K. A. Melik'-Ohanĵanyan, who produced an exhaustive work based on the existing forty or more manuscripts and on their different readings.[3]

The abundance of the manuscripts of the text has given Kirakos's work an unprecedented advantage. They date from the sixteenth century.[4] Twenty-eight of the extant manuscripts are kept in the Matenadaran in

T. Samuelian & M. Stone, eds. Medieval Armenian Culture. (University of Pennsylvania Armenian Texts and Studies 6). Chico, CA: Scholars Press, 1983. pp. 262 to 271.

Erevan, and the rest are catalogued in Venice, Jerusalem and Paris.

The author is known as a thirteenth-century Armenian historian, a cleric, whose surname identifies his home as Ganjak, in Eastern Armenia, near the borders of Caucasian Albania. He was born in 1203 and was from the "province of Ganjak," rather than from the city of Ganjak. Kirakos informs us that Mxit'ar Goš, his famous contemporary author of Datastan-agirk' (Code Book), "was from the city of Ganjak, whereas others, such as Yovhannēs Sarkawag, Dawit' Alawka Ordi, were from the "province of Ganjak; so was I."[5] This obviously indicates a distinction between the two locations: the province of Ganjak and the city of Ganjak.

The most important manuscripts identify the author of Kirakos's History as "the worthy vardapet of Getik."[6] This designation is coupled with another name, "Arewelc'i," and is referred to a certain Kirakos, also of the thirteenth century, who has compiled the Yaysmawurk' (Menologion) in 1269. There are subsequently two legitimate surnames—Getikc'i and Arewelc'i—according to the different colophons of the same Menologion. Scholars have agreed that both designations belong to our historian Ganjakec'i, and that the latter was also the author of the Yaysmawurk'. Ł. Ališan has preserved the colophon which reads:

"With hope in God and by the love towards His saints I, Kirakos vardapet Arewelc'i, compiled the feasts of God's saints accord-ing to the commemoration of each (saint's) day. I also wrote their history which was not found in the book of Yaysmawurk' and edited it with the original (text) . . . This was done in 1269 in Sis, the capital of Cilicia, during the reign of King Het'um and in the first year of the crown-prince Levon, in the sixty-sixth year of our life, when (the book) came to its completion for the glory of God."[7]

This colophon is striking because it establishes the correct date of Kirakos's birth. In 1269 the author claims to have been 66 yaers of age, therefore, he must have been born in 1203. Moreover, the information given in the actual History of Kirakos supports this date. This is what we read:

"When this book was written in the year 1241, during the reign of King Het'um the Pious of Cilicia . . . it was in our fortieth year, more or less."[8]

Still another copy of the Yaysmawurk' whose colophon identifies Kirakos as Arewelc'i and from the monastery of Getik: "Kirakos vardapet

Arewelc'i, from the monastery of Getik, the compiler and the illustrator of this testament."[9]

Conclusion: (a) On different occasions Kirakos is identified by three surnames but is nonetheless one and the same author.   (b) He acquired different names from the different phases of his life. He was recognized as Ganjakec'i, because he was from "the province of Ganjak."   He was known as Getikc'i, because he studied at Nor Getik and lived there for a long time.[10]   And he was called Arewelc'i, because his ecclesiastical and literary activities flourished in "the district of the East."[11]

Kirakos is well acquainted with the Armenian historiography preceding his era. He also knows of the histories written by Xosrov, Šapuh Bagratuni, and Yovhannēs Vanakan, whose texts have not reached us. He specifically refers to John Catholicos's History, and uses the works of Movsēs Dasxuranc'i and Samuēl Anec'i.   He compiled a special chapter on the history of the Caucasian Albanians[12] following the longer version of the history of that nation by Dasxuranc'i.   He either copied portions verbatim from, or summarized the lengthy descriptions of his tenth century colleague.[13] Although Samuēl's name is only quoted twice by Kirakos as "Samuel the priest of the cathedral of Ani,"[14] his Chronology has served as another primary source to Kirakos.[15]

Kirakos is one of the very few Armenian historians who, along with historical events that he narrates, offers an interesting autobiography through chronology, names, and with expressions of gratitude towards his superiors. He is very much attached to the monastery of Nor Getik and to his famous teacher Yovhannēs Vanakan.   Although Kirakos speaks about Mxit'ar Goš at length, he was hardly a disciple of this great teacher, since Goš died in 1213 when Kirakos had barely reached the age of ten. His famous teacher was Vanakan who died in 1251[16] as he, Kirakos himself states: "This we (attest) not as hearsay but as an eyewitness, for we stayed with him (Vanakan) for a long time to study at the monastery of Tawuš."[17]

Vanakan left Getik for Tawuš where he established the school of Xoranašat around 1215-1220. Here Kirakos studied under his beloved teacher until 1225 when Jahal-ad-Din Mengubirdi, the last of the Khawarasm Shahs (d. 1231), invaded Georgia and Armenia, and destroyed Xoranašat soon after Kirakos was captured by Molar Nuin: "Then they captured me and separated me from my friends to use my services as secretray to read and write their correspondences."[18] This happened in the middle of the year 1236 when the

Mongols were ready to retire "from our country to go far away into foreign lands." Kirakos stayed with them in captivity "until (God) visited us, according to his will." He ultimately escaped by night on the day his teacher Vanakan was released in 1236.

Obviously Kirakos's intentional capture by the Mongols brings out the interesting question of language. Being from the "province of Ganjak," where Turkish and Persian languages were predominant, Kirakos must have been well versed in these tongues. Actually there are indications which demonstrate Kirakos's knowledge of Persian and Arabic languages. For example, speaking of a certain fortress, Kirakos gives its name and says: "which was called xoyaxana in the Persian language;"[19] or a certain tree "which the Persians called chandarin."[20] He also translates the Arabic word khalifa by adding "because khalifa means a successor" or "they called khalifa, that is the sucecssor of Muhammad."[21] Kirakos even preserves words in the language of the Mongols: xunan (battlefield), t'un (fortress), t'anjah (stronghold). We should remember that the official language of the Seljuks and of the Shah Armens was Persian. Only later, in mid-1280s, after Jimri's revolt, it was replaced by the Turkish.[22] During the Ilkhanid period, the Mongols came under the influence of Iran and adopted the Persian as their official language.[23] As for Ganjak itself, the rulers were Muslim and the population was Persian: "This city (Ganjak) was well inhabited by Persians" who lived together with the Armenians.[24] Moreover, Mongol armies comprised considerable number of Turkic and Persian descendants who were in direct contact with Vanakan and his captive disciples.[25]

Extensive description is provided by Kirakos concerning the monastery of Nor Getik since he was one of the important pillars of that school. Here he assumed the leadership of the doctrine which emphasized the "Eastern" tradition of the Armenian faith as against the "Cilician," the latter being more Latinized and under the constant influence of the Crusaders. As he himself states: "on the question raised among the Christians pertaining to the Holy Spirit of God" Kirakos sided strongly with the doctors of the East (Armenian proper), following the teachings of Vanakan, Vardan Arewelc'i, and others. This question of dogma is directly connected with the Synod of Sis, convened by Catholicos Constantine in 1252, upon the receipt of Pope Innocent's letter. The Catholicos, persuant to the conciliar decision, had written "to the province of the East, in Great Armenia, to the learned vardapet Vanakan, to Vardan Arewelc'i, and to Yovsēp'," who were the leaders of the doctrinal formulations and men of authority.[26] It is obvious that here there is dependence on the "east" on matters of doctrine and authority, notwithstanding the political and ecclesiastical power which is centered in the "west."

In 1255 Kirakos met Het'um, the Armenian king of Cilicia, while the latter was returning from his trip to Samarkand, the capital of Mongolia. It was in the village of Vardenis, in the district of Aragacotn, where Kirakos heard Het'um speak on "the barbarous nations whom he had seen and heard."[27] The Mongol hordes had swept through Armenia and Georgia far into Anatolia. Het'um recognized that only in alliance with them his kingdom could be saved. He first sent his brother Smbat the Constable on an official embassy to Karakorum, who returned with the guarantee of Cilicia's integrity. Smbat's departure and return are dated by the Constable himself in his Taregirk', i.e. "the year 697 (=1248) when I went" and "the year 699 (=1250) when I returned to my brother Het'um."[28] In 1253 Het'um visited Great Armenia on his way back. It is assumed by Melik'-Ohanjanyan that it was at that time that Kirakos must have received an invitation to go to Cilicia. One thing is clear: by this time and until 1260 Kirakos was still at Nor Getik according to a record preserved in an inscription on the walls of the monastery, which mentions Kirakos's name twice, first as a donor, and then as a mediator who exercised his power to relieve his people from the heavy taxes.[29] In any event Kirakos was in Sis, Cilicia, in 1268/69, at the time when he was working on the Menologion, and this is the last date that we know of Kirakos's life. Probably soon after he returned to his monastery and there he died in 1271, as we learn from his colleague Grigor Akanc':

"It was in the year 720 of the Armenian calendar (720 + 551 = 1271) when the glorious Armenian vardapets Vardan and Kirakos passed away."[30]

Kirakos began to write his History on May 19, 1241 on the Sunday of Pentecost: "This day when we undertook this work is the feast of the advent of the most holy Spirit in the upper room."[31] He worked on his book at least for two decades before it was completed. Whereas the first section of the History forms a compilation of events "from the previous historiography," the second part, the more interesting and valuable section, contains the contemporary history written by the author as "auricular and as an eyewitness."[32] It ends with the events of the year 714 of the Armenian era (1265), when the Ilkhan Abaghu, the mongol ruler of Persia, married

Despoina, the illegitimate daughter of the Paleologue emperor Michael VIII, after himself being christened by the Patriarch of Antioch.[33]   Hulaghu, Mangu's brother and the founder of the Mongol empire in Persia, died the same year (1265) according to Kirakos.[34]   The closing date of Kirakos's History is verified by Vardan who adds that "it was the period between 685 (1236) and 714 (1265) that was covered by Vanakan and Kirakos concerning the Mongols, the Persians, the Albanians, the Armenians, the Georgians, and the Greeks."[35]   There is also the extensive work of Jami' al-tawarikh[36] (The Assembly of Histories) left by the wazir Rashid-al-Din (1247-1318), who used materials collected by a number of collaborators and wrote in the colloquial Persian of his day. This work contains large sections of the history of the Mongols, of India and Europe and, being contemporary with Kirakos's work, can along with Vardan's History, help in reconstructing the unfinished ending of Kirakos.

In the last and inconclusive paragraph of his history, Kirakos tells about Abaghu's battle with Berke Khan (1257-1267), the leader of the Golden Horde, who led his army through the gates of Darband and encamped on the banks of the river Kura. The other bank of the river was kept by Abaghu's troops. The battle across the Kura is recorded by Rashid-al-Din which ends by the victory of Abaghu who was finally able to force Berke to leave the river bank and head towards Tiflis. Berke dies on the way and is buried in Saray, the capital of Batu, while Abaghu retires to Mazandaran and Gurgan to spend the winter of 1266/67. The same details are found in Vardan's History.[37]   All three—Rashid-al-Din, Vardan, and Kirakos—give the same date (1265/66) for the battle between Abaghu and Berke. In this way we can reconstruct the ending of Kirakos's work.

Kirakos essentially describes the political, social and economic events which resulted from the Mongol invasions of Eastern Armenia, Georgia and Albania. Such were, for example, the fading away of the minor kingdoms and the feudal lords of Armenia, the domination of the Seljuks, and the adherence of the Armenians to the Georgians, under whom the Zacharids enjoyed self-determination and independence. In addition to his account of the Mongol invasions, Kirakos has recorded certain policies of taxation, beliefs, even customs and the language of the Mongols. He has carefully described the gradual transition of the lands and the landholding privileges from the hands of the Armenian feudal lords to the Mongol rulers, then to the Armenian church hierarchy, and eventually to the mercantile class. The description Kirakos gives about the Mongol as a member of a distinct race with his peculiar appearance, behavior and manners is enlightening. In the chapter entitled "On the description of the appearance of a Mongol" Kirakos says:

> The way they looked was frightening. No beard at all, but sometimes a little hair on the jaw or around the lips. Narrow and penetrating eyes, sharp voice and a race which lived long. They ate meat of all animals, clean and unclean, but above all they preferred the horse meat which they broiled or roasted without salt. Then they dipped the meat in salty water piece by piece and ate. As they ate, some prostrated like the camels, and others sat, but all, lords and slaves, ate together. While drinking the wine one held the bowl and the other filled his cup from the bowl and scattered the beverage in the air in four directions—north, south, east and west—and then tasted, and finally gave it to the senior of the clan. Always the slave ate and drank first and then the elders, so as to avoid any risk of poisonous food or beverage. [38]

Kirakos, unlike his predecessors, utilized inscriptions preserved on monuments or on monastery walls as sources for his history. While writing on Mxit'ar Goš and on the famous monastery of Getik, he relied on the inscriptions that he found on the walls pertaining to the construction work, the builders, and those who contributed to the erection of the monuments. There is no doubt that Kirakos, enriched with vast and contemporary sources, became one of the indispensable authors of the Middle Ages, to be quoted by his successors. By later generations, Kirakos's History was considered as the only reliable source for the Mongol invasions in Armenia, and as such was quoted by subsequent historians. Vardan Arewelc'i has recorded that he had used Kirakos's History for the passages concerning "the nation of the archers, the Persians, the Albanians, the Armenians, and the Georgians, as well as the Greeks . . . the histories of which were written in detail by the blessed vardapets Vanakan and by our dear (brother) Kirakos . . . which history we did not dare write for the third time . . . but just summarized it by enumerating the events of importance and worthy of mention . . ."[39] Although Vardan in the main summarized Kirakos's passages, but in some cases important differences in information suggest that two different sources were used by each independently. Melik'-Ohanĵanyan is inclined to think that

Vanakan's lost work might have been the one used by Vardan; or that the difference may lie in Vardan's personal knowledge and observations.

NOTES

[1]The designation of the History as "Armenian" is not original and goes as far back as the first edition of the work by Oskan Tēr-Georgian Yovhanniseanc' of Erevan. Cf. Patmut'iwn Hayoc' arareal Kirakosi vardapeti Ganjakec'woy (Moscow, 1858).

[2]Kirakos Ganjakeci', Patmut'iwn Hayoc', ed. K. A. Melik'-Ohanjanyan (Erevan, 1961) VIII, XXX-XXXI.

[3](a) Patmut'iwn Hayoc' (ed. Oskan Ter-Georgian).

(b) Kirakosi vardapeti Ganjakec'woy hamaṙot Patmut'iwn i srboyn Grigorē c'awurs iwr lusabaneal (Venice, 1865).

(c) Patmut'win Hayoc' arareal Kirakosi vardapeti Ganjakec'woy (Tiflis, 1909) [Reprint of 1858 edition].

(d) Patmut'iwn Hayoc', ed. K. A. Melik'-Ohanjanyan (Erevan, 1961).

[4]Cf. Kirakos (ed. Melik'-Ohanjanyan) Int. 95-111.

[5]Ibid., 116.

[6]Cf. note 2 above.

[7]Ł. Ališan, Hayapatum (Venice, 1901) 472.

[8]Kirakos, 278.

[9]M. Awgerian, Liakatar Vark' Srboc', 76. Cf. No. 219 of Vienna in Tašian's Catalog der armenischen Handschriften der Mechitaristen Bibliothek zu Wien (Vienna, 1895-96) 559.

[10]Kirakos, 222: "Many brethren came to the famous monastery of (Nor Getik) which became the center of education for many, the same monastery where we ourselves were educated."

[11]The Armenian chieftains in the northeast of Armenia were backed by the Georgian kings and often resisted the Mongol invasions. The peaceful alliance between Armenia and Georgia availed time and effort for the culture to flourish in Eastern Armenia. Monasteries became the main centers for education of science and literature: Sanahin, Hałbat, Nor Getik, Xoranašat,

Hałarcin, Keč'aŕis, Ayrivank' are well known schools in the 13th century. The teachers in those centers of education were Yovhannēs Tawušec'i, Mxit'ar Goš, Vanakan Vardapet, Kirakos, Vardan Arewelc'i, and others.

[12]Kirakos, 192-201.

[13]Cf. Movsēs Kałankatuac'i, Patmut'iwn Ałuanic (Tiflis, 1913). English trans. by C. J. F. Dowsett, The History of the Caucasian Albanians by Movsēs Dasxuranc'i (London-New York, 1961).

[14]Kirakos, 8, 84.

[15]Cf. Samuēl Anec'i, Chronology, French trans. by M. F. Brosset, Collection des historiens anciens et modernes de l'Arménie, II (Paris, 1867-68).

[16]Kirakos, 348.

[17]Ibid., 218.

[18]Ibid., 249.

[19]Ibid., 313.

[20]Ibid., 235.

[21]Ibid., 376, 378.

[22]Cf. Siaset Nameh, the book about the office of the 11th century Vizir, by Nizam al-Mulk (Moscow-Leningrad, 1949) 242.

[23]Cf. Bertold Spuler, Die Mongolen in Iran (Politik, Verwaltung und Kultur der Ilchanenzeit 1220-1350) (Berlin, 1955) 59.

[24]Kirakos, 226.

[25]Spuler, Die Mongolen, 450-58.

[26]Kirakos, 310.

[27]Ibid., 371.

[28]Smbat the Constable, Taregirk' (Paris, 1859) 124; Cf. Kirakos, 364.

[29]Cf. H. Ačaŕyan, Hayoc' Anjnanunneri Baŕaran, II (Erevan, 1944) 625; H. Janp'olatyan, "Mxit'ar Goš ew Nor Getiki Vank'ě," Ašxatut'yunner Hayastani Petakan Patmakan T'angarani, I (Erevan, 1948).

[30]Grigor Akanc'i, History of the Nation of the Archers (ed. Patkanian; St. Petersburg, 1870) 52.

[31]Kirakos, 9-10.

[32]Ibid., 218.

[33]At the end of the first section the declaration and profession of the creed of the Armenian Church by the Armenian Catholicos Nersēs IV Šnorhali (1100-1173) is inserted by Kirakos (121-147). The text is authentic and identical with the original preserved and published in Šnorhali's Ēndhanrakan T'ułt'k' (Jerusalem, 1871) 87-107. Kirakos also includes in his History the encyclical of Catholicos Constantine I Barjrberdc'i (1221-1267) pertaining to the Council of Sis taken place in 1243. Cf. Kirakos, 259-300. The encyclical is followed by the twenty-five decisions adopted by the Council (Ibid., 301-310). Cf. Oramanian, Azgapatum (Constantinople, 1913) II.1626-1635. The History also contains a text on the doctrine of the procession of the Holy Spirit from the Father (Ibid., 329-333) which is "acceptable to the Armenian Church and to the spirit of Kirakos, the doctrine of the Holy Spirit which proceeds from the Father and is manifested through the Son." Ibid., 333.

[34]Kirakos, 398.

[35]Vardan Arewelc'i, Patmut'iwn Tiezerakan (ed. M. Emin; Moscow, 1861) 192.

[36]Russian trans. of Moscow-Leningrad is quoted by Melik'-Ohanjanyan, cf. Kirakos, 34, n. 4 (Int.). Also cf. The Cambridge History of Islam (Cambridge, 1970) I.168.

[37]Vardan, 213.

[38]Kirakos, 271-72.

[39]Vardan, 192.

CANON TABLES AS AN INDICATION OF TEACHER-PUPIL RELATIONSHIPS IN THE CAREER OF T'OROS ṚOSLIN

Helen C. Evans

Institute of Fine Arts (NYU)

The canon tables, Eusebius' concordance index of parallel passages in the gospels and the letter to Carpianus explaining their use—are placed at the beginning of most Cilician gospels and are among the most richly decorated of the pages in those texts.[1] Usually the ten indices, plus Eusebius' explanatory letter, are arranged on five pairs of facing folios with the letter on the first pair of folios. The distribution of the indices on the succeeding four pairs of folios varies considerably from manuscript to manuscript as does the decoration of all the folios. Such diverse canon table formats have been found on Cilician manuscripts that they often appear to have been created at the whim of the individual artist.[2]

However, the canon tables of T'oros Ṙoslin's manuscripts prove that the sense of freely chosen formats is inaccurate. T'oros, considered the finest Cilician artist, produced six signed manuscripts between 1256 and 1268 A.D. whose canon tables are preserved.[3] While no two sets of these tables are exact duplicates, each set uses the same sequence of bird types atop similar headpieces and the text is distributed in the same manner on each set of tables. Minor motifs are also related from manuscript to manuscript. T'oros's format for the decoration and the arrangement of the indices is evident on the relatively early manuscript, J. 251, which he executed at Hromklay in 1260 A.D. for the Catholicos Kostandin I and which is now in the Armenian Patriarchate in Jerusalem.[4] Pairs of peacocks surmount the letter of Eusebius atop rectangular headpieces filled with concentric arches on the first pair of folios (fig. 1). On the first folio, the peacocks' necks

T. Samuelian & M. Stone, eds. Medieval Armenian Culture. (University of Pennsylvania Armenian Texts and Studies 6). Chico, CA: Scholars Press, 1983. pp. 272 to 290.

entwine about a cross while on the second two, with flared tails, approach a fountain filled with water and flowers. The headpieces are supported by columns. Confronted lion capitals top the columns of the first folio, the same bodies, but with crowned human heads, those of the second folio. Index 1 and the first of index 2 are on the second pair of folios under pairs of cranes (fig. 2). The cranes flank a water filled fountain on the first folio and an altar on the second atop headpieces that stress a triangular format. The rest of the second index, all of indices 3 and 4, and the first of index 5 are displayed under groups of partridges on the third pair of folios (fig. 3). A pair of partridges approach a vase from which two grapevines grow on the first folio while on the second several flank a fountain with a pair of lions' heads for its spouts. The headpieces have differing interior layouts—concentric circles are the focus of the first folio's and the broad rectangular border band that of the second's. On the fourth pair of folios (fig. 4) opposed pairs of roosters surmount the rest of index 5 and all of indices 6, 7, and 8 where the headpieces are dominated by radiating ribs and an arch filled with a zig-zag pattern. The final pair of folios with indices 9 and 10 (fig. 5) have strange, long legged birds over the headpieces filled with concentric arches reminiscent of those on the first pair of folios.[5]

Most of the motifs used by T'oros on his tables are so common not only to those of Hromklay, but also to other Cilician works, that their use elsewhere is not in itself a proof of a direct relationship.[6] Rather the source must be sought for his tables as a unit. The search is for earlier manuscripts with the same distribution of the text and precisely the same distribution of the key elements of the decoration—the bird and headpiece sequence. Kirakos, a painter at Hromklay before T'oros, is typical of artists with only slightly differing canon tables. In his gospel of 1244 A.D., Venice 69/151, for the Catholicos Kostandin I, Kirakos used the same bird and headpiece sequence as T'oros except that the roosters precede instead of following the partridges.[7] It is Yohanēs, another artist of the generation preceding T'oros at Hromklay, who established the format for text distribution and bird sequence copied consistently by T'oros. Yohanēs's gospel of 1253 A.D., now in the Freer Gallery of Art, Washington, D.C., F.44.17 (fig. 6) (again for the Catholicos Kostandin I), provides even many of the subsidiary motifs of T'oros's tables—the column types, details of the headpieces, the designs flanking the headpieces and columns—as Narkiss has noted.[8] However, while every set of T'oros's canon tables derive from Yohanēs's tables, only the most basic elements of their formats remain unaltered—the distribution of the letter and the indices, the sequence of the bird types, and the general formats of the headpieces.

It is important to understand the complex interplay of innovation, revival, and continuity which defines the relationship of T'oros's tables to those of Yohanēs. This can be shown by a comparison of the formats of the first pair of folios of Yohanēs's manuscript with T'oros's first pairs in his texts as the relationships established demonstrate the pattern by which all the subsequent folios are created.

The pages by Yohanēs are beautifully executed in delicate, jewel-like detail. The first folio has a pair of peacocks whose heads entwine about a cross as their tails stretch furled behind them. The headpiece has sirens perched in the floral rinceau filled spandrels and a wide arch filled with peacocks in a delicate rinceau confronting a double-headed eagle over a portrait of Eusebius. Rearing, confronted lions form the capitals of the supporting columns with their floral patterned shafts. Elaborate birds with rigidly looped tails and ear tufts perched on umbrella-shaped trees flank the headpiece while the columns are flanked by trees with intricately entwined branches upon which hawks perch cleaning their claws. The facing folio is a mirror image of the first for most of the page. However, the peacocks atop the headpiece now stand with tails furled beside a fountain from which flowers grow. One twists its neck toward the preceding page; the other ducks his head for a drink from the fountain. The wide arch has a lush rinceau of thick leaved foliage filled with small naturalistic birds. At the apex cranes confront a long-necked vase over a portrait of Carpianus. The birds, flanking the headpiece, simpler than those on the preceding page, have straight tails.

While executed with less detail, the first folios preserved by T'oros continue the essentials of this format. The "Zeytun" gospel, done in 1256 A.D. for the Catholicos Kostandin I, is now in Istanbul (fig. 7).[9] On the first folio few changes were made—the sirens are bulky, an extra decorative arch is in the headpiece, the peacock band now parades in one direction, Eusebius is in a new pose, the birds in the trees by the headpiece are less exotic, and the lions of the capitals do not rear. The facing folio also changes little—the birds by the headpieces become parrots, the birds by the columns raise their heads, the broad arch of the headpiece continues the peacock parade of the opposing page, and both peacocks atop the headpiece have the reversed head pose of Yohanēs's left bird with their tails inverted to allow the eyes to drip down. Some of these details, such as the seated pose of the lions of the capitals, are innovations which T'oros will not repeat. Others will be seen to reappear on some of the later manuscripts—the extra arch in the headpiece, the continuous peacock parade in the broad arch, the bulky siren forms, and the new pose of the second folio's peacocks.

In his next preserved work, J.251, of 1260 A.D. (fig. 1), T'oros returned to a more exact copy of the Yohanēs tables for the elements outside of the headpieces—the peacocks match those of the Yohanēs types, the lions of the capitals rear (although only those of the first folio have lions' heads).[10] Within the headpieces the format is that of the "Zeytun" gospel with its extra decorative arch, and the first folio echoes its peacock parade. The innovation in the first folio is that the spandrel fillers are now a lion hunting a deer. The wide arch of the second folio is also new—the vegetative patterns that have previously been the background for animal forms now exist alone. As if to compensate, sirens, not unlike those by Yohanēs, fill its spandrels. Neither the figure of Eusebius or Carpianus relates to those in the earlier gospels, but the thoughtful, finger to cheek pose of Carpianus will be repeated in T'oros's two last works, J.1956 and M. 10675. The column bases are now elaborated versions of the Yohanēs/"Zeytun" type and will be continued.

From 1262 A.D. two T'oros manuscripts are preserved. One, J.2660, now in the Armenian Patriarchate in Jerusalem, was illustrated by T'oros for the son of King Het'um I and his wife (fig. 8); the other, W.539 (fig. 9), was done for the nephew of the Catholicos Kostandin I and is now in the Walters Art Gallery in Baltimore, Maryland.[11] Both manuscripts use the same formats for their peacock pairs—that of the Yohanēs tradition for the first pair and essentially that of the "Zeytun" gospel for the second although the left bird on the second folio holds its tail in the Zeytun style. The first folio of the Walters' manuscript is the closest copy of the Yohanēs folio that T'oros ever produced even to the double-headed eagle at the apex of the headpiece's wide arch. In contrast, the headpiece of the second folio copied only the layout of the Yohanēs manuscript. The spandrels possess two deer—in type, not pose—related to that of J.251's spandrels. The broad arch in its rinceau retains traces of the lush vegetation of the Yohanēs prototype, but the creatures are now carnivores after their prey in a cavorting parade, as if an expansion of the hunt theme of J.251. This is typical of the way

T'oros's tables evolve. Within the sequence established by Yohanēs, details change, elements from Yohanēs's or T'oros's earlier manuscripts are reintroduced, new motifs are added—the change is incremental.

On his other manuscript of the same year, J.2660, T'oros was more boldly innovative. He changed the motifs of both headpieces and the lower outside trees with standing figures of prophets. The other trees of the headpieces, however, are quite faithful to Yohanēs's pattern. The headpieces most often find their sources in J.251 where there is a similar concentration of the decorative arches about the portrait busts. The peacocks of both pairs of spandrels seem to be derived from the peacock parade of the first folio of J.251, and the vegetative design of the broad arch of the first folio was first seen on the second folio of J.251 as well. The animal band on J.2660's second folio uses the confronted creature format of Yohanēs's manuscript and T'oros's W.539, but the apex is a confronted pair of sirens. Their proportions resemble that of the "Zeytun" sirens while their crowns are like those on the human-headed lion capitals of J.251.

Three years later, in 1265 A.D., in his gospel for the Lady Keran, J. 1956 (fig. 10), now in the Armenian Patriarchate in Jerusalem, T'oros employed a similar assymetrical layout for each folio.[12] The trees by the colums and the headpieces, closely copied from Yohanēs's first folio, are placed only at the outer edges of the two folios making them explicitly one unit. Other elements are also revivals of Yohanēs's models: the pose of Eusebius (more like that in Yohanēs's gospel than any other by T'oros), the sirens of the second folio's spandrels, and the designs of the arches of the headpieces and the columns. Again there are elements from earlier Roslin works. The wide arch of the first folio is copied from J.2660 and the peacock band on the second folio from the "Zeytun" gospel. The pose of Carpianus on the second folio is also derived from that on the "Zeytun" gospel. And there are innovations, such as the exclusively foliate designs of the spandrels of the first folio, which will be repeated in T'oros's next and final signed work, M.10675. The head poses of both pairs of peacocks are also new. For the first time the peacocks of the first folio do not entwine their necks. Those of the second folio both face the fountain while otherwise having the bodies of the birds on the manuscripts of 1262 A.D., W.539 and J.2660.

In T'oros's last work, again for the Catholicos Kostandin I (now in the Matenadaran in Erevan, M.10675 (fig. 11)), the pattern continues.[13] Patterns true to Yohanēs's original gospel are seen in the entwined necks of the first peacock pair, the basic scheme of the headpieces, the flanking trees and birds, and the patterns on both the horizontal crossbars—the stepped pattern of the upper crossbar having been used consistently on every manuscript. While the columns for the first time replace Yohanēs's lion capitals with paired acanthus leaves, their bases are the purest copy of those on his folios since the "Zeytun" gospel, clearly a deliberate revival. Elements of T'oros's last works are also present. The pose of Carpianus and the purely vegetative designs of the spandrels and the broad arch of each folio are inspired by J.1956, done only three years earlier. The two narrow shell-patterned arches repeat a pattern established on the first folio of W.539. The new poses of the second folio's peacocks are merely a reuse of bird forms from earlier manuscripts. The bird on the left is from J.1956 while that on the right was first introduced in the "Zeytun" gospel and reused in the W.539 and J.2660 gospels. The real innovation on these folios is the use of long-necked birds beside the lower outside trees. Thus this last work by T'oros demonstrates anew his awareness of the motifs established by Yohanēs, his reuse of motifs initially innovations on earlier tables of his own, and his continued unwillingness to repeat a format without some degree of modification and innovation.

This rooting of a set of canon tables so specifically in a preceding master's work is not unique to T'oros. The unnamed painter of the Queen Keran gospel, executed at Hromklay in 1272 A.D., J.2563 (fig. 12), also used the same distribution of indices, birds, and headpieces as Yohanēs and T'oros.[14] Yet his tables are only indirectly copied from those of Yohanēs. The direct source is T'oros, especially his later works, as shown by the first pair of folios.[15] The peacocks of the second folio and the long-necked bird beside its lower tree are clearly derived from T'oros's last work, M.10675, while the pose of Carpianus and the rinceau-filled spandrels of the first folio are common to both of T'oros's last work, J.1956 and M.10675. The peacocks of the first folio have unentwined necks like the birds of J.1956. The trees to the side of the pages are in the tradition of Yohanēs, but the exotic tails of the upper birds curl in, a characteristic only of T'oros's last manuscripts. (The tails curl out on Yohanēs's tables.) Other elements echo T'oros's earlier manuscripts. The multiple arches of the headpieces follow the pattern of T'oros's earliest works, the Zeytun gospel and J.251. The broad arch of the first folio with its confronted peacocks and double-headed eagle could refer to Yohanēs's design, but more likely to its reuse on W.539 on 1262 A.D. And the same zone of the second folio with its confronted lions is most reminiscent of the confronted beasts on the other manuscript of 1262 A.D., J.2660. Thus this work too is clearly part of the highly specific canon table evolution which can be traced through T'oros to Yohanēs.

The existence of a common iconographic theme cannot explain this continuum. The Catholicos Kostandin I, as a patron of Kirakos, Yohanēs, and T'oros, may have influenced the choice of the formats of the tables. However, only Yohanēs, T'oros, and the painter of J.2563, who postdates the catholicos, consistently adhered to the same distribution of the text and sequence of key forms—the birds and their headpiece layouts. This fact combined with each artist's awareness of details of the preceding artist's work suggests instead a teacher-pupil relationship. T'oros continuously revived different details of Yohanēs's prototype in his manuscripts. The painter of J.2563 derived elements of his tables from a number of T'oros's works. All three used decorative patterns common at Hromklay so this intense loyalty to a specific predecessor's organization of those motifs can only be explained by a need to be associated with that artist.[16] The most logical explanation of this is that they chose to indicate their place in a master-pupil relationship through the continued use of the master's canon table format. This would fit the stress on continuity found in Armenian art in general and specifically in the manuscript tradition where leaves from older texts are bound into each manuscript as if to authenticate it.

It is possible that a more thorough study of Cilician canon tables by the sequence of the forms supported by the headpieces and the distribution of the text might enable us to demonstrate more extended master-pupil groupings and thus help explain the evolution of Cilician decorative art. Certain earlier Cilician manuscripts, such as M.7347 of 1166 A.D. or Venice 1635 of 1193 A.D., do share decorative formats with the Yohanes type tables, i.e. M.7347's rooster format (fig. 13) is very like that of the Yohanēs-T'oros type seen on J.251 (fig. 4).[17] However, no text with precisely the same format sequence and/or the same distribution of text is yet known. A later gospel, M.197 of 1287 A.D. (fig. 14), does have the same sequence of birds and the same distribution of text with the same type of incremental changes that have been observed in the Yohanēs/T'oros/J.2563 relationship as shown by its first folio.[18] Works like it might be proven to have a place in the same master-pupil continuum. The possibility that the complex decorative patterning known in Cilicia could be broken ino a series of steps from master to pupil does exist. This first step in that direction has sought only to demonstrate how the canon tables prove T'oros to be the pupil of Yohanēs and the painter of J.2563, the pupil of T'oros.

NOTES

[1]The research for this paper could not have been accomplished without the aid of a summer grant for 1981-1982 from Dumbarton Oaks, Washington, D.C., and a 1981-1982 Travel Grant from the Kress Foundation which allowed me to work with the manuscripts at the Armenian Patriarchate in Jerusalem; the Matenadaran in Erevan; the library of the Mekhitarist Congregation at San Lazzaro in Venice; the Walters Art gallery in Baltimore, Maryland; and the Freer Gallery of Art, Washington, D.C. My thanks must be given to the staffs of those institutions for their aid and cooperation as well as to Dr. Thomas F. Mathews and Alice Taylor of the Institute of Fine Arts, New York University, for their advice.

[2]L. Azarjan, Cilician Miniature Painting (Erevan, 1964) pls. 54, 61 [Russian]; S. Der Nersessian, Armenian Art (London, Thames and Hudson, 1977) pl. 115; S. Der Nersessian, Armenian Manuscripts in the Walters Art Gallery (Baltimore, pub. by the Trustees, 1973) pls. 13-22; S. Der Nersessian, Armenian Manuscripts in the Freer Gallery of Art (Washington, 1963) pls. 6, 7, 10; S. Der Nersessian, The Chester Beatty Library, A Catalogue of the Armenian Manuscripts (Dublin, Hodges Figgis and Co., 1958) pls. 8-12; S. Der Nersessian, Manuscrits Arméniens Illustrés de la Bibliothèque de Pères Mekhitaristes de Venise (Paris, E. de Boccard, 1937) pls. XVI-XXIII.

[3]The six manuscripts with canon tables associated with T'oros by colophons are:
1.   Istanbul, Armenian Patriarchate, "Zeytun" gospel, 1256 A.D.
2.   Jerusalem, Armenian Patriarchate, no. 251, gospel, 1260 A.D.
3.   Jerusalem, Armenian Patriarchate, no. 2660, gospel, 1262 A.D.
4.   Baltimore, Walters Art Gallery, no. 539, gospel, 1262 A.D.
5.   Jerusalem, Armenian Patriarchate, no. 1956, gospel, 1265 A.D.
6.   Erevan, Matenadaran, no. 10675, gospel, 1268 A.D., previously J.3627.
A final manuscript associated with T'oros by colophon is Jerusalem, Armenian

Patriarchate, no. 2027, which as a ritual has no canon tables. Der Nersessian, Walters Art Gallery, 15, except for the present number of J.3627 which was transferred to the Matenadaran after publication of her text.

[4]This text has been chosen as the exemplar since it is one of those in the Armenian Patriarchate in Jerusalem which has not been fully published. Ibid., 15; B. Narkiss & M. E. Stone (eds.) Armenian Art Treasures of Jerusalem (New York: Caratzas Bros., 1979) 148; N. Bogharian, Grand Catalogue of St. James' Manuscripts (Jerusalem: Armenian Convent Printing Press, 1967) II, 14-23 [Armenian].

[5]While there are alterations in the formats from text to cover, the only significant change in the bird sequence is on the last pair of folios where there is an evolution in the depiction of the long-legged creatures. Most seriously altered is the bird on the right side of the final folio. Beginning with J.2660 that bird's head is consistently catlike.

[6]Related motifs are found on Venice 1635, 1193 A.D.; Freer 50.3, a twelfth century gospel possibly from Hromklay; Walters 538, a Cilician gospel of 1193 A.D.; and Chester Beatty 588, a thirteenth century gospel from Hromklay. Der Nersessian, Manuscrits Arméniens Illustrés, pls. XVI-XXIII; Der Nersessian, Freer Gallery, 13 and pls. 6, 7, 10; Der Nersessian, Walters Art Gallery, pls. 13-22; Der Nersessian, Chester Beatty, 2, pls. 8-13.

[7]The photographs of Venice 69/151's canon tables have not arrived from San Lazzaro in time for this publication. Venice 69/151 is identified in Der Nersessian, Chester Beatty, 1.28. Her association of Chester Beatty 588 with Kirakos provides a parallel example of folio formats similar to the T'oros tables but associated with different indices. Ibid., 1.30 and 2, pls. 8-12.

[8]Der Nersessian, Freer Gallery, pls. 17-21; Narkiss & Stone, Armenian Art Treasures, 48. (Unlike Narkiss, I find only the canon tables of Yohanēs and T'oros's manuscripts to be compelling related. Within the body of the manuscripts, T'oros's pericope markings are elaborate while those of Yohanēs are simple circles; T'oros's initial at the beginning of each gospel is figurative, Yohanēs's not; the portraits of the evangelists vary, etc.)

[9]See footnote 3. Photographs of only the Eusebian letter and the dedicatory folios are available at Dumbarton Oaks, but they so closely match those of Yohanēs's manuscript and fit so well into the pattern established by

the rest of T'oros's manuscripts that there seems no reason to doubt that the other folios were also based on the Yohanēs prototype.

[10]See footnote 3; Narkiss & Stone, Armenian Art Treasures, 148; Bogharian, Grand Catalogue (1967) 2.14-23.

[11]See footnote 3; Narkiss & Stone, Armenian Art Treasures, 148-149; Bogharian, Grand Catalogue, VIII (1972), 277 for J.2660. Der Nersessian, Walters Art Gallery, 10-30 for W.539.

[12]See footnote 3; Narkiss & Stone, Armenian Art Treasures, 149; Bogharian, Grand Catalogue (1972) 6.526-530.

[13]See footnote 3; Bogharian, Grand Catalogue (1977) 8.263.

[14]Narkiss & Stone, Armenian Art Treasures, 64, 149.

[15]As in the T'oros/Yohanēs relationship, the pattern of exchange established on the first folios is followed throughout the entire set of tables.

[16]See footnotes 6, 7, and 16 for manuscripts with similar motifs from Hromklay and L. Durnovo, Armenian Miniatures (London: Thames and Hudson, 1961) 102-103.

[17]Der Nersessian, Walters Art Gallery, 7, 27, and Azarjan, Cilician Miniatures, pls. 41-42 for M.7347 in the Matenadaran. A study of its canon tables at the Matenadaran showed it to posess peacock, crane, and rooster formats very similar to the Yohanes type and in the same order in the manuscript. The text itself is not distributed in quite the same manner, i.e. fig. 13 has indices 6 and 7, not 7 and 8. The other two pairs of folios in M.7347 are topped by guinea hen like creatures and frontally posed peacocks, rather than partridges and long-ledgged birds. Der Nersessian, Manuscrits Arméniens Illustrés, pls. XVI-XXII for Venice 1635. There are similarities to the Yohanēs type are quite consistent until the final pair of folios.

[18]Der Nersessian, Freer Gallery, 60 and footnote 150. The principal colophon is lost. A notice of 1590 as tranlated by Der Nersessian states "written by Bishop John . . . in the year 1287, on March 13." The canon tables were studied at the Matenadaran.

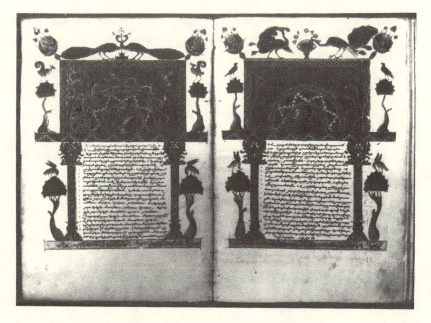

1.   Jerusalem, Armenian Patriarchate, ms. 251, Eusebian letter, by T'oros
Řoslin, 1260 A.D.   Courtesy of the Library of Congress.

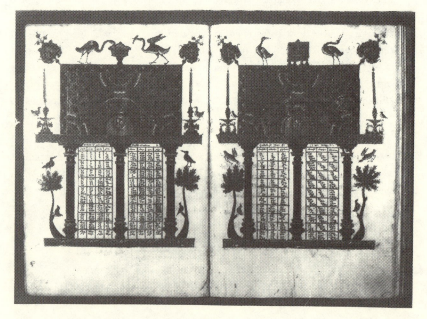

2.   Jerusalem, Armenian Patriarchate, ms. 251, Canon tables, indices 1
and 2, by T'oros Řoslin, 1260 A.D.   Courtesy of the Library of
Congress.

3.   Jerusalem, Armenian Patriarchate, ms. 251, Canon tables, indices 2, 3,
      4, and 5, by T'oros Ṙoslin, 1260 A.D. Courtesy of the Library of
      Congress.

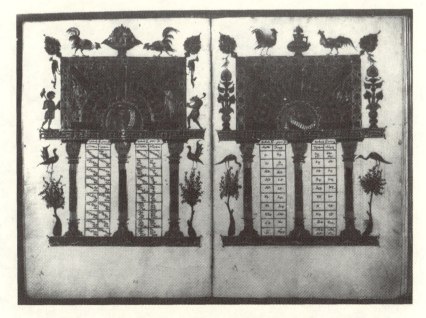

4.   Jerusalem, Armenian Patriarchate, ms. 251, Canon tables, indices 5, 6,
      7, and 8, by T'oros Ṙoslin, 1260 A.D. Courtesy of the Library of
      Congress.

5.   Jerusalem, Armenian Patriarchate, ms. 251, Canon tables, indices 9
and 10, by T'oros Ŕoslin, 1260 A.D.   Courtesy of the Library of
Congress.

6.   Washington, D.C., Freer Gallery of Art, ms. 44.17, Eusebian letter, by
Yohanēs, 1252 A.D.   Courtesy of the Freer Gallery of Art, Smith-
sonian Institution, Washington, D.C.

7.   Istanbul, Armenian Patriarchate, "Zeytun" gospel, Eusebian letter, by
      T'oros Roslin, 1256 A.D.   Courtesy of Photograph Collection, Dum-
      barton Oaks, negatives B52. 2188- B52. 2189.

8.   Jerusalem, Armenian Patriarchate, ms. 2660, Eusebian letter, by T'oros Roslin, 1262 A.D. Courtesy of the Library of Congress.

9.   Baltimore, Walters Art Gallery, ms. 539, Eusebian letter, by T'oros Roslin, 1262 A.D. Courtesy of Walters Art Gallery, Baltimore.

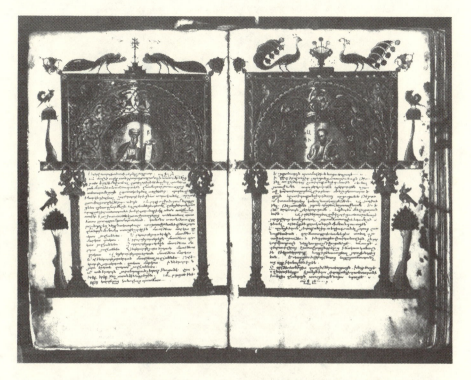

10.   Jerusalem, Armenian Patriarchate, ms. 1956, Eusebian letter, by
        T'oros Ṙoslin, 1265 A.D. Courtesy of the Library of Congress.

11.   Erevan, Matenadaran, ms. 10675, Eusebian letter, by T'oros Ṙoslin,
       1268 A.D.   Courtesy of Photograph Collection, Dumbarton Oaks,
       negatives B52. 1811 - B52. 1812.

12.   Jerusalem, Armenian Patriarchate, ms. 2563, Eusebian letter, 1272
       A.D. Courtesy of the Library of Congress.

13.   Erevan, Matenadaran, ms. 7347, Canon tables, indices 6 and 7, 1166 A.D. Courtesy of the Matenadaran, Erevan.

14.   Erevan, Matenadaran, ms. 197, Eusebian letter, 1287 A.D. Courtesy of the Matenadaran, Erevan.

ARMENIAN CILICIA, CYPRUS, ITALY AND
SINAI ICONS: PROBLEMS OF MODELS*

Valentino Pace

Università di Roma (Italy)

Years ago, Kurt Weitzmann published a double-sided icon from the Monastery of St. Catherine at Mount Sinai, representing the Crucifixion and the Resurrection (fig. 1). Together with other icons from the same collection, among them a diptych representing the Virgin with the Child on one side (fig. 4) and St. Procopius on the other side (fig. 3), he ascribed it to a Venetian workshop active at Acre around the third quarter of the thirteenth century.[1] In a paper read at the 1981 Symposium "The meeting of two worlds," I expressed my disagreement with Weitzmann's views.[2] My aim is to reexamine these icons and their possible models or prototypes. The cases I am going to make are concerned with the models. The line of reasoning, therefore, is not necessarily corroborated by the chronology of these works but simply testifies to the availability of such models in the workshop of the painter, without implying any further relation between him and his source. For this reason I am purposely avoiding to deal with questions of chronology.[3]

To begin with, in the Resurrection depicted in the double-sided icon (fig. 1), the crowned heads are clearly reminiscent of models like the David playing the harp in the Erznka Bible of 1268 (fig. 2).[4] The hairdoo may indeed have an ultimate Western, French, origin,[5] but the Cilician connection must not be ruled out for this reason. After all, the physiognomic type of Salomon—that is the crowned head on the right—is clearly non-Western, possibly aiming at a kind of Levantine physiognomy, somehow not distant from the types of Queen Keran's family as represented in her famous

---

T. Samuelian & M. Stone, eds. Medieval Armenian Culture. (University of Pennsylvania Armenian Texts and Studies 6). Chico, CA: Scholars Press, 1983. pp. 291 to 305.

Gospels (fig. 5).[6] Moreover, the heavy ornamentalism of both icons is often found in Cilician miniatures. Once again Queen Keran Gospels provide a good example.[7] Particularly relevant, beyond other similarities which are also found in Cypriote painting,[8] are the borders of the halos which we see around the heads of the Madonna and the Child, and of St. Procopius in these icons (fig. 3, 4) and around the Madonna of the Nativity in the Queen Keran Gospels (fig. 6) in a loose miniature sheet from the Stoclet collection (fig. 7) and elsewhere in the (Cilician) side.[9]

As I already said these similarities must be understood simply as possible proof of the availability of Cilician models in the workshop of our Sinai icons; a direct participation of Cilician artists in this workshop can surely be ruled out, since Cilician miniatures and Sinai icons do not share features which could support direct interrelations: a few similarities in the painterly treatment are not strong enough to prove this point.[10]

From this perspective, that is, the search for the origin of workshop which produced the Sinai icons, the comparisons with late thirteenth-century painting in Cyprus, proposed by Sotirious, who ascribed our diptych to a painter from that island, are just as unsatisfactory.[11] But Cyrpus certainly provided models for the iconography of the Virgin in the diptych (fig. 4), derivative from the "Kykkiotissa,"[12] for her physiognomic type,[13] and for the punched halos in the Resurrection.[14]

If the workshop which produced the Sinai icons had models not only from Cyprus (and elsewhere) but also from Cilicia, we would gain further evidence of a phenomenon which Kurt Weitzmann and Wolfgang Grape already pointed out, dealing with parallels between a Sinai icon of the Last Judgement and a miniature by T'oros Roslin[15] as well as between a Sinai icon of the Crucifixion and a miniature in the Queen Keran Gospels.[16]

Both cases bear on the "Cicilian question" within the Mediterranean context. Further cases will help us to understand better the many facets of this issue.

Sirarpie Der Nersessian drew our attention to the similarity of iconography between Duccio's "Madonna dei francescani" and two earlier Cilician miniatures (figs. 7, 8) based on lost models alleged to be of Western origin, which would have been influenced Duccio.[17] In my opinion it has not yet been demonstrated conclusively that this iconography is ultimately of Western origin. In this case, as well, the possibility of Cilician credit cannot be ruled out.[18] The same point can be made with another case which is

drawn from one of the two miniatures: Christ wears an "embroidered" white
tunic with a sash supported by   bracets (fig. 7).   A similar clothing is worn
by the Child in the diptych, (fig. 4) whose iconography, as noted before,
partially depends on the "Kykkiotissa."   Since this peculiar fashion occurs in
a number of Cypriote icons,[19] I feel that it is more likely that this fashion
was exported from Cyprus than from any other areas—for example, Italy—
where it is often misunderstood.[20]

The peculiarly embroidered white tunic of Christ is not necessarily
bound to Cyrpus.   Its use began to be fairly common in the fourteenth
century.   About 1270, the Cilician miniature seems to have been quite
innovative.   If such a feature of fashion should turn out to be a Cilician
innovation in this iconographic context, this would be another piece of
evidence supporting the hypothesis that Cilician models were available to the
workshop where these Sinai icons were painted.[21]

Cilicia and Italy shared other artistic contacts.   Wolfgang Grape has
devoted a careful study to the "Gaibana epistolary," a manuscript of the
Venice-Padua area, finished in 1259, whose miniatures bear outstanding
resemblances to Cilician manuscript painting;[22] he also pointed out some
examples of Byzantinizing painting in Central Italy; for instance, the
"Marzolini triptych" in the National Gallery of Umbria at Perugia[23] (figs. 9,
10).

There is no doubt that the Umbrian triptych must be seen in a wider
context than the Centro-Italian tradition provides.   In this context, which
should be sought in the East, not in the West as was believed,[24] the role
played by Cilicia in the larger framework of the "Byzantine question" cannot
easily be ascertained: buildings in the background, stylization of landscape,
physiognomical types, crysography make it possible for us to tie this triptych
also, to Cilician miniatures as well, but not exclusively to them.   Grape and
I have made comparisons between this Umbrian panel painting and the Second
Prince Vasak Gospels[25] (figs. 8, 9, 10); other comparisons could be made with
the Queen Keran Gospels,[26] further instances of parallelism or reciprocal
influences between Umbria and Cilicia should be carefully checked.[27]
Without any doubt the recorded gift of liturgical books to an Armenian
church at Perugia, in 1279, is a stimulus for further research in this
direction.[28]

I presented here some clues which would let us detect Cilician models
behind "Sinai" and Centro-Italian paintings.   We look forward to a time when

research on Cilician painting, and with it of the other Mediterranean areas "between East and West," will provide the kind of evidence which will either confirm or deny the hypothesis of this paper.

NOTES

*The Author wishes to express his gratitude toward those who enabled him to carry his program of research partially embodied in the present paper: Archbishop Shahe Ajemian and Archbishop Norayr Bogharian at the Armenian Patriarchate of Jerusalem; Archbishop Damianos, Higoumenos Sophronios at the Monastery of St. Catherine at Mt. Sinai; the N.C.R.D. of Israel and CNR of Italy.

[1]K. Weitzmann, "Icon Painting in the Crusader Kingdom," Dumbarton Oaks Papers, 20 (1966) pp. 49-83 (64-69).

[2]V. Pace, "Italy and the Holy Land: Import-Export. I. The case of Venice," Proceedings of the Symposium "The meeting of two worlds," Kalamazoo—Ann Arbor, May 1981; ed. V. Goss; in press.

[3]The double-sided Icon and diptych belong to a larger group of paintings whose chronology should be carefully checked. For some considerations on the difficult use of their stylistic data, see my "Possibilita e limiti dell'analisi stilistica come metodologia storica: 'Stile,' 'Maestro' e 'Bottega' in pittura': con particolare riferimento alle icone sinaitiche," Proceedings of the International Colloquium on "Artistes, Artisans et Production artistique au moyen-age" (Rennes, May 1983; ed. X. Barral i Altet; in press). As far as icon and diptych are concerned, I have the feeling that they are to be dated later than "before 1291" and that for this reason their origin at Acre should be ruled out. Unfortunately, I cannot prove my point with satisfactory comparisons: the complex shape of the "heaven" and of the starry halo within the mandorla behind Christ in the Resurrection are indeed motifs which were fairly widespread in the fourteenth and fifteenth centuries, but there is at least one instance of it in the early thirteenth century: San Cipriano, Murano (now Potsdam, Friedenskirche). See S. Badstubner-Groger, Die Friedenskirche zu Potsdam (Das christliche Denkmal. 85; Berlin: Union Verlag, 3. Aufl., 1980). H. Hallensleben correctly dates these mosaics to the first half of the thirteenth century. His article is due to appear in the

Zeitschrift fur Künstgeschichte. It was he who pointed to me this example. Moreover, the painterly treatment of the large figures of the Virgin and of St. Procopius show somehow an "academic" quality, which seem to me far from thirteenth century characteristics. For a good color plate of St. Procopius, see: K. Weitzmann, The Icon (New York: Braziller, 1978) pl. 37. See also pl. 38.

[4]On the Ernzka Bible, see: S. Der Nersessian, "La Bible d'Ernzka de l'an 1269: Ms. Jerusalem No. 1925," published 1966 and reprinted in her Etudes byzantines et arméniennes (Bibliotheque arménienne de la Fondation Calouste Gulbenkian, Louvain: Editios Peters, 1973) [hereafter quoted as BAS, followed by the year of the original publication] 603-609. For further illustrations see also: B. Narkiss & M. Stone, eds., Armenian Art Treasures of Jerusalem (Jerusalem: Massada Press, 1979) figs. 84-86.

[5]See, for instance, the hairdoo of the so-called Philippe Auguste and of the so-called St. Louis at Reims Cathedral: W. Sauerländer, Gotische Skulptur in Frankreich: 1140-1270 (Munchen: Hirmer, 1970) figs. 260-261.

[6]The famous Queen Keran Gospels, Ms. Jerusalem 2563, still needs an art-historical study. It is dated 1272. For some comments and splendid color illustrations, see: S. Der Nersessian, L'Art arménien (Paris: Arts et Metiers graphiques, 1977) 144-148 and figs. 104-107; or Narkiss & Stone, Armenian Art Treasures, 63-64, figs. 77-78.

[7]See, for instance, the throne of the Madonna in the Annunciation (f. 184) of the Queen Keran Gospels, or the frame of the window in the building to the left, behind the Evangelist Luke, in Ms. Erevan 9422 Matenadaren No. 9422 (see a color pl. in: B. Brentjes, S. Mnazakanjan & N. Stepanjan, Kunst des Mittelalters in Armenien (Berlin: Union Verlag, 1981) fig. 236.

[8]It may be remembered that it is also on the basis of their strong ornamentalism that a group of Sinai icons (among them the Procopius diptych) has been ascribed to Cypriote painters by G. and M. Sotiriou, in their Icones du Mont Sinai (Athenes: Istitut Francais, 1958) 2, .159, 170-173 [in Greek, with French summary].

[9]The miniature from the Stoclet collection was published by S. Der Nersessian, in her "Deux exemples arméniennes de la Vierge de Misericorde," REArm 7 (1970) 187-202 [BAS, 585-601]. Quite similar halos are also found in the Second Prince Vasak Gospels (figs. 8, 9, 13) and in other Cilician

manuscripts at Erevan: Matenaradan No. 197 and 9422 (see Brentjes, et al., Kunst des Mittelalters, figs. 234-238.

[10]Comparisons can be drawn between the Queen Keran Gospels (especially Moses and the Apostles in the Transfiguration, f. 69 or the angel in the Annunciation, f. 184) and the Resurrection (the figures of Adam and Eve). Compare also the crysography in the Queen Keran Gospels and in the Procopius diptych.

[11]Sotiriou, Icones di Mont Sinai I, figs. 188-190, 2, 171-173, with references to his Ta byzantina Mnemeia tis Kyprou (Athens, 1935), pls. 80, 86 and 117 [in Greek].

[12]Sotiriou, Icones di Mont Sinai, 171-172. It is the red veil over the maphorium on the Virgin's head which testifies to the dependence of this icon on the Kykkiotissa; the pose of the Child does not follow that prototype. For a later copy of the Kykkiotissa, see: A. Papageorgiou, Ikonen aus Zypern (Munchen, Geneve, Paris: Nagel, 1969), 48.

[13]Papageorgiou, Ikonen aus Zypern, 25.

[14]D. T. Rice, "Cypriot Icons with Plaster Relief Background," Jahrbuch der osterreichischen Byzantinistik (1971), 21. M. S. Frinta, "Raised Gilded Adornment of the Cypriot Icons, and the Occurrence of the Technique in the West," Gesta 20 (1981) 333-347.

[15]Weitzmann, Icon Painting, 59, figs. 14-15; W. Grape, Grenzprobleme der byzantinischen Malerei (Dissertation, Wien, 1973) 82-85, fig. 38a-b. S. Der Nersessian, Armenian Manuscripts in the Walters Art Gallery (Baltimore: The Trustees of the Walters Art Gallery, 1973) 20-21.

[16]Grape, Grenzprobleme, 79-81, fig. 36a-b.

[17]Der Nersessian, "Deux Exemples"; C. Belting-Ihm, Sub Matris tutela (Abhandl. der Heidelberger Akademie der Wissensch. Phil.-hist. Klasse, Heidelberg 1976), 68-70 agrees with Der Nersessian stating that the Cilician miniatures "entstanden offenbar unter franziskanischem Einfluss."

[18]Pace, Italy and the Holy Land, note 54. See also D. Kouymjian, "The iconography of the 'Coronation' Trams of King Levon I," Armenian Numismatic Journal, 4 (1978) 67-74.

[19]Papageorgiou, Ikonen aus Zypern, figs. on pp. 21, 36 and 46.

[20]An Italian origin for this fashion was guessed by Der Nersessian,

"Deux Exemples," BAS, 594, on the basis of the reference to a Sienese panel painting of 1262. This work, however, clearly testifies to misunderstandings of the original composition, since "dash" and "silk scarf" are made of two different materials. For a good colour illustration see: P. Torriti, La pinacoteca nazionale di Siena, 1 (Genova: Sagep, 1977) 22-23. For further examples of iconographic dependence on the Kykkiotissa, see: K. Weitzmann, "Crusader Icons and la 'Maniera greca,'" Il Medio oriente e l'Occidente nell'arte del XIII secolo (ed. H. Belting; C.I.H.A., Atti del XXIV Congresso Internazionale di Storia dell'arte, Bologna 1979; Bologna: CLUEB, 1982), 71-77 esp. 73-74 and P. Santamaria, "La Vergine Kikkiotissa in due icone laziali del Duecento," Roma anno 1300 (Atti della IV settimana di studi di storia dell'arte dell'Università di Roma, Roma 1981; Roma: L'Erma di Bretschneider, in press).

[21]To our present point, it would be enough that Cilician models transmitted such a feature to the workshop of the Sinai icons.

[22]Grape, Grenzprobleme, passim.

[23]Ibid., 145. See also: Weitzmann, "Icon painting," 82; Pace, "Italy and the Holy Land."   On the tritych: F. Santi, Galleria nazionale dell'Umbria.   Dipinti, sculture e oggetti d'arte di età romanica e gotica (Roma: Istituto poligrafico dello Stato, 1969), 37-38.

[24]M. Boskovits, Pittura umbra e marchigiana fra Medioevo e Rinascimento (Firenze: Edam, 1973) 7-9; M. Boskovits, "Gli affreschi della sala dei Notari a Perugia e la pittura umbra alla fine dei XIII secolo," Bollettino d'Arte 56 (1981), 1-41 esp. 7-8.

[25]Grape, Grenzprobleme, 144-146, fig. 77a-b; Pace, "Italy and the Holy Land."

[26]Compare the painterly treatment in the Queen Keran Gospels of the tunics of the apostles in the Washing of the Feet, or of the angel in the Annunciation, with the angel of the Annunciation in the Umbrian triptych; or, the crysography of both miniatures and panel.

[27]Pace, "Italy and the Holy Land."

[28]Der Nersessian, "Deux Exemples," 592 (quoting G. Hovsepian, Colophons des manuscrits, Antelias, 1951 [in Armenian]) was the first scholar to draw the attention of Art Historian to this important reference. See also:

Pace, "Italy and the Holy Land." Der Nersessian points out a number of parallels between Italy and Cilicia, explaining them as the result of a trend brought from Italy to Cilicia, in the wider context of historical events, which testify to the rising importance of the Western culture in the Cilician Kingdom. See, among the many works she devoted to Cilician Art, "Western iconographic themes in Armenian manuscripts," (1965), BAS, 71-94; "Miniatures ciliciennes" (1969), BAS, 509-515; "Deux Exemples" (1970) BAS, 585-601. Once admitted the "contacts" between the two areas, the artistic trends must not have followed however a one-way direction of influences. Grape, Grenzprobleme, passim, has taken, correctly in my opinion, a more cautious and balanced position. The history of Cilician Armenian has been surveyed by S. Der Nersessian, "The Kingdom of Cilician Armenia," A History of the Crusades, general ed. K. M. Setton (vol. II. The Later Crusades. 1189-1311; eds. R.-L.-Wolff and H. W. Hazard, Madison, Milwaukee and London: The University of Wisconsin Press, 1969), 630-659 [repr.: BAS 611-630].

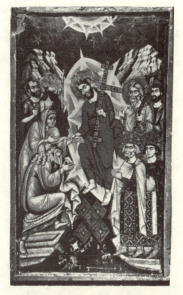

Figure 1   Crucifixion and Resurrection.   Monastery of St. Catherine,
              Mount Sinai.   (K. Weitzmann, Icon Painting in the Crusader
              Kingdom, Dumbarton Oaks Papers 20 (1966) fig. 28)

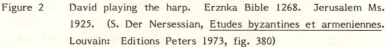

Figure 2   David playing the harp.   Erznka Bible 1268.   Jerusalem Ms.
              1925.   (S. Der Nersessian, Etudes byzantines et armeniennes.
              Louvain: Editions Peters 1973, fig. 380)

Figure 3   Diptych: St. Procopius, Monastery of St. Catherine, Mount Sinai.   (Courtesy Michigan-Princeton-Alexandria Expedition to Mt. Sinai)

Figure 4   Diptych: Virgin with Child. Monastery of St. Catherine, Mount Sinai. (Courtesy Michigan-Princeton-Alexandria Expedition to Mt. Sinai)

Figure 5   King Leo II, Queen Keran & family.   Jerusalem 2563, f. 380
(Narkiss & Stone, Armenian Art Treasures of Jerusalem,
Jerusalem: Massada Press, 1979. f. 77)

Figure 6   Madonna of the Nativity.   Jerusalem 2563, f. 21, 184

Figure 7   Madonna and Child.   Bruxelles, Stoclet collection.   (Der
Nersessian, <u>Etudes byzantines et armeniennes.</u>   f. 367)

Figure 8   Prince Vasak and sons, Virgin of Mercy, enthroned Christ.   Jer.
2568, f. 320.   (Narkiss & Stone, <u>Armenian Art Treasures of
Jerusalem.</u> p. 69)

Figure 9   Narzolini triptych.   Perugia, Galleria nazionale dell'Umbria.
(Carlo Fiorucci, Perugia)

Figure 10   Triptych: Angel of the Annunciation.   Perugia, Galleria
nazionale dell'Umbria.   (Carlo Fiorucci, Perugia)

VASPURAKAN MANUSCRIPT ILLUMINATION AND
ELEVENTH-CENTURY SOURCES

Alice Taylor

Institute of Fine Arts (NYU)

In the two centuries following the Mongol invasions of Asia Minor, manuscript painting flourished in the southern Armenian province of Vaspurakan. Hundreds of manuscripts have survived from fourteenth- and fifteenth-century Vaspurakan.[1] No manuscripts with illuminations can be attributed by colophon to Vaspurakan between the early eleventh and the late thirteenth centuries; this may merely indicate that the manuscripts produced in the Seljuk period were all destroyed. Scholars have maintained that traditions of manuscript illuminations survived unbroken from the eleventh to the fourteenth centuries. Lilit Zakarjan undertook to trace such a survival, basing her study on a group of manuscripts made in K'ajberuni from 1296 to 1316.[2] She showed that this group depends on an eleventh-century model and concluded that a local tradition in manuscript illumination linked the eleventh- and the fourteenth-century Vaspurakan.

A fourth manuscript dependent on the same eleventh-century model may join the K'ajberuni group. In establishing this, I will consider in more detail the exact relationship between the eleventh- and fourteenth-century manuscripts, and suggest that the fourteenth-century copies do not come out of a local tradition, but copy a very unfamiliar model.

The Metropolitan Museum in New York owns a single folio with illumination on both sides (figs. 1 and 2). Captions in Armenian identify the figures, but the fragment carries no other text, and there is no external indication of provenance. The folio finds close parallels in the eleventh-century.

T. Samuelian & M. Stone, eds. Medieval Armenian Culture. (University of Pennsylvania Armenian Texts and Studies 6). Chico, CA: Scholars Press, 1983. pp. 306 to 314.

306

The shorter dimension of the page is the height of the illustration and the longer dimension, its width. Bound in a codex of normal proportions, the picture would be sideways, with the spine of the book running along the feet of the figures. Since the feet in both illustrations fall to the same edge of the folio, when the page is turned, rotating the folio around the spine of the book, the other side comes out upside down.

A rather large group of eleventh-century Armenian Gospel manuscripts has illustrations laid out in the same way.[3] These illuminations form a cycle illustrating major events in the life of Christ, preceding the canon-tables and the text of the Gospels, which are mounted in the usual, vertical fashion. The orientation of the pictures means that turning from one illustration to the next requires turning the whole book around.

The fragment in New York (henceforth the Metropolitan fragment) very closely resembles a folio from one of these manuscripts, No. 6201 of the Matenadaran, a Gospel made in 1038.[4] Four folios carry the eight scenes of its preface cycle. The last of these folios corresponds to the page in the Metropolitan Museum. Recto shows the resurrected Christ at the tomb, and verso, four standing Evangelists. The scene at the tomb is the rarer of the two. It includes Christ, three women, and two apostles. A combination of any two of these elements would be surprising; all three occur together only in this manuscript and in its copies.[6]

This scene in the Gospel of 1038 does not correspond to any particular Gospel text. Rather, it compiles elements of all four accounts, straining the structure of the pictorial narrative to give as explicit a demonstration of the reality of the resurrection as possible without contradicting the Gospel story. As in Mark 16:1, three women approach the tomb, carrying the spices with which they intend to annoint Christ's body. The women look to the tomb, on which two angels are perched. Two angels figure in Luke 24:4, and in John 20:12. Below the women stand two men, the two apostles who visit the tomb as related in John 20:3-10, but not in any of the other Gospels. Matthew 28:4 alone mentions the sleeping guards, who appear below the tomb. Christ really has no part in the narrative at this point, since the mortals are to visit the tomb and leave without concrete proof that he has risen.

The artist has managed to include elements from differing versions of the story without allowing them to conflict. The three women, who should arrive at the empty tomb alone, see only the angels, as do the apostles. The angels look past these figures to Christ; they see him, but the other figures do not. Unlike the standard images of the discovery of the empty tomb, which do not include Christ,[7] this illustration reveals the resurrection explicitly.

This compositional device, the insertion of several separate incidents into one space, most distinguishes the Gospel of 1038, since this miniature, for all its rarity, does have ties to east Christian tradition. Most of the elements do occur, singly, in Armenian and Syrian iconography. Even the combination of Christ with the women at the tomb already appears in the Syriac Gospels of 586, where the monk Rabula included Christ meeting two women in the same landscape with the two women at the tomb.[8] This close connection of the two scenes became a common Syrian device for showing the resurrection more directly than the scene of the discovery of the empty tomb alone.[9] It occurs in the frescoes of Alt'amar.[10] as well. But this is clearly a juxtaposition of two moments in the narrative, and thus more traditional than the conflation of the Gospel of 1038. That the Gospel of 1038 departed radically from the norms of medieval Armenian iconography is demonstrated by its reception by later artists.

The Metropolitan fragment in New York is a later version of the Gospel of 1038. Clearly, the artist was uncomfortable with his model; he retained the composition of the Gospel of 1038, with the angels perched on the open tomb at the upper left and Christ standing at the right, but he simplified the narrative by representing only two moments from the Gospel of John. The two men preceding Christ at the tomb are the two apostles of John 20:4-9. The second is labelled "Petros" in agreement with the text. The Gospel does not identify the first apostle to arrive at the tomb, but he was commonly taken to be John, as he is labelled here (Yovhannēs). In the Gospel according to John, a moment later, Mary, after meeting the angels where she is expected to find Christ's body, turns her back on the two angels and the tomb. She appears in the illumination just below the tomb. The caption next to this figure reads kuysn 'the virgin.' Although the context of John's account clearly shows this person to be Mary Magdelene, the verses actually illustrated (John 20:11-14) do call her simply Mary, and it was fairly common to mistake her for the Virgin Mary.[11] The creator of the fragment was divided in his response to a venerable old manuscript. He retained as much as he could of the composition; however, he consciously and deliberately changed details to conform to the single text he had chosen and to simplify the space in the composition. Even so, to fully understand the image of the Metropolitan fragment, the viewer must look at different events simultaneously, but the consecutive moments of John's narrative have been spread out to minimize the problems of the Gospel of 1038.

The Gospel of 1038 and the other eleventh-century manuscripts with which it can be grouped[12] are all large codices. The Metropolitan fragment is smaller (19 x 29 cm. Its very bright colors contrast with the subtle harmonies of the eleventh-century manuscripts.[13] On stylistic grounds, the Metropolitan fragment may be placed in fourteenth-century Vaspurakan, where brightly colored figures were usually painted on blank paper with sparse indication of setting. It is not possible to assign the page to any of the published Vaspurakan artists, but the creator of the Metropolitan fragment may have come from the same circle as Melk'isedek, who painted a Gospel (Matenadaran No. 4813) in Berkri in 1338.[14] In that manuscript, Melk'isedek used decorative motifs very similar to those of the Metropolitan fragment, including the elongated, angular braid pattern of the frame, and the draperies decorated with simple scratches and circles. If the Metropolitan fragment was produced around Berkri, it joins the group of copies of the Gospel of 1038 that Zakarjan published. The creators of these copies—Xač'er and Yovsian—also adjusted it, changing the events depicted to simply chronology. In publishing them, Zakarjan concentrated on the similarities of the three Gospels to their eleventh-century model to the exclsuion of the significant divergences between the model and the copies, differences that characterize the circumstances in which the copying took place. All three of the later artists—Xač'er, Yovsian and the creator of the Metropolitan fragment—dealt with the same model, in the same area of Vaspurakan, and at roughly the same time, but they did so independently.

In the Gospel of 1294, Matenadaran No. 4814 (fig. 3), Xač'er replaced the complex overlapping of time and space in the Gospel of 1038 with one easy to read moment; two women together with John and Peter, arrive, evidently in a group, at the tomb. They look past the angels to the resurrected Christ. Xač'er has given up all fidelity to the Gospel texts to present one moment. This violence to the text demonstrates how extremely puzzling the Gospel of 1038 was to Xač'er.

Yovsian produced two nearly identical Gospels, Matenadaran No. 4806 of 1306 and No. 4818 of 1316.[15] His treatment of the discovery of the empty tomb shows him to have been just as uncomfortable with the iconography of the Gospel of 1038 as Xač'er or the artist of the Metropolitan fragment. Yovsian's solution differs from the model more drastically than does Xač'er's, but preserves the meaning of the Gospel texts (fig. 4). He broke the scene into separate episodes in order to resolve an ambiguous scene into familiar components. In his version, only Mary Magdelene sees Christ. She faces him in the upper right corner. John 20:14 says that she turned her back on the angels to see Christ, and so they are behind her. Below Christ and Mary stand two women. as in Matthew 28:1, facing away from the tomb. Peter and John are properly alone as they investigate the tomb (here rather quaintly filled with the dead).

These three variations on the eleventh-century model are not misunderstandings, but separate revisions. Zakarjan and H. Hakobyan have both adduced twelfth- and thirteenth-century manuscripts of uncertain provenance as evidence of a continuous local tradition linking the Gospel of 1038 to early fourteenth-century Vaspurakan.[16] There may have been some tie (besides that of the copying itself) between the eleventh-century Gospels and fourteenth-century Vaspurakan, since their most distinctive feature—the format of the pages—was adopted in many Vaspurakan manuscripts.[17] However, the evidence of the copies of the Gospel of 1038 indicates that there had been a significant break in local artistic production—exactly as indicated by the dearth of late eleventh-, twelfth-, and early thirteenth-century Vaspurakan manuscripts. Each artist who copied the Gospel of 1038 had to grapple with his model alone and devise his own solution, without the aid of a developed local tradition. This suggests that the Gospel of 1038 was not copied in K'ajberuni before 1294.

More research should show to what extent this pattern is repeated elsewhere in Vaspurakan from the end of the thirteenth century, but evidence already available points to a break in traditions of manuscript illumination before this period: Vaspurakan painting, as it appears in the late thirteenth and early fourteenth centuries, breaks down into many local schools. Sirarpie Der Nersessian focused on the schools of Van and Xizan;[18] Hakobyan has further noted that the independence of Arčeš, Ostan, Ałt'amar, Bałeš, Varag, and Xlat' and other highly localized iconographies coincides with the evidence provided by copies of the Gospel of 1038.[19] There was in Vaspurakan a great deal of activity in manuscript illumination in the late thirteenth and early fourteenth centuries, but this activity did not spring from local tradition. It was not until the many small schools of Vaspurakan coalesced later during the fourteenth century that a new local canon developed.

NOTES

[1]H. Hakobyan, Vaspurakani manrankarč'ut'yunĕ (Erevan: Haykakan SSH GA, 1976) 1, 6.

[2]L. Zakarjan, Iz Istorii Vaspurakanskoj Miniatjury (Erevan: AN ArmSSR, 1980) 14-35.

[3]The best discussion of the group, with a good survey of the earlier literature, is that of B. Narkiss, Armenian Art Treasures of Jerusalem (eds. B. Narkiss and M. Stone; Jerusalem: Massada Press, 1979) 36-40.   The manuscripts are treated more fully, but somewhat fancifully, by T. Izmajlova, Armjanskaja Miniatjura XI Veka (Moscow: Iskusstvo, 1979) 47-102.

[4]Izmajlova, XI Veka, 47-64 with the older literature.

[5]Ibid., pls. 28 and 29.

[6]E. Kirschbaum, "Frauen am Grab," Lexikon der Christlichen Ikonographie (Rome: Herder, 1970) 2, 54-62.

[7]Ibid.

[8]C. Cecchelli, The Rabbula Gospels (Otten and Lausanne: Urs Graf-Verlag, 1959) unnumbered plate labelled fol. 13a, and J. Leroy, Les Manuscrits syriaques à Peintures (Paris: Paul Geunthner, 1964) pl. 32.

[9]Leroy, Manuscrits syriaques, pls. 79 and 93.

[10]S. Der Nersessian, Aghtamar: Church of the Holy Cross (Cambridge: Harvard University Press, 1965) pl. 67, just visible in the lower right (and mislabelled "Harrowing of hell"), and S. Der Nersessian and H. Vahramian, Aght'amar (Documenti di Architettura Armena 8; Milan: Edizioni Ares, 1974) pl. 58, lower left.

[11]J. Breckenridge, "'Et Prima Vidit':   The Iconography of the Appearance of Christ to His Mother," Art Bulletin, 39 (1957) 13.

[12]Narkiss, Jerusalem, 36.

[13]Ibid., pls. 49-51, and Izmajlova, XI Veka, pls. 24-29, 38, 40, 42, 45-46.

[14]H. Hakobyan, Armenian Miniature: Vaspurakan (Erevan, Sovetakan Grol, 1978) pl. 20 [in Armenian, Russian, and English].

[15]Zakarjan, Vaspurakanskoj Miniatjury, 84 and 87. Only No. 4818 is reproduced, pl. 14.

[16]Ibid., 10-11, and Hakobyan, Vaspurakani manrankarč'ut'yunĕ, 19.

[17]Hakobyan, Armenian Miniatures, pls. 11, 19, 20-22, 27-29.

[18]The Chester Beatty Library: A Catalog of the Armenian Manuscripts (Dublin, Figgis and Co., 1958) xxxiii-xxxix.

[19]Hakobyan, Vaspurakani Manrankarč'ut'yunĕ, 67.

Fig. 1. New York, Metropolitan Museum of Art, 57.185.3. The Virgin, John and Peter at the tomb with Christ and two angels, fourteenth century. Vaspurakan (Deposited by J. C. Burnett, 1957, Metropolitan Museum of Art photo).

Fig. 2. New York, Metropolitan Museum of Art, 57.185.3, verso. Four Evangelists, fourteenth century, Vaspurakan (Deposited by J. C. Burnett, 1957, Metropolitan Museum of Art photo).

Fig. 3. Erevan, Matenadaran, No. 4814, fol. 6. John, Peter and two Holy women encounter Christ and two angels at the tomb, 1294, Argelan, artist Xačʻēr (after Lilit Zakarjan, Iz Istorii Vaspurakanskoj Miniatjury (Erevan: AN ArmSSR, 1980) fig. 13).

Fig. 4. Erevan, Matenadaran, No. 4818, fol. 11 verso. John and Peter at the tomb, two angels, Mary encountering the risen Christ, and two Holy Women, 1316, Hazarakn, artist Yovsian (after Lilit Zakarjan, Iz Istorii Vaspurakanskoj Miniatjury (Erevan, AN ArmSSR, 1980) fig. 14).

EVIDENCE OF ARMENIAN RUG-MAKING ON THE BASIS OF
THE ILLUMINATIONS OF ARMENIAN MANUSCRIPTS
FROM THE SEVENTH TO FOURTEENTH
CENTURIES

Viken Sassouni[*]

University of Pittsburgh

Introduction

With the exception of the Pasyrik rug, dated to the sixth century B.C. and uncovered by Rudchenko in 1949 in mounds of Altai, no earlier carpet from Armenia has survived other than rare samples dated to the thirteenth and fourteenth centuries, AD.

This hiatus is in part attributable to the accidental freezing of the Pasyrik and to the fragility of textiles in general. Small fragments have been unearthed from the excavation of Erebuni and elsewhere, proving that knotted rugs were being made toward the fifth century, AD.

Schurmann recently attributed the weaving of the Pasyrik rug to populations living in the sixth century, BC, in the Armenian Plateau.[1] Thus, it was established that knotted rugs were probably made as early as the eighth century, BC and that there was a continuity of weaving these rugs to the present day.

During the period extending from the seventh to the fourteenth centuries only indirect evidence has been quoted to establish that the Armenians were rug-weavers without interruption during this period. To a large degree these come from travelers and historians of the time.

The Arab historian Ibu Kaldoun wrote that in the eighth century rugs were given as payment of taxes by Armenia to the Caliph of Baghdad.[2] Marco Polo, passing through Armenia at the end of the thirteenth century,

T. Samuelian & M. Stone, eds. Medieval Armenian Culture. (University of Pennsylvania Armenian Texts and Studies 6). Chico, CA: Scholars Press, 1983. pp. 315 to 328.

reports that it was the Armenians and the Greeks in Turkomania who wove "the finest and most beautiful rugs in the world" not to mention "very beautiful and very rich silk cloth of many colors" whereas the Turkomans were a "simple people" who lived in the mountains of the Anatolian plateau. The Arab geographer Yakout, writing in the thirteenth century (1229) after having defined the geographical position and administrative dependency of the city of Van, indicates that large rugs were woven there.[3]

Thus it was established that rug-weaving was an active Armenian handicraft and home industry during the middle ages.

More precise documents about the existence and nature of Anatolian rugs are to be found in the Renaissance paintings in Italy, made during the thirteenth, fourteenth and fifteenth centuries. Artists of the time, such as Holbein, reproduced with great precision of detail oriental rugs which were highly appreciated as rare luxury items, thus permitting a precise dating.

It is a similar type of source that this study will concentrate on: Armenian manuscript illuminations as a source for the documentation of Armenian and oriental rugs. As direct examination of these manuscripts was not possible, in this report only published sources are utilized. A rapid survey of this material shows that only about 200-250 manuscripts have been reproduced out of a total store of 20,000. Their author's criteria of selection for publication being unspecified (some for their style, some for their beauty and degree of preservation), the present review should be considered only as preliminary due to uncertainties of sampling techniques.

There are five areas where the study of rug-making can be investigated from manuscript illuminations: 1. Dye similarities between illuminations and rugs; 2. Illustrations of actual rug-making processes; 3. General composition of a page, its parallel in rug design; 4. Details of decorations, especially borders similarities between illumination and rugs; 5. Actual illustrations of rugs in the illuminated pages.

1.   Dye similarities

Although illumination and rug-making have their own technical dictates, a large number of colors used in both have similar hues and probably derive from similar dye sources.

There are some obvious differences: The use in illuminations of gold foil either as an undercoat to make the colors more responsive to light or simply directly as a main color. There are greater freedoms in illumination design than in rug-making due simply to the technical dictates of warp, woof and knotting imposed by weaving.

There are also certain dyes (like the dark brown or black) which are harmful to wool's modulus of elasticity but not to the parchment of manuscripts.   On the other hand, there are certain mineral powdered and mixed with a suspension media which were used in illuminations, but were not really dyes which could be applied to wool.

A recent chemical analysis of dyes used from manuscripts[4] reveals that most of the dyes were extracted from similar vegetable or mineral sources such as Lapis Lazuli and Indigo for the blues, Red lake, Vortan Karmir, Madder roots for the reds, etc.[5]

Other studies are still needed for direct comparison.   However, at first glance there is no important discrepancy between the manuscript palette and the one of the rugs with Armenian inscription, as long as these were derived form natural sources and not, as after 1850, from aniline and chrome dyes.[6]

2.   Illustration of actual rug-making process

The Armenian illuminations often include on their margin, representations of people: their dress, their occupations. In this last category, it is common to find wine-making, hunting, fishing, navigating, building, warring, etc.   Among these occupations the weaver's arts are relatively frequently illustrated.[7]

3.   General composition

Others have mentioned before that the design of a manuscript page, a door of a church, an elaborate binding of a book, as well as rugs, have certain compositional characteristics in common. It is interesting that rugs with Armenian inscriptions have the border treatments which share similarities with those of illuminated pages. (Fig. 2a, Note the frame; Fig. 2b, a prayer rug with similar composition as 2a.)

In other cases there are close resemblances in the composition of the field. The frontispiece of the illumination in Fig. 4a is designed with oblique arms dividing the field which is filled by fantastic creatures.[8] Compare this to the "Armenian Dragon-Rug" in Fig. 4b: the composition of the field is very similar, as is the choice of colors. This type of similarity may explain the attribution to Armenians of the dragon-rugs, of which the seventeenth-century Koher Rug, with its Armenian inscription, is a derivative.[9]

In another frontispiece, there is a naturalistic representation of the Dragon-Phoenix (Fig. 5a) probably brought through the silk-road from China.[10] Compare this to the fourteenth- or fifteenth-century compartmented rug from the Berlin Museum, attributed to Armenians of Anatolia (Fig. 5b). The Dragon-Phoenix struggle here has evolved a geometric style.[11] One derivative of the dragon-rugs in the nineteenth century is the Chelabert Armenian Karabagh rug (Fig. 3b). Compare its composition with the manuscript in Fig. 3a.[12]

4.   Details of decoration

There are many details in the decorations of illuminations which are found in Armenian rugs. (Fig. 3a, note details on the cross; Fig. 4a, note detailed decoration of the columns; Fig. 7a, note decoration of the chair.) Some are seen in the border treatment; others are found in the rug designs typically associated with Armenian inscription, like birds, church floor plans, flowers, crosses, etc.[13]

Early illuminations of the ninth and tenth centuries have a clear geometric, angular style very close to Caucasian and certain Anatolian Armenian rugs. Later on, the Armenian illuminations show a strong tendency to curvilinear decoration and naturalistic representations of humans, animals and plants.

5.   Direct rug reproductions

There are a certain number of Armenian illuminations where actual rugs are represented. There are several types of rugs which can be distinguished.

a.   Rugs underfoot of apostles, saints and the Virgin

These rugs which are frequently represented, seem to be stereotyped; they usually have a single border made of geometric designs in subdivided squares, surrounding a plain field, often blue or red. Rarely a fringe is seen, which may even raise a question as to the real nature of what is represented. On the other hand, there are a number of rugs with Armenian inscriptions which seem to have these same characteristics—plain field, red-orange, surrounded by a simple and single border. Others, also small rugs with trellis design, are more individualistic (Fig. 6a); (compare with nineteenth-century Armenian rugs with similar designs (Fig. 6b)).

b.   Saddle rugs

Most of the horsemen are represented seated on saddle rugs. Fringes here are frequent. Although there is no way to affirm that they are pile-rugs rather than kilims. In much of the published material, these rugs have a horizontal-striped design which is not usually associated with those bearing Armenian inscriptions in the nineteenth century. One would therefore conclude that either those designs with stripes existed during the fifteenth and sixteenth centuries, disappeared and then were replaced by new designs in the nineteenth century; or that those saddle rugs were imported from other ethnic groups.[14]

c.   Full rug representation

There are finally some illuminations which illustrate actual rugs whose designs have been transmitted to the end of the nineteenth century. In the Gospel of Xizan[15] the rug spread under the Virgin's feet has all the characteristics of the "Mina Khani" design (Fig. 7a). Compare it with the Armenian Karabagh rug with a "Mina Khani" design dated 1904 and inscribed in Armenian (Fig. 7b).

Another example is found in the manuscript of the Alexander Romance.[16] Alexander as an infant is represented on a rug entirely decorated with latchhook rosettes (Fig. 8a). Compare it with the Armenian Kazak dated 1896 with similar design and colors (Fig. 8b).

Conclusions

From these few examples one is impressed by the parallelism and similarities between Armenian illuminations and rugs from areas inhabited by Armenians. While the profusion of rug illustrations does not compare to those of the Mogul or Persian manuscripts of the same period, one should realize that their manuscripts were mostly court-commanded products where luxury and courtly magnificence were to be glorified.

The most frequent Armenian manuscripts had primarily a religious theme. Furthermore there was a real tradition of austerity among the monasteries where these manuscripts were composed. The surrounding peoples, dwelling mostly in rural villages, led simple and austere lives. The domineering Islamic population had taught the minority populations to avoid ostentation or any visible indication of wealth.

In spite of all these limitations the illuminations being published are shedding new light on the rug-maker's craft and products.

Yet more light can be expected as more of the 20,000 manuscripts become available in published sources.

*Viken Sassouni died while these proceedings were in preparation. On behalf of the conference participants, the editors and convenors wish to express their grief at the loss of a valued colleague and friend.

NOTES

[1]U. Schurmann, "The Pasyrik Rug," Lecture to Armenian Rug Society, NY, Sept. 1982.

[2]A. Sarkissian, Two Studies on Armenian Rugs (trans. L. Amirian) The Armenian Review 33 (1980) 1-2 [first published 1929].

[3]Ibid.

[4]M. Orno & T. F. Mathews, "Pigment Analysis of the Glajor Gospel of U.C.L.A.," Studies in Conservation 26 (1981) 57-72.

[5]S. Dilanian, "Vordan Karmir" [Warm-red, Cochineal] Sovetakan Hayastan (1979) 11: 12-14.

[6]H. Bedankian, "Natural Dyes in Caucasian Rugs," Oriental Rug Review 2 (1982) 7: 25-26.

[7]A. Kevorkian, The Craft and Mode of Life in Armenian Miniatures (Erevan: Hayastan, 1983) plates 24-25 [In Armenian]. The three major methods are 1) thread twisting (M. 4223, la 1401, Xizan, Gospel by Yovhannēs) 2) spinning (M. 4818, la 1316—Hazarka, Gospel by Xač'ēr) 3) weaving (M. 5472, 516-52a—16th century Rome. (Bishop Zakaria Alexander Romance).

[8]L. Durnovo, Miniatures arméniennes (Paris: Editions Cercle d'Art, 1960) 125, 127. Ms. of the middle 13th century by T'oros Roslin and Gospel of 1316, virgin spinning wool.

[9]Sarkissian, "Two Studies," 1-2.

[10]Durnovo, Miniatures, 127.

[11]N. Fokker, Caucasian Rugs of Yesterday (London: Allen & Unwin, 1979) 42.

[12]H. & H. Buschhausen, The Illuminated Armenian Manuscripts of the Mekhitarist Congregation of Vienna (Vienna: Mekhitarist Press, 1977) pl. 60, fig. 168. [Hymnal, Lake Van, 16th cent.].

[13]V. Sassouni, "Armenian Rugs," The Armenian Review (1980) 4: 383-411.

[14]Durnovo, Miniatures, 159 [Gospel of 1332]; 167 [Gospel of 1397]; 170 [Hymnal 1482]; 183 [Alexander Romance, 16th century]; 99 [Gospel, mid-thirteenth century].

[15]H. Hakopian, Armenian Miniatures of Vaspurakan (Erevan: Sovet-akan Grol, 1978) pl. 6 [Evangelist Mark Gospel, 1303, Arces]; pl. 56 [The Annunciation, Gospel 15th century, Xizan Rug].

[16]B. Narkiss & M. Stone, Armenian Art Treasures of Jerusalem (New Rochelle, NY: Caratzas Bros., 1979) pl. 127 [The Alexander Romance of 1536].

Fig. 1.   Illustration of actual
rug-making.   Notice the warp being
stretched.   (Manuscript 15th cent.
Rome, Bishop Zakarian Kevorkian,
The Craft, pl. 25.)

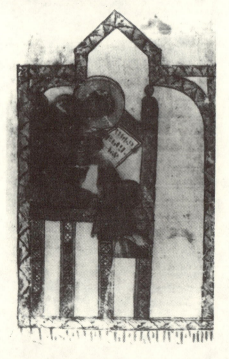

Fig. 2a.   The total frame of the
illumination represents a vertical
section of a typical Armenian
church.   (Manuscript of Arčēš of
1303. Gospel of Mark after
Hakopian, Armenian Minatures, pl. 6)

Fig. 2b.   A Caucasian rug with a prayer
Mihrab similar to the illumination in
2a.   (Private Collection.)

Fig. 3a.   A central cross with angel's
wings radiating (Cross of Navakalik,
Hymnal of Van. 16th cent. in Armenian.
Ms. Mekhitarist, Vienna, after
Buschhausen, Armenian Manuscripts of
Vienna, pl. 60).

Fig. 3b. An Armenian "Chelabert" rug
from Karabagh. Notice the central
cruciform design with arms radiating.
(Private Collection.)

Fig. 4a. The frontispiece of this
illumination is sub-divided boldly
by oblique blue arms. Fantastic
creatures fill the sub-divided field.
(Manuscript of the second half of the
13th century: Canon of Concordance
after Durnovo, Miniatures arméniennes,
125.)

Fig. 4b. A "Dragon Rug" attributed
to Armenians in the 15th, 16th, 17th
and 18th centuries. Notice the field
divided by intersecting blue and golden
arms. In the resulting subdivisions
are representations of the Dragon and
Phoenix in combat. Notice the
similarity of design and colors with
frontispiece of the illumination in
Fig. 4a. (Courtesy of the Textile
Museum.)

Fig. 5a. A naturalistic representation
of the Dragon-Phoenix struggle, probably
inspired from China and brought through
the Silk-Road. Frontispiece of an
illumination from Cilicia, 1288,
after Old Armenian Manuscripts (Erevan,
1952) pl. 35.

Fig. 5b. A 14th or 15th century rug
attributed to Armenians from Anatolia.
The Dragon-Phoenix is represented in
linear geometric style. (Berlin
Museum after Fokker, Caucasian Rugs, 42.)

Fig. 6a. The rug underfoot has a trellis design on a clear field and
light borders. (Manuscript of 12th century. In Der Nersessian:
L'Art arménien (Paris: Art et Metiers Graphiques, 1977) pl. 126.)

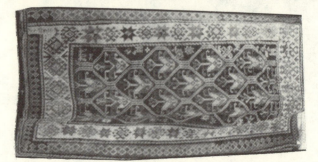

Fig. 6b. An Armenian Kazak rug dated 1884 (AMI) with a similar
design as in Fig. 6a. (Private Collection.)

Fig. 7a. The Annunciation. The large rug underfoot has the typical
trellis design called "Mina Khani." Notice the Virgin spinning wool.
(Gospel of Xizan. In Kevorkian, <u>Armenian Manuscripts</u>, pl. 56.)

Fig. 7b. An Armenian Karabagh Rug with a typical "Mina Khani" design.
Notice the date 1904, and the Armenian inscription which read
"Varsenig SAHAGIAN." (Harold Bedoukian's Collection, Montreal.)

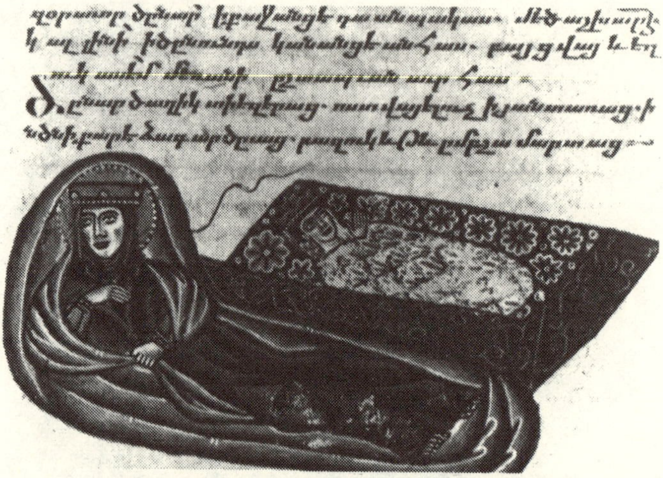

Fig. 8a. Alexander at his birth is stretched on a rug with typical
latchhooks. (The Romance of Alexander. In Narkiss & Stone,
Armenian Treasures of Jerusalem, 127.)

Fig. 8b. An Armenian Kazak dated 1896 with a very similar design
and color palette as in Fig. 8a. (Private Collection.)

THE KAFFA MANUSCRIPT OF THE LIVES OF
THE DESERT FATHERS

Nira Stone

Hebrew University of Jerusalem

I wish to present the manuscript of the Lives of the Desert Fathers
of Egypt, manuscript no. 285 of the Library of the Armenian Patriarchate
in Jerusalem. It was written in 1430 C.E. in Kaffa in the Crimea in the
Monastery of St. Anthony. Its substantial content is parallel to its substantial
physical format. It numbers 823 paper pages measuring 2.7 x 18 x 9 cms.
The script is a transitional bolorgir-notragir in black ink with the titles and
the names of the saints written in red. Each page has 37 lines of writing,
in two columns. The book is in a fairly good state of preservation, although
it has been repaired at some points and there is worm damage at others.

The manuscript contains 38 full or half-page miniature paintings and
a further 500 or so small illustrations which decorate the text. These are
chiefly heads or groups of heads related to the stories in the corresponding
text (fig. 1).[1]

The Crimea was a cross-roads of cultures of the busiest kind in the
fourteenth and fifteenth centuries and formed a meeting point for eastern
and western art. The Venetian and Genovese colonies brought with them
their Italian character, and Greece and Byzantium made their own contribution, while the Russian proximity also contributed not a little to the
contacts between the various cultures and artistic traditions. This was also
true of the local Armenian art which, naturally, developed in this well-to-do
and firmly established community. There was a very significant Armenian
colony there, active in the ferment of international commerce and the
Armenians formed a foreign colony second in size only to the Greeks.[2]

T. Samuelian & M. Stone, eds. Medieval Armenian Culture. (University of
Pennsylvania Armenian Texts and Studies 6). Chico, CA: Scholars Press,
1983. pp. 329 to 342.

According to the colophon of our manuscript, it was written and illuminated by the monk Thaddeus Avramec' in the monastery of St. Anthony in Kaffa. He tells how he carried out extensive scientific research in order to locate the most appropriate texts to include in the composition which we now possess. He relates his search for the best texts in Armenian and, when he did not find them, he searched among the Greek texts and copied from them as well. He illuminated and illustrated the whole so that the painting would attract and give pleasure to the reader.[3]

Now, Armenian texts of the Lives of the Desert Fathers exist in abundance from earlier periods, but not a single copy known to us is illuminated. A search among similar manuscripts in Greek was equally fruitless—no manuscript was found which might have served as an examplar for Avramec''s rich and artistic illuminations, which are highly original and highly creative. This accords with the painter's own witness in the colophon.

The possibility always exists that the copyist of our manuscript copied the colophon and that Avramec', instead of being an energetic researcher was only a very faithful copyist. There is a measure of scholarly disagreement on this point.[4] One thing seems quite incontrovertable—he was an extremely talented painter, even if he copied his paintings from some lost exemplars. On this point, one further small detail may be added: in the Library of the Mekhitarist Fathers in Venice there are, still unpublished, a number of pages containing illuminations almost identical to those in our manuscript, where they survive.[5] Professor Der Nersessian directed my attention to them and is of the opinion that Avramec' also painted them. Her evidence for this is the accuracy of the copy. Thus, the discomfort of the figure seated on the chair recurs in both manuscripts, a clear indication, in her opinion, that both were painted by the same artist (fig. 2).

Yet, we may question whether Avramec', so great an artist that he created the total corpus of illuminations in the Jerusalem manuscript, was still able to make copies so slavishly exact as the Venice pages, in which no hint of creativity can be discerned. However, one might postulate one of two things: (1) that his rigorous training as a scribe prepared him for these two seemingly incompatible activities; or (2) that one of his apprentices did it, hinting at the existence of an unknown atelier, a subject to which we will return later.

The originality of the illuminations in our manuscript enhances its intrinsic value while at the same time creating those problems that generally accompany such uniqueness. We often feel some discomfort where we are suddenly confronted by an artistic work that does not belong, at first glance, to any readily recognizable school, style, atelier, or other category. We always tend to search for influences, relationships, exemplars, and so forth, the more so when the work of art is not based on any known previous creation which could have served as its iconographic or stylistic exemplar.

The paintings of our manuscript were not the work of an amateur or a beginner. These are paintings of highest professional standards, of excellent precision and quality. There is, of course, the outside possibility that among the Greek manuscripts that he investigated one or more were illuminated, upon which he based himself and that these may have since disappeared. This is, of course, at most only a supposition and, in view of the evidence that we now have (or do not have), we assume that Avramec' was in fact a talented and creative painter and he created and executed the illumination of our manuscript.

If, indeed, we accept the assumption that Avramec' is actually the originator of these paintings, why did he do it at just that moment of history and no other? Why did Armenian art wait until the year 1430 to illuminate a manuscript of this type? After all, manuscripts of The Lives of the Desert Fathers and similar works were plentiful before, yet none of them was illustrated. Why did artists illustrate Gospels, Psalters and even Menologia and Synaxaria, but not the Lives of the Desert Fathers of Egypt? The creation of a cycle of illustrations clearly indicates the special importance attributed to the text at that particular time and the value seen in making it attractive. From the time of Avramec' on there are rather numerous illuminated manuscripts of this type—before him there are none.

The answer may lie in the general social and political unrest of the period. Civil upheavals were not uncommon in the Crimea towards the middle of the fifteenth century.[6] The Muslims were already knocking on the gates of Byzantium. The time had come to turn to the world of the ascetic saints. At Mount Athos the Hesychastic movement was flourishing and spreading fast. It summoned Eastern Christians to flee the corrupt world and seek solace in solitude and prayer. Monasticism became an ideological as well as a political aim of many Eastern Christians.[7] It may be that this new atmosphere gave artists the incentive to create rich and elaborate illustrations of stories about the famous solitary monks of earlier ages. The fact that a real need was fulfilled is borne out by the numerous later copies of our manuscript, which thus takes on very great importance indeed. Chronologically and artistically our manuscript belongs in many respects to the Palaeologian renaissance which attributed great significance to saints and their icons.

Avramec' generally based the portraits in his manuscript on well-known stereotypes (fig. 3). In the iconography of the scenes, however, he is quite unique and without predecessors. Moreover, the combination of the scenes and portraits to form the illustrative cycle of Avramec' manuscript is equally new. Nonetheless, although it was thus a unique creation, our manuscript was copied in the succeeding centuries in its complete form at least six times and it provided many iconographic models that became stereotypes for single scenes or parts of them.[8] The most prominent of these is the presentation of the luscious garden as the Garden of Eden with the four rivers (fig. 4). The rivers flow upwards out of a rocky background and appear later in all copies of the Kaffa manuscript, as well as in another type of manuscript, a Synopsis of Biblical History.[9]

As to the stylistic affiliations of the manuscript—most Armenian painting in the Crimea followed the Cilician style. Our manuscript, however, forms a clear exception to this and, as we shall demonstrate, it is not alone. Its style we dub Armeno-Crimean.[10]

On the one hand the Armeno-Crimean style exhibits some well-known characteristics of contemporary Byzantine style: (1) the division of the background in the proportions of one-third to two-thirds (figs. 3 and 5); (2) the attempt to create realistic pictures as seen in the paintings of the rocky mountains; and (3) the grouping of figures so that they penetrate the depth of the background (fig. 6). Indeed, the problem of depth occupied our painter and we can observe another interesting attempt to solve it in his painting of the sea (fig. 7). In that painting, he uses a gradual lightening of lines of blue as a technique to give the impression of depth for the sea and its waves. A strikingly similar technique is employed in a fresco of the year 1479—just 49 years later than our manuscript—in the Cathedral of the Assumption in Moscow to represent the depth of the heavens.[11]

In contrast to its Byzantine aspects, the chief distinguishing characteristic of the style of the manuscript is that it rendered the human form more correctly, gradually moving away from a flat presentation of form. As in other Crimean manuscripts of this group, our manuscript also shows additional signs of simplification of detail and the shortening of the proportions of the figures (fig. 8).

The artist, however, goes even further. He tries seriously to give as realistic a description as possible of the figures. Instead of anonymous figures, he attempts to attribute individual traits to each of them. For example, the usual clothing of desert fathers and other saints receives a personal touch when a group of monks appears in turban-like headgear which identifies them as Egyptians (fig. 9).

Yet another characteristic of the Armeno-Crimean manuscripts is the generally limited palette. The colors are indeed brilliant, but they are special in character and include many shades of brown, purple, green, yellow and white.[12]

All these features differentiate the style of our manuscript and its congeners from the bulk of "Cilician-type" Crimean manuscripts. Moreover, the uniqueness of much of its iconography and of its overall illustrative cycle may also be due to its creation in a distinct tradition.

We have, indeed, been able to locate a number of other manuscripts which were painted in the Crimea in a style similar to that of our manuscript. This justifies the new conclusion that in Kaffa there was an atelier that painted in this distinct, Armeno-Crimean style.

> 1. A page that is sewn inside a Kaffa manuscript of the year 1449 (Matenadaran, no. 1203) presents Gregory Tat'ewac'i among a group of disciples or admirers. Dr. Korkhmazian, some time ago, pointed out the stylistic similarity between it and paintings in our manuscript, particularly in the traits of the faces of many of the small marginal figures. The painter of this portrait may have belonged to the same school as Avramec' and have come from the Crimea. This is plausible since many of the young Armenians from the Crimea went to Tat'ew to study.[13]

Other clearly Crimean manuscripts which belong to the Armeno-Crimean school are the following:

> 2. Ms. Matenadaran, no. 7337 of 1352.[14]
> 3. Ms. Matenadaran, no. 3863 of 1401.[15]

These two manuscripts contain figures similar, among other features, in their stance and form.

> 4. Ms. Jerusalem, no. 773, a Miscellany from Crimea, has a frontispiece with a portrait of Nersēs Šnorhali, stylistically

belonging to the Armeno-Crimean school.[16]

5. The Venice manuscript pages mentioned above are also evidence that someone carefully copied the manuscript of the Lives of the Desert Fathers which was apparently important when it was painted.[17] As we stated, these pages might have been painted by Avramec' himself, or by one of his students.

At this time, then, there existed in the Crimea an atelier or school painting in the Armeno-Crimean style. Furthermore, we can discern in its work both eastern and western influences, as indeed we would expect in this area, a cross-roads of cultures. Some of these are:

1. The faces of the figures are elongated, their hair is fair and sometimes even their eyes are light. These features give a western rather than Armenian cast to the faces. This phenomenon might be explained in a number of ways. It could indicate that the painter realized that these were foreigners and not Armenians and, even though they were in fact Egyptians, he used as his model the faces of the European foreigners who were in the Crimea at his time.

2. The limited palette is characteristic of Armenian painting from the Crimea while the mountains and the buildings are in Byzantine style.

3. The purple marble looks Italian (fig. 4).

4. The red carved table appears to be Mongol or Chinese in character (fig. 7).

5. There seems to be a Russian connection.

The geographical proximity of the Crimea to Russia is reflected in its art as well. Thus there is considerable resemblance between the stance of the figures in Avramec''s manuscript and in the paintings of a much earlier, very important artist, Theophanes the Greek, in Moscow.[18] This is particularly true of the bent-over figures in the manuscript (fig. 8). We know that Theophanes worked for some time in the Crimea before he moved to Moscow. Perhaps he left an atelier there, or at least a pervasive influence which is still to be felt in the somewhat later Armeno-Crimean style.

6. Russian proximity is also expressed in a certain similarity between the painting of Avramec' and the Novgorodian school.

The influence of this school may be a contributory factor in the sudden popularity of the Lives of the Desert Fathers, for it has a particular penchant for hagiographical icons which provided amazingly descriptive representations of scenes from the lives of the saints.[19]

CONCLUSIONS

The conclusions that are to be drawn from the above analysis of the Jerusalem manuscript of the Lives of the Desert Fathers are the following:

a.   The manuscript has no clear exemplar, Armenian or Byzantine, Eastern or Western.

b.   The scenes represented are usually directly related to the narratives contained in the text.

c.   The popularity of this particular cycle of illustrations in the mid-fifteenth century is probably related to the rise of the Hesychian movement in the contemporary Greek Church. This in turn was stimulated, partly at least, by the disruptive political situation at that time.

d.   The study of at least five other examples of painting from the contemporary Armenian Crimea indicates the probable existence of a distinct atelier of which the Avramec' manuscript is a chef d'oevre.

e.   The style cultivated in this atelier is quite separate from the more widely known Armenian style of the Crimea, the so-called "Crimean Cilician style," although it shares certain characteristics with it.[20]

f.   The analysis of the manuscript's paintings from a stylistic point of view indicates a number of interesting affiliations: western, Byzantine, Mongolian-Chinese, and particularly Russian—both of the school of Theophanes and of the later Novgorodian type.

This preliminary analysis suggests that our continuing study of the Kaffa manuscript will illuminate still other unknown aspects of Armenian art in the Crimea.

NOTES

[1]Bogharian, Grand Catalogue of St. James Manuscripts (Jerusalem, 1967) 2. 107-112 (in Armenian).

[2]J. L. Lamonte, The World of the Middle Ages (New York, 1949) 625.

[3]See above, note 1.

[4]There are different opinions on this matter. Dr. Der Nersessian expressed to me the view that Avramec' copied not only the paintings but also the whole colophon. Dr. Korkhmazian claims that Avramec' did not copy the paintings, mainly because no possible model has been found. See E. Korkhmazian, The Armenian Miniatures of the Crimea (Erevan, 1978) [in Russian]. Archbishop Bogharian communicated orally that he thinks that the colophon may be authentic and the Avramec' translated the text from a Greek manuscript which was possibly illuminated.

[5]These pages, from Ms. no. 1922 of the Mekhitarist Library in Venice will be published soon with a description by S. Der Nesessian.

[6]D. Obolensky, The Byzantine Commonwealth: Eastern Europe 500-1453 (London, 1971) 260-261.

[7]J. Meyendorff, Byzantine Hesychasm: Historical, Theological and Social Problems (London, 1974) chaps. 1, 8, and 9. See also chap. 11 as an example of its influence on art.

[8]The copies are: BM Ms. no. add, 27.301: Armenian Patriarchate of Jerusalem Mss. nos. 23, 228, 268, 293, 410, 971 and 1409; Venice, Mekhitarist Library, Ms. no. 1922.

[9]See S. Der Nersessian, The Chester Beatty Library: A Catalogue of the Armenian Manuscripts (Dublin, 1958) 6.

[10]Some observations on components of the artistic style in the Crimea are to be found in H. & H. Buschhausen, Armenische Handscriften der Mechitaristen in Wien (Wien, 1981) 43-44. This analysis does not conflict with ours and they do not discuss the manuscripts we have identified as coming from the Armeno-Crimean group. Indeed, they only mention Ms. Matenadaran No. 3863, justly citing it as an example of Italian influence.

[11]This composition is known in at least three manuscript copies, one

in the Chester Beatty Library and two others in Jerusalem—one in the Library of the Armenian Patriarchate and the other in the Jewish National and University Library.

[12]See M. Ilyin, Moscow Monuments of Architecture of the 14th-17th Centuries (Moscow, 1973) 22.

[13]This new trend in colors may be attributed to the development of new paints in Trebizond. See G. Mathew, Byzantine Esthetics (London, 1963) 153-4. These may have been shipped to the Crimea.

[14]Korkhmazian, Crimean Miniatures, 66. See also L. A. Dournovo (ed.) Miniatures arméniennes (Erevan, 1969) plate 69.

[15]Ibid., plate 24.

[16]Ibid., plate 52.

[17]This manuscript is located in the Library of Manuscripts of the Armenian Patriarchate of Jerusalem and Archbishop Bogharian kindly drew it to my attention.

[18]See note 5, above.

[19]See Ilyin, Moscow Monuments, 43.

[20]This matter is the subject of a separate study by the writer which will be completed soon.

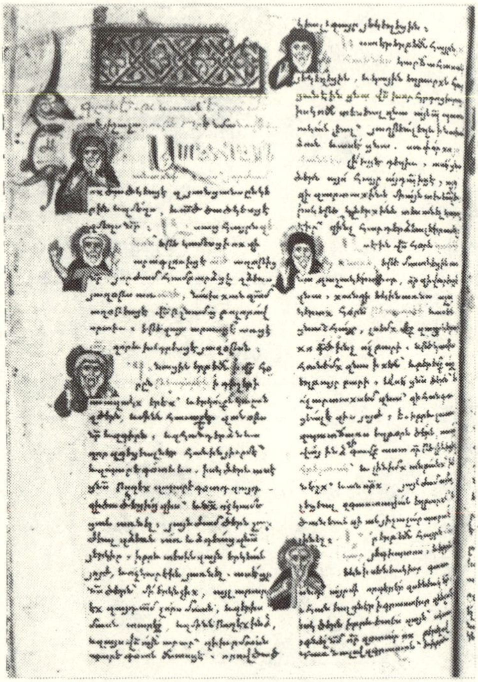

Figure 1.   Page with marginal heads

Figure 2.   Marcarius, Marcus and the Sick Cub

Figure 3.   Mary the Egyptian

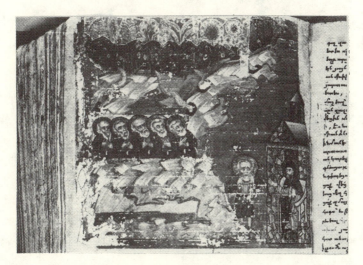

Figure 4.   The Six Brethren who found Paradise

Figure 5.   Paphnutius meets Onophrius

Figure 6.   Theophilus and the Monks

Figure 7.   Marcus and Serapion

Figure 8.   Paphnutius and the four old Monks

Figure 9.   Pambo and Visitors

THE ANNUNCIATION AT THE WELL:

A METAPHOR OF ARMENIAN MONOPHYSITISM*

Thomas F. Mathews

Institute of Fine Arts (NYU)

Specifically Armenian developments in Christian iconography have not
yet been systematically studied in any depth, for it is generally assumed that
Armenian iconography departs from the accepted language of Byzantine
iconography only occasionally and incidentally. The iconography of the
Annunciation, however, sometimes makes a specifically Armenian statement
that has interesting implications. A hitherto unpublished manuscript,
University of California, Los Angeles, ms. Arm. 4, offers a good example (fig.
1). The background consists of a high wall with occasional windows, that
recedes zig-zag to the left; above the wall, elements of city-scape appear
including the Virgin's house on the right that breaks through the upper frame.
In the foreground the angel makes a bold gesture of speech while the Virgin,
occupied with spinning, bends slightly to give ear to his message. Overhead,
the dove, encircled by an aureole, flies down along a path of light that
consists of two beams pouring out of the semicircle of heaven at the top of
the picture. Below, in the center, there is shown a well on which the Virgin
has placed her pitcher. The well is framed with a shouldered arch beneath
which two streams of water fall into a single basin. It is this well with its
two jets of water that excites the viewer's curiosity. For unless one supposes
that Armenia invented hot-and-cold water plumbing, the two spouts of water
are a perfectly gratuitous detail, quite unnecessary to the depiction of the
well. We lack colophon information about the place where U.C.L.A. ms. 4
was executed, but the painter, named Yovhannēs, is mentioned in an
inscription on the front fly-leaf, and the scribe entered his name at the end

T. Samuelian & M. Stone, eds. Medieval Armenian Culture. (University of
Pennsylvania Armenian Texts and Studies 6). Chico, CA: Scholars Press,
1983. pp. 343 to 356.

of the gospel of Mark on p. 229, saying: "I beseech you to remember me, the unworthy scribe Vrt'anis, in the year 1643."[1]

The iconographic tradition of this Annunciation can be shown to be much older than the seventeenth century. Virtually identical with the iconography of the U.C.L.A. manuscript is the Annunciation in a very handsome gospel prepared for the chief vardapet of Glajor, Esayi Nč'ec'i, in the year 1323 (fig. 2).[2] The manuscript, Erevan, Matenadaran ms. 6289, is signed repeatedly by the painter T'oros Tarōnec'i. The background wall zig-zags off to the left with similar architecture behind it, and the dove descends on the same stream of light. The Virgin stands more erect but the two figures are otherwise rather similar, and between them we discover a little arched well in which two streams of water fall into a basin, with the Virgin's pitcher above. It cannot, and need not, be demonstrated that the artist of U.C.L.A. ms. 4 copied directly from Matenadaran ms. 6289, but it is obvious that he depended on the same iconographic tradition.

The appearance of this iconography in the work of T'oros Tarōnec'i can be followed fairly closely. The earliest work in which T'oros Tarōnec'i's signature appears is U.C.L.A. ms 1.[3] This gospel was already half finished when T'oros started work on it, and the Annunciation was one of the scenes that had been completed (fig. 3). Nevertheless, T'oros could not resist the impulse to improve on the work of his predecessors. He repainted the face, hands and mantle of the Virgin to make her better match his rendering of the Virgin elsewhere in the gospel, and he added the dove in sketchy white outline pouring down a stream of grace. The iconography includes a palm tree and a hexagonal well-head from which a single stream of water flows into an amphora. T'oros later repeated this iconography in a gospel that is totally his own work, Venice ms. 1917 dated 1307 (fig. 4).[4] The domes and gables echo the earlier miniature, and the Virgin repeats the same awkward gesture, holding her spindle to one side. The dove, again in sketchy white, descends from the hand of God; the tree has been somewhat reduced in scale and the well has been somewhat simplified and its stream of water omitted.

The next dated Annunciation in T'oros's oeuvre occurs in 1318 when he was called upon to illuminate an entire Bible for Esayi Nč'ec'i, Erevan, Matenadaran ms. 206.[5] Richly illuminated with preface miniatures for the books of the Old Testament and text miniatures within the four gospels, this bible is T'oros's finest and most consistent work. In the Annunciation it is clear that T'oros's style has matured, his figures have relaxed and acquired a gentle grace, and his composition works together as a unit instead of as a collection of pieces (fig. 5). At the same time it is clear that T'oros is trying to integrate new iconographic sources into his painting. Perhaps taking his cue from Syrian painting, T'oros now places the dove against a disc of light (fig. 10);[6] on the other hand, the way he has bent the ray of divine grace to make it enter the Virgin's ear is a distinctly Western element, a literal translation of the theologian's speculation on "conceptio per aurem."[7]   A wide variety of non-Armenian material appears to have been in circulation in Glajor in the early fourteenth century; this very manuscript includes as its front fly-leaf a page from a Latin gospel book. For the representation of the well, however, T'oros depends on no known foreign source.   Beneath a shouldered arch a large amphora sits on a shelf; under the shelf a pair of spouts of water pour into a wide basin.

A similar iconography is repeated by T'oros three years later, in 1321, in a gospel book in Jerusalem, ms. 2360.[8] The dove appears on the disc of light following the ray toward the Virgin's ear; in the arched well T'oros has represented two spouts over a basin but he has carelessly forgotten to show the water flowing from the spouts (fig. 6). This manuscript is a work of tiny dimensions, a mere 11 cm. high, in which the paintings were executed without a great deal of care. Still the omission of the flowing water may tell us something about T'oros; namely, that he is probably not the inventor of this iconographic detail. Had he invented the well with the two spouts it is unlikely that he would have forgotten to show it correctly in this instance. Two years later he corrected his mistake when he painted Matenadaran 6289 with the water flowing, as we have seen (fig. 2). It should also be noted that in ms. 6289 he abandoned the Western iconography of "conceptio per aurem" and represented the rays spreading out as if to "overshadow" the Virgin, in the expression of the evangelist (Lk. 1:35).

Who was the inventor of this iconography cannot now be determined, but it is clear that it gained considerable popularity in Glajor in the fourteenth century.   It appears in a somewhat different form—with a cinq-foil arch and a rather ornate basin—in Nor Juła ms. 47 which was executed in Glajor around 1330 (fig. 7); and it appears with still other variations around the turn of the century in Matenadaran 6305 executed in nearby Tat'ew.[9]

To interpret properly this development of iconography in late Armenian painting one must really ask two questions: first, how has the

Armenian iconographer re-worked the tradition of the Annunciation at the Well; and secondly, why has he so re-worked it.

The Annunciation, marking the decisive moment when God entered human history through the Incarnation, is one of the commonest subjects in Christian art; nevertheless, the Annunciation at the Well is an unusual subject. This is all the more surprising in view of the wide circulation given to the aubject in three interdependent extra-biblical accounts: the Protoevangelium of James, Pseudo-Matthew, and the Armenian Infancy Gospel.[10] According to these accounts the Virgin had gone to drawn water when she first heard the angel address her, "Rejoice, Virgin Mary." Though she did not actually see him, she was frightened at the voice and hastened home to return to her assigned work of spinning for the temple veil. The angel, however, pursued her in order to continue his message as narrated in Luke.

In Early Christian art the Annunciation at the Well appears only twice, once on a pilgrim's flask from the Holy Land and once on an ivory book cover.[11] In both instances the well is intepreted as a natural spring coming out of the ground; the Virgin kneels to draw water and she turns back to catch sight of the angel who appears behind her (fig. 8). In Middle Byzantine art the subject is equally rare, and when it appears the iconography is somewhat different.[12] Now the well is a man-made well-head; the Virgin may kneel or walk, and the angel still approaches from behind, but now he flies. This version of the iconography remained current through the Paleologan period and was used at the Kariye Camii in Constantinople (fig. 9).

In contrast to Byzantine or Western art, artists in Syria and Armenia show a special predilection for the Annunciation at the Well, and they develop in the course of the thirteenth century a new iconography for conveying the theme. This new iconography combines the Annunciation at the Well with the traditional "at-home" Annunciation. The Virgin is shown sitting or standing in front of her house, her spinning in her hand, but between her and the angel is shown the well and sometimes the tree. This version of the subject first appears in a very handsome Syriac manuscript in London, British Library, ms. add. 7170, fol. 12v, dating 1216-20,[13] and in the nearly contemporary twin manuscript in the Vatican (fig. 10).[14] It then occurs again in a Syriac ms. of 1226 and in one of ca. 1250[15] before it is employed in the famous Armenian Gospel of Queen Keran in 1272.[16] This is clearly the tradition that stands behind the Annunciation as it appears in the first two manuscripts of T'oros Tarōnec'i—the U.C.L.A. ms. 1 and Venice ms. 1917 (figs. 3 and 4).

As we have seen, the painters of Glajor in the early fourteenth century re-worked this iconography by transforming the free-standing well-head into an arched well containing two spouts (figs. 2 and 5-7). On one level this may be seen as simply an Armenian appropriation of the iconographic vocabulary, for it should be observed that in medieval Armenian architecture the well actually took the shape of an arched enclosure.[17] The thirteenth century well in Tat'ew may be taken as typical: a slightly ogive vault shelters the place where water ran into a basin or trough. The artist's re-working of the well into an arched enclosure adds a note of local color to the iconography. But this does no explain the two spouts.

In thirteenth century Syrian and Armenian painting the preference for including the well must be taken as a Mariological metaphor. The Virgin from whom man's salvation was to spring was commonly referred to as the "well" or the "source" in homiletic literature and hymns.[18] When the well image was re-worked in Glajor, however, the metaphor seems to have shifted: the well is now Christological rather than Mariological. The evidence is circumstantial but considerable, for a mixing or commingling of liquids is one of the earliest analogies used to explain the union of the human and the divine nature in Christ. Thus Augustine described the mystery of the Incarnation in the term "mixtura": "In hac persona mixtura est Dei et hominis."[19] Similar uses of the terms mixtio, mixtura, krasis, synkrasis might be found in discussions of the hypostatic union in Irenaeus, Tertullian, Cyprian, Apollinarius, Epiphanius, or Gregory Nazianzenus.[20]

The Council of Chalcedon, however, changed all of that. In their denunciation of Eutyches, who had spoken of two natures before the union and one nature after the union, the fathers of the council insisted on the perfect integrity of both the human and the divine nature after the union in Christ. They therefore rejected the earlier language of "mixture" pro-claiming a union asynchytos, i.e. "unconfused in two natures."[21] The root meaning of the term asynchytos, "unconfused," is precisely "not-poured-together," being derived from syn-cheo, "I pour together, or mix." After the Council of Chalcedon Greek theologians generally tried to avoid all metaphors of mixture in speaking of the Incarnation; Armenian theologians, however, never seem to have abandoned the archaic terminology. Having formally rejected Chalcedon at the Council of Dvin in 506/8, Armenian theologians continued to refer to the Incarnation as a mixing or mingling of the two natures.[22]   Thus, in the words of Nersēs Šnorhali, "The incorporeal Word commingled with the body, making it divine by the mixture (xaṙnmamb), but not undergoing any change or alteration in this union."[23] Further, when the Synod of Hṙomkla tried to formulate the Armenian position for the benefit of the Byzantine emperor Manuel Comnenus, they fell back on the same expression: "The body commingled (xaṙnec'aw) with the divine nature, without at the same time being estranged from its natural essence."[24] This pre-Chalcedonian, not to say anti-Chalcedonian, formula was evidently a line of continuity in Armenian theology that was important to maintain.

It has not yet been possible to trace this metaphor of mixing into the theological literature of the school of Glajor where our iconography first appears. Esayi Nč'ec'i, the principal luminary of that school, does not seem to have been wedded to any rigid formula for expressing the Armenian position on the natures in Christ; he goes so far as to say that one could with orthodoxy speak either of two natures or of one nature in Christ, if one qualified the statement properly.[25]   Yet it is clear from the pressures exerted by the Dominican Unitores on the church in Greater Armenia that the Chalcedonian issue was very much on peoples' minds in the first decades of the fourteenth century. Indeed it was the only substantive dogmatic issue that seemed to stand between the Armenian and the Roman churches, the other issues being questions of rite and calendar.[26] It is significant, then, that at precisely this time an iconography appears to give expression to the ancient metaphor of the mixing of natures in Christ.

While the iconography of the Annunciation with two jets of water in the well remains a minor theme in the overall development of Armenian art, it is a theme worth noting. Dogmas are not generally susceptible to translation into images; the issues are far too subtle and abstract. Efforts to represent the equality of Persons in the Trinity by images of three bearded men or a three-headed man only succeed in making the mystery ridiculous or monstrous. The suitability of the Armenian image is therefore all the more remarkable. The symbol is placed in parallel to the narrative image: at that moment in which the human nature of Christ was fused with the divine nature, when the Virgin accepted the message of the angel, the nature of the union is expressed in the iconography of the well. It is a specifically Armenian image invented to express a specifically Armenian understanding of the mystery of the Incarnation.

NOTES

*For their kindness in providing me with photographs of material in their care I would like to thank Archbishop Norayr Bogharian of the Armenian Patriarchate of Sts. James, Jerusalem, Father Nersēs Nersēssian of the Biblioteca S. Lazzaro, Venice, and Mr. Babgen Choukasezian of the Matenadaran, Erevan. For the photograph of figure 7 I am indebted to A. Mekhitarian of Brussels.

[1]U.C.L.A. Arm. ms. 4 was purchased by Dr. Caro Minasian from one Grigor Davitian on 27 July 1950, prior to which it is said to have belonged to the family of Hoja Petros Veligian. Executed on paper and measuring 186 x 250 mm., it includes miniatures of the four evangelists and the following six subjects from the life of Christ: the Entry into Jerusalem, the Crucifixion, the Annunciation, the Baptism, the Presentation in the Temple, and the Transfiguration. The canon tables are missing and the scenes from the Life of Christ are in scrambled order at the beginning of the book; the style, however, confirms that they belong to the book and were executed by the same painter as the evangelists. The catalogue of this and the other Armenian mss. in the U.C.L.A. Collection will be published shortly by Avedis K. Sanjian.

[2]This ms. is discussed by A. N. Avetisyan, Haykakan Manrankarč'ut'yan Glajori Dproc'ē (Erevan, 1971), pp. 124-35; the Annunciation is published in fig. 41.

[3]The Second Storm at Sea (p. 227) and the Ascension (p. 453) are signed by an artist named T'oros who, on the grounds of style, can be shown to be T'oros Tarōnec'i. The manuscript will be published by T. F. Mathews and A. K. Sanjian in Armenian Gospel Iconography: The Glajor Gospel of U.C.L.A.

[4]Sirarpie Der Nersessian, Manuscrits arméniens illustrés des 12e, 13e et 14e siècles de la Bibliothèque des Pères, Mekhitaristes de Venise (Paris, 1937) 1.112-36; 2, fig. 102.

[5]This ms. is discussed in Avetisyan, Haykakan Manrankarč'ut'yan

Glajori, 90-91.

[6]The dove against a halo of light appears in Syrian mss. of the second decade of the thirteenth century, Vatican Syr. 559, fol. 8v, and British Library 7170, fol. 15 (cf. Jules Leroy, Manuscrits syriaques à peintures [Paris, 1964], pl. 73, 3 and 4. By the end of the century it was taken up in Cilician painting as in Vienna, ms. 278, fol. 161 (Heide and Helmut Buschhausen, Die illuminierten armenischen Handschriften der Mechitaristen-Congregation in Wien [Wien, 1976], fig. 82).

[7]Gertrude Schiller, Iconography of Christian Art, trans. J. Seligman (New York, 1971), vol. 1, pp. 42-44. The notion that the Blessed Virgin conceived per aurem was expressed already in the Armenian Infancy Gospel: "Bann Astuac emut ěnd unkn Iseleanc'n i nerk's." Esayi Tayec'i, Ankanon Girk' Nor Ktakaranac' (T'angaran Haykakan Hin ew Nor Dprut'eanc'; Venise, 1898) 19. Cf. Paul Peeters, Évangiles Apocryphes, II: L'Évangile de l'Enfance (Paris, 1914) 97. Nevertheless it is in the West that this notion is first expressed in iconography.

[8]Bezalel Narkiss and Michael E. Stone, Armenian Art Treasures of Jerusalem (Jerusalem, 1979) 76, 150.

[9]L. A. Dournovo and R. G. Drampyan, Haykakan Manrankarč'utyun (Erevan, 1967), fig. 62. [Text in Armenian, Russian, and French.]

[10]The Protoevangelium of James, chap. 11 in Edgar Hennecke and Wilhelm Schneemelcher, New Testament Apocrypha (trans. R. McL. Wilson; Philadelphia, 1963) 380; The Gospel of Pseudo-Matthew, chap. 9 in The Ante-Nicene Fathers 8 (New York, 1926) 272; The Armenian Infancy Gospel, chap. 5, Tayec'i, Ankanon Girk' 14; cp. Peeters, Évangiles Apocryphes, 2.89-90.

[11]For the pilgrim's flask see André Grabar, Ampoulles de Terre Sainte (Paris, 1958), pl. 31.

[12]For the Middle Byzantine version see Vat. Gr. 1162, fol. 117v, C. Stornajolo, Miniature delle omilie di Giacomo monaco (rome, 1910), pl. 50.

[13]Leroy, Manuscrits syriaques, pl. 73, 3.

[14]G. de Jerphanion, Les miniatures du manuscrit syriaque no. 559 de la Bibliothèque Vaticane (Vatican City, 1940), pl. III, 3; Leroy, Manuscrits syriaques, pl. 73, 4.

[15]Midyat, Syro-orthodox Episcopacy, Evangelary, fol. 14v, and Deir es-Za'faran, Mar Hanania, Evangelary, fol. 22.   J. Leroy, Manuscrits syriaques, pl. 105, 1 and 127, 1.

[16]Jerusalem, Armenian Patriarchate of St. James, ms. 2563, fol. 184. Narkiss and Stone, Armenian Art, 63-64, 149, but without illustration of the Annunciation.

[17]O. X. Xalpaxčjan, Graždanskoe Zod'estvo Armenii (Moscow, 1971) 228-39.

[18]G. W. H. Lampe, A Patristic Greek Lexicon (Oxford, 1961) s.v. pēgē and phrear.

[19]Augustine, Epist. 137, 11 (PL 33, 520).

[20]See the citations given by Pascal Tekeyan, Controverses christologiques en Arméno-Cilicie dans la seconde moitié du XIIe siècle (1165-1198) (Orientalia Christiana Analecta 124; Rome, 1939) 86, n. 1.   Further see citations in G. W. H. Lampe, A Patristic Greek Lexicon, s.v. krasis and synkrasis.

[21]J. D. Mansi, Sacrorum conciliorum nova et amplissima collectio, VII, 115.

[22]For the Armenian reaction to Chalcedon see Karekin Sarkissian, The Council of Chalcedon and the Armenian Church (New York, 1965).

[23]Nersēs Šnorhali, Encyclical Letter as cited by Tekeyan, Controverses christologiques, 86, from the edition of Constantinople, 1825, 57.

[24]Synod of Hromkla as cited by Tekeyan, Controverses christologiques, 91, from the edition of Constantinople, 1825, 177.

[25]Letter of Esayi Nč'ec'i to Tēr Matt'ēos (dated 1321), cited by M. A. van den Oudenrijn, "Uniteurs et Dominicains d'Armenie," Oriens Christianus 40 (1956) 105-106.

[26]Ibid., 94-112.

Figure 1.   Los Angeles, University of California, Arm. ms. 4, p. 10.   The
Annunciation by the painter Yovhannēs, 1643.

Figure 2.   Erevan, Matenadaran, ms. 6289, fol. 143.   The Annunciation by
the painter T'oros Tarōnec'i, 1323.

Figure 3.   Los Angeles, University of California, Arm. ms. 1, p. 305.   The
Annunciation, retouched by T'oros Tarōnec'i, before 1307.

Figure 4.   Venice, Biblioteca S. Lazzaro, ms. 1917, fol. 153.   The
Annunciation by T'oros Tarōnec'i, 1307.

Figure 5.   Erevan, Matenadaran, ms. 206, fol. 474v. The Annunciation by
T'oros Tarōnec'i, 1318.

Figure 6.   Jerusalem, Patriarchate of St. James, ms. 2360, fol. 149. The
Annunciation by T'oros Tarōnec'i, 1321.

Figure 7.   Nor Juła, ms. 47, fol. 1v.   The Annunciation, 1330.

Figure 8.   Paris, Bibliothèque Nationale, ms. lat. 9384, ivory cover, detail.
              The Annunciation at the Well.

Figure 9.   Istanbul, Kariye Camii, mosaic of the inner narthex. The
Annunciation at the Well. (Courtesy of Dumbarton Oaks,
Center for Byzantine Studies, Washington, D.C.)

Figure 10.   Rome, Biblioteca Vaticana, ms. syr. 559, fol. 8v.   The
Annunciation at the Well, 1219-20. (From de Jerphanion.)

ARMENIAN BIBLICAL TRADITION IN COMPARISON WITH THE VULGATE AND SEPTUAGINT

Bo Johnson

Lund University (Sweden)

The history of the origin of the Armenian Bible is well known. The translation was made during the first decades of the fifth century, and, according to tradition, there were three stages in this work: first a translation from a Syriac text, then a new translation from a Greek text emanating from Asia Minor, and after that a final translation from a text brought from Alexandria.

Like other daughter versions of the Septuagint, such as the Ethiopian, Coptic, Georgian, Slavonic, and Gothic, this Armenian Bible lived a life of its own and was scarcely observed by those working with the biblical text. This isolation was broken in 1666, when the Armenian Bible was for the first time printed by Oskan and thus made available to the world of biblical scholars. This and the following editions awakened great interest among European scholars working in the field of biblical text research. During the eighteenth century there was an ongoing discussion about the Septuagint, and among the issues raised at that time were the place and value of the Armenian Bible as a witness of the text of the Greek Bible.[1] It was soon observed that the Armenian language was well adapted to provide a literal translation from the Greek, and so the Armenian translation would have almost the same value as its Greek Vorlage—granted that it really was a word for word translation. But there was an obstacle. The old tradition and the text itself offered possible hints of Syriac or Latin influences.

In a journal article of that time, Bredenkamp confirms that the Vorlage of the Armenian translation was the Greek Septuagint.[2] But he

---

T. Samuelian & M. Stone, eds. Medieval Armenian Culture. (University of Pennsylvania Armenian Texts and Studies 6). Chico, CA: Scholars Press, 1983. pp. 357 to 364.

357

observes that the Armenian translation does not follow the Greek text form of Codex Alexandrinus so closely as had been claimed by La Croze.[3] The Vorlage rather seemed to be a mixed text with certain affinities to the Greek text in the Complutensian Polyglott from the beginning of the sixteenth century.

Bredenkamp had no idea of the suggested Syriac influence, but so far as the Vulgate was concerned, he had no doubt that the Latin exerted some influence on the Armenian text. He enumerates several passages with marginal notes in the Armenian Bible emanating from the Vulgate and remarks on certain influences on the text itself.

The observations made by Bredenkamp were later taken up by Eichhorn in his Introduction to the Old Testament. In the fourth edition,[4] of 1823, he devotes 20 pages to the Armenian translation. Eichhorn finds corrections following the Syriac likely, but he leaves the question open. Concerning the influence from the Vulgate, however, he has no doubt. He devotes three pages to the passages 2 Sam 3:33 and Num 26:14, mentioned by Bredenkamp as proof of corrections following the Vulgate. But still, in 1823, he mentions that he has not seen the edition of Zohrab of 1805.[5]

In the nineteenth century and up to recent times, the Old Testament Introductions generally take very little notice of the Armenian translation. Scholars differ slightly concerning the possibility of Latin or Syriac infleunce, and the conclusion voiced is often that of Kenyon in 1903: the Armenian, Arabic, Georgian, and Slavonic translations appear to be of little critical value—although in the edition of 1939, this statement was replaced by "but they have been little studied."[6]

During this time another project had begun—the painstaking and careful collation of the text of the Armenian Bible for the Cambridge[7] and Göttingen[8] editions of the Septuagint. As a result, the question of the character and the value of the Armenian translation and also its supposed influence from Syriac or Latin sources was raised again. The basis for this new textual research was the Zohrab edition and a large number of Armenian Bible manuscripts.[9]

The Armenian Bible resulted from the activity of the translators at the beginning of the fifth century. Whether the old tradition concerning the three stages of the translation should still be regarded as valid is a question open to discussion. To me, the old tradition still offers the most likely explanation to what I observed in 1 Samuel. Cox, however, cannot find similar traces of the Syriac in the Armenian Deuteronomy.[10] I think we must await the full examination of the Armenian Bible for a final decision. At this preliminary stage, however, it is worth considering the different treatments of the Armenian Bible in the individual books of the Göttingen Septuagint, even if the basis for the work may not have been exactly the same all the time.

In any case, the Armenian Bible existed in the second half of the fifth century. And this Bible no doubt was quite uniform in character. In its final form, the text was, and still is, a good witness to the so-called 'hexaplaric' text, i. e. the Greek text emanating from the third century revision by Origen in the direction of the Hebrew bible using the three Greek translations by Aquila, Theodotion, and Symmachus.

It is not plausible that there were no contacts between the Greek and the Armenian Bible during the following centuries. The Armenian language and translation may have served as a bridge when the Bible was translated into Georgian. There is a parallel development in Greek and Armenian concerning the change from majuscules to minuscules (glxagir and p'ok'ragir respectively). At the same time the Arabic script developed, and this was certainly formed as a minuscule script.

In the thirteenth century, during the reign of King Het'um II, and, according to tradition, under his auspices, new efforts were made in the elaboration of the Armenian Bible text. Since King Het'um also kept contacts westwards with the roman Catholic Church, it has been suggested by Bredenkamp, Eichhorn, and others, that the corrections in the Armenian Bible in accordance to the Vulgate could already have been inserted into the text by Het'um himself. These corrections were mostly labelled as "falsifications in accordance to the Vulgate."

If, however, we go behind the edition of Oskan, the impact of the Latin Vulgate will faint considerably. Those two passages quoted by Bredenkamp as proof of an influence from the Vulgate are not convincing. The reading "300" instead of "200" in Num 26:14 was imputed to the influence of the Latin Bible on the basis of a marginal note in Oskan. Now this number "300," it turns out, is not to be found in the Vulgate at all, and so it has been suggested that Oskan thought that it must have been the Vulgate, even if he himself was not responsible for the change, because he took it to be a correction from the time of Het'um. But this is just a guess. In fact, the Armenian texts are divided. Jerusalem 1925, a manuscript dating to 1269, has "200" like the Septuagint, and so has one of Zohrab's eight manuscripts. The other manuscripts have "300." But the text here is confused with whole verses replaced, and the number "300" may have arisen from any number of sources.

The other passages, 2 Sam 3:33, is a doublet. The first line in the Armenian text is more similar to the text of the Vulgate than the second line, which is the text of the Septuagint. The first line is also missing in Jerusalem 1925. But the first line is almost identical with the text of Symmachus, according to a marginal note in the Greek majuscule M. The same is the case with a doublet in the following verse (2 Sam 3:34). The parallel text is missing in Jerusalem 1925, but appears both in the margin of Jerusalem 1928 (from the year 1648) and in the text and margin of Jerusalem 1934 (from the year 1646). This obviously indicates a new wave of influence from the side of Greek manuscripts on the Armenian manuscripts from the thirteenth century and onwards, but hardly testifies to any impact from the Latin Vulgate at this time.

There is, however, one influence from the Vulgate before Oskan that cannot be denied. It is the division of the text into chapters. This division was introduced by the English archbishop Stephan Langton who died in 1228. It was soon taken over by scribes and scholars and applied to several texts and later to printed editions, even editions of the Hebrew Bible, which of course does not imply that the text was in any way amended in the direction of the Vulgate. By the fourteenth century the Latin chapters begin to appear in some Armenian manuscripts, often together with older divisions of the text. From the middle of the seventeenth century, this division is made more explicit by the use of letters A, B, G, . . . within the chapters and by the numbering of single verses, all in accordance with the Vulgate and most western European translations and editions of that time.

Thus Latin influence on the Armenian Bible begins by gradually introducing the Latin division of the text in the thirteenth century. There seems to have been no influence on the text itself before Oskan, who, in his printed edition of 1666 introduced Latin names for certain books of the Bible, and inserted marginal notes and perhaps some corrections from the Vulgate. Nevertheless, he followed in the main the manuscript Erevan 180, from the year 1295, and his dependence on the Vulgate should not be overestimated. Gehman, in his examination of the Armenian text in Daniel, arrived at a similar conclusion.[11]

So we must look in another direction if we are to find the basis and the background for the activity in the field of the Armenian Biblical study during the thirteenth century. This background is obviously Greek.

One of the novelties in the Armenian text at this time is the division of the text into sections. Earlier there existed several systems for the division of the text. The Greek manuscripts of the Septuagint offer a wide variety of systems. It is important to distinguish here between the character and the history of the text itself and the sections marked in the text. In many cases a mere glance at the manuscripts shows that the signs indicating the text sections are by a later hand. But even when they were inserted by the copyist himself, they are of course not of the same age, nor necessarily from the same source as the text form. It makes sense that the division into sections took place at first in order to compare manuscripts with each other; that is, it emanated from the scribes or the scholars in monasteries and libraries. Consequently, the same system for the division of the text into a certain number of sections was applied to manuscripts of quite different textual character. In the Septuagint tradition there are several parallel systems, sometimes combined in the same manuscript and not always carried out completely. The length of the single sections can vary considerably and gives the impression that the work was conducted in a rather arbitrary way. One section may contain just a few lines and the next one several pages. A possible explanation of this might be that some signs indicating the sections were lost, and the next copyist changed the surviving numbers of the sections to the right sequences.

The existing division of the Armenian Bible into sections is not complete in the earliest manuscripts (from the thirteenth century) and seem to have been introduced at the same time. This division is the same in the Armenian manuscripts and was taken over by Zohrab in his printed edition. This indicates that it was taken over from a single or a few Greek manuscripts at a time. I have checked several Greek manuscripts for 1 Samuel also in this respect. In 1 Samuel there are eighty sections in the Armenian text. The same division of the text is found in the old Codex Vaticanus (the majuscule B) from the fourth century, where the signs are obviously inserted by a later hand, and in thirteenth-century Codex Vaticanus no. 330, Rahlfs's Number 108.[12] This manuscript contains the first half of the Old Testament. The division into sections is very different in the various books, and sometimes in the same book there is competition between parallel systems. Only Joshua (30 sections) and 1 Samuel have the same division that was taken over by the Armenian Bible.

Rahlfs remarks that this manuscript, according to Mercati and Guidi, has marked the layers with Greek, old Slavonic and old Armenian number letters. An examination of the manuscript shows that every eighth sheet has a Greek and an old Slavonic number, but there are hardly any Armenian letters in this connection. The third sequence of numbers is rather a series of Georgian number-letters. There are, occasionally, some signs, possibly Armenian, in the margin, but they have hardly anything to do with the division of the sections. But the Slavonic and not least the Georgian signs show that this manuscript might have been involved in the work with the biblical text in the Eastern churches.

Another indication of the influence exerted by the Greek on the Armenian text at this time are the marginal notes. They are found in several Armenian manuscripts and were also taken over by Zohrab and printed as variant readings. These notes are very uniform in the Armenian tradition, and they were obviously taken from a specific Greek manuscript in the same way as the division of the text had been. In the Greek manuscripts these notes usually refer to variant readings from the three Greek translations parallel to the Septuagint, and attributed to Aquila, Theodotion, and Symmachus. An examination of the marginal notes in 1 Samuel shows that they often appear in the same Greek manuscript 108.[13]

The conclusion to which these facts lead is that the Armenian Bible kept its uniform character even though, in the thirteenth century, the text was divided into sections and supplied with marginal notes and parallel readings from one or a few Greek manuscripts. Later, the Latin tradition exerted a similar, though limited influence. As for the text itself, it does not seem to have undergone any revision as a consequence of these influences.

NOTES

[1]A good representative of the discussion is to be found in the numerous references to the Armenian translation in letters received or written by La Croze. The correspondence is gathered in Thesauri epistolici Lacroziani (ed. I. L. Uhlius; Lipsiae, 1742-46) 1-3.

[2]H. Bredenkamp, "Ueber die Armenische Uebersetzung des Alten Testaments," Eichhorn's Allgemeine Bibliothek der biblischen Litteratur 4 (1937) 623-652.

[3]Thesauri epistolici Lacroziani, 3. 201.

[4]J. G. Eichhorn, Einleitung in das Alte Testament (4th ed.; Gottingen, 1823) 2.329-349.

[5]Ibid., 348.

[6]F. G. Kenyon, Our Bible and the Ancient Manuscripts Being a History of the Text and its Translations (4th ed.; London, 1903; Revised, rewritten and enlarged, London, 1939).

[7]A. E. Brooke and N. McLean, eds., The Old Testament in Greek according to the Text of Codex Vaticanus, Supplemented from other Uncial Manuscripts, with a Critical Apparatus Containing the Variants of the Chief Ancient Authorities for the Text of the Septuagint (Cambridge: University Press, 1906-) 1-.

[8]A. Rahlfs, W. Kappler, J. Ziegler, R. Hanhart and J. Wevers eds., Septuaginta Vetus Testamentum Graecum Auctoritate Societatis Litterarum Göttingensis editum (Göttingen: Vandenhoeck & Ruprecht, 1931-) 1-.

[9]H. S. Gehman, "The Armenian Version of the Book of Daniel and its Affinities," Zeitschrift für die Alttestamentliche Wissenschaft 48 (1930) 82-99; B. Johnson, Die armenische Bibelübersetzung als hexaplarischer Zeuge im 1. Samuelbuch (Coniectanea biblica Old Testament Series 2; Lund: CWK Gleerup, 1968); B. Johnson, "Fünf armenische Bibelhandschriften aus Erevan," Forschung zur Bibel. 1. Wort, Lied und Gottesspruch. Beiträge zur Septuaginta. Festschrift für Joseph Ziegler (ed. J. Schreiner; Würzburg: Echter Verlag, 1972) 67-72; B. Johnson, "Some Remarks on the Marginal Notes in Armenian 1 Samuel," Armenian and Biblical Studies (ed. M. E. Stone; Jerusalem: St. James Press, 1976) 17-20; C. E. Cox, The Armenian Translation of Deuteronomy (University of Pennsylvania Armenian Texts and Studies 2, Ann Arbor, Michigan: Scholars Press, 1981). See also the penetrating studies of the Armenian text in certain volumes of the Göttingen edition of the Septuagint.

[10]Cox, Deuteronomy, 6; 301-327.

[11]Gehman, "Daniel," 95.

[12]A. Rahlfs, "Verzeichnis der griechischen Handschriften des Alten Testaments," Nachrichten von der Koniglichen Gesellschaft der Wissenschaften zu Göttingen (Philologisch-historische Klasse 1914 Beiheft, Berlin, 1915) 248.

[13]Johnson, "Marginal Notes," M. E. Stone, "Additional note on the Marginalia in 4 Kingdoms," Armenian and Biblical Studies (ed. M. E. Stone; Jerusalem: St. James Press, 1976) 21-22.

THE USE OF LECTIONARY MANUSCRIPTS TO ESTABLISH
THE TEXT OF THE ARMENIAN BIBLE

Claude Cox

Brandon University (Canada)

The textual critic of the Armenian Bible has available to him the following tools: 1) Armenian manuscripts (mss); 2) the Georgian version, if indeed the Georgian is a daughter version of the Armenian; 3) quotations of the biblical text in historical and ecclesiastical writings; 4) lectionary manuscripts; 5) editions of varying quality of the parent text (Greek, Syriac) of the Armenian version.[1]

Until now, the textual criticism of the Armenian Bible has generally limited itself to 1 and 5. The chief exception to this is Lyonnet who employs 1 through 5 in an attempt to recover a form of text of the Gospels older than that preserved in Zohrabian's edition.[2] Lyonnet was trying to discover evidence of the existence of a translation of Tatian's Diatessaron but his attempt to "get back behind" Zohrabian's text-type has a much wider application. Put most simply, the Armenian Bible was translated in the early fifth century but mss of the complete Bible do not predate the twelfth or thirteenth centuries.[3] The question, then, is, "Can we and, if so, how do we get back to a text that is closer to the date of translation than is the form of text, e.g., in Zohrabian who printed a fourteenth-century ms?" The answer lies in a methodology that employs 1, 2, 3, 4 and 5 each of which has its own special challenges. As for 1, we possess different text groups within the Armenian textual tradition of the various biblical books. These groups can be compared and more original types of text determined.

2)   The use of the Georgian version may be of value for the textual criticism of some books of the Armenian Bible. However, repeated attempts

T. Samuelian & M. Stone, eds. Medieval Armenian Culture. (University of Pennsylvania Armenian Texts and Studies 6). Chico, CA: Scholars Press, 1983. pp. 365 to 380.

at revision of the Georgian Bible make its use as a daughter version quite hazardous.[4]

3)   Quotations from the Bible in Armenian ecclesiastical writers and historians are an important potential means of access to an early form of the Armenian biblical text. The same problems that face the use of the quotations to establish the text of the Septuagint are present here: citation from memory, alteration in the course of recopying, lack of critical editions.[5]

4)   The extent to which the Armenian Lectionary may prove to be a valuable means of access to an early text has not yet been assessed. As with quotations one can expect that scribes would alter an older type of text to agree with a later one with which they were familiar. As with 2 and 3 one is faced with the problem of not having a critical edition: one must use individual mss.

5)   The use of the Greek and Syriac translations is an important control in the textual criticism of the Armenian Bible. However, both the Greek and Syriac texts, and especially the Greek, represent developing textual traditions. As a result one is forced to ask concerning "what kind of" Greek or Syriac text the Armenian is related to. Further, though Koriwn seems to suggest a relation to the Syriac, the nature of that relation is not yet clear. Armenian Deuteronomy (Dt), e.g., derives its present form at least from a particular type of Greek text.

*   *   *

The purpose of this paper is to call attention to the potential text-critical use of the Armenian Lectionary by offering the results of the collation of lectionary citations from Dt.

The lectionary citations of Dt were collated against the text printed in Deuteronomy. The text printed there is that of ms 61 (San Lazarro ms 1007). This ms belongs to the "group a" group of mss, the text-group which offers the purest form of text.

Ms 61, dated 1332, and other mss of group a are medieval or later in date. The question naturally arises about the extent to which this type of text preserves the translation made in the fifth century. Concerning the text-critical usefulness of scriptural citations in the Lectionary, it seems to me that the following possibilities emerge:

1)   Lectionary mss take us back earlier than the best type of text extant in biblical mss of the Middle Ages.

2)   Lectionary mss provide a type of text as good as our best extant type of text = group a in Deuteronomy. In this case, the Lectionary could offer corroborating evidence that would help to establish the best extant type of text.

3)   The type of text preserved in Lectionary mss is a developed type of text such as is preserved in 57 (= Zohrabian's ms). In this case, the collation of Lectionary citations will not add significantly to ms evidence and will be of little use for establishing the original text.

In all of the above it would be more precise to say "the earliest type of text preserved in lectionary mss" rather than "lectionary mss" or "the type of text preserved in lectionary mss." This is so because one should not expect all lectionary mss to offer the same type of biblical text: Lectionaries from different localities and of different dates likely will reflect the type of text in use in particular localities at particular dates. Therefore the same guidelines likely apply to lectionary mss as apply to biblical mss: the earliest lectionary mss from Armenia proper likely will preserve the most valuable text.

The collations of the Lectionary texts offered here are limited to Dt. The Lectionary contains the following selections from that book: 6:4-7:10; 7:11-8:1; 8:12-9:10; 9:11-9:24; 10:1-10:15; 11:10-11:25. These 113 verses represent more than one-eighth of the text of Dt.

The three lectionary mss collated are:

1.   Jerusalem 121, dated 1192, copied in Mashkevor monastery which is located in the Amanus Mountains which are, in turn, located north of Antioch of Syria. This ms is designated below as L1.

2.   Jerusalem 1998, dated 1374, copied in Tiwrik in the Turkish province of Sivas; Tiwrik = Divrigi, Diwrigi, or Difrigi and is located about midway between Ankara and Lake Van.[6] This is designated L2.

3.   Leiden, Rijksuniversiteit Or. 5479, 15th century, origin unknown.[7] This ms is designated L3.

The list given below is the list of readings collected from the collation of the lectionary mss against the text in Deuteronomy. The following are the sigla employed. Ms 9 appears in full collation (not partial as in Deuteronomy) as does 57 (= Zohrabian's base ms) which does not appear at all in Deuteronomy. (See appendix for collations.)

Biblical mss:

9-13-61	aI	Group a
233	aII	
13' = 13 + 233		
33	bI	b
218	bII	
33' = 33 + 218		
38	cI	c
57	cII	
38' = 38 + 57		
162		d
174		e

Lectionary mss:

L' = L1 + L2 + L3
L = L1 + L2

For other signs and abbreviations see Deuteronomy, xvii-xix.

*   *   *

From the collation of the three lectionary mss the following conclusions can be drawn.

First, the text of the lectionary mss belongs within the textual tradition known previously from the biblical mss. Put differently, the lectionary mss do not take us back closer to the date of translation than do the biblical mss. There appear to be no original readings attested only by these lectionary mss: L1 and L2 alone attest the use of the demonstrative nu with the pronoun at 7:1 and with the verb at 9:7. These are noteworthy readings but it cannot be proven yet that they are more likely to be original than the forms without the nu.[8]

Second, the textual character of the lectionary mss can be determined generally. This can be done by assessing the amount of deviation from the group a type of text. From the apparatus of Deuteronomy one can assemble lists of readings characteristic of the different text groups. There are 28 group bc readings and the agreements of the lectionary mss with these readings are as follows:[9]

Total bc readings	Attested by	L1	L2	L3
28		5	11	18

What this means is that L1 is basically a group a type of text while L3 is much more a group bc type of text; L2 is more a bc type of text than L1 but less so than L3.

Do the lectionary mss belong with group b or with group c? In the passages of Dt found in the Lectionary there are 14 group c readings.[10]

Total c readings	Attested by	L1	L2	L3
14		0	2	3

The conclusion to be drawn from this is that L1 is not influenced by the group c text: it is a group a type of text but shares a few readings with group b. L2 and L3 have few group c readings: they do have substantial agreements with bc readings and this can only mean that the text-types they attest are more group b than group c text-types. If group c is a more developed text-type than group b then L2 and L3 offer a text that is less developed than group c.

Third, as must be clear from remarks just made, these three lectionary mss do not offer among themselves a homogeneous type of text. This can be demonstrated further by comparing the numbers of shared unique readings among the three mss:

Mss	Shared unique readings
L1 + L2 + L3	0
L1 + L2	12
L1 + L3	3[11]
L2 + L3	5

It is clear from this comparison that L1 and L2 are more closely related to each other than is L1 to L3 or L2 to L3.

Finally, to respond to the questions posed at the outset concerning the text-critical value of lectionary mss: the earliest type of text preserved in these lectionary mss, i.e., the text in L1, is about as good as that preserved by the best extant type of text known from biblical mss. The types of text offered by mss L2 and L3 are more developed, but not yet so developed as the group c type of text. One may conclude that the lectionary mss can offer corroborating evidence that would help to establish the earliest recoverable text. If among the three lectionary mss the purest type of text is offered by the earliest ms and the most developed by the latest then the text-critic may expect to find the earliest lectionary witness the most valuable. This conforms with general text-critical principles.

NOTES

[1]These tools coincide with those available to an editor of the
Gottingen edition of the Greek OT (The Septuagint [LXX]), a model of
text-critical methodology: 1) Greek mss; 2) the versions, such as the Latin
or Armenian, into which the Greek was translated; 3) quotations of the
biblical text in commentaries of the church fathers; 4) lectionary mss; 5)
edition(s) of the biblical text in the parent language, Hebrew. As an example
of the Göttingen approach cf., e.g., J. W. Wevers, ed., Genesis (Septuagint,
Vetus Testamentum Graecum, Auctoritate Academiae Scientarum Gottingensis editum, I; Göttingen: Vandenhoeck and Ruprecht, 1974).

From the start the Gottingen LXX has disregarded Greek lectionary
mss in the belief that they represent late, mixed text forms and therefore
have little text-critical usefulness. See J. W. Wevers, Text History of the
Greek Genesis (Mitteilungen des Septuaginta-Unternehmens XI, Abhandlungen
der Akademie der Wissenschaft in Gottingen, Philologisch-Historisch Klasse,
dritte Folge, Nr. 81; Göttingen: Vandenhoeck and Ruprecht, 1974), 176-185.

[2]S. Lyonnet, Les origines de la Version arménienne et le Diatessaron
(Biblica et Orientalia 13; Rome: Pontifico Istituto Biblico, 1950).

[3]The earliest complete Bible listed in my The Armenian Translation of
Deuteronomy (University of Pennsylvania Armenian Texts and Studies, 2;
Chico, CA: Scholars Press, 1981) is San Lazarro ms 1311, dated 12th-13th
century; the next oldest is Yerevan ms 178, dated 1253-1255.

[4]It was for this reason, based on conversations with Mzekala Shanidze
in Tbilisi, that it was decided not to try to use the Georgian in preparing
Deuteronomy.

[5]See "Cyril of Alexandra's Text for Deuteronomy," Bulletin of the
International Organization for Septuagint and Cognate Studies 10 (1977) 31f.

[6]For information on Jerusalem 121 and 1998 see N. Bogharian, ed.,
Grand Catalogue of St. James Manuscripts (Calouste Gulbenkian Foundation
Armenian Library; Jerusalem: St. James Printing Press, 1966-). For the
location of place names I am indebted to A. K. Sanjian, ed., Colophons of

Armenian Manuscripts 1301-1480:   A Source for Middle Eastern History
(Cambridge, MA: Harvard University Press, 1969), Appendix C, 388-429. A.
Renoux's Le Codex armenien Jerusalem 121 (Patrologia Orientalis Tome
XXXVI, Fascicule 2, No. 168, ed. F. Graffin; Turnhout/Belgique: Brepolis,
1971) is devoted to ms 121 but does not reproduce the biblical citations.
Renoux dates the Jerusalem lectionary reflected by the later Armenian mss
to the 5th century.

Ms 121 and 1998 were collated in Jerusalem at St. James Monastery
in the summer of 1975. In this connection I would like to recognize the
helpfulness of Archbishop Norair Bogharian, Keeper of Manuscripts at St.
James.

[7]Rijksuniversiteit Or. 5479 was collated in Leiden in July 1978. I am
grateful to J. J. S. Weitenberg for checking information concerning this ms.

[8]There are a number of issues which at present remain unresolved in
the textual criticism of the Armenian Bible. One of these is the use of the
demonstratives -s -d -n: among the readings listed below some 43 involve
confusion in this regard. Another concerns confusion among various forms of
the subjunctive, between present and aorist and between different forms of
the present and different forms of the aorist (e.g. կեցցէ ք   or   կեցէք   at
8:1: both are aorist subjunctives). There are some 24 cases of this type of
variation in the list above. Still a third area of confusion concerns the
number of a relative pronoun when the antecedent is plural in number:
should the pronoun be plural too? There are 8 cases of this in the list.

[9]Group bc readings are those attested by: 33' 38 162 174; 33' 38 162;
33' 38 174; 33 38 162 174; 33 38 162; 33 38 174; 218 38 162 174, 218 38 162.
Group c appears to be a development of the group b type of text: cf.
Deuteronomy, 219f. In the collation of the lectionary mss the distinction
between ղ and ե is not counted, nor is the presence or absence of final յ .
(1) refers to a change of line or column.

[10]Group c readings are those attested by: 38 162 174 or 38 162.

[11]Includes 9:17 where the reading of L1 is L1*vid.

Appendix   Collations
6:4   ｂēզ] ｂēｌ   L2 L3
       ﾃｅｐ] ｐｎ   233 L

6:5   fin]+ ｅｌ ｊｍﾃｎｍｊ ｎ ﾃｍｍｇ ｐｎｇ 13 162 L3

6:7   զ ｎｍｌ]pr ｂ 9 33' 38' 162 174 L3
       ﾃｍｎｍｕｍｐ ﾃ] ﾃｍｎｍｕｍｐ ﾃｂ   L' 9 rell
       om ｂ 4   Ll(1)

6:8   զｕ ｎ ｕ ｍ] զ ｎ ｎ ｕ ｍ 233 218 174 L2* L3
       om ｅｌ 2* L3(1)
       ｅｑ ｂ ｇｂ] ｅｑ ｂ ｇｂ ｎ   233 L

6:10   ｍ ｎ ｂ ｇē] ｍ ｍ ｎ ｂ ｇｂ 13' 33' 38' 174 L'
       om ｍｐ 2 L3
       om ｅｌ 2 L2
       ｊ ｍｕ ｎ ｖｅ ｎ ｌ] ｊ ｍｕ ｎ ｖｅ ｍ 13, ｊ ｍｕ ｎ ｖｅ ｍｊ 33' 38 174 L',
             ｊ ｍｕ ｎ ｅ ｍｊ 57 233 162

       զ ｐ ｍｑ ｍ ｐ ｓ] ｐ ｍｑ ｍ ｐ ｓ 38 162 L3(1)
       զ ｎ ｐ] զ ｎ ｐ ｓ 13 L'

6:11   զ ｎ ｐ 1] զ ｎ ｐ ｓ 13 L'
       զ ｎ ｐ 2] զ ｎ ｐ ｓ 13' L'
       ｅｌ   3   5   Ll*
       զ ｎ ｐ 3] զ ｎ ｐ ｓ 13' 38' 162 Ll^C L2 L3
       ｊ ｍｑ ｂ ｇ ｂ ｓ] −ｅ ｕ ｇ ｂ ｓ 13 174 L2 L3,   −ｅ ｕ ｇ ｅ ｕ 218,
             −ｂ ｇ ｅ ｕ 162

6:12   ｍ ｎ ｄ ｂ ｎ] + ｐ ｎ ｌ ﾃ 233mg 33 38' 162 L3

6:13   ｅｌ 1 2   L3
       ｐ ｍ ｚ ｍ ｅ ｕ ｇ ｅ ｕ]−ｂ ｇ ｅ ｕ 218 Ll, pr ﾃｂ ｍｊ ｎ 57 L2
       ｊ ｍ ｐ ｅ ｕ ｇ ｂ ｓ] −ｂ ｇ ｅ ｕ Ll

6:14   ｍ ｑ ｑ ｍ ｇ ｎ] ｍ ｑ ｑ ｍ ｇ Ll
       զ ｄ ｅ ° ｐ] զ ｄ ｅ ｌ ｐ 9 57 L

6:15   ｎ ｍ ｘ ｍ ｄ ｎ ｍ] + ｅ 162 L'
       ｍ ｄ 1] + ｐ ｎ 9 13' 33' 174 L'

6:16   ｖ ｎ ｐ ｄ ｅ ｕ ｇ ｅ ｕ] −ｂ ｇ ｅ ｕ Ll
       ｖ ｎ ｐ ｄ ｎ ｌ ｔ ｂ ｎ] −ｔ ｅ   L3

6:18   զ ﾃ ｍ ﾃ ｎ ｊ ｎ] զ ﾃ ｍ ﾃ ｎ ｊ ｕ ｎ 9 33 38' 162 174 L3
       զ ﾃ ｍ ﾃ ｎ ｊ ｎ   զ ｐ ｍ ｐ ｂ tr 218 38' 162 174 L2
       զ ｐ ｍ ｐ ｂ] զ ｐ ｍ ｐ ｂ ｎ 13 218 38' 162 174 Ll L3
       ｌ ｂ ｇ ｂ] ｌ ｂ ｎ ｂ ｇ ｂ 38' 162 174 L2
       ｅ ｐ ｑ ｎ ｌ ｍ ｌ] ｅ ｐ ｑ ｍ ｌ Ll
6:19   fin] + ｍ ｐ   233 162 L3

6:20   ｇ ｐ ｅ ｑ] զ ｐ ｅ ｑ 13 33' 38' 162 174 L2 L3
       ｂ ｐ ｍ ｌ ｎ ｌ ｎ ｐ] + ｎ 13 174 Ll L3,   ｂ ｐ ｍ ｌ ｎ ｌ ｎ ｐ L2
       ｑ ｍ ｍ ｍ ｕ ｍ ｍ ｐ] + ｎ 13, L3 inc

6:21   ծառայ p] ծառայ 218 174 L
        որ] աձ 38' 162 174 L3, om L
        աղդի prae որ tr L3
        fin] + եւ մեծամեծ տեսլեամբբ (եամբ L3) 13' L3

6:22   om մեծամեծս L3
        շարաշարս] շար շարանս L3
        յերկրին]pr ի L2
        փարաւունն] փարաւունն L3

6:23   տաւ] որ L2
        Հարg] + ն 9 L3 rell

6:24   զիրաւունս] իրաւունս 33' 38' 162 174 L2,
                իրաւունս Ll*, զիրաւունսս Ll^c

        Լեգի] Լենեգի 218 38 162 174 L'
        այսօրս] այսօր 13 38' 162 174 L'

6:25   պատուիրանս] pr զ 162 L3, + ս Ll
        fin] + որ L3

7:1   տարգի] տարգէ 162(1) L3
        յոր] զոր 162 Ll L3
        դու] դուն L
        զազգսն] զազգս 13 Ll
        զամուր Հագին] զամով Հագին 33 38' 174 L2
        զփերեզգացին] փերեսացին L2
        զերուսացին] զյերուսացին 9-13' 33' 38' 162 Ll
        զմեզ] զքմեզ 233 38 L3

7:2   ընդ նոսա post ուխտ tr L2 L3

7:3   զդուստր 1] զուստր L2, + ն L3
        տայցես]. տացես 9-233 218 57 162 174 L2,   տացցես Ll
        եւ 2]pr եւ զ Ll*(1)
        առնուgու] առgես L2*(c pr m)

7:4   պատամբեgուցանիցէ] -եgուսgէ L2 L3
        զորդին] զորդի 233 L2
        պաշտիgէ] -եսgէ L3
        զմեզ] զմեզ 13 38' 162 Ll'

7:5   այլ] այզ Ll
        եւ 2   3 L2
        քում] քո L2

7:7   զամ ազգս] զազգս ամենայն Ll
        Հանեgաւ] pr եւ 33 L3
        ընդ] ի L2
        սակաւաւորք (-աւաւուրբ9) 9-61-233   ] սակաւաւոր
                13(1) L' rell
7:8   այլ] այզ Ll

7:8   զերղումնն] զերղումն 174 L3
       Հարց] + ն 9 Ll L3 rell
       եՀան] pr եւ 13 174 L2
       փարաւովնի] փարաւոնն 9-233 38' 162 L2
       եգիպտացոց] -ւոցն L3

7:9   init ----- իւրոց om L3
       աղգ] աղգս 13 57 174 L'

7:10   յատելեաց] ատելեաց 233 174 L2
       այլ] այդ 218 Ll

7:11   զկատուիբանս] + իմ L2

7:12   Լևիցէք] Լևիցէք 9-13' 218 174 L
       om եւ 2   L3
       om քեզ L3
       զուխտն] զուխտ 13 162 L

7:13   գձնունդս գձնունդ 9 L3
       զգործեան] pr եւ 57 L2
       եւ 6 prae զգործեան tr 162 L3
       զեղ] զիւղ 162 L2 L3,   զեւղ 9 Ll rell
       զանդեայս] զանդայս Ll
       որ Հարցն քոց prae զոր tr L3* (c pr m)

7:14   Լիցի] եղիցի L3
       om ի 233 L3(1)
       յանասունս] յանասուն 13 33 38' 162 L2

7:15   ախտ] ախտս 174 L
       եկիպտացոցն] -ոց   L3
       զորս] զոր L2
       այլ] այդ Ll
       աձցէ] աձէցէ Ll

7:16   զկապուտ] կապուտ 13 218 L2 L3

7:17   ապ եթէ] ապա եթէ 9 Ll, ապա թէ 13 33' 38' 162 174 L2 L3

       մոի] սրտի 9-13 218 L'
       զի] թէ L3
       զիւրդ] զիւեւրդ Ll

7:18   երկնչիցիս] երկիցես Ll
       նոցանէ] + ն 9 L

7:19   մեձամեձս 1   2 L3
       զբազուկն] զբազուկ 13' 218 L'
       om քո 2 L3
       աձն 9-61-233] աձ L' rell
       յերեսաց] յերեսացք Ll*(c pr m),   յերեսաց L2(1)
7:20   զձիստատան] -տանանան 174 L3, -տանց Ll, տացն L2

7:21   զանդխիցես]-ես ցես L3

7:22   Լինիցի] Լիցի 13 57 162 L2 L3

7:24   զանուն] զանունս L2
    տեղեոջէն] տեղեոոջէն Ll
    կեցցէ 9] կայցէ 13' 174 L'

7:25   զդրօշեալս] pr եւ L2, զդրօշեալ 218 57 162 L
    դիg] դդիս 162 L
    արձաթոյ et ոսկոյ tr 13 L2
    ի նոցանէ] նոցա Ll

7:26   տանիցիս] -իցես L3
    Լինիցիս] մի Լինիցես L
    նզով] նզովս 162 L3
    զնոյն] զնայն L2
    այլ] այղ Ll
    om եւ 3 Ll*(c pr m)

8:1   պատուիրանաց] -նացս L2
    om ես Ll
    քեզ 9] ձեզ 61[C] -233[C] 33 38' 162 L3
    կեցցէք] կեցջիք L2 L3
    բազմապատիկք] -տիկ 218 L3
    Լինիցէք] Լինիջիք L2 L3
    ժառանգիցէք] pr եւ 13 L3, եւ ժառանգեսջիք L2

8:12   շինիցես] -եսցես 9-13 33 38' 162 174 L2 L3
    բնակիցես] -եսցես 13 33 38' 162 174 L2 L3

8:13   արջառ] + ք ն
    om քո l L2
    յաճխիցէ]-եսցէ 9 38 L2
    իցէ] է L3* (c pr m)

8:14   om եւ 1 9L' rell
    մռասցիս] մռանայցես L

8:15   om ընդ 1 L3

    անապատն] pr ի 233 L3, անապատ 13 L2
    om ընդ 2 L3
    կարիճն] կարիճ 33 38' 162 L2 L3
    աղբեր] աղբեւր 9 218 38' 174 L, աղբիւր 233
        33 162 L3
    ջրոյ] ջուրց 13 33 38' 162 L,   ջիւր L3

8:16   կերակրեցան] -կրեաց 9 L' rell
    քեզ մանա 61-233*] զքեզ մանանիւ (յիւ 9 Ll) 9-13
        Ll, քեզ մանանիւն 233[C], զքեզ մանանիւն L2*,
        զքեզ մանանայիւն L2c pr m L3 rell
    Հարք] + ն 33 38' 162 174 L'

8:17   արար] արարին Ll
    զզօրութին] թիս 33 38' 162 L3
    զայն 61sup lin 218 txt] զայս 33-218mg 38' 162 174 L3
    զմեծ] մեծ 9 L' rell

8:18   այլ] այղ 162 L1
       ոյճ] ուճ L2
       զօրութի] pr զ L2

8:19   եթէ] թէ L2
       մոռացիս] մոռանայ գես L2
       երթիցես] երթայ գես 33' 38 162 174 L3
       պաշտուցես] -իցէք 33(1) L3
       om եւ 4 L1*(c pr m)
       պազանիցես] պագ գես 9-233 L1,   -իցէք 33 38' 162 174 L3
       վկա այօր tr L1
       կորստեամբ] կորրստեամբ L2
       կորնչիցեք] կորնչիչէք 13 L2

8:20   զորս] զոր L3
       կորնչիչէք] կորիչէք 9-233 33 38 L'

9:1   եեղ] եեղ 9-13' 38' 174 L2 L3
       անցանես] անցանիգես L2 L3
       om եւ 1 38' 162 174 L2
       զօրագոյնս] pr զ 57 L1, զօրագոյն 174 L3
       զերկինս] յերկինս 33 38' 162 L2 L3

9:2   զորս] զոր 13 218 57 L3
       թէ] եթէ 13 33 38' 162 174 L3

9:3   om այսօր L3
       երթիգէ] երթայ գէ 33 38' 162 174 L2 L3
       հուրն] հուր 162 L2 L3
       om նա 2 L
       առաջի post զնոսա tr L
9:4   թէ] եթէ 33' L3
       որ 1] + աճ 233 L3
       զբարի] բարի 13 33 38' 162 174 L'
       այլ] այղ 218 L1
       որ 2] + աճ 233 L3

9:5   ամբձութե] ամձութեան L1
       զերկիր] +ն 9-13' 33' 174 L2 L3
       այլ] այղ L1
       զի 61-233] եւ L, pr եւ L3 rell
       զուխտ] որ L2
       om որ 2 174 L3
       om եւ 2 233 L
       յակովբու] յակովբա 13, յակովբաJ 33 38 174 L2 L3,
           յակոբայ 9-233 218 57 162

9:6   քո 1   2 L2
       զբարի 9-61] բարի L' rell

9:7   եղէք] + ն L
       վարեթիք ---- կոյս] վակոյս L1(1)

9:9   լեառնն] լեառն 57 L2 L3
       զտախտակս ն] զտախտակս L2

ուխտի] +ն 13 57 L2

9:10 զերկուսին] երկուս L1*(1) զերկուս L1c pr m L2

քարեղէնս] քարեղէն L2
գրեալս] գրեալ 13 218 174 L2
յաւուրն] յաւուրս L2

9:11 տախտակս ն] -կս 174 L

քարեղէնս] +ն L3

9:12 արդէն] անտէն L3
  զճանապարհաւն] զճանապար հաւ քո L1
  ձուլածոյ] ձուղ- L, ձուլածոյս 13' 33 38' 162 174 L3

9:14 թոյլ] թուղ L1
  om իմ L3(1)
  առաւել] pr եւ 174 L1 L3

9:15 դարձեալ] դարձայ L2
  լերնէ] լեառնէ L3
  լեառնն] լեառն 9-13 L2 L3
  քորրոքէր] քորրոքեալ էր L3
  երկոքին] երկուս 174 L2, երկու L1 L3 rell
  տախտակքն] -կք L3
  յերկուսին] յերկուսին L1 L3
  ի ձեռս] om ի 13 L3, ձեռին 174 L

9:16 ձուլածոյ] ձուղ- L1, ձուլածոյս 13 33 38' 162 174 L

9:17 զերկուսին] զերկուսին L1* vid L3

9:18 զառաջինն] -ջին 174 L2(1)
  զջար] ջար 218 174 L'

9:19 սրտմտութե] -թեն 13 57 162 L2, L1inc
  զի] զոր L3
  իմ post լլաւ tr 13 218 38' 162 174 L'
  om եւ 4 13 218 57 162 174 L'
  ժամանակի] +ն 162 174 L2

9:20 om եւ 2 13' L
  ժամանակի] +ն 13 38 174 L2

9:21 զմեղս ն] զմեղս 13 L2 L3
  իջանէք] իջանէ L2
  լեռնէ] լեառնէ L3

9:22 om ի 2 L1
  զերեզմանս ն] -մանս 33' 38' 162 174 L2 L3
  ցանկութե] -թեն 13 33 38' 162 174 L'
  մեր] ձեր 9-13 33 38' 162 L'

9:23 կադեսբառնեայ] կադեսզբառնեայ L2
  ասէ] pr եւ 233 33 L3
  om զերկիրն L2
  ձերում] ձերոյ 33' 38' 162 174 L1 L3

ՀայնԷ] բանի L3
տն 2] նորա L

9:24   տնակողմանն] pr ի 38' 162 174 L3,   տն կողմանն 218,
տնակողմն(տնակողմ   L1) կոյս 13 L

10:1   ժամանակի] + ն   233 218 38' 162 174 L2 L3
ասաց] ասէ 13 L'
Լեառնն] Լեառն L3
տապանակս] տապանակ 9 L' rell

10:2   պատգամն] −գամս 33(1) 57 L1
զորս] զոր   233 162(1) 174 L2 L3
դու] դուն 33' 38' 174 :'

10:3   Յանիուտ] Յանիոյտ L2
կոկեցի] −եցի L3
Լեառնն] Լեառն L3
երկոքին] երկու L rell
ի ձեռս] om ի 13 L1,   ձեռին 174 L2 L3

10:5   om եւ 4 13 L'
10:6   աՀարովն] աՀարոն 233 33 38' 162 L3
եղէզգար] եղիգար 9-13 57 174 L'
նորա 2] նմա   9-13 L3

10:7   init]pr եւ 233 L3
Յեռեկա 13-61] Յեռեկայ 162, Յեռեկայ 9, Յետակացg L2,
Յետակայ L rell
Չուրg] Չրոցg L2*vid,   Չրոg 33' 174   L'-L2*

10:8   om   տն L3
ցայսօր] Յայսաւր L1

10:9   այնորիկ] այսորիկ 13 L3
ժառանգուԹի]pr մասն եւ 33' 38' 162 L3

10:10   կայի] կացի 33' 38' 162 174 L'
om   տր 1 L2
ժամանակի] + ն 13' 38' 162 174 L
տր 2 9-61-233 L   ] om L3 rell

10:11   Հարgն] Հարg   218 L

10:12   եեղ] եէլ 9-13' 38' 174 L2 L3
այլ] այդ L1
om   ի 3   13' 218 57 L'

10:13   Լեgի] Լինեgի 13 218 174 L2
10:14   om   քո L1
երկիրը]pr եւ 33 38' 162 174 L3, om L2
om   եւ 2 L2

10:15   զզաւակ] զաւակ L1*

գ ձեզ] pr եւ L
աւուր 9-61 218(1)   ] աւուրս 13' 33 38' 162 174,
        աւուրg L3

11:10   է 1 61 33] om 9 L' rell
 յորժամ] pr որ 233 L3
առողանեն] ուռղանեն 9-13' 33 38' 162 L'

11:11   այլ] այղ Ll
om դուք 13 L2
լեառնային] լեռնային 9 L' rell
դաշտային 61 162   ] դաշտական 9 L' rell

11:12   om քո 2 162 L3
նորա] նորայէ L3

11:14   om եւ 1 33 38' 162 L3(1)
ձերոյ] ձերում 9 33 38' 162 Ll*(c pr m) L2 L3
զեղ] զեւղ 9-13' 33 38' 174 L',   զիւղ 162

11:15   անասնոյ] արջառոյ L2

11:16   յագեցիս] -իցիս 174 Ll
յանդին] յանձին Ll*
յուլանայgէ] յուլղ- Ll, յուլանայgէ p L3,
        յուլանայgեն 1 3 38' 162 L2
om սիրտ ---- յանցանիցէ p L3
սիրտ] սիրտp 13 38' 162 L2

11:17   կորնչgէp]   -իՉէp Ll, կորնՉէp 13 L3
ձեղ] ինձ L2

11:18   արկՉէp] արասՉէpL
զնոսա 16-233] զսոսա 9 L' rell
եղիցին] եղիցի 218 L2
անշարժ] անշարժp L3

11:18   om ի 3 13 L2
om եւ 3 162 L3
om ի 6 Ll L3

11:20   զսոսա] զսոա L3

11:21   լինիցէp] -իՉէp L2
երկիի] + ն 218 38' 162 174 L2
աւուրg] + ն 33 L'
երկիին 61 L3] երկիի 9 L rell

11:22   եթէ] թէ 162 L2
լնիցէp] լուիՉէp L2
ձեղ] pեղ 9 L2 L3
աձ] + pn 218 38' 162 174 L2 L3
գնալ] pr եւ L3

11:23   որ] + աձ L3

ազգս ն] pr զ 9 L1
ձերոց] քոց 13 L2
զազգս] + ն 13 218 L
Հզ•բազոյ նս] pr զ L2

11:24   որ 9]   ուր 233 33' 38' 162 174 L2
կոխիցեն] —եսցեն L1
Լեցէ] եղեցէ L2
մեծէ] մեծ 13 L2
միՆչեւ] միՆչ L1
սաՀմանքն] սաՀմանք 13 33' 38' 162 L'

11:25   զերկիղ] զերկիւղ   233 33' 162 174 L'
արկցէ] արասցէ L2
որպէս] + եւ 233 L2

THE ARMENIAN GOSPEL TEXT FROM THE FIFTH
THROUGH THE FOURTEENTH CENTURIES

Joseph M. Alexanian

Trinity College, Deerfield, Illinois

The Armenian version of the Bible has been of interest to textual scholars since the beginnings of modern New Testament textual criticism.[1] Studies by European and American scholars during the past forty-five years have corroborated the testimony of Movsēs Xorenac'i and the shorter Koriwn that the Armenian New Testament was translated first from Syriac in the early fifth century (Arm 1), and was revised following the Council of Ephesus in 431 A.D. from Greek manuscripts (Arm 2).[2]

Although scholars have been able to identify the Syriac base of Arm 1, the nature of the Greek text underlying Arm 2 is still a matter of debate.[3] Progress in this area has been hampered by the lack of a critical edition of the Armenian New Testament based on the earliest extant manuscripts and by a scarcity of scholars trained in both classical Armenian and the science of New Testament textual criticism.

In a study begun about ten years ago, the author analyzed the texts of fifty-five Armenian gospel manuscripts and nineteen Greek, Latin, Syriac, and Georgian witnesses in Luke 11 using the Colwell-Tune Method,[4] and compared forty-seven of the above Armenian manuscripts, plus nine others, regarding their omission or inclusion of seven test passages in the four gospels.[5] The Armenian manuscripts, sixty-four in all, date from the ninth through the seventeenth centuries and are located in Soviet Armenia, Jerusalem, Venice, and the United States of America.

Our purpose was to solve certain problems in text-critical methodology, investigate the nature and development of the Armenian gospel text,

---

T. Samuelian & M. Stone, eds. Medieval Armenian Culture. (University of Pennsylvania Armenian Texts and Studies 6). Chico, CA: Scholars Press, 1983. pp. 381 to 394.

and clarify the relationship of Armenian to the various families of Greek manuscripts in order to shed light on the history of the gospel text. In this paper we will limit our remarks to the development of the Armenian gospel text from the fifth through the fourteenth centuries, focusing on the nature of the fifth-century text, the forces that shaped it during ten centuries of transmission, and the differences between the Arm 2 text of the majority of our manuscripts and the text normally used by scholars, the printed Zohrabian edition of 1805.

The Fifth-Century Text

Arm 1 was translated from the Syriac in the early fifth century.[6] The archetype was not the Diatessaron or the Peshitta Syriac but an Old Syriac four-gospel text similar to the Sinaitic Syriac.[7]   Arm 1 is found in the fifth-century fathers and the earliest liturgical manuscripts and is reflected in the earliest Georgian manuscripts and fragments.   Traces of Arm 1 are also found in some of our extant Armenian manuscripts.[8]

Old Syriac and Tatianic readings, harmonization, avoidance of participles, addition of personal pronouns, and proper nouns transliterated from Syriac characterized the Arm 1 text.[9]   In the test passages from the four gospels, Arm 1 included Luke 22:43-44, the account of the Bloody Sweat, but supported the critical text in the other six passages.[10]

Arm 2 was the result of the revision of Arm 1 by Greek manuscripts brought from Constantinople after the Council of Ephesus in 431 A.D.[11]   All Armenian gospel manuscripts examined thus far derive from this revision, since they all share certain free renderings and mistranslations of the Greek.[12]   The earliest Armenian and Old Georgian manuscripts and fragments suggest that the original form of Arm 2 was closer to Arm 1 than the text found in the extant manuscripts.   Minor corrections, probably during the fifth and sixth centuries, eliminated Old Syriac and Tatianic readings and conformed Arm 2 more closely to the Greek.[13]

The nature of this Greek base has concerned textual critics for over eighty years.   Virtually every type of Greek text has been suggested.   Until recently, most scholars assumed that the Greek underlying Arm 2 was a manuscript (or manuscripts) of the Caesarean text-type.   However, as the evidence against the existence of a Caesarean text-type has become overwhelming,[14] the need for a reassessment of the relationship between the

Armenian and Greek texts has become urgent.

Our research suggests that the base of the Arm 2 revision was a manuscript of the Early Koine text similar to the Greek codex 1 (XII). "Early Koine" is our designation for an influential text which developed out of the Alexandrian text-type in the second century and became the base for the earliest translations into Latin and Syriac. It continued unchanged in wide-spread use into the Middle Ages and at the same time evolved into the medieval Byzantine text-type.

The Early Koine text is the text of Origen (III) and the Greek family 1 (X-XV). It is found in Jerusalem in the fourth century, in Constantinople in the ninth century, and has been traced even to Caesarea of Cappadocia, which had close ties with the Armenian Church until the late fourth century. Codex 1, the primary witness to the Early Koine text, is one of the primary witnesses to our majority text in Luke 11. The other primary witnesses are Old Syriac, the base for Arm 1, and Old Georgian, which was translated from early Arm 2.[15]

Arm 2 is an accurate and sensitive translation of the Greek text. It faithfully represents Greek word order, tenses, grammatical constructions, and proper nouns without becoming slavish.[16]

In Luke 11, Arm 2 avoids the longer additions from Matthew which are characteristic of the Byzantine text, but does contain short harmonizations. In company with the Alexandrians, the Sinaitic Syriac, and the Early Koine, Arm 2 rejects the additions to the Lord's prayer (11:2-4, cf. Matthew 6:9-13), the request for bread (11:11, cf. Matthew 7:9), the reference to the bushel (11:33, cf. Matthew 5:15), and the phrase "scribes and Pharisees, hypocrites" (11:44, cf. Matthew 23:27). In short harmonizations, of which the following are representative, Arm 2 follows the Early Koine in adding iwr/autou in 11:11 (cf. Matthew 7:9) and in reading the future tense ełic'i/estai in 11:34 (cf. Matthew 6:22). In substituting pargews baris/agatha for pneuma hagion in 11:13 (cf. Matthew 7:11) and tačarn/naou for ǒikou in 11:51 (cf. Matthew 23:35), Arm 2 follows its Old Syriac base.[17] During the first eight centuries (mid V—mid XIII), Arm 2 read the critical text in all seven test passages.[18]

The Text of the Sixth through Eighth Centuries

During these centuries, the Armenians fought repeatedly, first against the Persians and later against the Arabs, to preserve their church and culture. We have no gospel manuscripts from this period, but written sources and archaeological remains testify to monasteries and scriptoria throughout Armenia and in major cities throughout the Near East, where no doubt thousands of Biblical, liturgical, theological, and secular manuscripts were produced.   Opportunities for contact with the Byzantine Church and the Greek gospel text were plentiful in western Armenia, Jerusalem, and elsewhere.[19]

Certain evidence suggests that Arm 1 continued in use, competing with Arm 2 for acceptance, until the eighteenth century.   Four minority readings with strong Armenian and Greek support appear to be original Arm 2 readings which were displaced by Arm 1 readings in our majority text. Such readings witness to the presence of Arm 1 during this period, before the Armenian manuscript tradition diverged into two branches.[20] The seventh-century father T'ēodoros K'řt'enawor refers to Arm 1 while debating with anti-Chalcedonians.   He notes their rejection of the "first translation" and the "old edition of the Gospel" because it contained the account of the Bloody Sweat (Luke 22:43-44).[21]

Arm 2 steadily gained acceptance during this period probably due to ecclesiastical pressure and to the destruction of outlying monasteries where conservative tendencies would prefer the Arm 1 text.   At the same time, Arm 2 underwent gradual modification, though the changes were relatively minor.   The many examples in our extant manuscripts of harmonizations, random corrections from Greek manuscripts, and intra-versional variants involving spelling, grammatical constructions, omission, addition, transposition, substitution, and article usage illustrate what must have been occurring prior to the ninth century.[22] While many such variants remained minority readings, some gained sufficient acceptance to enter the majority text.

Divergence of the Manuscript Tradition

Sometime before the ninth century, the Arm 2 manuscripts divided into two branches, Group Z and Group W.[23] Group Z comprises the vast majority of manuscripts, while Group W contains only a few. Out of our corpus of fifty-five manuscripts, fifty-one belong to Group Z, four to Group W. The manuscripts of Group Z share eight distinctive group readings in Luke 11 which distinguish them from Group W. In 145 variation-units in Luke

11, pairs of Group Z and Group W manuscripts show only 53%-77% agreement, with most of the percentages being below 70%. Percentages of agreement between pairs of Group Z manuscripts are above 70% for the vast majority, with some percentages reaching 90% and above. Percentages of agreement for Group W manuscripts are only 56%-67%.[24]

Our Group Z manuscripts date from the tenth through the seventeenth centuries. They have higher percentages of agreement, fewer errors, fewer singular readings, and fewer minority readings than the manuscripts of Group W. They are the product of a relatively controlled textual tradition.[25]

Frédéric Macler and August Merk believed that Group Z faithfully preserves the original Arm 2 text.[26] Stanislas Lyonnet, Arthur Vööbus, and Louis Leloir, on the other hand, view Group Z as only one stage in the process of conforming Arm 2 to the Greek gospel text.[27] Our research suggests that the truth is somewhere between these two extremes. As we shall see, the Group Z text did change over the centuries. But these changes never assumed the proportions of a thorough revision, nor did they result in an Arm 2 text conformed to the Byzantine text. They occurred within the context of a scholarly and ecclesiastical concern for an accurate, understandable, and uniform Biblical text. The Group Z manuscripts reflect political, intellectual, and religious forces which resisted arbitrary change and which encouraged—perhaps at times demanded—careful transmission of the gospel text.

The Group W manuscripts date from the ninth through the eleventh centuries. Among them are M1111 (887, Rhodes #991),[28] the earliest dated Armenian gospel manuscript and the one with the most random Greek readings; E3784 (1057, Rhodes #863), the manuscript with the most harmonizations; and J2562 (XI, Rhodes #502), which together with E3784 contains the most readings from Arm 1. These manuscripts contain more errors, singular readings, minority variants, and especially harmonizations than the manuscripts of Group Z. As we have seen, percentages of agreement among them are low.[29]

Any attempt to reconstruct the history of the Armenian gospel text must explain satisfactorily the rise of Group W. Macler attributed their peculiar characteristics partly to error and harmonization, but primarily to random contact with Greek manuscripts.[30] Later armenologists refined his theories and added Arm 1 as another important source of the Group W readings.[31]

Our examination of the Group W manuscripts confirmed the findings of these scholars and contributed one additional source for the readings of Group W.   Some of the singular and minority readings found in these manuscripts, and in some Group Z manuscripts as well, appear to be readings from the original Arm 2 revision which uiltimately failed to displace the Arm 1 readings in the accepted gospel text.[32]

Thus, the divergence of Group W from the textual mainstream was caused by scribal carelessness, absence of control, and provincialism. Because of constant persecution and warfare, clergy were sometimes uneducated and ill-prepared for the demanding task of copying the Biblical text.   Circumstances did not always allow for the control and correcting of texts provided by a scriptorium.   A provincial spirit clung to dialectal spellings, and preserved Arm 1 and original Arm 2 readings lost in the majority of manuscripts.   Contributing factors were the geographic isolation imposed by the Armenian terrain, the availability of Greek manuscripts, and the textual struggle between Arm 1 and Arm 2 during the fifth, sixth, and seventh centuries, all operating independently on each manuscript.

Group W did not survive the political, religious, and cultural catastrophes of the eleventh and twelfth centuries, although some Group W characteristics persist in a few later Group Z manuscripts.

The Text of the Ninth through Eleventh Centuries

The ninth, tenth, and eleventh centuries were a period of cultural splendor.[33]   Politically divided, the several kingdoms in the Armenian homeland built magnificent churches and cathedrals and decorated them with carvings and paintings, some of which were executed by European artists. Ani, the capital of the Bagratid kingdom (859-1045), was filled with palaces and "a thousand and one churches" at the height of its power.   There are scholars who trace the origins of the European Gothic style to the Armenian architecture of this period.

Monasteries and scriptoria flourished. Beautifully illuminated Biblical manuscripts were produced for royalty, clergy, and wealthy noblemen and merchants.[34] Nineteen of our sixty-four manuscripts come from this period, including E229 (989, Rhodes #724) and E3793 (1053, Rhodes #866), the Group Z manuscripts closest to our majority text with 92%-93% agreement in Luke 11, and the four manuscripts of Group W.

During this period, errors, singular readings, and variants in Luke 11 are generally high. However, in the Group Z manuscripts closest to our majority text, they are greatly reduced. In the test passages, the critical text is read in all seven cases by all manuscripts except E7737 (965, Rhodes #1019), which reads Mark 16:9-20 after a subscript, and E229, which reads Mark 16:9-20 and John 7:53-8:11.

The period came to an end with the onslaughts of the Seljuk Turks from the east and the Byzantine armies from the west. Two hundred years of independence and glory passed, and hundreds of priceless manuscripts were destroyed.

The Text of the Twelfth through Fourteenth Centuries

Two of our manuscripts are dated in the eleventh or twelfth centuries, and two in the twelfth. The two earlier manuscripts, K1 (Rhodes #1048) and K2 (Rhodes #1049), read the critical text in all five passages where they are extant. J1796 (late XII, Rhodes #475) reads the critical text in six of seven passages, but includes Luke 22:43-44, as did the ancient Arm 1 text. Only K20 (XII, Rhodes #1067) departs from the prevailing Arm 2 text of the preceding six centuries in reading the critical text in only one of the three passages where it is extant.

Copied probably in Xarberd, west of Armenia proper within Byzantine territory, K20 illustrates the extent of foreign influence on individual Arm 2 manuscripts. The name of the scribe's mother is Greek. The miniatures are strongly Byzantine in character, and many of them are labelled in Greek. The manuscript even contains a prayer written in Greek.[35] It is not surprising to find the text of K20 influenced by the Byzantine text.

As historic Armenia was invaded by the Byzantines and the Seljuk Turks, Armenians emigrated southwest into Cilicia, where a prince of the Bagratid house of Kars founded a barony which was later elevated to a kingdom. Once again culture flourished. Scriptoria were established in Hŕomklay, Sis, and elsewhere. The power and wealth of the Armenian kingdom of Cilicia (1080-1375) are reflected in the beautifully written and lavishly illuminated manuscripts produced for catholicoi, archbishops, priests, and members of the royal family. The graceful and creative artistry of T'oros Roslin and Sargis Picak illuminated the Biblical narratives.[36]

The Bagratid kingdom had preserved and enhanced native Armenian culture. The kingdom of Cilicia exposed Armenian culture for the first time to the full force of European—especially Frankish—culture. As a result, Armenian social structure, religious life, law, art, and even the alphabet were Europeanized. The power and influence of the Roman Catholic Church were introduced into the life of the Armenian Church. These dramatic changes in Armenian society are reflected in the texts of our eighteen manuscripts from the thirteenth and fourteenth centuries.

Whereas virtually all manuscripts prior to the thirteenth century had read the critical text in all seven test passages, thirteen of the fifteen manuscripts examined in the four gospels now adopt the reading of the Latin Vulgate in one to six passages, the average being between three and four. The only two manuscripts to preserve the original Arm 2 text, C949 (XII-XIII, Rhodes #1038) and J1925 (1269, Rhodes #477), come from the far north-eastern and northwestern corners of historic Armenia, where there was considerable animosity toward Cilicia.[37]

This shift from the Early Koine toward the Vulgate text is seen most dramatically in the test passage from Luke. Whereas all but one of the fourteen manuscripts from the ninth through the twelfth centuries omit Luke 22:43-44, all but five of the thirty-four manuscripts from the thirteenth through the seventeenth centuries read it. This overwhelming acceptance of the account of the Bloody Sweat beginning in thirteenth-century Cilicia is probably due to Latin influence. Pro-Latin clergy may have introduced the passage as a means of assuring the Chalcedonian West of the orthodoxy of the supposedly Monophysite Armenian Church.[38] It may also reflect an awareness in the Armenian Church that this passage, unlike the other six, was found in the "first translation" (Arm 1).

Vulgate influence is seen also in the introduction of Western art forms into manuscript illumination, the addition of the letters "ō" and "f" to the alphabet, the adoption of the Frankish chapter divisions for the gospel text, the Latinized spelling of Solomon (Luke 11:31) in some Cilician manuscripts, and the rapid shift from erkat'agir (uncial) to bolorgir (minuscule) script at the beginning of the thirteenth century.[39] There is no evidence, however, that the influence of the Latin Vulgate resulted in a thorough revision of the Arm 2 text. Rather, the changes appear to be limited to proper names and conspicuous passages such as the ones we have noted.

An interesting example of conformity to the Vulgate text is seen in J1941 (1334-1349, Rhodes #484). The text of this manuscript agrees with the

Vulgate text in Mark 16:9-20, Luke 22:43-44, and John 5:4. In the remaining four test passages, the original text follows the critical text, the original text of Arm 2. However, a later hand has added Matthew 16:2-3 and "the Son of God" in Mark 1:1 in the margins. In Mark 1:2, "Isaiah" has been erased by a later hand and the sign of the plural added to "the prophet." John 7:53-8:11 is absent, but a note in the lower margin, perhaps by the original scribe, indicates that the story of the woman caught in adultery belongs there. Next to the note is the Frankish designation for chapter eight. Although the Frankish chapter numbers are rarely found in Armenian gospel manuscripts until the fifteenth century, J1941 has them throughout the four gospels. J1941 is also the earliest of our manuscripts by far to use the Latin letter "o" for the diphthong "aw."

In Luke 11, there is evidence of firmer control over the production of manuscripts in Cilician Armenia. All Arm 1 and early Arm 2 readings are eliminated. Errors, singular readings, and random Greek readings are reduced to their lowest point. On the other hand, Cilician manuscripts have ten harmonizations (mostly intra-versional) and other minor additions not found in our majority text. Percentages of agreement between Cilician manuscripts are high, with many pairs of manuscripts agreeing 88% and more.[40]

The adoption of the Vulgate readings in the test passages and the textual changes in Luke 11 produce a gospel text in fourteenth-century Cilician Armenia which is smoother and fuller than the early Arm 2 text and our majority text. It is this text which is found in the Zohrabian edition of 1805. In the test passages, Zohrabian agrees with our fourteenth-century Cilician manuscripts in reading the critical text in only two passages, omitting Matthew 16:2-3 and John 7:53-8:11.[41] In Luke 11, Zohrabian differs from the Cilician manuscript J1930 (1323, Rhodes #480) only once, apart from minor orthographic differences, in supplying the omitted ełew/egeneto in 11:14.

The kingdom of Cilicia fell before the ravages of the Black Death and the repeated attacks of the Mamelukes of Egypt and their Syrian allies. The inhabitants of Cilicia fled, taking with them their cherished Biblical manuscripts. In scriptoria throughout Greater Armenia and in cultural centers as widely scattered as Constantinople and New Julfa in Persia, the artistic and textual traditions of Cilicia continued to influence Armenian manuscript production for centuries.

NOTES

[1]See, e.g., R. Simon, Critical Enquiries into the Various Editions of the Bible (London: Tho. Braddyll, 1684) 208.

[2]Surveys of text-critical studies in the Armenian version may be found in F. Macler, Le texte arménien de l'évangile d'après Matthieu et Marc (Paris: Imprimerie Nationale, 1919) xxxiv-lxxii; A. Vööbus, Early Versions of the New Testament (Stockholm: Estonian Theological Society in Exile, 1954) 138-171; B. M. Metzger, The Early Versions of the New Testament: Their Origin, Transmission, and Limitations (Oxford: Clarendon Press, 1977) 157-171, especially 166-167; and J. M. Alexanian, "The Armenian Version in Luke and the Question of the Caesarean Text"   (Unpublished Ph.D. dissertation, University of Chicago, 1982) 5-34.

[3]Compare K. Lake, R. P. Blake & S. New, "The Caesarean Text of the Gospel of Mark," Harvard Theological Review 21 (1928) 255-256, 310; Vööbus, Early Versions, 170; L. Leloir, "La version arménienne du Nouveau Testament," 300-313 in K. Aland (ed.), Die alten Ubersetzungen des Neuen Testaments, die Kirchenvaterzitate und Lektionare (Arbeiten zur Neutestamentlichen Textforschung, 5; Berlin: Walter de Gruyter, 1972) 305; and R. Kieffer, Au delà des recensions? (Coniectanea biblica, New Testament Series, 3; Lund: CWK Gleerup, 1968) 236-237, 244-249.

[4]See E. C. Colwell, Studies in Methodology in Textual Criticism of the New Testament (New Testament Tools and Studies, 9; Grand Rapids: Wm. B. Eerdmans, 1969); G. D. Fee, "Codex Sinaiticus in the Gospel of John: A Contribution to Methodology in Establishing Textual Relationships," New Testament Studies 15 (1969) 28-31; E. J. Epp, "The Twentieth Century Interlude in New Testament Textual Criticism," Journal of Biblical Literature 93 (1974) 407-410; and Alexanian, "Armenian Version in Luke," 85-122.

[5]The seven test passages are as follows: Matthew 16:2-3, Mark 1:1 ("the Son of God"), Mark 1:2 ("in the prophets" or "in Isaiah the prophet"), Mark 16:9-20, Luke 22:43-44, John 5:4, John 7:53-8:11.   The earlier Greek witnesses generally support the reading "in Isaiah the prophet" in Mark 1:2 and the omission of the remaining six passages. We will refer to this older and usually shorter text as the "critical" text.

[6]See the surveys listed in footnote 2. Every text-critical study of the

Armenian gospels published since 1938 has supported a Syriac base for Arm 1. It should perhaps be noted that, in the same manuscript or version, different sections of the New Testament may have very different textual histories. See Colwell, Studies in Methodology, 21-23. The statement that Old Syriac, not Greek, was the base of the Arm 1 gospels implies nothing regarding other sections of the Armenian version. Compare J. A. Robinson, Euthaliana (Texts and Studies, Vol. III, No. 3; Cambridge: University Press, 1895) 83-92; L. Leloir, "Versions armeniennes," cols. 810-818 in L. Pirot, A. Robert & H. Cazelles (eds.), Supplement VI of Dictionnaire de la Bible (ed. F. Vigouroux; Paris: Librairie Letouzey et Ane, 1960) col. 812; and H. J. Lehmann, "Some questions concerning the Armenian version of the Epistle of James," Acta Jutlandica (Humanities Series, 56, entitled Aarhus Armeniaca) 56 (1982) 57-82.

[7]Robinson, Euthaliana, 76-82; F. C. Conybeare, "The Growth of the Peshitta Version of the New Testament," American Journal of Theology 1 (1897) 883-912; Voobus, Early Versions, 138-159. Compare S. Lyonnet, Les origines de la version armenienne et le Diatessaron (Biblica et Orientalia, 13; Rome: Pontificio Instituto Biblico, 1950) 195-274.

[8]Lyonnet, Les origines, 55-194.

[9]Ibid., 51-54; Vööbus, Early Versions, 148-149.

[10]Lyonnet, Les origines, 12-13; Alexanian, "Armenian Version in Luke," 188.

[11]Voobus, Early Versions, 168-169.

[12]A. Merk, "Die Einheitlichkeit der armenische Evangelienuber-setzung," Biblica 4 (1923) 356-374; Lyonnet, Les origines, 180.

[13]Lyonnet, Les origines, 160-161, 185-194, 264-265, 274-277.

[14]See Epp, "Twentieth Century Interlude," 393-396; Alexanian, "Armenian Version in Luke," 35-79.

[15]Alexanian, "Armenian Version in Luke," 273-284, 288-290.

[16]Compare F. C. Conybeare, "Armenian Language and Literature," Encyclopedia Britannica, 11th ed. (1910) 2.572; Vööbus, Early Versions, 162-164; and E. F. Rhodes in Metzger, Early Versions, 171.

[17]Alexanian, "Armenian Version in Luke," 290-291.

[18]Ibid., 188-189.

[19]See, e.g., A. K. Sanjian, "Anastas Vardapet's List of Armenian Monasteries in Seventh-Century Jerusalem: A Critical Examination," Le Muséon 82 (1969) 265-266, 287-292; and R. W. Thomson, "Seventh Century Armenian Pilgrim on Mount Tabor," Journal of Theological Studies 18 (1967) 27-33.

[20]Alexanian, "Armenian Version in Luke," 221-223.

[21]Ibid., 292; F. C. Conybeare, "Armenian Version of NT," in James Hastings (ed.), A Dictionary of the Bible (New York: Charles Scribner's Sons, 1898-1905) 1.153-154; G. Garitte, La Narratio de Rebus Armeniae: Édition critique et commentaire (Corpus Scriptorum Christianorum Orientalium, Vol. 132, Subsidia tome 4; Louvain: Imprimerie Orientaliste L. Durbecq, 1952) 329-331.

[22]Alexanian, "Armenian Version in Luke," 199-223.

[23]Frédéric Macler was the first scholar to note the two branches in the Armenian gospel manuscript tradition. See Macler, Le texte arménien, 1-2, 165-166, 315. The designation "Group Z" indicates the manuscripts closest to Zohrabian. "Group W" (for "wild") indicates manuscripts whose texts do not agree closely with one another or with any known textual group. See P. R. McReynolds, "The Claremont Profile Method and the Grouping of Byzantine New Testament Manuscripts" (Unpublished Ph.D. dissertation, Claremont Graduate School, 1968) 133.

[24]Alexanian, "Armenian Version in Luke," 169-171, 180-181.

[25]Ibid., 170-180.

[26]Macler, Le texte arménien, 315; A. Merk, review of Le texte arménien de l'évangile d'après Matthieu et Marc by F. Macler, Biblica 4 (1923) 229.

[27]Lyonnet, Les origines, 264-274; Vööbus, Early Versions, 167-171; Leloir, "Versions arméniennes," col. 813; Leloir, "La version arménienne," 305.

[28]Armenian manuscripts are identified by manuscript number followed by their date, by year or century, and the catalog number in E. F. Rhodes, An Annotated List of Armenian New Testament Manuscripts (Tokyo: Rikkyo [St. Paul's] University, 1959). The manuscript number includes a letter, which usually indicates the city where the manuscript is located (C =

Chicago, E = Erevan, J = Jerusalem), and the library number. In the case of M1111, the letter refers to Moscow, where the manuscript was located when it first drew the attention of European scholars. Manuscripts formerly in the H. Kurdian collection, Wichita, Kansas, but now in the library of the Mechitarist Monastery in Venice, Italy, are identified by the letter "K."

[29]Alexanian, "Armenian Version in Luke," 180-183.

[30]Macler, Le texte arménien, 2, 94, 165-166.

[31]See A. Merk, "Die armenische Evangelien und ihre Vorlage," Biblica 7 (1926) 69-71; Lyonnet, Les origines, 180-190; Voobus, Early Versions, 154-167.

[32]Alexanian, "Armenian Version in Luke," 221-223.

[33]Useful, though popular, accounts of Armenian history and culture will be found in L. Arpee, A History of Armenian Christianity (New York: Armenian Missionary Association of America, Inc., 1946); Y. Astowrian, Patmowt'iwn Hayoc' (Buenos Aires: Sipan Press, 1947); S. Der Nersessian, The Armenians (Ancient Peoples and Places, 68; New York: Praeger Publishers, 1970); V. M. Kurkjian, A History of Armenia (New York: Armenian General Benevolent Union of America, 1964); D. M. Lang, Armenia: Cradle of Civilization (London: George Allen & Unwin, Ltd., 1970); and H. Pasdermadjian, Histoire de l'Armenie (Paris: Librairie Orientale H. Samuelian, 1964).

[34]S. Der Nersessian, Armenian Art (Paris: Thames and Hudson, 1977) 80-122.

[35]H. Kurdian, "An Important Armenian MS with Greek Miniatures," Journal of the Royal Asiatic Society (1942) 155-162.

[36]Der Nersessian, Armenian Art, 123-162; S. Der Nersessian, An Introduction to Armenian Manuscript Illumination (Baltimore: Walters Art Gallery, 1974) cols. 3-8; Der Nersessian, The Armenians, 149-153; B. Narkiss (ed.), Armenian Art Treasures of Jerusalem (New Rochelle, New York: Caratzas Brothers, Publishers, 1979) 47-62, 81-88.

[37]Alexanian, "Armenian Version in Luke," 189, 296.

[38]It is interesting to note that, during the doctrinal controversies of the seventh century, the theologian Yovhan Mayragomec'i charged that this

passage had been interpolated into the Lukan text by the pro-Chalcedonian party in the Armenian Church. See Garitte, La Narratio, 45, 326-334.

[39]Alexanian, "Armenian Version in Luke," 191, footnote 1, 223-226.

[40]Ibid., 175-177, 186-187.

[41]The pericope adulterae is given at the end of the Gospel of John.

THE SOURCES OF THE ISAIAH COMMENTARY
OF GEORG SKEWṘAC'I

David D. Bundy

Université Catholique de Louvain (Belgium)

The exegetical literature on Isaiah is vast and for the most part has not yet been critically examined or published. It is a significant literature because the Isaiah text provided a common matrix upon which the patristic writers could restate and reaffirm the tenets of their spirituality and of their theology. The Gēorg Skewṙac'i's commentary on Isaiah is one of the most voluminous produced after the golden age of Greek patristic literature. It is important in its own right as a monument of Armenian literature in the thirteenth century. It is also a witness to the critical and synthetic use of Greek and Syriac as well as Armenian sources. These sources are the primary concern of this article in which we shall provide biographical information about the author/compiler, an indication of the sources identified, observations about the use of those sources and a comparison with other Greek and Syriac commentaries.

Gēorg Skewṙac'i (1301)[1]

Gēorg Vardapet was born at Lambron Castle (therefore also listed as Gēorg Lambronac'i) and studied at several monasteries before returning to the Monastery of Skewṙa[2] to write and compile his commentaries on the Acts of the Apostles and on Isaiah as well as a number of other theological and philological works[3] before his death in 1301 C.E.[4]

The Commentary on Acts was published in 1839 at Venice on the basis of two manuscripts from the library of St. Lazarus.[5] This work depends heavily on a version of the Chrysostomian Commentary on Acts[6] and

T. Samuelian & M. Stone, eds. Medieval Armenian Culture. (University of Pennsylvania Armenian Texts and Studies 6). Chico, CA: Scholars Press, 1983. pp. 395 to 414.

incorporates much material taken from a commentary attributed to Ephrem of Nisibis/Edessa (c. 309-373)[7] the Armenian version of which is probably from the fifth century.[8] It also contains citations attributed by the scholiast to Cyril of Alexandria, Cyril of Jerusalem, David (the Philosopher), Dionysius, Kirakos and the Catholicos Nersēs. This commentary has been studied primarily for its contribution to our knowledge of the Ephremian commentary.[9] Unfortunately it did not come to the attention of Prof. Geerard as he was compiling the fourth volume of the Clavis Patrum Graecorum.[10]

The commentary on Isaiah[11] is preserved in some 38 manuscripts, the oldest of which is Yerevan 4825 (1295 C.E.) which was copied only three years after the actual composition of the commentary in 1292 C. E.[12] Whereas the projected critical edition will use all of the textual witnesses, the observations of this essay are based on a collation of the seven oldest texts: Yerevan 4825 (1295 C.E.), Yerevan 4214 (1298 C.E.), Jerusalem St. James 365 (1299 C.E.), Yerevan 4119 (1307 C.E.), Yerevan 1138 fol. 143 v-153 r (1347 C.E.) (fragment only), Yerevan 4141 (1351 C.E.) and Yerevan 1209 (undated, probably 13th-early 14th century). These manuscripts are carefully copied and present relatively few variants apart from the normal spelling errors and differences of abbreviations. Yerevan 4825 is a paleographical masterpiece and happily free from orthographical problems and from innovative abbreviations.

The Isaiah Commentary:

(Scope, Genre and Structure)

What we have termed a commentary, following the indications of the manuscript catalogues and because of structural and methodological considerations to be indicated below, is actually generically a catena. Françoise Petit who has worked extensively with the Greek and Latin exegetical catenae has suggested a definition for the genre: "One labels as 'catenae' the biblical manuscripts in which the sacred text is accompanied by juxtaposed exegetical citations deriving from the commentators of the first six centuries with their respective attributions."[13] This is accurate for the Greek compilations but must be amended for the Armenian and Syriac materials. It is in these catanae that many of the exegetical traditions of the church have been preserved. More than the great systematic commentaries, they confirm what was appreciated and read.

The work of making this material available has just begun. There is of course, the fundamental classification of the Greek catanae by Karo and Leitzmann,[14] and there is the magisterial status quaestionis of Robert Devreesse.[15] Devreesse also edited fragments taken from certain catenae on the Octateuch and the Kings.[16] Most helpful and methodologically the most sound has been the work of Françoise Petit on the catenae of Genesis and of Exodus. She has devoted much effort to the diachronic examination and publication of these texts.[17]

The analysis of the Greek exegetical literature in the catenae devoted to Isaiah has not been taken beyond the pioneering work by Faulhaber of the catenae on the prophets found in selected Roman manuscripts.[18] There is of course the work of L. Eisenhofer on the Procopius Commentary on Isaiah (P. G. 88, 1817-2718) which depended upon the catenae and commentaries for its materials and which Eisenhofer was able to document.[19]

The commentary of Gēorg Skewřac'i has affinities with this corpus of materials and divergences. It is similar in its method of documenting sources, in its method of using sources, and in the scope of the sources cited. It is different in structure and brings to bear material not found (to our knowledge) in the Greek catenae. Some of this difference in structure and sources is due to the Syriac influences. The proclivity of the Greek scholiasts toward citing the entire parent text gives way to the Syriac scholiast methodology. Only the texts to be commented upon are cited and only in so far as is relevant to the comment envisaged. A text is cited and the comments immediately follow from one or several authors. This method (not unlike that of Procopius) had been practiced in the Syrian church since the fourth and fifth centuries if the commentaries generally agreed to be authentically from Ephrem are any indication. The scholia were no longer scholia properly so called but a terse, sparse commentary preserved apart from the main biblical text and organized (and no doubt supplemented and edited) as an integral unit. Isaiah commentary materials preserved in Syriac include the Ephremian scholia (known from the Severian catena), Iso'dad of Merw, Dionysius bar Ṣalibi, Barhebraeus (Gregory abū-l-Farağ) and the Gannat Bussame.[20] The Syriac commentators sometimes documented their work, but unfortunately they were neither consistent or systematic in the identification of their sources.

Fortunately, Gēorg Skewřac'i follows the tendency of the Greek catenists in documenting the material used. When the indications of the sources can be verified, the attributions of the manuscripts are remarkably accurate. However, as was suggested by Faulhaber, it is not always clear where a citation begins or ends.[21]

This documentation poses most accutely a methodological problem for the study of this and similar works. It lends itself to serve as a mere repository of data illuminative of the Greek and/or Syriac traditions. This is certainly an important legacy of Gēorg Skewr̄ac'i. However the primary contribution which this text can make is to help us understand more fully the history of commenting on the Isaiah text and the process of selection and appropriation of three exegetical heritages (Greek, Syriac and Armenian) in thirteenth-century Armenia. As Devresse argued, this genre of literature deserves to be studied as having worth on its own merits and not merely as a source for establishing texts from earlier and therefore presumably more worthwhile periods.[22]

Sources Indicated in the Prologue and Lemmata

The commentary begins with a superscription indicating sources employed, the king for whom it was written and the author. The text, taken here from Yerevan 4825, reads:[23]

Հաւաքումն ժողովումն
մեկնութեան սուրբ մարգարէին
Եսայեա ի Լուսաւոր
մեկնչաց սրբոյ Հաւրն
Եփրեմի յովՀաննու ոսկեբերանին
եւ կիւրղի աղեքսանդրու Հայրա-
պետին Հրամանաւ տեառն
Հայոց Հեթմոյ [   ]
վարդապետին գէորգեա արարեալ

A concise collection of the commentary on the holy prophet Isaiah from the illustrious interpreters, the holy father Ephrem, John Chrysostom and Cyril Patriarch of Alexandria. Commanded by the Lord of the Armenians, Het'um . . . done by Gēorg Vardapet.

There are, however, other sources indicated by the lemmata of the manuscripts. These were written, in the manuscripts examined, in black ink in the outer margins. The hand is always the same as that of the copyist. Those commentators thus indicated by abbreviations of their names include: Ephrem, John Chrysostom, Cyril of Alexandria, Sergius (Sarg), Evagrius, Severus, Athanasius, Epiphanius, Gregory, George, Gregory of Nazianzus and a source identified by the abbreviation, bara.

The abbreviations proffered by the lemmata are for the most part accurate insofar as resources are available to control the sources used. However, there has been enough confusion to warrant a caveat to anyone who would attempt to reconstruct the work of a particular commentator. Sometimes the scribe (or compiler) failed to note a sentence or paragraph taken from say, Ephrem, in the midst of a lengthy citation from the Chrysostomian commentary.   And occasionally, a comment is simply attributed to the wrong author.   More often the lemmata are missing.   For example the entire body of material dealing with Isaiah 47 is not documented although Ephremian and Chrysostomian materials are used along with others which cannot at this stage of the investigation be identified.

Then too, the citations appropriated are often reworked so as to make positive identification of sources a hazardous enterprise.   In addition, Gēorg Skewṙac'i (or his sources) often supplements the text used with comments or clarifications.   The lack of critical editions of the extent exegetical literature and the regretted loss of many important works militates against the exhaustive identification of the sources of this work.

The chart 1 in the Appendix indicates the sources and their frequency according to the lemmata accompanying each chapter of the Isaiah text.   It is to be noted that Cyril is cited in the prologue and consistently up to chapter 11: 1. It is in chapter 10 that Sergius (Sarg) is first mentioned and becomes a consistently exploited source until chapter 30 after which this work is infrequently mentioned.   Gregory is cited only in chapters 53 and 54. From the number of attributions, it appears that much more care was taken with the documentation in the first half of the commentary.   There is little difference in the documentation of the manuscripts examined.   The chart is based on Yerevan 4825 and Jerusalem St. James 365.

The Use of Sources

Having described the commentary and indicated the scope of sources acknowledged, we proceed now to an examination of Gēorg Skewṙac'i's method of using his sources.

John Chrysostom.   The most important source for this work is the commentary on Isaiah attributed to John Chrysostom.   This commentary is preserved most completely in an Armenian version.   The edition published by the Mekhitarist fathers of St. Lazarus includes material on Isa 2:2-21:2, 28:16, and 30:6-64:10.[25]   The Latin translation published separately depends for Isa 1:1-8:10 on the translation of the Greek text provided by Montfaucon and reproduced in Migne (P.G. 56, 11-94).[26]   The Armenian text of the prologue and commentary on Isa 1:1-2:2 was published later by Avetisian.[27]

The authenticity of the Chrysostomian commentary on Isaiah has been inconclusively discussed. The Mekhitarist fathers affirmed its authenticity[28] as did L. Dieu[29] and J. Quasten.[30]   J. Ziegler argued that the biblical text used and complemented in the commentary did not coincide with the traditional style of the assuredly authentic commentaries, nor did the style and method observable in the work.[31]   Nevertheless M. Geerard included it with the authentic works of Chrysostom.

More recently, J. Dumortier has suggested that what one finds in the Greek text is from Chrysostom himself, but that the remainder is based on a stenographic record which the Greek scribe could not decipher but which served an Armenian translator/writer a framework for his own work and a screen behind which he could publish it.[32]   J.-N. Guinot accepts this as a working hypothesis[33] and further argues that the lack of dependence of Theodoret of Cyrrhus on the work attributed to Chrysostom to Chrysostom, and in fact the radical differences between the two works augers poorly for the authenticity of the commentary.[34]

The question of authenticity cannot be settled, if ever, until there is a critical edition of the Armenian text, until the exegetical catenae and commentaries are edited, and until the fragments attributed to Chrysostom on Isaiah extant in Greek and Syriac catenae on Isaiah are carefully examined and compared with the Armenian materials. Of the Greek scholia, Faulhaber lists five scholia found in Ottob. 452 dealing with Isa 6:2, Isa 37:33, Isa 49:15, Isa 57:17 and Isa 57:18ff.[35] He notes that others are to be found in Vat. Gr. 450, 459, 465, 570, 576, 577, 807, 1146, 1190, 1225, 1785 and Palat. 11 and Ottob. 7.[36]

The Armenian corpus of the Chrysostomian commentary material on Isaiah has been examined by Akinian.[37]   The date of the translation or writing of this work is uncertain. However the Seal of the faith[38] does provide a terminus a quo. This is a florilegium of theological and exegetical works assembled in the early 7th century at the behest of the Catholicos Komitas (612-628 C.E.).[39] In this collection is found one passage from the Chrysostomian commentary on Isaiah taken from the discussion of Isaiah 11:1-2. Thomson has suggested that the text represents, probably, an earlier translation than that published.[40]   However, as he suggests, "in places his extracts make better sense than the Armenian edition."[41] In several cases the text found in the Seal of the Faith makes grammatical items less ambiguous and reads much more smoothly. Some changes also resolve theological ambiguities and may well reflect a response to the Chalcedonian and Julian crises.[44]   But, the resolution of the question of the number of translations or revisions can be achieved only after a careful examination of the Armenian exegetical traditions.

The excerpts from the Chrysostomian commentary on Isaiah in the work of Gēorg Skewṙac'i do not follow a particular pattern in their fidelity or lack thereof to the original text.   Often the Chrysostomian text is slavishly followed.   For example, the text of the comment on Isa 2:1-3 follows exactly the Chrysostomian as does that on Isa 12:1-6.   However, Gēorg Skewṙac'i often reworks his text to restate the ideas and/or to edit out technicalities which were for him irrelevant.   Credit is usually given, and accurately.   That there is a relationship between the cited source and the resultant text is usually beyond doubt.   What remains unclear is whether these revisions are due to the genius of Gēorg Vardapet or to one of his predecessors.

Let us take for example, the passage commenting on Isa 11:2.   The text of the Chrysostomian commentary is juxtaposed to that of Gēorg (with parallels underlined), in Chart 2 of the Appendix.

Ephrem.   The second most exploited source is the commentary attributed to Ephrem, presumably Ephrem the Syrian (c. 309-373 C.E.).   The citations are less frequent than is the case for the Chrysostomian commentary and less lengthy.

However, the critical problems are no less serious.   A portion of a commentary attributed to Ephrem was published by Moubarek (alias Petrus Benedictus) in the Roman edition of Ephrem's works.[45]   Here were included material on the prologue of Isaiah and on Isa 1:1-43 and 66.   The source of this edition is problematic.   There are an enormous number of variants between the published text and Vat. Syr. 103 to which the editor had access, not the least of which is commentary on Isa 43-65. This lacuna was filled by Lamy who published the text of the commentary on Isa 43-66 which he extracted from B. L. 12, 144.[46]   This manuscript, a copy of Vat. Syr. 103, contains a catena on the entire Old Testament compiled by a certain Severus in 861 C.E. at Edessa.[47]

The materials attributed to Ephrem in the work of Gēorg Skewṙac'i are mostly taken from the same corpus of material as that found in the Severian catena.   Whether it was taken from the Syriac catena, from a previously existing Armenian translation of that catena or from an Armenian translation of the Ephremian commentary is difficult to ascertain. The latter two possibilities are more likely to have been the case, since there are citations attested in earlier commentators as well.[48]   However the "Catalogue of Ancient Armenian Translations" does not mention such a translation having been made.[49]

The question of the authenticity of this material has not been decisively addressed. Lamy assumed the scholia to be from Ephrem[50] and Bardenhewer[51] stated that their authenticity was beyond doubt. Pohlmann[52] and Bravo[53] were more cautious. Burkitt[54] and Ortiz de Urbina[55] rejected their authenticity. More recently, Murray suggested some of the material of the severian catena may be authentic.[56]

Once again the relationship between the text cited and the version preserved in Gēorg's commentary varies greatly. Sometimes the Armenian version presents a woodenly literal translation of the Syriac. At other times the relationship is tenuous at best. A detailed study of the Syriac and Armenian materials is now in preparation.

Cyril. The large commentary of Cyril of Alexandria is preserved in its entirety in Greek.[57] It was used widely in Greek exegetical catanae,[58] and is partially preserved in a Syriac version, the most extensive fragment which is in the Severian catena.[59]

How and when the work was translated into Armenian is unclear.[60] There is no citation in the Seal of the Faith but the commentary was cited in the Isaiah commentaries of David K'obayrec'i, Grigor Abasu and Sargis Kund.[61] Gēorg Skewŕac'i used Cyril extensively for the first portion of the commentary. The borrowed passages are heavily revised, and interestingly, delete much of the anti-Jewish rhetoric.

Sergius. The commentary of Gēorg Skewŕac'i cites that of Sargis Vardapet Kund a total of 51 times as acknowledged by the lemmata. This commentary was described briefly by Akinian[62] but has not been published nor have I yet been able to obtain a microfilm. It does raise the question of sources to a more complicated level. In the copy examined, the lemmata are few and far between. Thus when Gēorg was citing the commentary taken, as the prologue indicates, "from all of the commentaries,"[63] he was probably at least on occasion citing from another commentator. However, none of the citations coincide with the commentaries of John Chrysostom, Cyril or Ephrem.

Athanasius. Indicated as the source of the commentary on Isa 7:14,

45:14-15 and 57:16 is Athanasius but the source or sources have not been identified. The fragment listed in Mai (on Isa 7:3) is not used.[64] The incipit of the scholia indicated by Faulhaber are not related.[65]

    Evagrius. The attribution in Isa 10:17 is probably to Evagrius Ponticus. Neither Faulhaber nor the CPG reflect citations dealing with Isaiah in the catanae examined.

    George. The source suggested by the lemma at Isa 3:12 has not been identified.

    Gregory of Nazianzus. This author is cited for Isa 2:2, 5:29, 41:2, 45:16, 55:11 and 64:5 and is acknolwedged by the abbreviation Acaban, "the theologian." These scholia have not been found in the Greek corpus of Gregory's works and should probably be added to the scholia on Isaiah listed in the CPG.[66]

    Gregory. The writer so designated is not to be identified with Gregory of Nazianzus.[67] There is no indication in the 25 lemmata (all having to do with chapter 53 of Isaiah) as to which Gregory is intended. Zanolli, following a suggestion of Akinian, discovered these fragments are taken from a homily by Grigor Skewřac'i, Gěorg's uncle and mentor.[68]

    Severus. The lemmata attached to the commentary on Isa 21:9 and 32:2 indicating their source to be Severus are probably referring to Severus of Antioch who was often cited in the Greek exegetical catenae on Isaiah.[69] However there is not precise reference to specific works in the text and the sources have not been identified.

    Bara. The source intended by the abbreviation bara at 42:3 has not been identified.

Conclusions

    Gěorg Skewřac'i thus used for his commentary on Isaiah a wide range of sources from three exegetical traditions: the Syriac work attributed to Ephrem of Edessa; the Armenian works of Sargis Kund and Grigor Skewřac'i; and the Greek works of Chrysostom, Cyril of Alexandria, Athanasius, Gregory of Nazianzus, Severus of Antioch, and Evagrius. All of the Syriac and Greek works appear to have been already extant in Armenian versions. Later sixth-through thirteenth-century Syriac and Greek commentaries were apparently unknown.

    The use of sources is not a slavish copying but rather shows a creative adaptation of materials available. It indicates that a commentary tradition was being developed on the basis of the patristic traditions. The scope of this freedom and creativity is best seen by comparing Gēorg's work with contemporary Syrian and Greek writers. The Syriac writers had developed a rather closed indigenous tradition; within the Greek church the recopying of patristic catenae indicates the parameters of the possible were defined. The commentary of Gēorg Skewṙac'i on Isaiah is an important milestone in the history of exegesis.

APPENDIX

Chart 1

Chapter of Isaiah	John Chrysostom	Ephrem		
Prologue	2 cit.	1 cit.	Cyril, 1	
1	40	18	Cyril, 34	
2	20	12	Cyril, 17	Greg. Naz., 1
3	20	12	Cyril, 15	George, 1
4	4	4	Cyril, 3	
5	30	15	Cyril, 24	Greg. Naz., 1
6	15	5	Cyril, 13	
7	19	6	Cyril, 17	Athanasius, 1
8	13	9	Cyril, 12	
9	16	8	Cyril, 12	
10	12	11	Cyril, 15	Evagr., 1 Sergius, 1
11	12	10	Cyril, 1	
12	2	–	Severus, 1	
13	6	7	Sergius, 1	
14	8	10	Sergius, 2	
15	2	3	Sergius, 1	
16	2	2	Sergius, 1	
17	2	1	Sergius, 2	
18	2	3	Sergius, 1	
19	10	10	Sergius, 1	
20	4	4	Sergius, 1	
21	1	3	Sergius, 1	Severus, 1

22	5	4	Sergius, 1	
23	4	2	-	
24	4	5	Sergius, 5	
25	5	5	-	
26	8	7	Sergius, 1	
27	3	3	Sergius, 1	
28	16	17	Sergius, 2	
29	8	10	Sergius, 6	
30	10	9	Sergius, 4	
31	4	3		
32	3	4	Sergius, 2	Severus, 1
33	7	8	Sergius, 3	
34	2	3		
35	2	2		
36	1	1		
37	1	1		
38	4	5		
39	3	4	-	
40	10	9	-	
41	6	5	Sergius, 2	Greg. Naz., 1
42	20	18	Sergius, 1	<u>Bara</u>, 1
43	7	7	-	
44	6	6	-	
45	7	7	Sergius, 1	Greg. Naz., 1, Athan.
46	2	5	-	
47	No sources indicated			
48	7	6	-	
49	14	14	Sergius, 2	
50	3	5	-	
51	6	7	-	
52	10	7	-	
53[24]	31	12	Gregory, 24	
54	10	11	Gregory, 1	
55	5	5	Greg. Naz., 1	
56	5	5	-	
57	5	5	Athanasius, 1	
58	8	4	-	

59	3	4	Sergius, 2
60	5	7	Sergius, 1
61	6	5	Sergius, 1
62	3	2	-
63	6	4	Sergius, 1
64	3	3	Greg. Naz., 1
65	8	9	Sergius, 1
66	6	5	Sergius, 1

Chart 2

Chrysostom on Isaiah 11:2[42]	Georg Skewrac'i on Isaiah 11:2[43]
Եւ հանգիցէ ի վերայ նորա	Եւ հանգիցէ ի վերայ նորա
հոգի աստուծոյ հոգի	հոգի աստուծոյ եւ արդ ասեն
իմաստութեան եւ հանճարոյ։	հերձուածողքն
ամաչեսցեն հերձուածքն որ	
հրեայերէն կամին մեկենել	
զգիրսս։ Հոգի ասէ խորհրդոյ	
եւ զաւրութեան հոգի գիտութեան	
եւ աստուածապաշտութեան.	
եւ այլք երկիւղի եւս յաւելուն	
եթէ լցցէ զնա հոգի երկիւղի	
աստուծոյ։ ակիդաս եթէ	
հաստեսցի ի նա երկիւղիւն տեառն	
սիմաքոս եւ թէոդոտիոն եթէ	
կոտտեսցի նա յերկիւղ տեառն։	
եւ արդ ընդէր լնուցու	թէ ընդէր լնու զնա հոգւով
հոգւովն զաստուածն։	թէ աստուած է քրիստոսն։ առ
գրեսցուք թէ ի	որս իդեւէ ասէ թէ գրեսցուք
Հաւրէ երկնչիցի որպէս դուք	թէ ի Հաւրէ երկնչի որդի վասն
Հայ հոյէք	ասելոյն թէ լցցէ նա հոգւովն
Հոգւովն եւս զինչ կարաստեր	երկիւղի որպէս դուք Հայ հոյէք
զոր դուք	Հոգւոյն զինչ կարաստէ զոր
իսկ ասէք թէ փոքր է քան զնա.	դուքդ Հայ հոյէք փոքր է քան
այլ վասն մեր յիւր շնչական եւ	զորդի։ այլ վասն մեր յիւր
ի մարմնական մարմին ընդունի	մարմին ընդունի զհոգին
զհոգին զիմաստութեան եւ	զգիտութեան. զհանճարոյ.
եւ զգիտութեան եւ	զգիտութեան

Chrysostom on Isaiah 11:2[42]

եւ զաստուածապշտութեան զի մեզ

ինքեամբ ցուցցէ աւինակ եթէ մեք

մեք կարաատ եմք այնպիսի պարգեւ-

աց Հոգւոյն ասառւծոյ

եւ ոչ նա որ տէրն է կարաատ

ինչ է Հոգի ընդունելով այլ ի

նմա երեւելով Հոգւոյն մեզ

Լինիցին Հաւատարիմ նորա

երախտիքն զի որպէս մարդն

Լինել ոչ եթէ կարաատ ինչ էր

եւ վասն այնորիկ եղեւ մարդ

այլ զի մարդն Լինել աբաս ցի

զմարդիկն որդիս ասառւծոյ

նոյնպէս եւ ընդունել զՀոգին ոչ

եթէ իբրեւ զկարաատ օք ընկալաւ

այլ զի կարաատութեանց ինքեամբ

բաշխեսցէ զՀոգին։

Georg Skewrac'i on Isaiah 11:2[43]

զաստուածապշտութեան զի մեզ

ինքեամբ ցուցցէ աւբինակ թէ

մեք կարաատ Հոգւոյն

եւ ոչ նա այլ զի նովաւ մեք

դարձեալ Հարատացուք Հոգւովն։

զի որպէս մարդն եղեւ ոչ զի

կարաատ էր այլ զի զմեզ

որդիս ասառւծոյ աբասցէ

նոյն պէս առ եւ զՀոգին զի

ինքեամբ մեզ բաշխեսցէ։

NOTES

[1]H. Ačaṙyan, Hayoc' anjnanunneri baṙaran, v. I (Haykakan SSR Erevani Petakan Hamalsaran, Gitakan Ašxatut' yunner, v. XXI; Erevan, 1942) 465 no. 86. See also: E. M. Baghdassarian, "La 'Vie de Georges de Skevra,'" Banber Matenadarani 7 (1964) 399-435. K. K'iparian, Patmut'iwn hay grakanut'ean I: skizbēn minč'ew 1700: v. I: skizbēn minč'ew 1300 (Venetik: S. Lazar, 1944) 350; Vincent Mistrih, Trois biographies de Georges de Skevra. Presentation, texte et traduction (Studia Orientalia Christiana Armenica; Le Caire: Ed. du Centre Franciscain, 1970); N. Polarian, Hay groṫner ē - žē dar (Erusalem: Tparan S. Yakobeanc', 1971) 324-329; P. S. Somal, Quadro della storia letteraria di Armenia (Venezia: S. Lazaro, 1829), 106 (Note that the last author confuses two Georges, one from the 12th, the other from the 13th century); L. G. Xač'eryan, "Grč'ut'ean Arvesti" Lezvakan - K'erakanakan Tesowt'yune Mijnadaryan Hayastandum (Erevan: Hayk. SSR Akad. Hratarak, 1962) 99-171, 288-320; G. Zarbhanalian, Patmut'iwn Hay Hin Dprut'ean d - žg dar (Venetik: Mxit'arean Tparan, 1932) 717-721.

[2]H. Oskian, "Skewṙac'i Vank'ē," Handēs Amsōreay 69 (1955) 17-42, 207-236, esp. 38-42.

[3]Mistrih, Trois biographies, 19-26; Vincent Mistrih, "Sur la confession et la communion par Georges de Skevra, texte, traduction et notes," Studia Orientalia Christiana Collectanea 16 (1981) 209-250, 2 plates.

[4]Ačaṙyan, Anjnanunneri baṙaran, 465 no. 86.

[5]Meknut'iwn Gorcoc' Aṙak'eloc' Xmbagir arareal naxneac' Yoskeberanē ew Yep'remē (Venetik: S. Lazar, 1939); Mistrih, Trois biographies, 21.

[6]The Chrysostomian text found in this commentary is quite different from that published by Montfaucon (P. G. 60, 13-384) but was found by F. C. Conybeare, "The Commentary of Ephrem on Acts," in F. J. Foakes-Jackson and Kirsopp Lake, The Beginnings of Christianity, Part I, The Acts of the Apostles (Grand Rapids: Baker, 1979, repr.) III, 375, to be identical with a Greek version preserved in a "New College Ms. of Chrysostom on Acts." A new edition of the Greek text is being prepared by F. T. Gignac (CPG, 2, 4426).

[7]N. Akinian, Surb Ep'rem: Meknut'iwn Gorcoc' Aṙak'eloc' (K'nnakan

Hratarakut'iwn Matenagrut'ean ew T'argmanut'ean naxneac' Hayoc', II.1; Vienna: Mxit'arean Tparan, 1921). Examined by August Merk, "Der neuentdekte Kommentar des hl. Ephraem zur Apostelgeschichte," Zeitschrift fur katholische Theologie 48 (1924) 37-58, 226-260 and Conybeare, "Commentary," 373-379. A new edition is being prepared by Charles Renoux.

[8]G. Zarbhanalian, Matenadaran haykakan t'argmanut'eanc' naxneac' dar d - žg (Venetik: Mxit'aran Tparan, 1889), 443; Conybeare, "Commentary," 376; Akinian, Surb Ep'remi Meknut'iwn Gorcoc' Aŕak'eloc', 6-7.

[9]Akinian, Surb Ep'remi Meknut'iwn Gorcoc' Arak'eloc', 3-6; Conybeare, "Commentary," 376-453.

[10]M. Geerard, Clavis Patrum Graecorum II (Corpus Christianorum: Turnhout: Brepols, 1980) 4.249-250.

[11]A. Zanolli, "Notizie sulla catena di Giorgia di Skewra e su dua codici Armeni della Casanatense," Giornale della Società Asiatica Italiana 3 (1935) 307-318; Mistrih, Trois biographies, 20.

[12]N. Bogharian, Grand Catalogue of St. James Manuscripts (Calouste Gulbenkian Foundation Armenian Library; Jerusalem: Armenian Convent Printing Press, 1967) 269.

[13]Françoise Petit, "Les "chaînes" exégétiques grecques sur la Genèse et l'Exode, Programme d'exploration et d'édition," Studia Patristica XII (Texte und Untersuchungen, 115; Berlin: Akademie Verlag, 1975) 46.

[14]G. Karo, H. Leitzmann, "Catenarum graecorum catalogus," Nachrichten von der königl. Gesellschaft der Wissenschaften zu Göttingen. Ph.-Hist. Klasse, 1902 (Gottingen: L. Harstmann, 1902) 334-342.

[15]Robert Devreesse, "Chaînes exétéques grecques," Dictionnaire de la Bible, Supplement 1 (1928) col. 1084-1233.

[16]Robert Devreesse, Les anciennes commentateurs grecs de l'octateuque et les rois (fragments tirés des chaînes) (Studi e testi, 201; Citta del Vaticano: Bibliotheca Apostolica Vaticana, 1959).

[17]Françoise Petit, "Les fragments grecs du livre VI des "Questions sur la Genèse" de Philon d'Alexandrie," Le Muséon 89 (1971) 93-150; F. Petit, L'Ancienne version latine des questions sur la Genese de Philon d'Alexandrie (Texte und Untersuchungen, 113, 114; Berlin: Akademie Verlag, 1973); F. Petit, Catenae graecae in genesim et in exodum, I. Catena Sinaitica (Corpus

Christianorum, Series Graeca, 2; Turnhout: Brepols; Leuven: University Press, 1977).

[18]M. Faulhaber, Die Propheten-Catenen nach römischen Handschriften (Biblische Studien, 4, 2-3; Freiburg i. Br.:   Herder, 1899).

[19]Ludwig Eisenhofer, Procopius von Gaza.   Eine literarhistorische Studie (Freiburg i. Br.:   Herder, 1897).

[20]For bibliography, see D. Bundy, "Isaiah 53 in East and West," Typus, Symbol, Allegorie bei den östlichen Vätern und ihren Parallelen im Mittelalter hrsg. M. Schmidt (Eichstatter Beiträge, 4; Regensburg: Friedrich Pustet, 1982) 53-74.

[21]Faulhaber, Propheten-Catenen, 40.

[22]Devreesse, "Chaînes exégétiques grecques," col. 1097-1098.

[23]Yerevan 4825, folio col. 1 lines 1-6.

[24]Zanolli, "Notizie," 311-312.

[25]Eranelwoyn Yovhannu Oskeberani meknut'iwn Esayeay margarēi (Venetik: Tparan S. Lazar, 1880).   Herafter, Chrysostom, Isaiah.

[26]A. Tiroyan, In Isaiam prophetam interpretatio S. Joannis Chrysostomi (Venetiis: St. Lazarus, 1887).

[27]J. Avetisian, "The Newly Discovered part of the Armenian Version on St. John Chrysostom's Commentary on Isaiah," Sion 9 (1935) 21-24 (Armenian).

[28]Chrysostom, Isaiah, introduction.

[29]L. Dieu, "Le Commentaire arménien de S. Jean Chrysostom sur Isaie est-il authentique," RHE 16 (1921) 7-30.

[30]J. Quasten, Patrology (Amsterdam: Spectrum, 1963) III.435-436.

[31]J. Ziegler, ed. Isaias (Septuaginta Vetus Testamentum Graecum . . . Gottingensis, XIV; Gottingen: Vandenhoeck und Ruprecht, 1939) 13, 73-74.

[32]J. Dumortier, "Une énigme chrysostomienne: le commentaire inachevé d'Isaïe," Mélanges de Sciences Religieuse. Universitas (Lille, 1977) 43-47.

[33]Theodoret de Cyr, Commentaire sur Isaïe.   Introduction, texte

critique, traduction et notes par Jean-Noël Guinot (Sources Chretiennes, 276; Paris: Ed. du Cerf, 1980) 19.

[34]Guinot, Theodoret de Cyr, 25-26.

[35]Faulhaber, Propheten-Catenen, 68-69.

[36]Ibid. 69.

[37]N. Akinian, "Des hl. Chrysostomus Kommentar zu Isaias in der armenischen Literatur," Handēs Amsōreay 48 (1934) 43-55 (Armenian).

[38]Catholicos Komitas, Le Sceau de la Foi (Bibliothèque arménienne de la Fondation Calouste Gulbenkian; Louvain: Ed. Peeters, 1974).

[39]J. Lebon, "Les citations patristiques grecques du 'Sceau de la Foi,'" RHE 25 (1929) 1-3.   On the citation of Chrysostom on Isaiah see p. 23.

[40]R. W. Thomson, "The Fathers in Early Armenian Literature," Studia Patristica, XII (Texte und Untersuchungen, 115; Berlin: Akademie Verlag, 1975) 464.

[41]R. W. Thomson, "Fathers," 464.

[42]Chrysostom, Isaiah, 132.

[43]Yerevan 4825, fol. 105 col. 1 line 28 - col 2 line 11.

[44]Catholicos Komitas, Le Sceau de la Foi, 318-319.

[45]Ephrem Syrus Opera omnia quae exstant graece, syriace, latine, in sex tomos distributa, ad mss. codices vaticanos allosque castigata, multis aucta, nova interpretatione, praefationibus, notis, variantibus lectionibus illustrata; nunc primum sub pontificis maximi e Bibliotheca vaticana prodeunt . . . (Romae: Ex Typographia vaticana, apud J. M. H. Salvioni, 1732-1746. [Syriac volumes 1737-1743.]

[46]Thomas-Joseph Lamy, Sancti Ephraem Syri hymni et sermones, II (Mechelen, 1882-1904).

[47]J. S. Assemani, Bibliotheca Apostolica Vaticanae Codicum Manuscriptorum Catalogus (Paris: Librairie Orientale et Americaine, 1926, repr.) III, 25-28.

[48]Akinian, "Chrysostomus Kommentar," 51-52.

[49]Zarbhanalian, T'argmanut'eanc', 443-466.

[50]Th. J. Lamy, "L'Exégèse en orient au IVe siècle ou les commentaires de Saint Ephrem," Revue Biblique 2 (1893) 5-25, 161-181, 465-486.

[51]Otto Bardenhewer, Geschichte der Altkirchlichen Literatur, Bnd. 4 (Darmstadt: Wissenschaftliche Buchgesellschaft, 1962), pp. 347-348. (Reprint from edition of Freiburg i. B. Herder, 1924.)

[52]A. Pohlmann, S. Ephraem Syri commentariorum in Sacram Scripturam textus in codicibus vaticanis manuscriptus et in editions romans impressus (Brunsberg: Eduard Peter, 1864).

[53]Carlos Bravo, "Notas introductorias a la noematica de San Efren," Ecclesiastica Xaveriana 6 (1956) 243-246.

[54]F. C. Burkitt, S. Ephraim's Quotations from the Gospel (Texts and Studies, VII, 2; Cambridge: University Press, 1901) 4-5.

[55]I. Ortiz de Urbina, Patrologia Syriaca (Roma: Pont. Inst. Ori. Stud., 1965) 73-74.

[56]Robert Murray, Symbols of Church and Kingdom. A Study in Early Syriac Tradition (Cambridge: University Press, 1975), 32 note 2.

[57]P. G. 70, 19-1499.

[58]Karo and Leitzmann, "Castenarum graecarum catalogus," passim; CPG 4, 185-259 passim.

[59]Vat. Syr. 103, fols. 218-238.

[60]Zarbhanalian, T'argmanut'eanc', 507, 509.

[61]Akinian, "Chrysostomus Kommentar," 51-52.

[62]Ibid.

[63]Ibid., 52.

[64]Angelus Mai, Novae patrum bibliothecae (Romae, 1853) 7, 2, 239.

[65]Faulhaber, Propheten-Catenen, 63.

[66]CPG, 2, 3052.

[67]Cfr. Faulhaber, Propheten-Catenen, 41; Zanolli, "Notizie," 310-311, 318.

[68]Zanolli, "Notizie," 318 ("Annotizione"). The homily is preserved in Venice, S. Lazarus 741 fol. 31ff.

[69]CPG, 4, pp. 216-217; Faulhaber, Propheten-Catenen, 75-78.

SOME REMARKS ABOUT THE ARMENIAN TRADITION OF
GREEK TEXTS

Andrea Tessier

Università di Padova (Italy)

From the point of view of a classical philologist the value of the Armenian translations of Greek texts, whose source has been transmitted to us through its 'direct' tradition, lies in the fact that they may cast some light on a lost segment of this tradition, insofar as its lectiones may survive in the translation.

Although it is often hard to determine the age of a translation and of its lost Greek antecedent, sometimes a translation (not, of course, its tradition) turns out to be prior to the whole extant direct tradition: the value of such a witness, even though it mirrors its antecedent distortedly, is quite great. On the other hand, even the translation of a manuscript, whose place within the traditional hierarchy is surely low, should not be hastily discarded (medieval variants are often ancient), unless we possess some plain evidence that the underlying manuscript source is copy of another extant manuscript; in which case the eliminatio would apply.

This definition of the connections between Classical and Armenian philology might sound too narrow, because the Armenian translations of Greek texts, besides providing the critic and the editor of the latter with important data, belong to Armenian civilization and mirror outstanding philosophical, religious and literary trends. However, such narrowness is intentional, for I deem it necessary to circumscribe the field of a definite philological domain, where the subservience of broader cultural data to the critical procedure is, at first glance at least, unavoidable.

First I shall try to point out some major problems, and faults, which

T. Samuelian & M. Stone, eds. Medieval Armenian Culture. (University of Pennsylvania Armenian Texts and Studies 6). Chico, CA: Scholars Press, 1983. pp. 415 to 424.

in recent times affected this domain. A makeshift inventory might be the following:

a.   Most nineteenth-century editions of Armenian texts are of poor value; this owing to the unsatisfactory recensio and to the old-fashioned philological procedure from which they stem. In a recent and outstanding book[1] Moreno Morani has re-examined the manuscript sources of the Venetian Mekhitarist edition of Nemesius' περὶ φύσεως ἀνθρώπων   (1889)[2] and showed that the single manuscripts offer, in many cases, a better reading than the one the Venetian editor chose.

b.   Some editors of Armenian translations were influenced by the Greek originals and, on this basis, they edited some difficult passages of their text and divested it of any critical value for the original. An example of this faulty procedure will be given below, concerning Aristotle's De Mundo.

c.   The 'division of labour' between Armenian and classical philologists is likely to bring about some common mistakes, which will be accounted for afterwards.

A concise survey of some of the problems that arise in Greek-Armenian philology cannot proceed without stressing the fact that the above-mentioned critical operations must be deemed typical of a "synchronic" or "horizontal" philology, viz. the work of an editor of a Greek classical text who makes use of its Armenian translation in the apparatus criticus he is constructing or, sometimes, through the choice of some good readings, in his text. Let us turn now to the outermost region of this domain, i.e. the "diachronic" procedure that rightfully belongs to the history of the tradition of a   text and, dealing with a "closed recension,"[3] aims at placing its translations within the frame of the stemma codicum. With reference to this I can quote an excellent book by the above-mentioned Moreno Morani,[4] where the Armenian translation of Nemesius' text is convincingly shown to be prior to the whole of its direct tradition and free from the widespread contamination that would have affected the latter.

An overview of the fate of the Classical Armenian translations of Aristotle as shown in critical editions of the Greek text will give ample opportunity to illustrate the philological method in practice. The aim of my research has primarily been the rearrangement of these oriental translations as they bear on Greek philology rather than first-hand research in the field of Armenian philology. I recently completed a comprehensive revision of the apparata to Aristotelian and pseudo-Aristotelian treatises which made use of data from the Armenian versions, omitting the Categoriae, where a recent edition of the translation[5] fills the gap and makes modern reference available to the philologist planning a new edition of the Greek text. I will take the liberty of giving some examples of faults and misunderstandings which bear on the above-listed problems.

Two Aristotelian treatises, the Categoriae and the De Interpretatione, and two pseudo-Aristotelian ones, the De Mundo and the De Virtutibus et Vitiis, were handed down to us in a Classical Armenian version: for the first two the date of the fifth century A.D. is generally agreed upon. The second two have been dated by Frederick Cornwallis Conybeare to the seventh to ninth centuries A.D.,[6] contradicting the Venetian Mekhitarist editor, who, in his foreword to the 1833 editio princeps, judged them as being contemporary to the two previous works.[7]

It is beyond my aim to inquire into the identity of the translator (or translators), though undoubtedly the traditional attribution to David the Invincible (Dawit' Anyałt'), a Christian Neoplatonist of Armenian origin, must be rejected.[8] Whatever date we choose for our translations within the above-mentioned limits, it is beyond doubt that their Greek antecedents are very old, older in any case than the manuscript tradition we possess: they are therefore to be numbered among the most valuable witnesses for a correct reconstruction of the Greek originals. As a matter of fact the Armenian translators practically reproduced verbatim their Greek model ("indeed"—as F. C. Conybeare points out—"it is little more than the Greek written with Armenian words"[9]), according to the fashion of the so-called Hellenizing school (Yunaban dproc'), operating in that time. Nevertheless, I must stress the point that the Armenian text of the two pseudo-Aristotelian treatises, as Conybeare says, "has undergone the most wholesale corruption."[10]

I have already mentioned the Armenian editio princeps of these four treatises: it was completed and printed in Venice, in 1833, in the island of San Lazzaro, on the basis of the manuscripts held in the monastery. At the end of the last century, in 1892, Conybeare collated this text with the Greek original, using, for the treatises included in the Organon, the Waitz edition,[11] and, for the pseudo-Aristotelian ones, the Bekker edition;[12] in the same volume he added the results of the collation to other Armenian manuscripts perused in Paris, Jerusalem, Pavia and Ejmiacin. It is particularly significant that Conybeare did not complete the collation with consistent standards, but when dealing with the pseudo-Aristotelian, texts he "even hesitated to print the variants of the Armenian, because most of them were so evidently due to the corruption of the version itself."[13]   The limits of Collation are therefore acknowledged even by the author, who, unfortunately, seldom seems to aim at scientific exactness.

From 1893 to the present two noteworthy events took place in this field, in 1966 the aforementioned new edition of the Armenian Categoriae and in 1977 the most recent inventory of the Armenian Aristotelian manuscripts accomplished by H. Anasyan in his weighty Armenian Bibliography:[14] the scholar enumerates some forty manuscripts for each treatise; on such basis we may expect new and satisfactory editions of the Armenian texts.

The Logical Treatises in Armenian

In his Oxford edition of the two logical treatises (Categoriae and De interpretatione) in 1949 Lorenzo Minio-Paluello inserts the Armenian translation in the critical apparatus to the Greek text,[15] relying ex-professo[16] on Conybeare's Collation. In spite of the already mentioned inaccuracy of the latter, Minio-Paluello's apparatus, owing to its "negative" structure (i.e. only the testimonies for the variants to the printed text are accounted for[17]), succeeds in overcoming some of Conybeare's faults.

Let us examine instead a couple of passages where, according to the author, the translation seems to bear ambiguous evidence to the Greek tradition, whereas the Armenian text allows us to easily spot which of the known variant readings was in the translator's antecedent manuscript.

a.   Int.20a4 οἷον ἐπὶ τοῦ ὑγιαίνειν καὶ βαδίζειν

M.-P.'s apparatus:ὑγιαίνει...βαδίζει B:ᵃ ς: [ΔΣΓ]

Conybeare's text: makoł
ĕin ew gnay[18]

It is plain and evident to the reader of the Armenian version that it actually confirms the reading of B (Marcianus 201), yet in Minio-Paluello's apparatus the square brackets enclosing the siglum of the version (the capital Δ stands for Dawit') mean:[19] "quid translator legerit ignoramus."   This note, owing to Conybeare's silence in the Collation, is misleading: as a matter of fact the latter critic never stresses the coincidence between Waitz's Greek text and the Armenian version, whereas Minio-Paluello should remark that his text, when innovative as compared to Waitz's, does not coincide with the Armenian either.

b.   Int.22b4 καὶ γὰρ αὕτη γίγνεται ἀντίφασις τῇ ἑπομένῃ
M.-P.'s apparatus: τῆς ἑπομένης   n' ΣΛ: [Δ]
C.'s text: hetewelumn[20]

The dative of the version, that in Minio-Paluello's apparatus is stated as not bearing sufficient evidence to the Greek, evidently mirrors the reading of n (<u>Ambrosianus</u> L 93), supported by the <u>Syra anonyma</u> (Σ) and the Latin version by Boethius (Λ).

The fault is once more engendered by Conybeare's silence, because Waitz's text coincides in this reading with the Armenian. Paradoxically enough, the absence of any remark as to **Δ** in Minio-Paluello's apparatus would be less misleading, for its 'negative' structure would then imply that **Δ** supports the <u>lectio recepta</u>.

The Armenian Translation of the De Mundo

This version is used by W. L. Lorimer in the apparatus to his edition of the Greek text.[21] "Omnia fere quae de hac interpretatione lectionibusque ejus scio, Friderico C. Conybeare accepta refero":[22] herewith the editor himself states his dependence upon Conybeare's data, which are particularly discontinuous and faulty as regards this treatise. The edition is further vitiated by the 'positive' structure of Lorimer's apparatus,[23] which mercilessly exposes Conybeare's omissions and faults.

Unfortunately Lorimer occasionally tries to restore the Greek text on the sole authority of the Armenian translation against the evidence of all direct tradition, after the example of Wilamowitz, who had published some remarkably innovative <u>excerpta</u> of the treatise in his <u>Griechisches Lesebuch</u>;[24] with some conjectures relying on the Armenian, avowedly due to Paul Wendland, the editor of Philo Judaeus.

Furthermore, Lorimer assumes that the Armenian translation stems from two different Greek manuscript sources. He counterposes the tradition on which the Venetian edition is based with a codex Conybeare found in Ejmiacin and edited in Vienna,[25] including the last third of the treatise (397a13 to 401b29). With reference to this, I hope to have demonstrated in a recent paper[26] that such opposition can hardly be proved on the ground of the manuscripts hitherto published, even though in few cases the Venice edition and the Ejmiacin manuscript actually display alternative readings, which had already been transmitted through the direct tradition.

Moreover, some alleged 'separative mistakes' arise from patent misunderstandings of the Armenian version. Let us examine a couple of passages.

a.   Mu.399b23 τὰ γὰρ πάθη, καὶ τὰ δι' ἀέρος ἅπαντα

Lorimer's apparatus: πάθη ÷ Mon 287 R 188 bᵉ m n : ἐπάνω Fᶜ Mutᴾ Neap R 256 : ἐπάνω Fl 33 : (ἐπ)άνω πάθη s : οὐ(ρά)νια πάθη Z : aut hoc aut illud aᵛ : οὐράνια bᵛˢ (?) : ἐπάθη Mutˢ.

Venice edition (V) 624, 16-17 erkin
Ejmiacin ms. (E) 230a25-26 kirk'n

First of all, erkin of V does not meanοὐράνιαas Conybeare's backversion doubtfully[27] states, for we would expect to find in the Armenian the adjective erknayin. I think that the editor was biased by the reading οὐ(ρά)νια πάθη – Parisinus 2381 (Z). We can easily get rid of this alleged 'Leitfehler'[28] by assuming that erkin represents the corruption of the reading kirk'n to be found in E, which mirrors πάθη of the direct tradition.

In my opinion V and E are likely to display two Armenian variants rather than two Greek ones.[29]

b.   Mu.401a11   "πᾶν γὰρ ἑρπετὸν πληγῇ νέμεται" ὥς φησιν Ἡράκλειτος

Lorimer's app.

πληγῇ Ⓢ a (vel θεοῦ πληγῇ): πληγὴν bᵉ (ganiw) : πᾶν γῇ vel πᾶν γῆν s : τὴν γῆν + (÷ γῆν B) Fl 2 Fl 13 Lp Maz O Par 166 Par 2494 R 58 R 70 R 223 R 1314 (τὴν γῆν) R 1908 Ven 215 bᵛ (hhoghov) m n : λόγον Capelle ex b cod. Par. Arm. 106 (baniw = λόγον : sic et cod. Vind. Arm. 320)

V 627,10 hołov
E 231a44 ganiw

The Aristotelian passage quotes Heraclitus (fragment B 11 DK): the meaning is that every animal 'which goes on all fours'[30] is driven to pasture by the blows of God, and this fits with the general sense of the passage, i.e. that every animal obeys the laws of God (401a10 τοῖς τοῦ θεοῦ πειθόμενα θεσμοῖς).

Surprisingly the whole direct tradition carries the reading τὴν γῆν, which must be rejected here, though τὴν γῆν νέμεσθαι [31] is not nonsensical in itself; the right reading πληγῆ·, we can see from the apparatus, is handed down through the indirect tradition, namely Stobaeus (the capital Gothic s stands for the excerpts from this author).[32]

Let us turn now tho the Arm. version: no doubt that E mirrors Stobaeus' reading, since ganiw is an instrumental from gan, that represents the proper Armenian equivalent for πληγή.[33] The faulty backformation πληγήν (Lorimer's apparatus) is sheer forgery, and is due to Conybeare, who could not have known Stobaeus' variant because his Greek model was Bekker's De Mundo, and translated ganiw bearing in mind τὴν γῆν: hence the accusative.

As for baniw =λόγῳ, this reading was found by Wilhelm Capelle in a Paris manuscript (106, now 240 Biblioteque Nationale) of the Armenian version; the scholar improved on this basis the Aristotelian text and translated: "wird doch alles Getier [...] von der Weltvernunft geleitet."[34]   This seemingly persuasive emendation once more testifies against the misleading practice of intervening on the Greek original by means of an isolated Armenian reading, since baniw represents an obvious corruption of the difficilior lectio, ganiw, and, far from affecting the Greek text, must be eliminated from its apparatus.

The third Armenian reading, hołov, also an instrumental, is likely to stem from an antecedent τῇ γῇ, which might be a corruption of πληγῆ. If we are right in assuming this, τὴν γῆν of the direct tradition is but a syntactical adjustment of this mistake, for the dative would not make sense here: a clue to this might be the reading τὴν γῆν, with 'iota subscript,' of the Vaticanus 1314.

This is briefly the status quaestionis. To sum up, when I faced the problem of the value of these Armenian translations in order to reconstruct their Greek antecedent manuscripts, and considered the use hitherto made of them, I met a fairly discouraging situation. Broadly speaking, the apparatuses hitherto completed suffer from one major fault: they always deal with second-hand data drawing on Conybeare's work which, in my opinion, is an extremely misleading instrument. The only correct philological procedure is, of course, the re-examination of the data, at least on the evidence of the Armenian printed editions we possess. I would even suggest that a complete absence of these data may turn out to be less deceiving than their misuse.

The work I have done in this direction, samples of which I just presented, does not provide final solutions. I only hope to have redressed some patent misunderstandings stemming from the misuse of the Armenian versions of the Aristotelian treatises. Yet the Armenian side of the problem must be more deeply explored: the above-mentioned work by H. Anasyan finally offers an almost thorough catalogue of the manuscript tradition of the translations and it is to be hoped that on this basis new editions will be prepared in the near future and that the new editions of the Greek originals will correctly take them into account.

NOTES

[1] M. Morani, Contributo per un'edizione critica della versione armena di Nemesio (Memorie dell'Istituto Lombardo—Accademia di Scienze e Lettere; Classe di Lettere—Scienze Morali e Storiche Vol. 33 Fasc. 3; Milano: Istituto Lombardo di Scienze e Lettere, 1973).

[2] Nemesiosi p'ilisop'ayi Emesazioy, Yałags bnut'ean mardoy (Venetik—S. Lazar, 1889); on the authorship of the edition cf. Morani, Contributo, 112.

[3] G. Pasquali, Storia della tradizione e critica del testo (Firenze: Le Monnier, 1952) 126 ff.; D'Arco Silvio Avalle, Principi di critica testuale (Padova: Antenore, 1972) 23 f.

[4] M. Morani, Le tradizione manoscritta del "De natura hominis" di Nemesio (Pubblicazioni della Universita Cattolica del Sacro Cuore—Scienze filologiche e Letteratura, 18; Milano: Vita e Pensiero, 1981).

[5] V. K. Č'aloyan & S. P. Lalap'aryan, Ananun Meknut'iwn Storogut'eanc'n Aristotēli (Erevan, 1961).

[6] F. C. Conybeare, A Collation with the Ancient Armenian Versions of

the Greek Text of Aristotle's Categories, De Interpretatione, De Mundo, De Virtutibus et Vitiis and of Porphyry's Introduction (Anecdota Oxoniensia, Classical Series 1, 6; Oxford, 1892) XXXII.

[7]Koriwn vardapeti, Mambrēi vercanoḥi ew Dawt'i Anyaḥt'i, Matenagrut'iwnk' (Venetik, 1833).

[8]Conybeare, Collation, VII; Kroll, "David," 2232-33 in Paulys Realencyclopädie der classischen Altertumswissenschaft (neue Bearb. G. Wissowa; Stuttgart: J. B. Metzlersche Verlagsbuchhandlung, 1901) 4.2.

[9]Conybeare, Collation, V.

[10]Ibid., XXXII.

[11]Aristotelis Organon Graece (ed. T. Waitz; Lipsiae 1844).

[12]Aristoteles Graece (ed. I. Bekker; Berolini 1831) I 391-401.

[13]Conybeare, Collation, XXXII.

[14]H. S. Anasyan, Haykakan Matenagitut'yun, II (Erevan, 1976).

[15]Aristoteles Categoriae et Liber de interpretatione (ed. L. Minio-Paulello; Oxonii: Oxford University Press, 1949).

[16]Ibid., XII: I would not term Conybeare's work an edition "ad artis criticae rationem."

[17]M. L. West, Textual Criticism and Editorial Technique (Stuttgart: Teubner, 1973) 87.

[18]Conybeare, Collation, 168, 19.

[19]Aristotelis Categoriae, 2.

[20]Conybeare, Collation, 178, 4.

[21]Aristotelis qui fertur libellus De Mundo (ed. W. L. Lorimer; Paris: Les Belles Lettres, 1933).

[22]Aristotelis De Mundo, 20 n.l.

[23]West, Textual Criticism, 87.

[24]U. von Wilamowitz-Moellendorff, Griechisches Lesebuch (6th ed.; Berlin, 1926) I.2.186-199.

[25]F. C. Conybeare, "Aristoteli yaḥags Astucoy ēndōrinakut'iwn," Handēs Amsōreay 7 (1893) 227-232.

[26]A. Tessier, "Leitfehler nella traduzione armena del De Mundo pseudo-aristotelico?," Bollettino del comitato per la preparazione dell'-edizione nazionale dei classici greci e latini—Accademia Nazionale dei Lincei 27 (1979) 31-40.

[27]The double quotation mark after the siglum of the version (here the small Gothic h stands for the Armenian version) means, according to Lorimer's practice: "Lectio exemplaris Graeci Armeniaci probabilis quidem, minime tamen certa."

[28]P. Maas, "Leitfehler und stemmatische Typen," Byzantinische Zeitschrift 37 (1937) 289-294.

[29]For an example of an almost 'reverse' corruption, see Mu. 395b35-36 = V 615, 7,— πάθος of the original has been rendered in Armenian with yerkir.

[30]Thus H. G. Liddell & R. Scott, A Greek-English Lexicon (9th ed.; rev. H. S. Jones; Oxford: Oxford University Press, 1940) 691, s.v. ἑρπετόν
That ἑρπετόν here means "something that moves with its trunk parallel to the ground" rather than "a creeping thing" was satisfactorily pointed out by G. S. Kirk, Heraclitus. The Cosmic Fragments (Cambridge: Cambridge U.P., 1954) 260.

[31]Liddel & Scott, Lexicon, 1167, s.v. νέμω.

[32]I cannot hold that a similar reading may be drawn from Apuleius' Latin version, where this passage looks hopelessly corrupt.

[33]Thus G. Avetik'ean & X. Siwrmelean & M. Awgerean, Nor baṙgirk' haykazean lezui (Venetik, 1836-37) I 528, s.v.

[34]W. Capelle, Die Schrift von der Welt, ein Weltbild im Umriss aus dem I. Jahrh. n. Chr. (Jena: Eugen Diederichs, 1907) 94. The scholar will subsequently adopt the right readingπληγῇ and translate: "Wird doch alles, was da kreucht und fleucht, durch den Schlag (Gottes) getrieben" in his work Die Vorsokratiker (Leipzig: Alfred Kroner Verlag, 1935) 36.

DATED ARMENIAN MANUSCRIPTS AS A STATISTICAL TOOL
FOR ARMENIAN HISTORY

Dickran Kouymjian

California State University, Fresno & Paris

A question which always disturbs historians writing about social or economic conditions of earlier centuries is whether generalizations or hypotheses about relative prosperity or decline in a given period are in fact correct. This is especially true when the historical sources are either few or do not supply more than a superficial catalogue of wars, famines, or the progress of great men. Armenian historians often face this problem. For long periods, such as the sixteenth century, no histories in Armenian exist at all.

Independent corroboration of hypotheses derived from analyzing primary sources, even when relatively rich in details, is something all scholars long for. One of the classic ways of confirming notions derived from texts is the qualitative and quantitative measure of the material culture produced in that era. In the Armenian case this would include principally church construction and manuscript illumination. Almost no attention has been given to using the material remains of Armenian culture statistically, quite apart from their value as artistic monuments, as independent verification of textual testimony about good times and bad, victories and defeats.

A decade ago, during the initial stages of the compilation of the Index of Armenian Art, it became clear that mere visual inspection of the number of cards arranged chronologically in the files could furnish a reasonably accurate idea of the relative production of miniature painting at any given period.[1] A glance at the file arranged iconographically would demonstrate the preference for one image over another during the course of centuries.

T. Samuelian & M. Stone, eds. <u>Medieval Armenian Culture.</u> (University of Pennsylvania Armenian Texts and Studies 6). Chico, CA: Scholars Press, 1983. pp. 425 to 439.

Gradually the data base increased to over 10,000 individually indexed items (illuminations). It became clear that, independent of strictly artistic considerations, this base might serve as a mode of statistical evidence.

In 1980, while the author was engaged in preparing a chapter on the historiographically obscure fifteenth and sixteenth centuries for the new collective Histoire des Armeniens,[2] it was decided to utlize the material already collected in the Index of Armenian Art. It was augmented to include data from all Armenian manuscripts and not just those with miniatures or illuminations. It seemed likely that by simply plotting manuscript production chronologically, graphic results would visually and instantly confirm or deny the validity of historical impressions of the period. The results of this statistical analysis supported in a striking way many of the conclusions reached about the history of Armenia from the fall of the Cilician kingdom in 1375 to the deportations of Shah Abbas in 1604. They were partially presented in the new Histoire.[3]

In the following pages the methodology developed will be presented in some detail accompanied by (1) an indication of the limitations of the work already achieved, (2) the effort necessary to carry out and complete the project, and (3) refinements of the system needed to make the results more credible. It is hoped that others will engage in this work with additions, corrections, and suggestions for improvement. The premises and the resources were as follows.

It is usually said that some 25,000 Armenian manuscripts have survived to our day. The majority of them are in Armenian repositories, either church or state controlled. Thanks to the aggressive work of the 1960s undertaken by the Matenadaran in Erevan in issuing a two volume summary catalogue[4] of the largest single collection of Armenian manuscripts, and the publication program of the Calouste Gulbenkian Foundation toward the completion and printing of catalogues of the major collections in the diaspora,[5] the vast majority, perhaps 90 percent or more, of all Armenian manuscripts have been identified and recorded according to accepted norms.

The idea of tabulating all Armenian manuscripts is hardly original. But thus far no single published guide nor detailed report offering a profile of the corpus of Armenian manuscripts is available.

For our survey the following major collections were used through their published catalogues: Erevan, Matenadaran, 10,408 manuscripts; a group comprising those of Venice, Mekhitarist Congregation, Volume III, Rituals, 136 manuscripts;[6] Vienna, Mekhitarist Congregation, 1,304 manuscripts;[7] Bzom-mar, Lebanon, monastic collections including that of the Antonian fathers, 683 manuscripts;[8] New Julfa, Isfahan, Patriarchal collection, 811 manu-scripts;[9] and a composite group including collections in the United States, the Vatican, German collections, Dublin (Chester Beatty), and Cyprus, 738 manuscripts.[10] The total of these codices, all thoroughly tabulated for all periods, is thus 13,944. In addition 2,800 manuscripts from the Jerusalem Armenian Patriarchal collection were examined,[11] but only recorded for a fixed time span. Altogether, a total of 16,744 Armenian manuscripts entered in the statistical analysis. The future addition of all other published material not included in this survey would bring the manuscripts close to 20,000, and the utilization of catalogues and inventories which are not yet published, such as the 3,500 or more in the Venice Mekhitarist collection and the 1,000 remaining in the Jerusalem collection, would bring the number very close to the overall total of 25,000 believed to be extant. Our dual sampling represents respectively 55.8 percent (13,944 ms) and 67.0 percent (16,744 ms) of surviving data.

In order to guarantee a degree of certitude and to facilitate the recording process, it was decided to use only specifically dated manuscripts; that is, those with a colophon indicating the precise year or years of execution. If more than one year was mentioned, only the first year was counted. Approximately dated works, for instance "second half of the fourteenth century" or "last decade of the fifteenth," were excluded. Of the sampling of 13,949 manuscripts all dates were recorded even into the late nineteenth century; for the additional Jerusalem series, manuscripts dated between 1300 and 1620 only were tabulated.

The first observation to be made is, that of the smaller sampling of 13,944 manuscripts, 57.2 percent of 7,973 were precisely dated. Calculating the percentages of individual collections within this sampling produces remarkably similar results: Matenadaran, 57.9 percent or 6,030 dated manuscripts; Vienna, Bzommar, New Julfa together, 54.5 percent or 1,521 dated manuscripts; the composite group, 57.2 percent or 422 out of 738 manuscripts. A general figure of 57 percent would mean that of the 25,000 known Armenian manuscripts we can expect to have 14,250 dated bits of material culture produced over a period beginning in the ninth century and extending through the nineteenth century. Our statistical analysis makes use of 7,973 dated manuscripts for this broad period, and by extrapolating from the Jerusalem collection (57 percent of 2,800 or 1,596 additional dated items), a total of 9,569 pieces of evidence for the period 1300 to 1620.

Methodologically the easiest way to perceive these data is to plot them on a simple graph. The resulting curve with its peaks and valleys should instantly reveal the trends in manuscript production. Since manuscripts were usually commissioned and since they are probably to be considered luxury items, increased production should coincide with the increase in relative prosperity. Thus, a series of charts was plotted of both individual collections and groups of them. Because of the scarcity of surviving manuscripts copied before 1190, the graphs were designed to begin with the year 1200 and terminate with the year 1790. There are fewer than 100 dated manuscripts up to the end of the twelfth century with perhaps twice that many undated from the same period.[12] Since we have reliable historical witness to the willful destruction of whole libraries with thousands of codices, especially during the Seljuk Turkic invasions,[13] an adequate notion of production cannot be obtained statistically. Though there was obviously continued destruction and loss in the centuries which followed, the number of surviving manuscripts for the thirteenth, fourteenth and succeeding centuries is sufficient to obtain meaningful results.[14]

Three major charts were plotted. 1. The entire Matenanadarn collection of more than 6,000 dated manuscripts as a control group, since it is itself made up of diverse collections from a broad geographical area. 2. A chart of the combined collections, except Jerusalem, of nearly 8,000 dated items. 3. A chart for a limited moment in Armenian history, the one the author was most concerned with at the time of the initial research, 1300 to 1620,[15] which includes the previous material plus all dated manuscripts from the first eight volumes of the Jerusalem catalogue for this time span. Figure I combines these three curves on a single graph. In addition, various individual collections were plotted with varying coordinates. The three major tabulations plotted the frequency of manuscript production by decade. Other charts plotted output year by year and in five, ten, twenty-five, fifty, and 100 year periods; each produced a somewhat different type of curve for the same material. The one using ten year periods seemed to be the most appropriate for the data at hand and was chosen as the best for illustrative purposes.

The results clearly reveal that in the sixteenth century for the first time the level of manuscript production fell below that of the previous or fifteenth century. The decline is palpable: the fourteenth century records 593 dated manuscripts, the fifteenth 832, the sixteenth only 627, and just the first fifty years of the seventeenth 1,250, while the entire century leaves us more than 2,750 dated manuscripts. These figures are based on the larger sampling of 16,744 items.

A more detailed analysis the period most intensively investigated—the fourteenth to the early seventeenth century—shows that production begins to decline sharply between 1340 and 1350, a time of unrest in the Near East as Mongol Il-Khanid rule ends and successors fight over the pieces. There is a recovery in the next decade, but then a deeper and deeper decline during the successive campaigns of Timur which devastate Armenia from 1387 to 1402. Only after these are over does production begin to increase and sharply so during Qara Qoyunlu rule. However, another decline in quantity is apparent in the two decades after the death of Qara Yusuf (1420), rising again in the 1450s and 1460s, declining in the next decade, and then once again increasing until the year 1500.[16]

Then, from 1500, really 1505, to 1520 there is the severest drop in Armenian manuscript production ever recorded. These are the years of Ottoman sultan Selim's campaigns against the Safavids and his conquest of Egypt, Syria, and Armenia. The decline remains generalized during the next decades corresponding to the eastern campaigns of sultan Sulayman in the 1530s and 1540s. The half century from 1500 to 1550 represents the absolute lowest point in the production of Armenian scriptoria until printing finally replaced the manual copying of manuscripts altogether in the eighteenth century. From our sampling of nearly 17,000 manuscripts there are five years—1513, 1519, 1520, 1538, 1540—from the sixteenth century for which not a single one is recorded, whereas for the previous and following century, the fifteenth and seventeenth, there is not a single unproductive year and for the fourteenth only one, 1374, for which no manuscript is recorded.[17]

Just as clearly and perhaps even more dramatically, visual inspection of the graphs shows a steady rise in manuscript copying starting in the 1550s, rising sharply, especially after 1610, to reach the absolute historic high point of productivity in the decade ending in 1660. Slight declines are marked during the last Ottoman campaign of the century toward the east in 1575-1580, again during the great famine and Jelali revolts of 1595-1600, and during the forced immigration of the Armenians out of the Arax valley instigated by Shah Abbas in the years 1604-1611.

Certainly refinements in the system employed would produce even clearer results. For instance, instead of basing the statistics on all dated Armenian manuscripts, if one were to choose only those executed in greater Armenia, eliminating works form Constantinople, western Anatolia, the Crimea and Poland, the picture would no doubt be made to appear even worse in periods of decline and less brilliant for Armenia proper, at least in the fifteenth and sixteenth centuries, during apparent revivals. On the other hand, the results under discussion can be controlled or at least checked to some extent by plotting the frequency of other surviving cultural vestiges, provided such works are of a kind that would have been produced by all Armenians at all times and in every environment. Obvious examples would include sub-categories within manuscript production—all illuminated codices or all Gospel manuscripts—and, of course, architectural monuments. For the latter there has been a recent survey limited to eastern Armenia in the fourteenth century by Jacques Sislian which shows fluctuations in monumental building corresponding almost exactly to our charts.[18] In the entire second half of that century, when manuscript production was in sharp decline, there is almost a total absence of church construction.

Another such control can be seen in the chart, Figure II, which plots Armenian Gospel manuscripts as well as the few extant Old and New Testaments and complete Bibles. It is based on information taken from Erroll Rhodes' survey of Armenian Gospels.[19] The various indices indicate that of 1,244 manuscripts, 809 or 65 percent, are dated, a higher than average figure. The curve of dated Gospels executed from 1200 to 1750, bears out, almost without exception, the results of the other graphs. Plotted on this same Gospel chart is another block of information, the frequency, once again by decade, of the number of Armenian printed books from the first issued in 1512 to 1800.[20] This curve shows not the number of actual books, for there were tens of thousands printed in the period, but only separate works. There are listed altogether 968 titles with the exact date of publication.

From these two graphs (Figure II) it becomes immediately clear that the first decade of massive distribution of Armenian printed books beginning in the 1660s corresponds exactly to that of the highest level of manuscript production (Figure I). This probably reflects a large rise in literacy and certainly in demand. With the first Armenian Bible printing in 1666, Armenian Gospel manuscript production shows a precipitous drop, the copying of Gospels ceasing completely in 1750 as the production of printed texts further increased. However, a comparison between the Gospel graph, Figure II, and the general manuscript graphs, Figure I, shows that just at this moment, the second half of the eighteenth century, despite the halt in the manual production of the Gospel, the single most copied Armenian text by a margin of ten, there continued to be a steady and relatively high number of manuscripts executed, even increasing toward the 1790s. Surely this reflects the new variety of secular works which are preserved in the manuscript repositories: dictionaries, travel accounts, memoires, account books, text books, various kinds of essays.

There is almost no limit to the amount and kinds of information available from the statistical analysis of these relatively large bodies of data. The individual production of scores of separate scriptoria and localities can be plotted. Several have been test-chartered, including Erzerum. Its graph, Figure III, is based on some 45 manuscripts from the larger sampling dated between 1180 and 1700. Turkish and Armenian sources on the city indicate that by 1523, as a consequence of the Turko-Persian wars during which it was used as a frontier garrison by the Ottoman army, Erzerum had become totally deserted by its civilian population.[21]   There are no manuscripts in our sampling for Erzerum from 1488 to 1570. By 1540 there were once again about 100 citizens, mostly Armenians. But, from then on, the city prospered steadily to become in the next century the third most important trading center in the Ottoman empire. The burst of Armenian activity is reflected in the dramatic rise in manuscript production.

The city of Julfa on the Arax is also a case in point. Its total destruction and abandonment in 1604 presents us with an interesting terminus ad quem.[22]   Ten dated Julfan manuscripts are known from the large sampling. The earliest is from 1325, then another from the mid-fifteenth century (1456), four from the second half of the sixteenth century, the frequency increasing as the century comes to a close paralleling the city's rapid rise as the most important Armenian merchant center in the east. Finally, for the half-decade before its final destruction at the start of the seventeenth century there are four manuscripts. Graphically this data confirms our notion that Julfa was a city in dynamic ascension just at the moment it was definitively condemned.

Evidently, further effort on statistical analysis of Armenian manuscripts will prove fruitful. Ideally, the data base should be completed to include all existing Armenian manuscripts, with or without a date. In the catalogues undated manuscripts are already ascribed to a period, "sixteenth century," "first quarter of the fourteenth century," by evidence other than colophons.   The eventual computerization of this information would not be very difficult, especially if one initially limited the categories say to date, place of execution, type of text, and identifying number.   It has been the hope of the computerization program designed for the Index of Armenian Art to input all manuscripts, not just illuminated ones as is now the case.[23]   Thus far inadequate resources have prevented the execution of this work.   Perhaps younger scholars more adept and specifically trained in computerization and statistical analysis will be intrigued enough by this preliminary study to carry on the work.

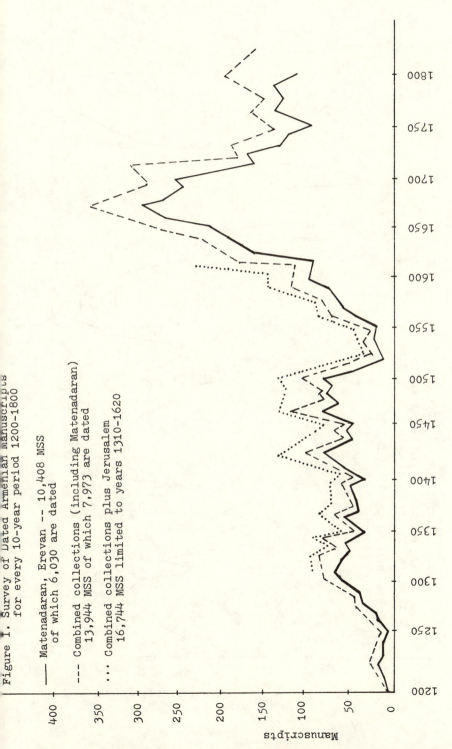

Figure 1. Survey of Dated Armenian Manuscripts
for every 10-year period 1200-1800

—— Matenadaran, Erevan -- 10,408 MSS
of which 6,030 are dated

--- Combined collections (including Matenadaran)
13,944 MSS of which 7,973 are dated

••• Combined collections plus Jerusalem
16,744 MSS limited to years 1310-1620

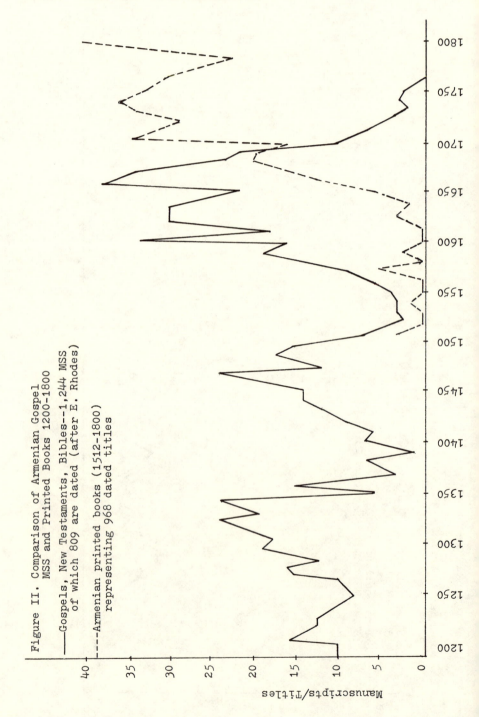

Figure II. Comparison of Armenian Gospel
MSS and Printed Books 1200-1800

——— Gospels, New Testaments, Bibles--1,244 MSS
of which 809 are dated (after E. Rhodes)

------ Armenian printed books (1512-1800)
representing 968 dated titles

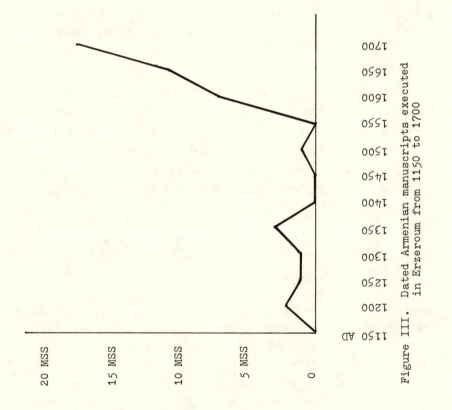

Figure III. Dated Armenian manuscripts executed
in Erzeroum from 1150 to 1700

NOTES

[1]D. Kouymjian, IAA: Index of Armenian Art, Part I: Manuscript Illuminations, Fascicule I, Illuminated Armenian Manuscripts to the Year 1000 A.D. (Fresno and Paris: Armenian Studies Program, California State University, and Center for Research on Armenian History and Art, 1977), xi; see also, Kouymjian, "IIAA: The Iconographical Index of Armenian Art," Journal of Armenian Studies I (1975) 1:65-67; Kouymjian, "Illustrated Armenian Manuscripts to the Year 1000 A.D.," Arkheion Pontou, 36 (1979) 249-252.

[2]Kouymjian, "Sous le joug des Turcomans et des Turcs ottomans (XVe-XVIe siècle)," 343-376 in Gérard Dédéyan, ed., Histoire des Arméniens (Toulouse: Editions Privat, 1982).

[3]Ibid., 370-1.

[4]O. Eganyan, A. Zeyt'unyan & P'. Ant'abyan, C'uc'ak jeṙagrac' Maštoc'i anvan Matenadarani, 2 vols. (Erevan: HSSH GA, 1965 & 1970).

[5]A more or less complete list of these can be found printed at the back of each issue of the Revue des Etudes Arméniennes.

[6]For Erevan, see note 4; for Venice, B. Sargisian & G. Sargsian, Mayr c'uc'ak hayerēn jeṙagrac' matenadaranin Mxit'areanc' i Venetik, III, Maštoc' - - girk' jeṙnadrut'eanc' (Venice: Mekhitarist Congregation, 1966). The first two volumes devoted to 319 Gospels and religious manuscripts (Venice, 1914, 1924), were not tabulated because of lack of indexes. The Gospels, however, representing 199 manuscripts are incorporated in Rhodes' list; see below notes 11, 16, and 19.

[7]J. Dashian, Catalog der armenischen Handschriften in der Mekhit-aristen Bibliothek zu Wien (Vienna, Mekhitarist Congregation, 1895), text in Armenian with resume of each manuscript in German.   This represents volume I with 575 manuscripts; volume II contains numbers 574-1304, H. Oskian, same title (Vienna, 1963).

[8]M. K'ēšišian, C'uc'ak hayerēn jeṙagrac' Zmmari vank'i matenadaranin (Vienna: Mekhitarist Congregation, 1964), 422 manuscripts; N. Akinian & H. Oskian, same title, Vol. II, "Antonean hawak'acoy" (Vienna, 1971), nos. 423-682, plus 37 additional manuscripts.

[9]S. Ter-Awetisian, C'uc'ak hayerēn jeṙagrac' Nor Juɫayi Amenap'rkič'

Vank'i, I (Vienna: Mekhitarist Congregation, 1970); L. G. Minasian, C'uc'ak jeṙagrac' Nor-Juɫayi S. Amenap'rkč'ean vanac' t'angarani, II (Vienna: Mekhitarist Congregation, 1972).

[10]A. K. Sanjian, A Catalogue of Medieval Armenian Manuscripts in the United States (Berekeley-Los Angeles-London: University of California Press, 1976), 180 manuscripts; E. Tisserant, Codices Armeni Bybliothecae Vaticanae Borgiani Vaticani Barberiniani Chisiani Schedis Frederici Cornwallis Conybeare Adhibitis (Rome: Typis Polyglottis Vaticanis, 1927), 127 manuscripts; N. Karamianz, Die Handschriften-Verzeichnisse der Königlichen Bibliothek zu Berlin. Verzeichniss der Armenischen Handschriften (Berlin: Asher, 1888), 99 manuscripts; G. Kalemkiar, Catalog der Armenischen Handschriften in der K. Hof- und Staatsbibliothek zu Munchen, in Armenian with German title and resume (Vienna: Mekhitarist Congregation, 1892), 22 manuscripts; J. Assfalg & J. Molitor, Verzeichnis der Orientalischen Handscriften in Deutschland, Armenische Handschriften (Wiesbaden; Franz Seiner Verlag, 1962), 28 manuscripts; S. Der Nersessian, The Chester Beatty Library. A Catalogue of the Armenian Manuscripts, 2 vols. (Dublin: Hodgis Figgis, 1958), 67 manuscripts; N. Akinian, C'uc'ak hayerēn jeṙagrac' Nikosiayi i Kipros (Vienna: Mekhitarist Congregation, 1961), 69 manuscripts.

[11]N. Poɫarian, Mayr c'uc'ak jeṙagrac' Srboc' Yakopeanc' I-VIII (Jerusalem: Armenian Covenant Printing Press, 1966-1978).

[12]See Index of Armenian Art, Fasc. I, op. cit., 14 manuscripts; and D. Kouymjian, IAA, Fasc. II, Illuminated Armenian Manuscripts of the 11th Century, Preliminary Report and Checklist (Fresno: Armenian Studies Program, California State University, 1977), 40 manuscripts.   Since the majority of early manuscripts are Gospels, E. Rhodes, An Annotated List of Armenian New Testament Manuscripts (Ikebukuro, Tokyo: Rikkyo (St. Paul's) University, 1959), is of help, listing some 90 manuscripts to the year 1220, see below notes 16 and 18.

[13]In the 1160s some 10,000 were destroyed in the monastery of Tat'ev alone, Step'annos Ōrbēlean, Histoire de la Siounie, trans. M. Brosset, I (St. Petersburg: Imperial Academy of Sciences, 1864) I.191.

[14]If, as is suggested later in this paper, all manuscripts, dated and undated alike, from all collections are plotted, the resulting data would produce meaningful curves for the tenth through the thirteenth century too.

[15]Actually the dates were originally 1375 to 1604, but curiosity about the period just before and after stretched the limits.

[16]The historical details for this and other sections below will be found in Kouymjian, "Sous le joug des Turcomans," esp. 341-358.

[17]These empty years have been checked against Rhodes, Armenian New Testament Manuscripts, making the basis for our results dependent on a much larger sampling than that of 16,744 manuscripts.

[18]J. Sislian, "L'Activité architecturale en Arménie orientale au cours du XIVe siècle," REArm 16 (1982) 289-299, see especially the table given in Pl. XXX.

[19]Rhodes, Armenian New Testament Manuscripts, the various indices are very useful.

[20]Hay hnatip grk'i matenagitakan c'uc'ak 1512-1800 (A Bibliographical List of Early Armenian Printed Books 1512-1800), collective authorship (Erevan: Myasnikyan Library, 1963), updated information on early printed books will not change the basic outline of the curve.

[21]The information is based on Ottoman defters, R. Jennings, "Urban Population in Anatolia in the 16th Century: A Study of Kaiseri, Karaman, Amasya, Trabizon and Erzeroum," International Journal of Middle Eastern Studies VII (1976) 21-57, cf., Kouymjian, "Sous le joug des Turcomans," 362-3.

[22]J. Baltrušaitis & D. Kouymjian, "Julfa on the Arax and Its Funerary Monuments," Etudes Arméniennes/Armenian Studies. In Memoriam Haïg Berbérian, D. Kouymjian (ed.), (Lisbon: Calouste Gulbenkian Foundation, in press).

[23]D. Kouymjian, "Computerization of Manuscript Illuminations: The Index of Armenian Art (IAA)," XVI. Internationaler Byzantinistenkongress Wien, 4.-9. Oktober 1981, Akten (Vienna: Der Österreichischen Akademie der Wissenschaften, 1981), 10 pages.

THE ARMENIANS IN THE BYZANTINE RULING CLASS
PREDOMINANTLY IN THE NINTH THROUGH
TWELFTH CENTURIES

Alexander Kazhdan

Dumbarton Oaks

In the eleventh-century life of a Byzantine saint, Lazarus of Mount Galesius by name, the following episode is related: young Lazarus, who longed for a journey to the Holy Land, found a companion in a monk from Paphlagonia, but this monk happened to be a vicious and perfidious; as they arrived in Attaleia, the major Cilician harbor, the monk met a ship-owner, naukleros, talked to him "in Armenian dialect" and agreed to sell him Lazarus. Only by the intervention of a sailor who understood Armenian and revealed the treacherous plan to Lazarus was the boy saved from slavery.[1] Another contemporary Saint's life transfers us into another area, far away from Cilicia or Paphlagonia: Nilus of Rossano is said by his hagiographer to have found a fox skin on the road; he bound the skin around his head, took off his clothes and hung them on the stick he carried on his shoulder (Byzantine saints sometimes had strange and hard-to-explain ideas). In such unusual garb he entered the kastron, the small local center, and children who saw him walking "in such a shape," as the hagiographer modestly puts it, began to throw stones at him and to yell. Some of them called him "Bulgarian kalogeros," a word that does not have an English equivalent but can be rendered in Russian as starec; it is quite plausible to surmise that by this name the children meant Bogomil. Other kids, however, called him Frankos, an ethnonym that designated in Byzantine texts first and foremost the Normans. But what matters for our purpose is the third group of local children—they called Nilus Armenian.[2]

T. Samuelian & M. Stone, eds. Medieval Armenian Culture. (University of Pennsylvania Armenian Texts and Studies 6). Chico, CA: Scholars Press, 1983. pp. 440 to 452.

An Armenian ship-owner with an Armenian crew would have been quite a natural sight in eleventh-century Attaleia, next to the heart of Armenian territory, but from the life of Nilus we learn that even boys in a small South-Italian kastron were not unaware of Armenians, though they considered Armenians as strange as the warlike Normans and the heretical Bogomils.

Geographically seen, the Armenians were ubiquitous throughout the Byzantine empire; they were ubiquitous from the social point of view, as well. We find them on all rungs of the social ladder, including the topmost, the imperial throne. Among Byzantine basileis of Armenian descent there is Leo V (813-820) explicitly described by Nicephorus Skeuophylax as a man "who originated from the Armenians and Assyrians";[3] though I cannot guess who the Assyrians of Nicephorus were, there is no doubt about the Armenian origin of Leo V. Basil I (867-886), Romanus I Lecapenus (920-944), John Tsimisces (969-976), all were definitely of Armenian stock, and their Armenian origin was understood by contemporaries and emphasized by chroniclers. This fact is well known and clearly demonstrated by Peter Charanis, whereas Elisabeth Bauer repeats these data without any substantial change or addition.[4]

Even among the higher echelon of clergy we find people of Armenian descent. Andronicus I (1183-1185), enraged by Patriarch Theodosius Bora-diotes (1179-1183), called him "the crafty Armenian," and Nicetas Choniates, the historian who preserved this scene, comments that the patriarch was Armenian "by his father's kin."[5] Another twelfth-century patriarch, Michael II (1143-1146), belonged to the famous Armenian family of the Curcuas that flourished in the tenth century, when John Curcuas was one of the foremost Byzantine generals; another John Curcuas, magistros during Tzimisces reign, was killed during the war against the Rus, and still another John Curcuas held the very important post of the katepana (governor) of Italy in 1008. We could suggest that by the time of Michael II Curcuas, in the mid-twelfth century, the family had been Hellenized, but his contemporaries did not forget the Armenian roots of the family: Michael Italicus, skillful rhetorician of the twelfth century, in his panegyricus dedicated to the patriarch claims that his hero's fatherland was "the divine paradise planted in the East,"[6] and such a vague expression could aptly, in the Byzantine rhetorical language, designate Armenian territory.

Armenian Theoctistes was an influential monastic leader in the second quarter of the eleventh century. In the purchase deed of 1030 he is named monk and hegumenos of the monastery of Esphigmenu (Esphagmenu in the charter); in 1034 he acquired for his monastery a virgin land nearby the monastic allottment Mauros Kormos; as the protos of Athos he signed two charters now in the archive of the Laura of Saint Athanasius (1035 and 1037) the first of which has his signature not in Greek but in Armenian.[7] Another charter of 1037 sheds some new light on the activity of Armenian monks within the framework of the Byzantine church. This charter contains a list of privileges bestowed by protos Theoctistes on his spiritual brother Nicephorus: Nicephorus should be entertained together with the protos, unless he preferred to eat in his own cell, receiving the same meal as Theoctistes; he retained a servant who was to be fed with the brethern; after Theoctistes' death, Nicephorus was to get an estate with various buildings and vineyards. It is worth mentioning that among witnesses who signed the charter of 1037 was at least one Armenian, John Petroses, who evidently belonged to the same noble family as Smbat Petruses; Smbat in 1064 held the post of strategos in the Thracian town of Apros.[8]

Why did Nicephorus receive this exceptional endowment? The charter of 1037 contains the explanation: Nicephorus diligently served thirty-six years in the theme of Charsianon (probably from 1001 through 1037), where he founded a monastery and gathered a number of monks.[9] We can conclude from this charter that the monastery of Esphigmenu had a certain number of monks who were not only still connected with Armenian literacy but who also participated in the organization of missionary activity on the eastern borders of the Byzantine empire. The date of 1001 when Nicephorus, the spiritual brother of the Armenian Theoctistes, was sent to Charsianon ought to make us especially alert: that was the time of the death of David Curopalates and of the annexation of his principality by Basil II (976-1025), emperor of Byzantium. The Empire apparently needed missionaries of Caucasian origin on the eastern frontier.

The role of the Armenians in the Byzantine army is well known. Nicephorus (963-969), in his Strategicon, acknowledges that the eastern army would be recruited from two elements, Rhomaioi and Armenians;[10] by so saying he emphasizes the specific role played by Armenian contingents at least on the eastern frontier. According to Kamal ad-Din, Roman III's (1028-1034) guard was formed of Armenians, and due to them the emperor was able to survive the flight from Aleppo in 1030.[11] However, in numerous

<u>chrysobulls</u> issued by Alexius I (1081-1118) Armenians are not listed among the foreign mercenaries (including Abchasians and Alans) who would be billeted throughout the Empire.[12]   How can this puzzling silence be explained? Does the imperial court consider the Armenians as the emperor's subjects, not foreigners? Or had the role of Armenian contingents drastically decreased by the end of the eleventh century?

Here we confront a very important question. We can take it for granted that the Armenians played a very significant part in Byzantine society—but has this part remained always the same? Can we reveal any changes under the smooth and pleasant surface of the overall statement that some Byzantine emperors, patriarchs, abbots and generals belonged to Armenian families?

The search for changes necessarily presupposes certain operations with figures but it is well known that Byzantine state archives perished and Byzantine demographic data are vague and unreliable. Can we find a means to hurdle this seemingly insurmountable barrier, the lack of precise information?   Tentatively we can, although for only a socially and temporarily restricted segment of the Byzantine population. I mean the ruling elite of the eleventh and twelfth centuries. The ruling elite is the single social stratum located, with a certain degree of consistency, within the spotlight of our sources; even if we do not know all the members of the Byzantine ruling class, we can be pretty sure that we will meet almost all the leading families if we choose for our investigation a relatively broad period of time. The eleventh and twelfth centuries present a particularly favorable period, since the Empire, until the catastrophe of 1204, was not yet transformed into an insignificant city-state on the edge of the Christian world, doomed to be gobbled up by the Turkish superpower; on the other hand, Greek sources of these centuries are relatively abundant. Moreover, the habit of using family names was established in Byzantium only in about 1000, whereas before this date they were used sporadically and not consistently.

The results of my calculations have been analyzed in two monographs published in Russian and therefore practically unavailable to Western scholars.   One of these books is dedeicated to Armenians within the framework of the Byzantine ruling elite.[13]   I will take a moment to summarize its conclusions shortly, but first I wish to expose one of many difficulties a scholar has to cope with while investigating the problems of medieval demography. This difficulty can be flatly defined as follows: Who should be included among Byzantine Armenians?

Of course there are some families whose Armenian descent cannot be questioned: they are explicitly named Armenians by our sources, they were closely connected with Armenian territories, their names are without any doubt Armenian. I couted fourteen families of unquestionably Armenian origin, such as the Musele, Curcuas, Taronites, Aspietes, and I can add to them now the fifteenth, Petruses, whom I have just mentioned. There is another group consisting of twenty families who have been described by various scholars as Armenians, even though we have no direct indications concerning their Armenian descent, only more or less vague hints. Let us take as an example the family of Sclerus, the first of whom, the strategos of Peloponnesia at about 805, originated, according to the Chronicle of Monembasia, in Lesser Armenia.[14] Is this testimony sufficient to enlist the Sclerus into the Armenian nobility? The case is ambiguous, especially if we take into consideration that skleros 'austere or severe,' is a Greek word and that later sources never mention the Armenian origin of the Sclerus family.

An even harder nut to crack is the small group of four families (Tornices, Pacuriani, Vichkatzi and Apuchap) who were intermittently called in our sources both Armenians and Iberi. The problem of their ethnic origin (especially that of Pacuriani) produced a hot dispute predominantly between Armenian and Georgian scholars; sharp words have been said by both parties and much poisoned ink spilt. As a matter of fact, the problem is not as insoluble as it seems from the heat of the dispute: the difference between Georgians and Armenians of Chalcedonian creed was not unbridgeable, especially in the region of Taiq, and we know some Byzantine subjects who spoke and wrote, besides the Greek, both Georgian and Armenian. The term introduced by C. Toumanoff, the "Caucasians,"[15] seems to me to provide a happy outlet from a "patriotic" but barren discussion.

If we assume that there were about thirty or forty Armenian families within the Byzantine ruling elite of the eleventh and twelfth centuries, we establish a starting point for deliberation about the role played by the "Caucasians" in Byzantine society. The general number of "aristocratic" families in Byzantium is approximately 340, so the Armenians made up a good ten percent of the whole.

Other ethnic minorities played a lesser role than Armenians. The Southern Slavs gave sixteen aristocratic families at that period, about ten or eleven were of "Latin" origin (mainly from Norman Italy), a few less—of Arab descent, approximately five—Turks.

The Armenian group within the Byzantine ruling class was far from uniform. Some of them retained their language, culture and Monophysite religion, even though the most cultivated of them could not resist the charm of Byzantine civilization: Gregory Pahlavuni Magistros had profound knowledge of Greek literature and devoted many years to translation from Greek.[16] Relations between the Monophysite (Gregorian) Armenians and the Byzantine state, church and population were tense, and the story of Gagik of Ani is perhaps the most eloquent episode of this incessant struggle: Gagik left Ani in 1045 and the emperor endowed him with a part of Cappadocia (perhaps also some lands in Charsianon and Lycandus); he murdered the metropolitan of Caesaria but was captured by local magnates, brought to their castle and hanged on the wall in 1079/80. But there was another group of Armenian aristocracy which accepted Chalcedonian creed and joined the ranks of the Byzantine elite.[17]

No less important was another distinction: some of the "Byzantine Armenians" belonged to the military aristocracy and served the Empire as generals and governors of provinces, some of them were civil officials, According to my calculations, the role of the Caucasians within the military aristocracy was much more significant than their part in the civil official-dom. Within this group four families are represented by civil functionaries only; we could add to them also the Machitarii, although the functions of the first among them, Basil Machitarius, are not clear enough—he was the governor of Melitene and Lycandus, but at the same time he functioned as judge. On the contrary not less than twelve or fifteen families belonged to the military aristocracy, whereas a considerable group of families began as generals and governors and eventually found their place within the civil officialdom. In other words, Armenians occupied about 10% of the civil elite and about 25% (or even more) of the Empire's military aristocracy whose origin we know (the figures seem to be higher than the overall percentage produced above; the discrepancy is to be explained by the fact that the origin can be determined only for approximately a half of the whole bulk of registered families). Thus we suggest that the Armenians in the Byzantine service were predominantly warriors or military administrators; they played an enormous role in the Byzantine army, even if the figure of 25% is exaggerated, whereas their impact on the civil service was not that significant.

We can reach the same conclusion in a different way. If we analyze the correlation of various groups within the Byzantino-Armenian aristocracy, we get, approximately, the following figures: 8% of old noble families had lost their importance by the eleventh century: 42% of families which can be determined as military aristocracy; 37% of families which had belonged to the military aristocracy but eventually changed face and became civil officials; and 13% of families who served in the civil service. Even if these figures should not be accepted as precise and impeccable data, we have no reason to doubt that the Armenians entered the ranks of the Byzantine elite mainly as warriors.

We have now to study the "geographical distribution" of Armenian commanders and governors on Byzantine service: in which regions did thy predominantly serve? The first conclusion we are able to draw is that some Byzantino-Armenian families, in their service, were connected with particular areas. Thus the Taronites functioned in the districts of Thessalonike, Macedonia and Skoplje; the Dallasseni were active in Antioch; the Apuchap, in Edessa. But the stable links of this kind can be traced in other, not Caucasian groups of Byzantine aristocracy. What is more relevant for our aim is the fact that Armenians were used, above all, for service in the frontier zone. In the eleventh century this zone included the eastern themes—from Antioch up to Iberia, as well as the island of Samos, that was to thwart the access to the Aegean Sea, and also Italy and the north-west regions; the latter encompassed at the beginning of the century, during the reign of Basil II, Thessalonike, Macedonia and Philippopolis; by the way, Philippopolis had a considerable, even though not measurable Armenian population. Later, after Basil's annexation of Bulgaria, the area of "Armenian activity" shifted westward—to Devol, Skoplje and Sirmium.

It is well known that the Armenian population was especially dense in the Eastern provinces of the Empire, in the themes of Antioch, Edessa, Melitene, Taron, Vaspurakan, Iberia and Sebasteia. Armenian governors were especially abundant just in these districts. In Vaspurakan and Iberia, which were annexed by Byzantium during Basil II's reign, the first governors were recruited from Greeks but very soon after that the administration of these themes was transferred to governors of Armenian stock.[18]

The social basis of the Byzantino-Armenian aristocracy is very difficult to describe since our sources are particularly scanty in determining economic positions and economic activities.   Nonetheless, we are able to state that landed estates are mentioned in the hands of fifteen Armenian families adding up to 40%; some of these estates (those of Pacuriani, Burtzes, Gabras, Pahlavuni and so forth) were large according to Byzantine standards. These figures do not imply that 60% of Armenian aristocratic families were landless; the silence of medieval sources is a very unreliable agument, even though it is worth noting that those Armenian families which belonged to civil officialdom stand outside this list of landowners.   But we can render these figures eloquent if we compare them with the data concerning other groups of Byzantine elite: thus among the uppermost echelon of the Byzantine ruling class, the so-called Comnenian clan (the Comneni and their relatives), 68% of families owned landed estates of various sizes, whereas among Byzantine civil aristocracy only about 16% of all the families can be described as landowners.

Now we come to another puzzling problem. Armenians formed an important part of the Byzantine military aristocracy; they—at least a substantial part of their elite—belonged to the landowning class. Thus both functionally and socially they joined the ranks of those who appeared to provide the main support of the Comnenian dynasty. Surprisingly, however, Armenians remained outside of the Comnenian clan and quite seldom concluded marriages with representatives of the imperial dynasty. Whereas the Comnenian clan consisted of around fifty families, only five Armenian families happened to be among them; but it is not only the figures that matter—none of the Armenian families have a position equal to that of the Ducas or Palaeologi, Batatzes or Contostephani. Let us study all the cases of the "Armenian marriages" to the Comnenian house.

Anna Dalassena married to John Comnenus, the father of the future emperor Alexius I; Michael Taronites's spouse was Maria, Alexius Comnenus's sister—the marriage was concluded still before 1081, before Alexius's ascent to the throne.   The relations of the Curticii with the Comneni are questionable: even if Constantine Curticius was married to Theodora, Alexius I's daughter, the alliance was of short duration, and quite soon Theodora found another husband, Constantine Angelus.   The marriage of Gregory Gabras with Alexius's other daughter, Maria, was planned but not concluded. Gregory Pacurianus Junior was the son-in-law of Nicephorus, Alexius's youngest brother. There are no evidences about "Armenian marriages" of the Comneni in the twelfth century, except in the case of Michael Gabras, who married the niece of Manuel I and that of John Comnenus, Manuel's nephew, who took his bride from the "Euphratian branch" of the Taronites.

Thus we can surmise that in the eleventh and especially in the twelfth century the Armenians were in a sense restricted in their climbing up the social ladder: they formed a significant part of the Byzantine elite but—unlike the tenth century—they had no access to the topmost echelon of the Byzantine ruling class.

Can we find an explanation of this puzzling situation?   In a recent article, S. Vryonis drew attention to the ambiguity of the Byzantine images of the Armenian.   It was well known, even before Vryonis, that strong anti-Armenian prejudice existed in Byzantine society; his merit lies in demonstrating that side by side with this hostile attitude Byzantium knew a milder language, and very often "Armenian physical prowess, bellicosity, and physical beauty" were praised by Byzantine authors.[19]   This ambiguity of images coincides with the ambiguity of behavior of the Byzantino-Armenian aristocracy with respect to the Byzantine state: they formed a solid body of imperial military commanders and provincial governors sent to the most responsible posts on the frontier; on the other hand, they frequently sided with rebels or even headed dangerous insurrections—I counted about 25 cases of mutiny from 976 through 1204, in which Armenians participated; some of them were Hellenized, whereas a considerable group preserved their language, dress and religion.   They were consistent supporters of the regime, but they were "dissidents."

This observation, however, does not bring us the final solution of the puzzle: neither the ambiguity of images nor the ambiguity of behavior prevented the Armenians from seizing the leading positions in the Empire of the ninth and tenth centuries.   We ought to acknowledge that in the eleventh and the twelfth centuries the Armenian situation in Byzantium grew worse.

If we summarize the data concerning the Armenians in Byzantine service during the eleventh and twelfth centuries, we get the following figures:

From the reign of Basil II we have data concerning 40 noble Armenians in Bynzatine service, including 33 military commanders and one official, Basil Lecapenus, of exclusively high rank;

From the second quarter of the eleventh century we have data concerning 38 noble Armenians, of whom only 23 can be determined as military commanders;

From the third quarter of the eleventh century about 50 noble Armenians are mentioned, of whom about 30 were military commanders;

There are also evidences (mainly provided by the seal material) that can be dated only approximately to the eleventh century—among these 26 noble Armenians only eight or nine were military commanders.

Alexius I's reign forms a turning point: we can collect testimonies on 63 noble Armenians of this span of time, but only about 20 of them were warriors; of the ten people whose activity can be dated roughly to the eleventh or twelfth centuries only one was involved military service.

During the reign of his two descendents, John II (1118-1143) and Manuel I (1143-1180), 40 noble Armenians are recorded; the number of warriors among them seems to have decreased even more—only eleven or twelve of them; at the end of the twelfth century (up to 1204) we know 19 noble Armenians, of whom only five were military commanders. Four persons more are dated roughly to the twelfth century, and none of them belonged to the military class.

Thus we can observe two tendencies of development: first, a general narrowing in the role of the Armenian element within the ruling elite of Byzantium; second, a decrease in the number of warriors (and provincial governors) within the Byzantino-Armenian aristocracy, its shift toward the civil service. Both tendencies could find, it seems, their explanation in the realities of both Byzantine and Armenian history of the period.

In Byzantium the Comnenian dynasty that seized the power in 1081 was supported by the "clan" of families connected with the dynasty by relation or affinity. This clan of approximately fifty families included, prbably, the largest landowners, and monopolized the military command. Old families of the military aristocracy who did not join the ranks of the Comnenian clan were pushed into the background, transformed into civil officialdom, plunged into provincial life or even vanished completely. Many important Armenian families suffered such a fate.

On the other hand, from the end of the eleventh century new Armenian principalities started to appear in Northern Syria, Mesopotamia and

Cilicia. The most efficient representatives of Armenian aristocracy rushed there, and their influx into Byzantium declined considerably. Thus during Alexius I's reign the Aspietes and Coccobasilii were the only Armenian families who entered the ranks of the Byzantine elite, and perhaps also the Vaspurakanites, but the information concerning the latter is extremely vague. After Alexius's death the Armenian influx into Byzantium as a matter of fact would have stopped, were it not for the Rubenides whose stay in Constantinople, however, was against their will.   All this twelfth-century emigration differs signally from the emigration of Basil II's time when such families as the Pacuriani, Dalasseni, Theodorocani, Vichkatzi, Tornices, Artsrunides, Delphanas came to the Empire. Moreover, from the end of the eleventh century on, a sort of Armenian ebb-tide from Byzantium can be observed.   Philaretus Brachamius and Rubenides tried to create their independent principalities in the frontier zone between Byzantium and the Seljuqs, a development strongly reinforced by the First Crusade, which destroyed traditional links of relationship and dependency in Northern Syria and Cilicia.   Bagrat, whom Baldwin of Boulogne appointed governor of Ravendal, is a typical example of this new tendency: according to Albert of Aix, Baldwin met him during the crusaders' siege of Nicaea in 1097, where Bagrat came, having absconded from "the chains of the Greek emperor." Supposedly he served Alexius I, at any rate his brother Kogh Vasil (Coccobasilius) had the title of sebastos and commanded the tropps of the Byzantine Pečenegs. Albert describes Bagrat[20] as a perfidious man who was experienced in warfare and whose repute was high throughout Armenia, Syria and Greece. Gabriel (Khavril), hegumenos of Melitene (died about 1103), was another man who connected his destiny with the frontier zone. An Armenian "according to his origin, tongue and habits" in the words of William of Tyre[21]—he was at the same time very close to Byzantine culture: in any case, a certain Michael Andreopulus translated for him from Syriac into Greek the book of Syntipas; in the preamble Andreopulus addressed Gabriel with the Greek titles of dux and sebastos.[22]

Even though the flow of the Armenian aristocracy into Byzantium began to dwindle from the very beginning of the twelfth century, if not from the end of the eleventh century, the links of Armenian principalities with the Empire were not interrupted; they took on a different shape; the links between vassals and their sovereign. The Armenian aristocracy ceased to be incorporated into the ranks of the Byzantine elite, but appeared, time and again, in the Byzantine army as independent vassals with their own troops.

Perhaps, all these changes could shed light on the Armenian attitude during the Crusades—the Armenians were the staunchest supporters of the crusaders, and the Crusaders' "treacherous" behavior with regard to the Empire induced Byzantine animosity toward the Armenians.

The social role of the Armenians in the Byzantine empire should be considered within the larger framework of the problem of the Byzantine frontier zone. On the one hand, these territories on the border lay relatively far from the center of the centralistic and totalitarian state; on the other hand, they required prompter and more responsible decisions. There was the abiding menace of hostile invasions in this hotbed of anti-centralistic and parafeudal tendencies which, however, did not win the day in the twelfth-century Byzantium despite the temporary success of the Comneni.

NOTES

[1]AASS Novembris III, 511F.

[2]AASS Septembris VI, 286 D.

[3]Theophanes 2, 22.36.

[4]P. Charanis, The Armenians in the Byzantine Empire (Lisboa, 1963); E. Bauer, Die Armenier im Byzantinischen Reich und ihr Einfluss auf Politik, Wirtschaft und Kultur (Yerevan, 1978).

[5]Nicetas Choniates, Historia (ed. J. L. Dieten; Berlin: de Gruyter, 1971) 253.2-3.

[6]Michael Italikos, Lettres et discours (ed. P. Gautier; Archive de l'Orient Chrétien 14; Paris, 1972) 72.18-19.

[7]On him, A. P. Kazhdan, "Esfigmenskaja gramota 1037 g. i deja-tel'nost' Feoktista," Vestnik Erevanskogo universiteta (1974) 3: 236-238.

[8]A. P. Kazhdan, "Grečeskaja nadpis' XI v. s upominaniem armjanina-stratiga," Istoriko-filologičeskij žurnal (1973) 2: 189f.

[9]Actes d'Esphigmenou (ed. J. Lefort; Paris, P. Lethielleux, 1973) No. 1.

[10]Ju. Kulakovskij, "Strategika imperatora Nikifora," Zapiski Akademii

Nauk. Serija Istor.-Filol. 8 (1908) 9: 1.3. See also the commentary on p. 28.

[11]V. Rozen, Imperator Vasilij Bolgarobojca (Saint Petersburg, 1883), 319.

[12]A. P. Kazhdan, B. L. Fonkič, "Novoe izdanie aktov Lavry i ego značenie dlja vizantinovedenija," Viz. Vrem. 34 (1973) 49.

[13]A. P. Kazhdan, Armjane v sostave gospodstvujuščego klassa Vizantijskoj imperii v XI-XII vv. (Yerevan, 1975). See reviews by N. Garsoian in American Historical Review (June 1978) 703 f. and by W. Seibt in Byzantinoslavica 38 (1977) 50 f.

[14]W. Seibt, Die Skleroi (Vienna, 1976) 19 f.

[15]C. Toumanoff, "Caucasia and Byzantium," Traditio 27 (1971) 111-152.

[16]R. W. Thomson, "The Influence of their Environment on the Armenians in Exile in the Eleventh Century," Proceedings of the Thirteenth International Congress of Byzantine Studies (London, 1967) 436 f.

[17]V. A. Arutjunova-Fidanjan, Armjane-xalkedonity na vostočnyx granicax Vizantijskoj imperii (XI v.) (Yerevan, 1980).

[18]V. A. Arutjunova-Fidanjan, "Vizantijskie praviteli femy Iverija," Vestnik obščestvennyx nauk AN ArmSSR (1973) 2: 63-78; Arutjunova-Fidanjan, "Fema Vaspurakan," Viz. Vrem. 38 (1977) 80-93; Arutjunova-Fidanjan, "Vizantijskie praviteli Edessy v XI v.," Viz. Vrem. 35 (1973) 137-153.

[19]S. Vryonis, "Byzantine Images of the Armenians," 65-81 in R. G. Hovannisian (ed.) The Armenian Image in History and Literature (Los Angeles, 1981).

[20]J. Migne, Patrologiae Cursus Completus (Series Latina, Paris, 1878-1890) 166, col. 447 D.

[21]Ibid., 201, col. 178 A.

[22]Mich. Andreopulus, Liber Syntipae, Zapiski Akademii Nauk, Serija Istor-Filol. 11 (1912) No. 1, p. 2.9-12.